A CIRCLE OF FRIENDS

A CIRCLE OF FRIENDS

The Tennysons and the Lushingtons of Park House

JOHN O. WALLER

—————————————

Ohio State University Press
Columbus

**Library of Congress Cataloging in Publication
Data**

Waller, John G., 1916–
 A circle of friends.

 Bibliography: p.
 Includes index.
 1. Tennyson, Alfred Tennyson, Baron, 1809–1892
—Friends and associates. 2. Lushington, Edmund
Law. 3. Lushington, Henry. 4. Tennyson family.
5. Poets, English—19th century—Biography. 6.
Great Britain—Biography. I. Title.
PR5583.W34 1986 821'.8 [B] 86-25007
ISBN 0-8142-0424-4

For Roger and Diana Lushington
and
my wife, Elaine

Contents

Illustrations

Preface

A LIST OF Alfred Tennyson's five or six closest friends ought surely, I think, to include his brother-in-law, Edmund Law Lushington, and Edmund's brother, Henry. The preeminent friend, of course, was Arthur Henry Hallam, early to die but securely immortalized in Tennyson's masterpiece *In Memoriam*. James Spedding and, probably, Edmund FitzGerald (despite his habitual disparagement of Tennyson's post-1842 poems) would belong on the list; and after 1854 certainly the Isle of Wight neighbor, Sir John Simeon, whose death invoked the tender lines "Shadows of three dead men / Walked in the walks with me / . . . . / Three dead men have I loved." The other two were Arthur Hallam and Henry Lushington.

It was Henry whom Tennyson declared the most helpful practical critic of his poems, and to whom he dedicated the second edition of *The Princess*, having, as I hope to show, spent much time with Henry during the months he was composing or publishing that poem. The friendship of Tennyson and Edmund, firmly grounded in mutual respect for each other's total integrity and complementary intellectual powers, endured quietly and undemonstratively, with scarcely a trace of diminution for more than half a century, terminating only with Tennyson's death, less than a year before Edmund's.

It could be claimed, though perhaps too tenuously, that Tennyson semi-dedicated his *In Memoriam* to Edmund. Twice—indubitably in the Epilogue and almost as certainly in the final form of section 85—Edmund is directly addressed. "Ah, take the imperfect gift I bring," the poet bids the addressee in the final stanza of 85; and the Epilogue pointedly positions the new brother-in-law as close as possible to the place left vacant by Hallam ("Nor have I felt so much of bliss / Since first he told me that he loved / A daughter of our house, nor proved / Since that dark day a day like this"). If a depersonalized Christ ("Strong Son of God, immortal Love") is invoked in the Prologue, the endearing character and finely developed scholarly intellect of Edmund Lushington are celebrated in the Epilogue: "And thou art worthy; full of power; / As gentle; liberal-minded, great, / Consistent, wearing all that weight / Of learning lightly like a flower."

Not merely as satellites to the laureate but each man on his own merits, in distinctly divergent fields of endeavor, Edmund and Henry sufficiently impressed enough of their contemporaries that both appear in the *Dictionary of National Biography*. But so, of course, in scores of diverse professions, did hundreds of other persons now no less obscure and equally worthy of being remembered. It must necessarily be as an extension of Tennyson's biography if the Lushingtons' memories are to be revived. Yet we will not even start to know the men whom Tennyson knew, admired, and loved unless we can partially remove them from his magnified shadow, set them down in other contexts than his, savor their words, appreciate their accomplishments, delight in their differences from one another, respond to their quiet nobility, and empathize with their disappointments and heartbreaking sorrows. Both men in their time stoically endured perhaps more than their fair allotment of those.

I have attempted, then, a more or less conventional biography, dually composed, of Edmund and Henry Lushington, introducing ancestors and parents, pursuing the two precocious boys through their scholastic triumphs at Charterhouse School and Trinity College, Cambridge, then proceeding through the exigencies of their private lives and respective careers—Edmund's for thirty-seven years as professor of Greek at Glasgow University, Henry's for barely eight as chief secretary of the queen's government at Malta, a situation that precipitated his death. We will review a substantial body of long-forgotten writings of our two men, preponderantly Henry's; meet their parents, brothers, and sisters; present facts newly uncovered concerning the generally sad marriage of Edmund and Cecilia, never an ideal match and so extraordinarily weighted down by her illnesses, physical and emotional, and by the devastating early deaths of three of their four beloved children.

I strive to maintain a Lushington biography throughout, avoiding any distortion that would surreptitiously transmute it into a disguised Tennyson story. But wherever consistent with the natural configuration of events, we will keep to the foreground the interaction with Alfred Tennyson. Fortunately, that emphasis unfolds organically from the available manuscript sources, so many being from the papers of Alfred or Frederick Tennyson. Once the tall Lincolnshire poet strides into our Kentish story, from about 1839, his name through the next fifty-three years will appear on approximately half our pages.

My debts to others are so numerous that I cannot hope to mention all. I think first of Professor William Darby Templeman, who at the University of Southern California taught my three courses in Victorian literature, conducted the graduate course in methods of research, and directed both my master of arts thesis and my doctoral dissertation.

My greatest literary indebtedness is to the late, ineffable Sir Charles Tennyson, whose work *The Somersby Tennysons* (the 1963 Christmas Supplement to *Victorian Studies*, subsequently expanded in collaboration with the late Hope Dyson into a book, *The Tennysons: Background to Genius*, 1974) awakened a latent interest in finding out more about Edmund Lushington, that classical scholar with the resonant name whom *In Memoriam* had so generously praised. Then by sheerest coincidence, during my first visit to Britain in 1970, I had the remarkable fortune of dropping into the recently established Tennyson Research Centre in Lincoln only a few minutes before Sir Charles arrived from London to receive, next day, the honorary citizenship of the ancient city of Lincoln. In a brief conversation, he encouraged me, although I was then only casually a Tennysonian, to return and study at the Centre.

Accordingly, I went in 1972 and again in 1975, by which time I had worked intensively in Sir Charles's own principal sources for *The Somersby Tennysons*, the Frederick Tennyson papers, now at the Lilly Library at Indiana University, and had begun accumulating material for at least an article-length profile of Edmund. (Only later did I become equally interested in Henry.) At a tea in the White Hart Inn at Tetford, a mile from Somersby, after the 1975 annual Tennyson Memorial Service at Somersby Church, Sir Charles, impressively alert and responsive at nearly ninety-six, advised me to communicate with the surviving Lushingtons at Maidstone.

My doing so, by letter, after returning to this country was the beginning of a treasured friendship with Roger G. L. Lushington, of Dorking (great-grandson of Thomas Davies Lushington, brother of Edmund and Henry), and his hospitable wife, Diana. From our first meeting in 1978, the Lushingtons, with Roger's mother, Cicely Lushington, and his aunt, Betty Lushington, who remembers Cecilia ("Zilly") Lushington, daughter of Edmund and Cecilia, have generously assisted me in making free use of the family papers in their custody, and bestowed their blessing to publish whatever I can. One story has it that certain bundles of letters became patriotic casualties of the scrap-paper salvaging during World War II—a possible explanation for the nearly total absence of letters from Henry on Malta during 1847 to 1855. But a substantial body of invaluable material remains, strong in certain of the areas where other collections are weakest, especially in the family background, childhood, and youth of Edmund and Henry, extending through their years at Trinity College, Cambridge.

At the Tennyson Research Centre, during numerous visits between 1970 and 1982, I have invariably been received, first by Laurence Elvin and later by Susan Gates, with warm friendliness. Through the kind permission of Lord Tennyson and the Lincolnshire Library Service, I am publishing excerpts from their holdings, as well as words from several manuscripts of Alfred Lord Tennyson and Emily Lady Tennyson in other collections (with concurrent permission of their holders, duly acknowledged here).

The collection of manuscripts that crowned the others, making it feasible to think of a book rather than an article or two, has been the Llysdinam papers of the Venables family, recently deposited in the National Library of Wales at Aberystwyth. For a period of almost forty-five years (mid-1839 through 1883), the journals of George Stovin Venables, barrister and journalist, intimate associate of Edmund and Henry at Charterhouse School, and a devoted friend of all their family, supply the indispensable month-by-month continuity that the absence of any Lushington journals had left unobtainable. Lady Delia Venables-Llewellyn, of Llysdinam Hall, Newbridge-on-Wye, who has given me permission to publish from the journals and correspondence, drove me about the verdant Welsh countryside and invited me to a supper including game—salmon and pheasant—from her beautiful estate beside the Wye, where the various Lushingtons had so frequently visited. From the National Library of Wales as well, where Kathleen Hughes, cataloguer of the collection, has been of immense assistance to me, I also have permission to publish.

At several other libraries I have received courtesies well beyond the anticipated routine. At the Lilly Library, Virginia Mauch, associate curator of manuscripts, exhibited a personal interest in my work and extended permission to transcribe and publish material from the Frederick Tennyson papers.

At the beautiful Wren Library, Trinity College, Cambridge, Trevor Kaye, sub-librarian, welcomed me and assisted me in numerous ways. Through him, the Master and Fellows of Trinity College are extending permission to publish from the Houghton papers there.

The exemplary courtesies shown me in 1975 and 1982 at Glasgow University Library by the reference librarian, Jean Robertson, can not be praised too highly. In the first brief, late afternoon hour, she appraised my needs and afterward directed me to a comfortable hotel, lending me two histories of the university from her own office shelves. By next morning she had mapped my day, dispatching me first to the University Archives, where Elspeth Simpson was waiting with an array of archival materials (with permission to publish); arranged a luncheon appointment with Mr. John Knox, of the Greek department; and in the afternoon produced an expertly selected stack of research materials that launched me on a study of Edmund's career at Glasgow. Unsolicited, she has since mailed me discoveries she had made concerning Edmund. In 1982 she reserved a room in the Faculty Club, made an appointment with Professor R. M. McDowell, of the Greek department, in direct line of succession from Edmund; and introduced me to Bernard Aspinwall, of the history department, with whom I had previously corresponded, who whisked me off for a visit to Carstairs, the former mansion of the Lushingtons' friend Robert Monteith, but then St. Charles' Private Hospital, where Sister Hilda, the mother superior, and her associates showed us the house and invited us to supper, followed by an evening of fellowship. Subsequently, Sister Hilda sent me an invaluable outline of Monteith family history.

The James White Library at my own Andrews University, under the successive directorships of Mary Jane Mitchell and Marley H. Soper, has been a second home, where I have benefited in countless ways, including extensive use of interlibrary loan services.

Other libraries in Great Britain and the United States where I have worked include the British Library, main reading room and manuscript department; the Public Records Office (at both Chancery Lane and Kew Gardens); Cambridge University Library; the Bodleian, at Oxford; the Wellcome Library for the History of Medicine; the Kent County Archives; the Newberry Library; Indiana University Library; the University of Notre Dame Library; and the Wellesley College Library, where I was privileged to meet Professor Walter E. Houghton, Jr., since deceased, and his wife, Esther Rhoads Houghton.

Administrators through the years at Andrews University have helped me in countless ways, including sabbaticals, assistance on travel expenses, and a grant for the typing of my manuscript. Former and present administrators who have helped me most include Robert E. Firth, Richard Hammill, Gordon Madgwick, Humberto Rasi, Richard W. Schwarz, Joseph G. Smoot, and Robert A. Williams. My department chairman, Delmer I. Davis, Sr., has endorsed my applications for sabbaticals and stood by to help me in other ways. When formerly I was chairman, my colleague Edith Stone twice assumed the routine burdens of the chair so that I could work in Britain.

Professor Cecil Y. Lang, who read my manuscript, made invaluable recommendations for revising, and generously provided me with a print-out of the forthcoming second volume, and much of the third, of Tennyson's letters, with the annotations.

Other persons near and far who have assisted me with their expertise in ways too diverse to enumerate include the Reverend Malcolm Bradshaw; Joanna Collenbrander; the Reverend Canon Michael L. Cooper; Lieutenant-Commander Andrew David (Royal Navy); Roy Davids, of Sotheby Park Bernet and Company; Aidan Day; Major General A. H. G. Dobson (British Army); Mark Dobson; Robert H. Dunn, M.D.; Mrs. B. Freake, of the Charterhouse School Library; the late Alfred Friendly, of the Washington *Post*; Herald Habenicht, M.D.; Captain A. W. Hemsted (Royal Navy); the Venerable Owain Jones; Staff Sergeant R. D. Lucas (British Army); Mr. and Mrs. F. H. Mitchell; M. C. Morgan; Vivien Noakes; Daniel Ranisavljevic; Marion Shaw; Rosemary Blok van Cronesteyn; Rebecca Wedgwood; and Professors Peter Allen, Richard D. Altick, Daniel Augsburger, Jerome H. Buckley, Elly Economou, Lawrence T. Geraty, Barry Gordon, Estella Ramirez Greig, Michael Hyde, E. D. H. Johnson, John E. Jordan, Jack Kolb, Judson S. Lyon, Robert Bernard Martin, Ruth Murdoch, the late William D. Paden, William S. Peterson, Andre Rochat, Edgar F. Shannon, Jr., William H. Shea, Walter M. Sutton, Harry W. Taylor, and James Winter.

To any persons, equally helpful over a period of more than ten years, whom I have inadvertently omitted—and surely there must be some—I contritely apologize.

Nancy Hackleman, my typist, has given me admirably professional service.

The staff of the Ohio State University Press, in particular Peter John Givler, C. Kate Capps, and Robert S. Demorest, have more than fulfilled my most sanguine expectations—being deftly reassuring, expertly answering my questions, and generally leaving me unfettered. I feel signally fortunate in having for editor a person so long experienced and quietly encouraging as Mr. Demorest.

Finally, my indebtedness to my wife, Elaine, reaches beyond the boundaries of the easily expressible. To her with my love, and to Roger and Diana Lushington, I gratefully dedicate this book.

A CIRCLE OF FRIENDS

I

Family Background and Early Childhood

To 1823

T HE YEARS OF BIRTH of Edmund and Henry Lushington, 1811 and 1812, mark a watershed in English history: the divide between the two periods Sir Arthur Bryant has designated "Years of Victory (1802–1812)" and "The Age of Elegance (1812–1822)."[1] Bonaparte's fortunes had reached their zenith in 1812. On the Iberian Peninsula the two years saw Wellington's forces drive the French out of Portugal and on 6 April 1812, exactly a week before Henry's birth, break through "the gates of Portugal" at Badajos into Spain toward the steady and methodical expelling of the enemy, in 1812, across the Pyrenees into France. In England old George III was declared insane and the regency began. Before 1812 ended the regent was perfecting his plans to transform the West End of London by constructing Regent Street. On 12 May 1812 an insane assassin killed the prime minister, Spencer Perceval, whose successor, Lord Liverpool, would hold the office until 1827.

The lord chief justice of England since 1802 was a great-uncle of Edmund and Henry—Edward Law, first Baron Ellenborough (1750–1818), a formidable personage, learned in the law, blunt and merciless in his rhetoric, rigid on the bench, a man of strictest integrity no less incorruptible than stubbornly impervious to enlightened reform. His career, starting with few material advantages, had exemplified how a man with the requisite intellectual and temperamental endowments might, through unflagging diligence and well-spaced turns of fortune, rise to the peak in the so-often-unrewarding profession of the bar.[2] Although his father was a distinguished Cambridge scholar who late in life became bishop of Carlisle, his grandfather (the bishop's father) had been an obscure Lake Country village curate with no university education. The boy Edward Law attended Charterhouse School as a foundationer ("gownboy") and worked his way up to become captain of the school, a position attained more than sixty years later by both Edmund and Henry. At Cambridge, where he finished third wrangler, he won the Chancellor's Medal for highest excellence in classics, gained earlier by his brother John, future bishop of Elphin, later by another brother, George Henry, future bishop of Bath and Wells, and much later by his grandnephews Edmund and Franklin Lushington. In 1788 Law's earned reputation as an ingenious special pleader and successful barrister brought his appointment to lead the defense in the notorious treason trial of Warren Hastings, former governor-general of India. For seven dreary years the prosecution dragged on at Westminster before the House of Lords. Pitted against such redoubtable orators as Charles James Fox, Richard Brinsley Sheridan, and the obsessed Edmund Burke, Law remained undaunted and tireless. With Hastings's acquittal in 1795, Law's fame was assured. By 1812, however, he had passed his peak in health and energy and, despite his reactionary convictions, enjoyed comparatively little influence with the ruling Tory cabinet.[3]

Yet in the story of young Edmund and Henry, Lord Ellenborough remains undeniably important. He had been by far the crucial influence in the career of his nephew, their father, Edmund Henry Lushington. In the nephew's mind the chief justice stood uncomfortably tall: the prototype of public service such as Lushington himself had not managed to achieve but hoped that a brilliant son, given resolute diligence and kindly paternal encouragement, might. But young Edmund would possess neither temperament nor desire for that kind of activity; and Henry throughout his brief adulthood would lack the requisite good health.

At Cambridge before becoming bishop of Carlisle, Ellenborough's father, Edmund Law (1703–87), had been master of Peterhouse, principal librarian of the university, and professor of casuistical divinity. He was encyclopedically read in metaphysics, theological exegesis, Christian apologetics, and related disciplines. He published several pamphlets and books, some of them important, including an edition of John Locke's works with a biographical introduction. The bishop, unlike his imposing judicial son, was physically diminutive, temperamentally sweet and placid. Yet in his own quiet scholarly mode, he was no less fearless than his son and, it seems, ultimately more effective in gaining acceptance for his most cherished ideals. Although a devout Christian, he was perhaps the most broadly latitudinarian Anglican bishop of his century. Like the poet Milton, earlier, and others, he repudiated the doctrine of eternal fiery punishment and taught that souls lie asleep between death and the Judgment. He contended that the sixteenth-century Reformation, the rejection of arbitrary dogmatism, still remained partial, in need of completion. No one could more incisively oppose required subscription to creeds. For his controversial writings, and for his support of more overt movements for broader toleration, he became widely suspected and roundly denounced, even occasionally charged with deliberate subversiveness and near-atheism.[4]

Perhaps the most influential of Law's books in his time, and later the most esteemed by historians, was *Considerations on the State of the World with Regard to the Theory of Religion* (1745). In opposition to deism he freshly undertook to justify God's way with humanity: God has willed that religious truth be progressive, tailoring itself to the naturally developing receptivity of the human mind, as it broadens through the centuries with accumulated experience and new discoveries. As in no other kind of human endeavor—the sciences or the arts of life— can human beings possibly advance in other than natural psychological and historically contextual ways, so it must necessarily be with religious understanding. Truth, although immutable, must grow within each of us organically, as we ourselves grow, through an ever-widening association of ideas, the old slowly developing into the new. *Considerations* was acclaimed by an eminent intellectual historian in our century as a precursor of David Hartley, Joseph Priestley, and several other later eighteenth-century liberal writers. As the "decisive figure in this whole development," Law "deserves a prominent place" in the "history of the growing revolt against . . . primitivism and uniformitarianism" in the last half of his century.[5]

When Edmund Law was married, in 1740, he was thirty-seven, vicar of Greystoke in Cumberland, and author of three heavy scholarly works. His bride was Mary Christian, eighteen-year-old daughter of a wealthy Cumbrian barrister and landowner descended from a family prominent for centuries as sturdy local officials ("deemsters") on the Isle of Man. Mary, whose portrait shows a wide-eyed beauty, came to the gentle little scholar (twice her age) with a dowry of £3,000 and a charming list of self-composed prenuptial resolutions: always to be "frugal"; serve God "more sincerely" than ever before; "never . . . fret or fall into a passion about small matters"; "lay aside all fondness for dress, but . . . be always exactly neat and clean"; and "never . . . contradict my dear husband without it be quite necessary and then with the greatest good nature I am mistress of"![6] Law had not yet become a bishop when Mary died thirty-two years later, leaving eight sons and four daughters, including two future bishops, a future chief justice, and an enterprising individualist who would make a fortune in India but lose much of it in America, where he married the granddaughter of Martha Washington. *The Dictionary of National Biography* memorializes the careers of twelve male descendants of the bishop, all named Law. At least two more descendants are there: Edmund Law Lushington and his brother Henry.

Ironically, the one member of the family of Christian now most widely remembered was a nephew of Mary Law: Fletcher Christian, who led the mutiny on the *Bounty* against Captain Bligh. It must have been a galling annoyance to that stout conservative defender of all things legal, Lord Ellenborough, to have for a first cousin such a law-defying rebel.

The Lushingtons, into which another Mary Law—daughter of Edmund and Mary—would marry in 1764, were Kentish landowners with estates at Rodmersham, near Sittingbourne, and Norton Court, near Faversham.[7] The Norton Court property had come into the family through the marriage of Stephen Lushington (1675–1718) into the old Kentish family of Godfrey. One of these was the ill-fated justice of the peace for Westminster Sir Edmund Berry Godfrey (1621–78), whose never-solved murder played such a dramatic part in the sensational happenings surrounding Titus Oates and the alleged "Popish Plot" during the reign of Charles II.[8] By two wives Sir Edmund's father had sired twenty children, one of whom named Benjamin became an ancestor of our Lushingtons. Benjamin's only son, John, who predeceased his sister Catherine (wife of Stephen Lushington), left his estate to her. Their son, Thomas Godfrey Lushington (1700–1757), was the first of various Lushingtons who through the years up to the present have proudly borne the christened name of Godfrey.

Through two marriages Stephen Lushington founded the two lines that have since included most, if not all, Lushingtons of any note. The second of these lines produced several notable men, among them a survivor of the Black Hole of Calcutta and his brother, the baronet Sir Stephen Lushington (1744–1807), director and chairman of the East India Company, and Sir Stephen's descendants, including the eminent reformer and legal authority, Dr. Stephen (1782–1873), judge of the Admiralty Court and dean of the Arches (ecclesiastical court of appeal for the province of Canterbury).

From Stephen Lushington's first line descended the subjects of our biography. His son and heir Thomas Godfrey married Dorothy Gisbourne, of an old Derbyshire family; she died in 1748, leaving, with other issue, a thirteen-year-old son, James Stephen (1733–1801), the grandfather of our Edmund and Henry. He graduated in 1756 from Peterhouse, where Edmund Law was master, took M.A. in 1759, and won a fellowship in 1761. It was probably at Peterhouse that he met the master's daughter, Mary, his future wife. Although heir to the family estates, he entered the church, serving as vicar of the old church at Crosthwaite just outside Keswick (later attended by Robert Southey, his family, and that of his brother-in-law Samuel Taylor Coleridge) from 1770 to 1780; rector of Latton, Essex, 1782–87; vicar of Newcastle-upon-Tyne, 1783–1801; and prebendary of Carlisle, 1777–1901.[9] His first wife, Mary, dying in 1768 at the age of twenty-four, left him with two sons and a daughter, the eldest, Thomas Godfrey (1765–1819), only three years old. The second was Edmund Henry (1766–1839), the father of our two men. Thomas would attend Peterhouse for a year, then spend nine years in the Bengal Service, return to England, and eventually suffer a mental collapse and not recover. In 1772 James Stephen had married Mary Christian, his first wife's first cousin, with whom he had a second family. Of some of these we will hear more later.

Edmund Henry began a life course closely patterned upon his distinguished uncle Edward's. Like the future chief justice, he attended Charterhouse School as a "gownboy," then distinguished himself at Cambridge—B.A. as fourth wrangler, the M.A., a fellowship. He proceeded to the Inns of Court in 1893 and studied in the office of the same superb special pleader, George Wood,[10] where twenty years earlier his uncle had launched his career. Special pleaders, lawyers skilled at adapting the law to particular cases, assisted the attorneys in preparing difficult briefs, which were in turn handed to the barristers, who alone were permitted to argue in the courts. Without the patronage of the attorneys, few if any new barristers could dream of succeeding. Edward Law practiced special pleading seven years before attempting an active barristership. By then his reputation stood so high with the attorneys that they gave him all the briefs he could handle.[11]

Concerning Edmund Henry Lushington's life during the middle and later 1790s, up to his thirty-fifth year, very little seems traceable. For at least five years, he practiced as a barrister, going on the Northern Circuit as his uncle had done. By 1801 he was preparing, though reluctantly, to leave England and begin a new life as a judge in faraway Ceylon. So much for what is known. But anyone who would understand his sons must attempt to understand him. He adored them and they him. Both boys, each in his fashion, would model himself upon the father, who was in numerous respects an unexceptionable model. But, basically, he was not at all like his eminent uncle. Lushington would always labor under an ethically admirable but vocationally retarding conscientiousness; an introspective turn of indecisiveness, painful self-doubt; a need for slow undisturbed reflection and hard-won second opinions. He could never have imitated his uncle's gift for quick decision, his tenacious hold upon a principle whether or not it was ultimately tenable, or his overbearing manner when opposed. Without extensive rerouting Law's road could never have been Lushington's road.

Lushington had not enjoyed a happy childhood. He had never really known his mother, who had died when he was barely two. Evidently his rather rugged stepmother, coming into his life when he was about six, was never very congenial with him. (In later life they were for most of the time estranged.) She promptly began bearing her own children, at least five in the first seven years and seven in all. Her four talented sons would all achieve responsible positions in public service, the ablest of the quartet, Stephen Rumbold Lushington (1776–1868), becoming assistant secretary of the treasury and ultimately governor of Madras. Edmund Henry and his ill-fated older brother would apparently become rather lost in the shuffle. It must have been a sore affliction to Edmund Henry when that constant playmate of his childhood fell into mental breakdown.

With only a few exceptions, Lushington's closest friends at Cambridge or in London were thinkers rather than dynamic doers. The chief exception, James Scarlett (1769–1844), who became one of the most acclaimed barristers of his period and a tireless opponent of repressive laws, later attorney-general, chief baron of the exchequer, and the first Baron Abinger, lost touch with Lushington in their later years. Two of Lushington's most congenial friends became respected natural scientists. Smithson Tennant (1761–1815) was a medical doctor and an esteemed experimental chemist and agriculturalist who died in an accident shortly after being appointed professor of chemistry for Cambridge University. Even more noted was William Hyde Wollaston (1766–1828), Lushington's Charterhouse schoolfellow and Cambridge friend, whose varied contributions to medicine, chemistry, optics, and other branches of physics fill nearly nine columns in the *Dictionary of National Biography*. Lushington himself, though never more than an amateur, was attracted to the natural sciences, and, with his speculative bent and sense of reverent wonder at natural phenomena, might have had a more congenial calling in science than in law. By some obscure indications, during the 1790s Lushington was associating with a stimulating set of able young Whigs including, among others, Thomas Creevey (1768–1838), member of parliament and now famed diarist, and John Whishaw (ca. 1764–1840), chancery barrister and stander-behind-scenes in Whig politics, sometimes called "the Pope of Holland House," for his unique place in the famous Whig society there.[12] Surviving correspondence shows that Whishaw and Lushington were friends for the rest of their lives. But Lushington's two closest intimates were obscure, cerebral country clergymen—Whitehall Davies (d. 1824) and, even closer to Lushington, the tortured Wilfrid Clark (1766–1825), who suffered a melancholy deterioration involving alcohol. Fortunately, Lushington's own middle and later years would be moderately prosperous and, with plentiful reasons, signally happy, settled on his own country estate, retired from competitive strife, surrounded by a large and loving family. But contentment would follow a heavy portion of earlier agony.

After 1801 Lushington's story acquires palpable substance, adequately documented for the remainder of his life. For nearly nine years he was under appointment to the Supreme Court of the newly established British colonial government of Ceylon, first as puisne justice and finally as acting chief justice. These were frustrating years, lonely and heartbreaking, undertaken to serve sufficient time (seven years) to qualify for a lifelong pension, then return to England, and rear a family in his hereditary station of country gentleman. The term began, as we shall see, with two deaths, both painful for him to endure, and one of them devastating. And then, emotionally shaken as he was, the peculiar requirements of his office, for one with his brand of idealism and temperamental bent, in association with a particular set of uncongenial persons, proved too much to surmount. Finally, out of considerations of honor and a prudent concern for his own health, he resigned before completing his term, and thereby relinquished his pension. The crisis arrived when the governor of Ceylon, the redoubtable General Sir Thomas Maitland (1759?–1824), ordered him under threat of removal from office to cease dawdling (as the governor saw it) and immediately give a particular verdict that he, still indecisive, had thus far thought improper. When after further reflection he essentially adopted the governor's position, he gave the verdict demanded, but attached his resignation rather than appear to have compromised his conscience to retain his employment.[13]

By Lushington's own accounting, out of the "8 years & 8 months" during which the Ceylon position had put him out of circulation for "any other occupation" his "actual residence on the Island" of Ceylon was only about "4 years & a half." At the very outset in 1801 his sailing was delayed for various reasons not his fault. He was still in England restlessly marking time when his "excellent father," aged sixty-six, died at Newcastle on 17 June. Among the departed vicar's papers was a ten-page document carefully admonishing all his children to love and fear God, reverence the Scriptures, and live exemplary Christian lives. They would "meet with sincere friends (for where is the comfort of life without this consolation)," and should always be true to them; "however never imagine that it will be your lot to have more than a few friends." They should never make themselves "Slaves to Popularity," but should always "do what is right & just," as their Saviour had done, seeking "all opportunities of serving all worthy Persons in their different pursuits." There was more, but what must have echoed in Lushington's mind most resonantly during the difficulties of his next eight years was an elaborated exhortation always to "meet with the approbation of [his] own conscience" regardless of the cost in popularity. Such upright counsel was unassailable, but perhaps a few ounces too burdensome, a few degrees too perpendicular, for such an already conscience-heeding son to lug across the water into the nothing-if-not-pragmatic position of a newly

FIG. I. Edmund Henry Lushington. Artist and date unknown. By permission of Roger G. L. Lushington.

established judgeship on Ceylon. On occasions when the letter of a law may come into conflict with the probable intention of the legislators, a judge's nagging conscience may need a sedative more than a stimulant.

Already in grief, Lushington would soon receive a felling blow. On 2 January of that year, he had been married to Louisa Phillips, daughter of Faulkner Phillips, an active member of one of Lancashire's most dominant textile and manufacturing families.[14] Before the September sailing Louisa was in advanced pregnancy; but as Lushington later wrote in his "large family Bible," they had been reassured by what he "deemed the best medical authority" that it was safe to go ahead. From the first Louisa was almost continually seasick. After two weeks they disembarked at Madeira, where on 8 October, in "extreme pain and danger for nearly 24 hours" she gave birth to a daughter. While apparently recovering, she was "attacked by dysentery. After illness for many days, she was so exhausted that she was thought to be dead. She however, revived, and for a few days there was hope. She died on October 27th, 1801." Back to England went the heartbroken widower, taking the child. Louisa had charged him as "one of her last requests, 'Let my child learn her principles from Sophia.' "[15] Sophia Philips (her branch of the wealthy spinning and manufacturing family did not double the "l") was Louisa's second cousin and most intimate friend. Sophia's brother George would later sit in Parliament for most of two decades as the leading spokesman for the Manchester manufacturers and would ultimately receive a baronetcy.

It is hard for us to realize the tedious length of a voyage under sails from Britain to India in those times. Leaving the infant with Sophia, now her godmother, Lushington sailed again at the end of February 1802 and did not arrive in Ceylon until 3 September. He was haunted by the memory of Louisa, and no doubt by his conscience for having risked her life by putting to sea when they did. He needed to talk about her but could hardly do so. On 27 December 1801 he wrote to Clark, "Even now I cannot mention circumstances which must increase your esteem & admiration. At some future period I may collect soft calmness & fortitude to describe the nobleness & generosity which exceeded all that I was capable of conceiving. At present I am unable." To Tennant nearly a year later, he spoke of "a subject upon which I often think & always anxiously." He desired that his good friends would think as he did, that they "should esteem & love the memory of Louisa—that you should value as you ought her generosity & fortitude—who died for me—not once only but three times—& still retained the same unshaken attachment to me the same generous disregard of her own sufferings. . . . It will give me a consolation to know that you think of her as I do. God keep you for the present."

In India and on Ceylon, he found much to outrage his always strong humanitarian conscience: "The Europeans live in palaces, the natives generally in mud huts." Reportedly all natives were "very dishonest, but respecting this point I have some doubts excepting those who deal with the ship captains & lower Europeans who treat them like knaves & vile beasts & may well expect to be cheated." He was shocked by the Europeans' calling all natives "Black Fellows," and damning them all as rascals, even in the hearing of their servants "of which half understand English"; and he was appalled at a "vicious" native custom that the British had been unable to overturn, forbidding women of certain castes to cover their breasts.

His official situation presented daunting difficulties. A defect in the charter had left an inadequate demarcation of the relative powers of the governor and the commanding general. Fortunately, the first general was congenial and cooperative, but his successor was individualistic and irascible, setting off conflicts that engendered other conflicts, worsened by overreactions from the Supreme Court, until as one historian has truly put it, "the Government became totally paralyzed and reduced to a position bordering on chaos."[16] The basic dilemma was removed by the appointment of a military man, General Maitland, as governor with both civil and military responsibility. But earlier confrontations had fortified the determination of the justices to resist intrusion upon the separation of judicial and executive power. Within the court hearings themselves, another problem was the nearly universal proclivity for perjury by native witnesses on either side of a case. Lushington soon found that "the mind is kept for hours and even days together in painful suspense endeavouring to extract the truth from a mass of falsehood on each side." The justices had "hardly ventured as yet to convict anybody except the witnesses whom we have several times ordered from the court to the whipping post." Worse yet, the absence of a jury system left the justices with total responsibility for convicting and sentencing, often to the punishment of death. It was still more agonizing during periods when one judge was absent from the island, leaving a prisoner's life entirely within the hands of the other judge, unable even to confer with a colleague. This may have been a bearable responsibility for a strong-stomached jurist, but not for the tender-conscienced Lushington, who near the end of his tenure "acted by myself for about 9 months." In the case precipitating his resignation, he had pled for more time to decide because he was simultaneously trying a man for murder—"a case of life and death."[17] Governor Maitland reported that the number of acquittals in capital cases had "led to the most unfortunate of situations—that the Decisions of the Supreme Court have become proverbial among the Natives," who considered it "more dangerous to steal a Handkerchief as they term it, than to Murder a Man." Maitland urged that the judicial system be speedily reorganized to provide juries.[18]

In 1805 Lushington had quixotically embarked from Ceylon for England with his first governor's official permission, but not with his actual approval, to set before the Colonial Office various grievances of the Supreme Court against the commanding general. The chief justice, probably unwisely, desired Lushington to make the trip; but undoubtedly another impelling motive was Lushington's desperate desire to visit his little daughter and her godmother, Sophia. Politically the voyage was imprudent. It is doubtful that the mission to the Colonial Office did anything at all to improve the situation on Ceylon. Lushington's time at sea, at his own expense, going and returning was thirteen months. Before he would again land on Ceylon on 5 April 1807, his friend the first chief justice had resigned for health reasons, and the colony had its new civil and military governor, Maitland, who did not welcome Lushington back. Lushington returned as acting chief justice by orders from London, but quite against Maitland's preference. The tragicomedy would play itself out until Lushington's resignation and final departure for England in March of 1809. But two purposes of his 1805 voyage had been happily realized: he had seen little Louisa, and he had visited Sophia and was almost certainly resolved to become her husband soon after his return.

The nightmare of Ceylon behind him, he reached England late in November 1809, after nine long weeks sailing from Ceylon to Bombay, another five and one-half slow months from Bombay. Materially, his homecoming was inauspicious. He was forty-three years old, had little available money and no reliable prospects for soon acquiring more. He had left behind him a few thousand pounds of his painfully earned judicial salary, invested with a firm in Madras. (By the summer of 1812, the company would go into bankruptcy, and not until nine years later would he recover even a fraction of his investment.) He knew that he had at best only a forlorn case for any kind of pension. His late father's substantial estate—lands in Derbyshire, Leicestershire, and Kent—was out of everybody's reach. His elder brother, "poor Thomas," the nominal proprietor, was hopelessly insane, and the four half-brothers were poised to litigate for as large a portion as they could get, as soon as they could do so with a mentally competent heir.

Lushington, of course, was still a barrister, but had neither a following nor a base of operation. As a former judge, and a nephew of the chief justice, he feared he would not be accepted by fellow barristers. Early in his Ceylon years, he had decided that if he ever returned to England without pension and went back to "the painful and murderous contention of the bar," he could at least not "return with propriety of the Sessions." Ellenborough now would attempt to reassure him, writing in May 1811: "I see no objection whatever on the score of the strictest propriety of the resumption of the practice of your profession, &,

except . . . as you may feel a repugnance to practice at the Sessions, I see no reason why you should not even attend them. . . . I think you are *prudentially* right in not resuming the practice of your profession in town. . . . " But even back in Lancashire, where Lushington started again, he would painfully feel the awkwardness. In April 1812 Ellenborough wrote, "I am not surprised at what you mention concerning the *leprosy*," but surely "any momentary displeasure which any gentmn of the bar may feel at your return to *them* will soon be removed by more liberal & just consideration on their part, & by the correctness & liberality of your own professional conduct upon every occasion."

The return to the bar, relatively unsuccessful, would last for no more than about two years. After the first, Lushington reported to Ellenborough that though he had "made some little progress . . . as my juniors are in possession of the business and the public confidence I cannot flatter myself with any hope of considerable success." He had gained less than £100. More specifically, he told Clark that the expenses of his "professional debut" had been at least £500 and his profit only 40/2 guineas (under £45). A year later, in the spring of 1813, he complained to Clark that he was "without sufficient practice to overcome the disqualifying nervousness which affects most *young men* in the beginning of their career." Yet he had done better recently, clearing £89 in the first quarter of 1813.

He and Sophia were married on 12 April 1810. Though thirteen years younger, she was nearing thirty-one.

As her wedding approached, she composed an earnest prayer that survives in the family papers:

> O Lord God Almighty, the Creator & preserver of my life, who has hitherto blessed me far beyond my expectations and deserts, assist me with thy heavenly grace in that situation of life which I am now going to enter. O may I make it my constant study & delight to please him, on whom my thoughts and affections are placed. Teach me the several duties of a Wife, & enable me to fulfill them. Do thou abundantly bless my beloved friend. Let our union be in the Lord, that we may be helps meet for each other in reference to both worlds. May our affections be founded upon truly Christian principles, bless O Lord our union let our love be pure & holy, lasting without decay. In any trials or afflictions that thou mayst be pleased to send us, may we support & comfort each other, bearing each other's burthens & lifting up our hearts more & more to thee, who alone knowst what is best for us. Teach us to look beyond this world to that eternal state where sin and sorrow cannot enter. Let us live in a constant state of preparation for death that when we have fulfilled thy will on earth we may be received into thine eternal kingdom. These petitions I ask, O Lord, not

relying on my own merits (for thou who art a God of infinite purity knowst my unworthiness), but on the merits of my Saviour & Redeemer Jesus Christ. Amen.

A well-executed water color of Sophia with Lushington's little Louisa done at about this time shows a strikingly handsome woman probably of something more than medium height. During the next fifteen years, she would bear twelve children, five sons and seven daughters, eight of whom would reach adulthood.

Despite financial and professional worries and the still-nagging feeling of too little usefulness in the world, the long-lonely Lushington had finally established a setting for lasting happiness. The sons and daughters of their father's middle age would begin life in a joyous, love-filled environment. An aunt, Sophia's sister Catherine, would live with them much of the time, sharing in the rearing and educating of the rapidly increasing brood.

The first offspring, and the father's first son, born at Prestwich, Lancashire, on 10 January 1811, was christened Edmund Law Lushington, honoring Lushington's scholarly grandfather, whom his namesake would grow in several significant respects to resemble: the retiring and scholarly bent, the gentle otherworldliness, the freedom from dogmatism, the attraction toward metaphysics. The choice of name, bespeaking pride in the Law family heritage, was sure to please the chief justice as well.

Lushington himself could hardly contain his joy. "Even this country," he wrote that May, inviting Clark to Lancashire for a visit, "is beautiful now & will be more so in a fortnight's time. Quiet rides. Good music & good tempered females in the house, your god daughter so much the object of your kindness & her little laughing brother hers and her aunt's delight will I trust make you stay with us happily for some time. I am sure that a whole legion of devils would vanish before them & then I could not care whose herd they seize upon."

In November of that year came the first apparent upward turn in Lushington's material prospects. When Sophia's father died, she inherited the income from a substantial sum of money, approximately £10,000, most of the principal to be retained for her children. At a time of depreciating currency, Lushington thought it important that the money be invested in real property. From Sophia's trustees he could borrow part of the price of a home, supplement it from his own small funds, and secure the loan with the purchased property. This may have been how he would acquire their first home, at Hanwell near London, in 1814. Unfortunately, though, the improvement in his 1811 fortune was largely offset within the year by his losses in the Madras investment.

The second son, Henry, was born at Singleton, Lancashire, on 13 April 1812. During the latter half of 1812, and all of 1813, Ellenborough was patiently exploring with the prime minister, Lord Liverpool; the chancellor, Lord Eldon; and other officials what could be done for Lushington, what possibility of a pension or of a position on a board of inquiry, or the like. Liverpool was sympathetic but, after conferring with the colonial secretary, declared that Lushington simply did not qualify under the time rules for a Ceylon pension. The best that could be offered was a pitifully small Civil List pension (little more than "a matter of charity"), which after usual deductions would net no more than £230 a year.[19] Ellenborough reluctantly accepted the offer; but it is virtually certain that Lushington finally never drew upon the pension. Before it came through, he had received adequate public employment.[20]

Already, in June 1813, Ellenborough had appointed him to the lifetime position of master of the Crown Office, a quasi-judicial post paying somewhat more than £500 a year in the Court of the King's Bench, Ellenborough's own court. Lushington would be the chief administrator of the court's office, with responsibilities including collecting and recording fines and impaneling special juries. Now, in July 1814, Ellenborough was assisting him to secure a second appointment, to the Colonial Board of Audit, the committee that examined the accounts of all British colonies. Neither post was a sinecure. The audit board, in particular, entailed close, anxiously demanding work, especially for such a conscientious investigator as Lushington. He would work his way up to the board's chairmanship in 1818 and retire from it in 1824 "on very satisfactory terms."

After 1814, evidently, he had no great financial anxieties. By 20 March 1815 he told Clark that his annual income was about £2,000. The family had moved to Hanwell, about seven miles from central London. Even now the verdant hilly neighborhood (much of it a public park) retains a startling beauty quite unlike the present undistinguished Hanwell center. He had found a pleasing house with excellent gardens and twenty-four acres of land "at extremely reasonable price." When in 1819 "poor Thomas" fortuitously died, Lushington and his half-brothers could at last begin settling their differences concerning their father's properties, reaching an agreement in 1821. That same year Lushington regained a portion of his long-lost Madras investments. He could begin selling dispersed parcels of land, looking forward to locating and purchasing his own country retirement estate. By the end of 1822, his annual income had climbed "rather above £5,000." He would soon be "quite easy and ready to depart," although he would live another seventeen years.

But he had not liberated himself from personal anxieties: convictions of underachieved potentialities, memories of fumbled opportunities for serving humanity. Such regrets amplified themselves around 1816 as he neared and entered his fifties. Perhaps even yet he might discover a work more widely beneficial. Writing to Clark that March, he recalled one of Gibbon's characters who "passed the morning and evening of life in pleasure & inglorious indolence—but whose meridian burst forth with strong lustre." He and Clark, just then, were "*at* the meridian & if we cannot hope for splendour may be *more useful* than at any other period. This ought to be the main object. I feel the desire and aim at it."

Already in February he had confided a new idea. Working almost at the door of the King's Bench prison, and reading the works of John Howard, he recognized how sorely Great Britain needed some centralized prison reform. Surely a general inspector of prisons "would be extremely useful," one who in the "spirit of Benevolence" would coordinate all the local prison inspectors and personally inspect every prison in the nation at least once every three years. True, the work would be grueling, "intersecting each county backwards & forwards," but he (already the adoring father of five small children with others arriving almost annually) felt ready to put forth the effort if such should prove his calling. Of course, nothing of the sort materialized. The burden of sensed shortcomings continued to weigh upon him. In February of 1821 he wrote that "the only serious drawback" to complete happiness was "the lingering" consciousness of past "errors of judgment." In June, contemplating his half-brother William's service on a distinguished commission of inquiry in Ireland, he "could almost envy him a situation so honorable & with such opportunities of being *useful*." "Am I authorized," he asked Clark, "to ascribe to myself any such desire of utility after what I once relinquished? Let that however pass." And in December his return for a Founders' Day visit to Charterhouse School, thirty-nine years after his last schooldays there, left him brooding over a life where "so much time has been misspent & so many opportunities of living to more useful purpose have been lost."

Those feelings of comparative failure, that equating of idealized "usefulness" with some large public office, would magnify Lushington's ambitions that his sons, unlike himself, would prove their abilities and rise to national eminence, not for mere fame or wealth but for ampler service to humankind.

Even earlier than he might have hoped for, Lushington had found himself having to cope with the gratifying problem of how to manage the education of a precocious firstborn son. At the age of three years, ten months, with his half-sister Louisa for his teacher, Edmund, as Lushington informed Clark, "begins to read little books by himself & takes great delight afterwards in telling the stories to Henry." (Henry was two years, six months.) Before reaching five Edmund had "*played* himself through a long Manchester multiplication table as far as 12 times 16—192." By himself he was reading "with great delight Miss Edgeworth's tales," quickly memorizing hymns and little poems, and writing on a slate "better than most boys at 7." He was "full of spirit & fire the whole time that he is learning." When his mother would ask him, "How much dear is 9 times 6?" he would say "54 mama taking her by the chin & giving a skip & a jump." He was constantly asking, "What does that mean?" about "any new word or expression."

Would Clark, who had taught boys at the Charterhouse, give some professional advice? Should they begin the youngster in Latin? He could almost undoubtedly learn it, but would that be an advantage or otherwise in his later schooling? Clark promptly advised against the Latin. A boy starting school too far ahead of the others would be unpopular and have too little left to accomplish there. Instead he should work on mathematics and the other common branches, acquiring a lifelong practical advantage "in the pursuit of either fortune or fame, & a prodigious resource for happiness."

The Latin, accordingly, was deferred, though only for a year, while Edmund worked on arithmetic and put "together maps" drawn "in an extraordinary manner for a child of his age." He was entering his seventh year when his mother and half-sister began him on the Latin grammar book written by Dr. John Russell, headmaster of Charterhouse School. Within a year his progress "surprised his Uncle George" (Sophia's M.P. brother, later Sir George Philips).

All seemed briskly marching to schedule until the summer of 1818, when Edmund, aged seven years, seven months, broke ranks. While using "a Latin & Greek grammar in one," he moved out of the Latin section and on his own volition began to study Greek. Suddenly, for Lushington, "one morning upon my return from London he repeated to me a Greek noun." Four months later Lushington was telling Clark that "Edmund has repeatedly desired me to remind you of your promise to send him a *Greek letter.*" He was dutifully continuing with Latin, but enjoying better his self-assigned Greek. When he was three days short of eight, his father asked Clark to recommend "the best & easiest Latin poetry for lessons." Edmund had "found the Metamorphoses rather difficult & I am anxious not to dispirit him. He goes on well with the Greek grammar and the examples in Russell."

Edmund was displaying already two tendencies of his later life—the more or less resolute avoidance of Latin in favor of Greek, and a susceptibility to discouragement when he fell short of excelling. Greek was his language, Latin was not. Time spent on Latin afforded less satisfaction and distracted him from Greek. Greek quickly became, and remained, a calling, an absorbing personal fulfillment; Latin was a tolerated annoyance.

It was the agile-minded, more versatile Henry, coming along only fifteen months behind Edmund, who would develop an approximately equal bent for both Latin and Greek, and would soon begin developing a naturally easy, idiomatic written English. But the father, so far as his surviving letters show, had not yet discovered Henry's potentialities. Others soon would do so, and then, if not before, the father would, too.

Fortune was seeming kind to the Lushington family. Lushington himself suffered attacks of gout, becoming more frequent and severe, but bore them pluckily. By early 1819 Sophia had borne seven children, and an eighth would come that year. But three times between December 1818 and April 1819, death would strike persons Lushington loved. In December it was Lord Ellenborough, his uncle and benefactor; then in January, his full-brother, "poor Thomas," long mentally deranged but his closest boyhood companion. Most heartbreakingly, at the end of March came the loss of his daughter Louisa, only child of the other Louisa who died at Madeira, and the infant whom Sophia had reared and loved as her own. The studious girl, not yet eighteen, was adept in Latin and French and had begun studying Italian. Though known to be gravely "ill of a pleurisy," she had been expected to recover; but death struck with stunning quickness.

"Our dear Edmund," Lushington told Clark, "was at first severely afflicted, but at his time of life such impressions must be soon effaced." But would they, in truth, be so? Leaving aside the question of how soon, if ever, such traumas fade from the psyche of any eight-year-old, the precocious Edmund was no ordinary child. Louisa had initiated him in his studies. She had stood as a fourth, with his parents and his aunt, as a source of adult love and encouragement.

For Edmund, early in his ninth year, the death of this young woman was the first of a dauntingly long string of bereavements throughout his lengthy life. Before he died, at eighty-two, in 1893, he would outlive eleven siblings (including Louisa), his firstborn and only son, and two of his three daughters. During a terrible four-year period between 1854 and 1858, he and his family would endure the deaths of a 30-year-old sister, the 43-year-old brother Henry, the 12-year-old son, and the 44-year-old brother Tom. Edmund would long outlive, too, any hope he may once have entertained of a normally happy, mutually sustaining marriage. Time and again the tender Edmund, senior in his clan, would be obliged to summon inner resources, buttressed by an undogmatic Christian faith and a rare intimacy with great tragic literature, to sustain himself and others who looked to him for strength. As bereavement inexorably followed bereavement, he would speak of the profound "mystery" of it all. "What does that mean?"—the small child's early question about "any new word or expression"—was extended by Louisa's death to the ultimate question he would ask time after time in presence of enigmas more puzzling than words.

Yet for the eager child, in 1819, the Greek still consolingly beckoned. "Edmund proceeds," Lushington wrote in June, "with his Greek and his Euclid con amore." On 4 July the father's letter to Clark began with a letter from Edmund (now eight-and-a-half), in Greek. The Greek was "entirely his own, and he alone is responsible for the errors or progress which he has made. You will perceive that he indulges in the use of abbreviations, perhaps from the pleasure of overcoming a difficulty." But there was an ominous note: "Edmund is subject to nervous twitches arising from some ulterior cause which I do not understand." One suspects his recent bereavement.

In late September came two other displacements. Both Edmund and Henry were sent from home to live at a small school in nearby Brentford conducted by a Dr. Crane. Then, rather perversely it seems now, Crane would not permit Edmund to go on with Greek. He "was at first nearly heartbroken, not I think by going to school," but by the taking away of his favorite employment. Henry, it seems, quickly adjusted, thriving in the enthusiastic acceptance of Crane and his wife. Edmund, "his spirits extremely distressed," became "comparatively unhappy and dull," his literal Latin translations failing to "give the senses." When the Cranes discussed the brothers, they invariably praised Henry to Edmund's disadvantage. Henry, they declared, unlike Edmund, was determined "not to get anything as a lesson without understanding it thoroughly." The parents, on the contrary, had found Henry to be the one who relied on his quicker memory, learning rules "to a letter" but not always understanding, whereas Edmund "understood applied & marked the exceptions," but remembered less well verbatim. To the Cranes, Edmund seemed "very much given *to self* . . . extremely tyrannical over Henry." The parents had observed Henry showing a temper, Edmund "none from the beginning," and Edmund always seeming less domineering over Henry than Henry had been over the younger Tom. Mrs. Crane contrasted Henry's sensitive responsiveness "to the gentlest reproof" with Edmund's resistance to restraint when "in high spirits" and "particularly his contempt for *females*." Lushington's "difficulty" had been "to restrain Henry—I have none to restrain Edmund." When Edmund complained of illness, the Cranes intimated he was malingering, although after an apothecary had come and given medicine for constipation, he improved. To Lushington himself Crane had exhibited a pedagogical "mock importance & mystery," even seeming to insinuate that "overexaction" of Edmund's "understanding at present might terminate in feebleness."

Lushington, shaken, could admit that maybe he had "indulged" Edmund in some respects more than Henry. And maybe Edmund was too much feeling superior to the other boys. But, really, was Crane's opinion "well founded or mere prejudice? Have all of us been blind from his birth to this moment?" He was almost "inclined to cut the Gordian knot by his almost immediate removal." But the boys stayed at Crane's through the following spring. By December, Sophia reported Edmund happier than he had been, and in January,

Edmund himself wrote, "I like school very much. Lately I have learned to slide [skate] & so has Harry."

The time had come for Henry to enjoy some equitable recognition. Perhaps unwittingly the Cranes were responding to the spell of a personality that today would be termed more "outgoing," more "articulate," more (the ultimate compliment) "charismatic" than Edmund's. To the end of his life, Henry would be the more gregarious of the two. His interests would be wider, his learning quicker (though not deeper) than Edmund's. Family tradition still has it that Henry was, everything considered, even more than Edmund "the clever one." The children's old family nurse liked to say of Henry, "If he only looked at a thing he knew it."[21] His closest friend, George Venables, recalled the adult Henry's "wonderful memory" and his uncanny reading ability: "He scarcely ever read a book through, but while he was dressing or resting, or in an interval of conversation, he turned over the pages of miscellaneous volumes; and it always appeared that he afterwards knew better than others the material part of their contents."[22]

By April 1820, looking about for another school, Lushington ruminated about Edmund's limitations: "His disposition requires more management" than Henry's. Probably his elders had "praised him too much for his early progress," so that by then "the slightest reproof overwhelms him." His "whole habit is too sensitive. He is eager in everything—less eager indeed than formerly about his improvement but still unhappy if he fails." A Hanwell neighbor, Dr. John Bond, was planning to open a school larger than Crane's, taking "50 scholars upon moderate terms." Lushington hesitated to expose his boys to the "contagion" of such an "inveterate punster & coxcomb" as Bond. But the boys would be nearer home. The parents could watch Edmund's health until he became emotionally ready for a public school. He would "have the advantage of competition," completely lacking at Crane's where the oldest boy, two years Edmund's senior, did not even know his Greek letters.

As for Henry (not yet turned eight), Lushington thought he might "be trusted" to the Charterhouse "or any other public school tomorrow." Long after Clark and he were "asleep," the boys' characters would be developed; but he was "inclined to think that Hy's progress in life will be more certain & happy." Surely the "great object" of education "should be to form the disposition so that it may encounter with firmness the various ills of life & take advantage of the opportunities." By June, Lushington was declaring Henry probably "the more careful—& rather think that he retains more perfectly what he learns. He far excels in the expression of his thoughts. Upon the whole I certainly feel less hope abt Edmd than I did a year since." But his health was improving, "or I should rather say quite good."

In the world that Lushington knew, a topsy-turvy world it may seem to us now, "progress in life" for a talented young gentleman would be over and up a hazardous road leading to parliamentary or judicial eminence. Surefootedly the boy would run a charted obstacle course, triumphantly endure a succession of initiation rites. He would attend a prestigious public school, develop social aplomb while mastering the rudiments of Latin and Greek, rising steadily to the top of the school. His university would be Cambridge, where mathematics stood firmly beside the classical languages along the obstacle course. Undeviatingly he would shoulder his way through a set of increasingly crucial competitive examinations to the highest scholastic honors, a publicly announced numerical ranking in his class that always thereafter would go with him where he went, be virtually a piece of his name. Neither the languages nor the mathematics would he allow to become ends in themselves. If he became too enchanted with them, they would turn into sirens to lure him off the road. He prevailed in the examinations chiefly to post notice to the world that it would hear from him later, in areas of endeavor largely unrelated to those where he had hitherto excelled. Unhesitatingly he would turn his face toward London, toward the Inns of Court, master the law, and then somehow—here the outlines of the map became inconveniently hazier—would manage to prevail in the badly overcrowded profession of barrister. There and later, if Fortune smiled uncrookedly, the prestige of his university ranking would boost him toward the summit.

Although loving Edmund no less, Lushington was now observing that apparently Henry, more than Edmund, had the auspicious combination of qualities for traversing such a trail. Along with his apparently sturdier disposition, Henry would quickly begin to develop a lively interest in current affairs and a liberal indignation against injustice, both like Lushington's own, and a graceful, apparently effortless way with the English language quite beyond Lushington's own, or Edmund's. Venables later wrote that long before his Cambridge years Henry had "taken an eager interest in political questions, with a constant leaning to the liberal side, and sometimes to radical opinions," having derived "his first political impressions from his father, who shared in moderation the Whig opinions of the society in which he had chiefly lived."[23]

Where Edmund would remain extraordinary was in his single-minded devotion to Greek. To the child, the schoolboy, the undergraduate, the Fellow of Trinity College, the professor at Glasgow, Greek would remain the center of life, no mere steppingstone to some broader or higher goal. His would be the dedication of the specialist in an era that still offered dismayingly few careers for that kind of specialization. Father and son would never lose their mutual respect and love, but the father's goals for him would not be his for himself.

In the fall of 1820, our boys, along with their brother Tom, joined the new school of their neighbor Dr. Bond. That summer Edmund had repeated "very well the first 260 lines of the Iliad." After a year at Bond's, Edmund was the head monitor. By December 1821 Lushington was again worrying about his being "so far superior to all the boys at his present school." He had begun to compose alcaics "with considerable facility, considering his youth & very recent practice." Perhaps it was time to think of sending him to the Charterhouse. There "among 400" Edmund would "meet with competitors, not to eliminate for this is not wanted—but to repress that baleful destroyer of excellence—vanity."

The family, meanwhile, was flourishing, adding in June a drawing room and two bedrooms to their Hanwell home. By the summer of 1822, the decision was set to send Edmund and Henry to the Charterhouse in January. Lushington had spoken "in general terms" to the headmaster, Dr. Russell, about the boys, but had not yet mentioned Edmund's "peculiar ardour. We cannot keep him in bed after 5. . . . The little Henry is all health vigour and fun." By December, if not earlier, Dr. Bond was agreeing that "Edmund ought to go." Lushington was naturally "rather anxious" about the differences the boys would find between the two schools—"particularly Edmd who has been so long the little cock strutting about with the Masters." But it had been "partly from the *moral tendency* of this situation as filling him with notions of his own superiority & rendering more sensitive to opposition & defeat when they should come, as come they must, that I thought it right to remove him & on acct of their mutual devoted attchmt Harry with him."

On entering the Charterhouse, Edmund would be just twelve, Henry not yet eleven. The ages were not untypically young, not even Henry's, although the average entering age at such public schools was gradually rising. "At the Renaissance," according to R. L. Archer's *Secondary Education in the Nineteenth Century,* "the usual age was six; Fox [born 1749] entered Eton at nine, Salisbury [born 1830] at eleven; in the forties twelve was a usual age; by the sixties entrance was deferred till fourteen, and a preparatory school preceded."[24] That same January 1823, a boy named William Makepeace Thackeray, who had been born six months after Edmund and nine months before Henry, was starting his second full year at the school. At school Thackeray was never esteemed successful. His preschool grounding in the classical languages was sadly inadequate, his native genius did not bend toward philology, and such motivation as he might have developed was crushed by the wrongheadedness of his masters. But, ironically, a major part of what is now readily known about Charterhouse school in the 1820s comes from the pen of Thackeray or from the researches of his biographers.[25] Unfortunately, nothing in the contemporary record seems to authenticate any association between him and the Lushingtons.[26]

II

Charterhouse School

1823–1828

C HARTERHOUSE S CHOOL, founded in 1611 on the grounds of a dissolved Carthusian monastery, was the school Lushington himself and his elder brother, Thomas, had attended, and the school of their father, the Reverend James Stephen Lushington, and of their mother's three most eminent brothers, the bishop of Elphin, the bishop of Bath and Wells, and Lord Chief Justice Ellenborough. Ellenborough had been buried in the school chapel just four years before his grandnephews Edmund and Henry arrived at the school.

At that time Charterhouse—along with Eton, Winchester, Westminster, Shrewsbury, Harrow, and Rugby—was one of the seven great public boarding schools. Its distinguished graduates had included Richard Crashaw; Richard Lovelace; Roger Williams (founder of Rhode Island); Isaac Barrow; Addison and Steele; John Wesley; William Blackstone; G. Manners Sutton, archbishop of Canterbury; and the current prime minister, Lord Liverpool. Among relatively recent graduates to become more prominent in the future were the historian George Grote and two future Cambridge mentors of Edmund and Henry, Connop Thirlwall (later bishop of St. Davids) and Julius Charles Hare.

Lushington had never considered any other public school for his three eldest sons. But significantly, the fourth son, Franklin (born 1823), would go instead to Rugby. Although Edmund and Henry, thoroughly prepared and extraordinarily motivated, would rapidly rise to the top of the school, their years fell in times of disenchantment for the school itself, as well as for their father.

When Lushington had considered sending the boys there as early as Easter-time, 1822, his friend Clark, as a former Charterhouse teacher, was warmly and bluntly opposed. He conceded that Charterhouse was probably no worse than other public schools, but he "shd feel easier if a boy in whose welfare I feel interest were at a school I was less acquainted with." First, there was no assurance that Edmund would find the salutary competition Lushington desired for him. More likely he would be placed, "not according to his actual proficiency," but by some arbitrary formula involving age, and thus encounter even less competition than at Dr. Bond's. Emulation of boys in higher forms seldom operated at all. If a lower-form boy was not old enough or strong enough "to defend himself against the wanton & vexatious teazing & tyranny of the other lower boys, without accusing them to the monitors, &c I can hardly conceive a more miserable being." And should he be "protected from this by becoming a favourite of any of the large boys, it may be even worse. Do not let your pure-minded little fellows go to that, or any such school, till they have acquired the strength & determination of 12 or 13." Their minds would, "surely enough, be corrupted, more or less, in course of time. But let them not be put in the way of it earlier than may be needful."

During the 1820s all of the public schools were still what later historians have called "unreformed." But the setting of Charterhouse in an undesirable part of London, nestling close to unsanitary Smithfield, the world's largest cattle market, was surely one of the worst. Furthermore, the school just then was almost unbearably overcrowded. In 1818 the headmaster, Dr. John Russell, had introduced the "Madras system" of student teachers, by which lower-form boys were taught by other boys, some of whom may have known less Latin or Greek than the fellow pupils they were nominally teaching. Lowered tuition rates brought a rapid enrollment increase with no commensurate increase in adult teachers—from 238 boys and 5 masters in 1818 to 477 and 8 in 1823, when the Lushingtons arrived. The peak of 480 came in 1825. Then began a sharp reaction: by 1829 enrollment had dwindled to 289, and by 1832, when Russell resigned, 137 with 4 masters.[1] The lowest point came in 1835, with only 99 boys.[2] As Gerald S. Davies, the historian of the Charterhouse foundation, puts it, "the British parent, not always a far-seeing judge in matters of education, had got what he had asked for—a cheap education—and presently discovered the value of the article."[3]

But it was not only at Charterhouse that enrollments declined during the 1820s and 1830s. At a time when evangelical religion was spreading in England, the public schools collectively had acquired a scandalous reputation. Eton saw a drop from 627 in 1833 to 444 in 1835; Harrow from 295 in 1816 to 128 in 1828; Rugby from 300 in 1821 to 123 in 1827.[4]

The boys at Charterhouse were crammed with hardly breathing room into the homes of the schoolmasters. In one of the smaller houses, the Reverend Charles Rowland Dicken's, thirty boys of all ages, including Thomas Mozley, future editor of the *British Critic*, "lived in the same room, down which ran two deal tables, from breakfast to bed-time, doing all our work there, however elbowed, jostled, dinned, distracted."[5] In 1821 the Reverend Robert Watkinson's three-story house of 75 feet, 7 inches frontage and about 40 feet depth held 148 boys besides Watkinson's own family and the servants. The Reverend William Henry Chapman's house, evidently about the same size, had 144 boys. The crowding had somewhat eased before the Lushingtons came in 1823. Three additional houses had permitted a limit of 100 boys to a house, but still four times the standard of later nineteenth-century schools.[6]

Edmund and Henry landed in Chapman's house, presumably with 98 other boys. Lushington was soon writing that "their rapid progress has given them some consideration & induced some *stout fellows*, who at first compelled them . . . to do their exercises—to request their assistance as a favour." Luckily they had "for one of their protectors" a robust cousin called William "Bull" Lushington, son of Lushington's half-brother. They seemed "pleased with the school, though *shocked* with the swearing & hardly being permitted to say their prayers by their bedside." Lushington was disgusted with the living conditions—a broken window, and no fire, in cold weather. By mid-March both boys were home with whooping cough. Lushington was convinced that they had not received "*reasonable* attention," and now Edmund was dangerously ill.[7] By month's end the entire Lushington brood of ten children had whooping cough, often fatal to English children.

Lushington felt reluctant to return the boys to such a place, although "their progress . . . while there was astonishg." In two months Henry, not yet eleven, was in the fourth form (innovatively, under Russell the forms ran from a low of twelfth to the high of first), and Edmund had already been "removed from the fourth to be praepositus [student teacher] to the 9th—the regular step to be removed into the 3^d or 2^d." But Lushington was sure that the moral education was bad, and wished he could find "a proper person" for tutoring such boys "on reasonable terms." He was determined to keep the two together. Henry, "though quick & clever," was "very little inclined to exert himself except for play & mischief," and "much more liable to be misled by other boys." It was important "not to loosen the tie which we have over his conduct in his devoted admiration & love of his brother."

Fortunately the parents could oversee the boys' moral education because the school permitted them to go home almost every weekend. After "rather an unpleasant conference with Chapman about the entire neglect" of Edmund's cough, Lushington had tried unsuccessfully to get the boys removed to another house. But in a later conversation, Chapman appeared to be "an excellent man—& has assured me of his unremitting attention in the future to the state of their health."

In the absence of greater contrary evidence, it seems fair play to suppose that Mr. Chapman, like most functionaries around institutions, was a reasonable enough approximation to "an excellent," or at least a well-intentioned, man. In 1827 he was promoted to second master. But the unrepaired window in a dank-cold London February is not reassuring. The man was, after all, accepting boarding fees for a house packed with boys in a period of high childhood mortality. The extremely minor but popular versifier Martin Farquhar Tupper, a boy of our period whose autobiography recklessly denounces every aspect of the school, immoderately accused the "seven clergyman masters" of reaping "fortunes by neglecting five hundred boys," and singled out Chapman as one of the most "ignorant old parsons" on the generally undistinguished staff.[8] But Chapman, it seems, was taken off by the pen of a much greater old boy than any Tupper, being most probably Thackeray's model for "Mr. Chip, the second master," in the tale "Mr. and Mrs. Frank Berry." As a boy Frank had gone to "Slaughter House School, near Smithfield, London," where nobody in authority did anything to stop a savage fistfight between him and the overgrown bully, Biggs, lasting for 102 rounds. After the usual Wednesday boiled beef supper ("boiled child we used to call it . . . in our elegant, jocular way"), on the evening when everybody, Mr. Chip included, knew the fight would occur, Chip called Berry up to his study. The other boys were disappointed, thinking "he was going to prevent the fight; but no such thing." "The Rev. Edward Chip" merely "took Berry into his study, and poured him out two glasses of port-wine, which he made him take with a biscuit, and patted him on the back and went off. I have no doubt he was longing, like all of us, to see the battle; but *etiquette*, you know, forbade."[9]

The fictional Chip, of course is not identical with the irretrievably dead Chapman. But practice at the unreformed public schools did relieve the masters from interfering very much with the boys' corporate personal lives. Tupper charged that the masters "practically ignored everything out of School, much as a captain knows nothing of his company off duty."[10] Frank Berry, though improbably, might have been killed—or his face permanently disfigured, like Thackeray's own in a Charterhouse fight—but the system was larger than Chip. One can easily imagine Chip, giver of port and biscuits and pats on the back, gravely assuring an agitated parent of his future "unremitting attention" to his two sons' health before disappearing, as in Thackeray, "to his duties in the under-school, whither all we little boys followed him."

Back at Hanwell, while slowly recovering from whooping cough, Edmund was not idle. He worked at verse translations and kept a journal of his reading between 21 March and 7 April logging 7,308 lines of Greek and 676 of Latin. In late April the boys returned to the school, Lushington having decided to "try at least how they stand the summer campaign." By June, if not earlier, both were functioning as *praepositii* under Russell's "Madras system."

One can find very few good words for that system. True, Davies, though he declared it generally a failure, conceded that it "had a very real success with the boy of real ability"—such, in short, as the Lushingtons were. Boys like them could clarify and reinforce what they knew by attempting to explain it to others. But for the average or below-average boy "it proved, as it was bound to prove, a complete failure."[11] Gordon N. Ray, Thackeray's biographer, wrote that it is "perhaps too much to say" that the classical languages at Charterhouse "were *taught* at all."[12] One story often repeated in later years concerned the undersized *praepositus* whose unruly nominal pupils deposited him under the desk to get him out of the way.[13] It is tempting to speculate, but quite impossible to establish, that this boy might have been Henry Lushington. Thomas Mozley, unable to teach satisfactorily, having begun the Greek alphabet only two years before, was compelled to spend "a whole year" doing nothing besides teaching and paper work, although "the unfortunate and guiltless form" under him "had the largest share of the punishment." Expected to teach the *Iliad*, he happily discovered among his "pupils" a "very nice" boy named William Dobson, future headmaster of Cheltenham College (and lifelong friend of the Lushingtons), who sat beside him and coached him "every word, every aorist, every elision, every dialectic difference," all of which Mozley dutifully conveyed to the class. Mozley moved into the higher forms while Dobson unfairly remained far behind.[14]

Various accounts, as Ray points out, substantially differ concerning the mechanics of the system: Davies says that "a 'poz,' as he was familiarly called, was chosen from among the boys in the top half of the second form and set . . . above each of the lower forms"; H. G. Liddell, that "the *praepositus* was selected from the form to be taught and elevated to the form above after six weeks of service"; and H. W. Phillott, that "all *praepositii* were taken from the fourth form."[15] We recall that before his illness Edmund, then in the fourth form, had been made *praepositus* to the ninth, "the regular step," according to his father, for promotion into the third or second. This account seems more-or-less compatible with both Phillott and with Mozley's assertion that a boy "had to teach a form satisfactorily for at least six weeks if he would rise from the fourth form to the third," although Lushington appeared to think it possible for Edmund to be advanced after his teaching stint directly into the second. Mozley, however, said that promotion from the third to the second required another stint of teaching, and the step from second to first entailed another.[16] Paradoxically, all of the differing accounts may be correct: Russell, under pressure from parents and diminished enrollment, could have tinkered with details of the system from year to year until finally, as one old graduate recalled years later, "the forms were amalgamated and in nearly every case each had its own master."[17]

In a hastily written letter to his father on 26 June ("I have been so much occupied with various concerns that I could not spare a single moment, as it was necessary to spend a short time at play"), Edmund reported that "Harry [Henry] is praepositus to the 10th f in a week will be made praep to the 9th," and then would be promoted to the third. Edmund himself was "praep to the 6th and in 3 weeks shall be put up into the 5th, & then I shall be an *upper fellow*." (In writing "the 5th" for the form he would attain, Edmund was joining other nonconformist Charterhouse boys in reverting to the conventional public school designations for the "fifth" and "sixth" forms instead of Russell's innovative "second" and "first"; Edmund, of course, already in Russell's "third," was well above his "fifth.")

The irrepressible Henry, in the same packet, wrote, "I am very glad, as I dare say you are that little Edmund is now an *upper fellow*." Henry himself liked "being Praepositus to the 10th Form very well, & shall be glad when I get into the 3rd. They have sometimes very long exercises in the 3rd Form, such as parse 5½ of Greek, & to translate them which was the one we had last night." (Were the *praepositii* required to do some of the exercises of the next form up, or had Henry merely been sitting in with some third formers during study time?) On 28 July Henry reported that he was "at the top of the 3rd division" of the third form, "there being 3 divisions in the form, & the last by far the largest." Edmund was again teaching as "Praep to the 5th form in school; afterwards he will be Praep into the fourth, & then put into the first. By the time he is put up, I shall, I hope, be Praep for the 2nd." (Presumably, Henry meant that he hoped soon to complete third form and become a *praepositus* in line for promotion to second form.) The third form were doing *Antigone* and Horace "on most days."

At Hanwell terrible grief struck the family that summer, not once but twice. In mid-July the eldest daughter, Sophia (born 1814), had died from a croup condition, which Lushington thought might have been a relapse from the whooping cough the boys had brought from Charterhouse. After the parents had called "our apothecary," Sophia seemed to improve, but the throat inflammation passed to the trachea causing death "in a few hours." To avoid risk of contagion, Edmund and Henry were not called back from school. About a week later, Mary Anne (born 1818) died of the same malady "after suffering which it is horrible to think of." On medical advice the family fled to Broadstairs with the six surviving younger children (three of them slightly affected), not even stopping for the second funeral.

Mr. Chapman, Lushington wrote to Clark, had been "equally kind and judicious" in telling Edmund and Henry about the deaths. Chapman in a "long conversation" with the boys' Aunt Catherine "had expressed his delight that notwithstanding their extraordinary & sudden elevation in the school" the boys had "conducted themselves with so much good-humour & want of affectation that no envy or jealousy was excited."

Lushington, however, from a letter of Edmund's, knew something that the benignly neglectful Chapman did not. Edmund, recently promoted at the early age of twelve to the first form and already pressing for first place in the examinations, had enraged some of the "big" first-formers by "doing 12 stanzas of alcaics & being so high in them; but they excused me as it was the 1st time." As one boy explained, "they were in a rage only because I did so many, not because I was so high in them & that they will *let me do them well*, if I do not do so many." They tore some stanzas from his copybook, later giving them back with permission to hand them in, "but said the next time I did so many I would be *bumped*. I hope however I shall be high in them & that is all I now care about."

We may wonder if Thackeray, only six months younger than Edmund, but still mired in the seventh or sixth form,[18] remembered this very incident a quarter-century later when he described his young Pendennis: "If he was distinguished for anything it was for verse-writing; but was his enthusiasm ever so great, it stopped when he had composed the number of lines demanded by the regulations (unlike young Swettenham, for instance, who . . . would bring up a hundred dreary hexameters to the master after a half holiday . . .)."[19] The name "Swettenham" reaches the ear with an invidiously disquieting suggestion of "Lushington." Or if Thackeray did not recall exactly this story, had Edmund acquired a reputation among his older and huskier form-mates for that sort of thing?

To his father the incident indicated again "the want of more active superintendence." Also he entertained misgivings about scholastic standards where any boys, even his, could be promoted so rapidly. He was convinced that Henry, now at age eleven in second form (fifth under the older system), was not so good a scholar as Clark, years before, had been in the old fourth.

As a first-former, Edmund was now directly under Dr. Russell, where Henry soon would join him. At the height of the enrollment boom, even Russell's esteemed first form was grossly overcrowded. Davies "humbly" wondered "how anything got taught or learnt in that vast assembly."[20] But Russell worked deliberately, a few lines in a day, demanding first a literal word-by-word translation, then attempting to elicit an idiomatic English rendering that he would "criticize with unsparing dissection."[21]

In 1823, although headmaster for twelve years, Russell was still only thirty-six. Himself a gold medalist from the Charterhouse of his predecessor, Matthew Raine, he had gone up to Christ's Church, Oxford, taken B.A. and M.A., and returned as a master. When Raine died, the school's governors suspended the rules to allow the appointment of a headmaster under twenty-seven.[22] Two portraits of Russell at the present Charterhouse School (removed in 1872 to a spacious site near Godalming, Surrey) seem, at least to a predisposed eye, to depict a rigidly imperious countenance. History, influenced by the later writings of articulate unscholarly boys like Tupper and Thackeray, has not been kind to him. Davies calls him "a man of exceptional vigour and capacity, a born reformer, and possessed of imagination and of original ideas," but he ventures mildly that "perhaps he may have lacked something of that intimate knowledge of the human boy," without which no headmaster can succeed.[23] Other writers are blunter: "pompous and unsympathetic," "heavy-handed sarcasm," "clumsy witticisms," "merciless" to "diffident or incompetent students," "despotically drilled into passive servility and pedantic scholarship."[24] Insensitivity, a trait he evidently exercised, is hard to forgive in a teacher. Thackeray, in Pendennis, takes him off to the brink of infernal immortality:

"Pendennis, sir," he said, "your idleness is incorrigible and your stupidity beyond example. You are a disgrace to your school, and to your family, and I have no doubt will prove so in after-life to your country. If that vice, sir, which is described to us as the root of all evil, be really what moralists have represented, (and I have no doubt of the correctness of their opinion,) for what a prodigious quantity of future crime and wickedness are you, unhappy boy, laying the seed! Miserable trifler! A boy who construes δε *and*, instead of δε *but*, at sixteen years of age, is guilty not merely of folly, and ignorance, and dullness inconceivable, but of crime, of deadly crime, of filial ingratitude, which I tremble to contemplate. A boy, sir, who does not learn his Greek play cheats the parent who spends money for his education. A boy who cheats his parent is not very far from robbing or forging upon his neighbour. A man who forges on his neighbour pays the penalty of his crime at the gallows. And it is not such a one that I pity, (for he will be deservedly cut off;) but his maddened and heart-broken parents, who are driven to a premature grave by his crimes, or, if they live, drag on a wretched and dishonoured old age. Go on, sir, and I warn you that the very next mistake that you make shall subject you to the punishment of the rod.

Who's that laughing? What ill-conditioned boy is there that dares to laugh?" shouted the Doctor.[25]

Tupper, less talented, did not imitate Russell's invective, but provided a dampening surfeit of his own. Russell allegedly had "worked so" upon Tupper's "over-sensitive nature to force" him "beyond his powers" that he became and remained a stammerer "until past middle life." He claimed to have seen the "irate" Russell "smashing a child's head between two books in his shoulder-of-mutton hand till the nose bled"—and to have heard "the Reverend Doctor's terrible sentence" commanding his boy head-monitor to punish another boy's "slight fault of idleness or ignorance" with eighteen strokes, "most severely," from "five-feet bunches of birch armed with buds as sharp as thorns, renewed after six strokes for fresh excoriation!" The boy Tupper had grimly determined "to commit justifiable homicide" upon any person who ever tried to flog him so; and later had vowed to "desert the Church of England" if Russell ever was "made a Bishop (happily he was not)."[26]

But if even the Devil is accorded his advocate, should controversial headmasters alone be deprived? Ray declares that however Russell may have failed boys like Thackeray, "he was a very successful instructor with boys of precise, retentive minds, who had been well grounded in the classics by earlier preparation."[27] Furthermore, he believed, passionately, in the efficaciousness of the imbalanced educational tradition he had inherited, Greek and Latin and virtually nothing else. Himself shaped and nurtured by it, he was taxing his nerves, almost giving his life, to perpetuate it. He was frustrated and disillusioned by the near impossibility of broadly dispensing it, boys as always being individuals. He drove himself, as Mozley remembered, almost to the point of no endurance, throwing his "tremendous energy of voice, look, and manner" into getting and holding the attention of "a hundred and twenty boys single-handed an hour and a half before breakfast, three hours after, and two hours in the afternoon, and then looking over the frequent translations, verses, and themes," until finally, "soon after my time he almost sank under the long-continued strain."[28]

For the rare few boys equipped and disposed to meet him, Russell had great wealth to offer. The Lushingtons, especially Edmund, must from the first have brought him joy. And there were some others, despite the ineptness of his lower-school system. In the superb 1832 Classical Tripos group at Cambridge, three of the top five would be Russell's boys—Senior Classic, Edmund Lushington; third, William Dobson; fifth, George Stovin Venables, in a quintet rounded out by no lesser future luminaries than Richard Shilleto (second) and William Hepworth Thompson (fourth).

Russell was remembered for speaking "with a peculiarly distinct and syllabic utterance, and making a great point of it that every one in his form should do the same."[29] Edmund, in turn, was remembered to the end of his life for his own distinctive enunciation, "a certain peculiarity of utterance, that made the words seem to come from him reluctantly, producing an effect, not of hesitation, but of deliberate choice, which made his language more impressive."[30]

By the end of February 1824, Edmund had attained fourth place in the school, and Henry was in the second form, though temporarily in last place because of "a bad exercise." But Henry was causing his father to worry: "This dear fellow who is a delightful boy & of whose success as a lawyer I should predict with more confidence even than of Edmund's" had most unfortunately developed "an ardent wish to be a sailor." Knowing how opposed his father was, he had tried for several months to "subdue" the yearning, "but hitherto in vain." He "could not help shedding tears" when he thought of not going to sea. By July he had sufficiently repressed his nautical dreams to rise to second place in the select group (the "Emeriti") between second and first forms.

In April, Lushington gratified his long-felt ambition to become a member of the Royal Society: "Though not a man of science I love it & going there may bring me in contact with early friends & revive old associations which are upon the whole gratifying though somewhat melancholy." In July he retired from the Colonial Board of Audit, a demanding position that had been wearing him down, and at fifty-eight felt himself at last "comparatively at liberty with every adequate blessing of fortune & with leisure to watch over and assist in the education of my dear boys."

By December he was again worrying about what to do next with Edmund. Though not yet fourteen, he was first in the school and would probably be captain after the examinations. At what age would it be advisable to send him up to Cambridge? By the following summer, Lushington had evidently consulted at least one Cambridge don, the ineffable professor of modern history William Smyth, who advised him to place Edmund in "a French Boarding-house" to perfect his command of the French language. George Philips, M.P., Lushington's wealthy cotton manufacturer brother-in-law, was intrigued with the idea. Why not send the boy to Geneva, where "by attending the College" he could also improve himself in "science, & general literature" while being introduced "into the most intelligent society"? A family could no doubt be located where he would "meet only with educated, & active minded men of unostentatious character." Lord Landsdowne, Philips asserted, had "spent some time, as a young man at Geneva, & I have no doubt derived advantage from his residence there. I do not know any place where I should prefer passing some months myself." No doubt the pragmatic Philips would have been delighted by any unharmful arrangement that would have reduced his nephew's fixation upon Greek and rendered him generally more like the urbane Lord Lansdowne. But another old friend of Philips, no less a personage than the humorist clergyman Sydney Smith, reluctantly advised that Edmund stay at Charterhouse, further perfecting his classical languages, to "ensure high academick honours to him which he thinks (however absurd some may consider it) are important means of success in the profession of the law." Charterhouse School, quite predictably, won.

After Clark's death in April 1825 ended Lushington's confiding letters, we have little further record of the Charterhouse years. Both boys wrote on 18 December 1824, attempting to cheer the ailing Clark. Edmund, as he always would, found small talk difficult on paper. He duly reported that he and Henry were now in the "Sixth Form" (Russell's first form), modestly refrained from mentioning that he was himself at the top of the school, told about his father's shepherd who, when riding a Shetland pony, "looks as if he would outweigh him; he is, thus mounted, the drollest figure imaginable"; hoped Clark was "perfectly well," and then desperately confessed, "I have now I am afraid nothing more to say." By comparison Henry's letter seems almost effortless:

> My dear Mr Clarke [sic]: As Papa is very anxious to hear from you, and Edmund is now working at a most terrific Problem, I take the liberty of sending you a few lines. I am afraid I shall not be able to say anything to amuse you, except so far as you may be interested respecting what is now going on at the Charterhouse. The name of the orator this year is Berdmore, grandson of your quondom Schoolmaster.[31] He is a little short fellow with red hair, so that his grandfather might say of him, as he did of Dr. Heathcote, "Fine child, just such a boy as I was." He has a tremendous voice, and thunders out the oration with the greatest emphasis. Papa was very anxious to go to hear him, but could not. The best news is, that Russell in endeavouring to Macadamize our green, has made a lake of it, and we are in the most imminent danger of being swept away like Pharaoh and all his host. I am, dear Mr Clark,   Your affectionate friend, HL

The Charterhouse lists show that Edmund remained for two-and-a-half more years, until 1827, and that Henry stayed a year after Edmund left. Edmund is listed as school captain for 1825, 1826, and 1827. Henry was captain in 1828. In verse competitions Edmund won silver medals all three years for translations of poems in Greek, and one for English verse in 1827. Henry won a silver medal for Latin verse in 1827 and in Greek verse in 1828, and a gold medal in 1828 for Latin verse.

During Henry's final year, being for the first time separated from Edmund, he developed a close friendship with a scholarly older boy, George Stovin Venables (born 1810), himself newly separated that year from his own elder brother, Richard Lister Venables, who had gone up from Charterhouse to

Cambridge. For both boys, until Henry's early death with Venables among those at his bedside in Paris in 1855, this association would be the closest attachment outside their own families; and Venables's intimacy with the Lushington brothers and sisters would long outlast Henry's death. The daily journals Venables kept from 1839 to 1883, when he retired from the leadership of the Parliamentary Bar, are indispensable sources for the history of the Lushington family.

It would be instructive to know how Russell kept an ambitious, work-obsessed boy like Edmund profitably occupied during his nearly three years in first form at the top of the school. Were the assignments varied from year to year to keep such first-form holdovers on fresh materials? Mozley, who finished in 1825, the year Edmund became captain, said that Russell himself, feeling the need of more variety, once devoted a term to the rapid, uncritical, reading of the *Odyssey*, and another time invited some of the first form to a private class in Theocritus.[32] What, specifically, were the responsibilities of a school captain under Russell? Edmund's anonymous obituary sketch in the *Athenaeum* (22 July 1893) would state that being "delicate in physique" and having risen to "the top of the school at a phenomenally early age," he "was exposed to more than the common share of difficulty in maintaining his authority as captain." Mozley, mentioning no names, wrote that in the ferment that was Charterhouse in those years, "boys were arriving at all ages; . . . 'taking places' over one another's heads, and rising in a year to the top of the school." In such circumstances, whether "very big fellows or very little . . . they might be equally unfit to make a good use of personal authority."[33]

Three testimonials of 1838, supporting Edmund for the Greek professorship at Glasgow University, touch upon the captain's duties. Edmund's great-uncle, the bishop of Bath and Wells, wrote that the post trained him "in the habit of superintending of the education of Boys, of various habits, & dispositions," including many considerably "older than himself, at a time of life indeed, when a few years difference in age, constitutes in general the chief test & standard of superiority."[34] William Dobson, Edmund's Charterhouse contemporary, stated generally that Edmund's "position in the school rendered him constantly liable to be called on to instruct the higher boys in such subjects as they happened to be occupied with from time to time." Russell himself was even less specific, saying only that "the post of captain, under the system which I had adopted, was one that required continued activity and vigilance, and I never found him wanting at the head of his class."[35]

Russell, by then six years out of his headmastership, went on to detail his admiration of Edmund:

He was always the same: industry was habitual with him: he was not content with the ordinary routine of school work, but was always improving himself to the utmost of his power; and the exercises which he wrote from day to day, never failed to deserve praise. The prizes which he gained were numerous in every kind of composition: in Greek composition . . . none . . . could compete with him; and while the soundness of his critical scholarship was far beyond the average of schoolboy attainments, his memory . . . enable[d] him to cite or refer to almost any passage in authors whom he had read, and his taste was equal to his memory. Since he left me, I have watched his progress with affectionate interest, and have still found him ever the same, making the most of every opportunity of improvement, and increasing his fame with unvaried success.

Poor Russell, reliving the disturbing years when his greatest apparent success had begun to turn into his greatest failure, could well sigh for the stability of one thing, one boy sculptored after his own heart, who had been always and "ever the same"!

Edmund in his turn might or might not have felt so laudatory of Russell. Certainly Henry would not. Henry too had won prizes, including a gold medal, something Edmund had not; and he too had been the school's captain. But Henry had the heart of a libertarian, an exposer of injustices, inequities, and abusers of authority; and he could not condone Russell's overbearing treatment of so many of his boys. Venables thought Henry was never quite fair to Russell: "He retained through life a strong sense of the harsh and unsympathetic system." Venables could never "induce him to share my own appreciation of the intellectual benefits, derived by himself and many others, from the most logical and masculine of teachers." Henry would have been "happier, if not better taught, under a master who had resembled the Dr. Arnold of popular tradition."[36] Henry himself, while captain of the school, wrote in February 1828:

Russell is turned out of his house, which is about to be pulled down, and a much better one built; he now occupies a brace of rooms where he can hardly stretch himself. However, though his lodgings are diminished, his spirit is increased; he is more ferocious than ever, and shows strong symptoms of magesterial insanity.

After Henry left the school, his brother Tom remained. Tom, or "Tod" as the family called him, was earnest and openhearted, admirably able to express his feelings and ideas, but he evidently had little calling for classical scholarship. Perhaps the Charterhouse masters, at a time of general frustration, felt personally affronted by a Lushington who did not match their stereotype of a Lushington. Henry felt they were persecuting Tom. He indignantly wrote his father in early November 1828, tactfully soliciting "more attention than the opinion of a boy of 16 is likely to deserve." Tod's "unfortunate situation at C.H." ought not to be "considered a proof of innate idleness," not while "every tendency to exertion, every wish for distinction, were damped by what I could readily call persevering spite and malice, and to which no easier name can be given than that of capricious injustice." What boy so maltreated could "be expected to surpass in industry others who met with no such chilling opposition?" The school had "thwarted Tod where he ought to have succeeded neither once nor twice." An "organized system of persecution seems to have been carried on against him, both by R1 and his subordinates." Russell himself had said of Tom that "he 'would not spare him as long as he was under him'." Henry would be happy to have Tod come up to Cambridge with him next year, and would do all that he could to help him succeed.

> If I could exert myself for my own advantage—and I have shown that it was not quite out of my power to do so—should I not be much more ready, much more eager, in the pursuit, when on my steadiness depended in great measure the future prospects of one so dear to all of us? All this I leave to your impartial consideration.

Henry complained to a friend that one of Tod's Charterhouse instructors seemed "to have taken a lesson in cruelty from Smithfield, and to have almost outdone his masters in the art of barbarity."

So the last word we have from one of our boys concerning the school where they had distinguished themselves is rather in the strain of Tupper and Thackeray. Tod, instead of to Cambridge, went on to Haileybury College to prepare for the Indian Civil Service. He would die off the coast of Ceylon in the summer of 1858 while attempting to return to England. When the youngest Lushington boy, Franklin, was ready for public school in 1835, it was Henry who took the lead in persuading their father to put him under Thomas Arnold at Rugby. And so it would occur that the long association of the Lushingtons with the unreformed Charterhouse was terminated in favor of the public school that had begun in the English mind to exemplify reform.

III

Park House and Trinity College

1828–1838

F ROM THE RECTORY in the parish of Hanwell, where the Lushington family had lived since 1814, six parishioners on 15 July 1828 joined their rector, T. F. Walmsley, in signing a statement of appreciation. Having "learnt with sincere regret that Mr and Mrs Lushington" were "about to take their departure from hence," they could not "forbear expressing" their "sense of loss which we shall sustain; and of acknowledging Mr Lushington's uniform endeavours to promote the harmony and welfare of the Parishioners, and the benevolent attention of himself and family to the wants of the Poor, more particularly their very liberal Patronage of the Hanwell National School." The Lushington's could be assured "that when they quit the Parish, they will carry with them the most cordial respect and esteem of its inhabitants."

Lushington at the age of sixty-two was realizing his long-cherished dream of residing on his own country estate. Already the absentee proprietor of three other small estates, he had now located, just out of Maidstone, the county town of Kent, the property he wished for himself. The auction sale, a year earlier on 5 July 1827, had offered the mansion and 232 acres, divided into eighteen parcels, several having houses or cottages for renters and farm buildings of various kinds. Surrounding the mansion were "Pleasure Grounds . . . tastefully disposed in Shrubberies, Lawns, and Walks"; and nearby were an "Orchard and

Productive Kitchen Garden enclosed with lofty walls, fully stocked and planted with choice Fruit Trees in high perfection." The outlying properties included hop fields, various orchards, woods, a chestnut grove, a plot of oziers (willows used in basketmaking), and other arable and meadow lands.[1] It remains unclear how many of the parcels Lushington obtained at the original sale; but with subsequent purchases he would eventually consolidate more than 299 acres.[2]

In a riot of diverse typefaces, the auction brochure acclaimed the late eighteenth-century mansion, called Park House: "STONE BUILT . . . OF HANDSOME UNIFORM ELEVATION, WITH PORTICO ENTRANCE, DELIGHTFULLY PLACED ON A COMMANDING EMINENCE, IN THE CENTRE OF A SMALL PARK, ORNAMENTED WITH STATELY TIMBER, Situated on the HIGH ROAD from MAIDSTONE to ROCHESTER . . . Embracing Delightful Views of the River Medway, Allington Castle, and the surrounding Picturesque Scenery." Actually, the house, still standing, is large but not immense. On the "Principal Story," the "spacious and handsome Vestibule, and Back Hall, Capital Dining Parlour 28 feet by 20, and Drawing Room of the same Dimensions, a Library or Breakfast Room 20 feet square, a Back Parlour, or Housekeeper's Room, of the same Dimensions, and a Water Closet" seem more than adequate. But unless the advertisement omitted some rooms, the first floor sleeping quarters, with a "Music Room 24 feet by 20," "four excellent lofty Bed Chambers, about 20 feet by 17, with Dressing Rooms, a Nursery, and a Water Closet," would hardly seem equal to the requirements of the immediate Lushington family, to say nothing of all the guests, including various Tennysons, who in future years would arrive, at times in clusters, and not always readily depart. Perhaps during the year between Lushington's purchase and occupancy he substantially remodeled that floor. When his descendants sold the house in 1936, the first floor still had a "Music Practice Room," but the number of "Principal Bedrooms," double or single, was eight. Of course, the house had also a "lofty Kitchen," and a top-floor servants' hall, and for wines and other purposes, "capital Cellaring."

In this house Lushington and Sophia would serenely live out their lives and quietly die. Edmund's home it would then become but for half of every year, during his long service at Glasgow University, not his residence. Here in the autumn of 1842 he would bring his bride, Cecilia Tennyson, but before the month's end cart her off to Glasgow, a place she would quickly learn to loathe. Nor even at Park House, until her advanced old age, would she ever feel quite fully at home.

That summer of 1828, undistracted by the confusion of the family's moving, Edmund and Henry were reunited, at a small private school at Bovingdon, near Hemel Hempstead in Hertfordshire, conducted by a former Fellow of Christ's

FIG. II. Park House. 1975. Photograph by author.

College, Cambridge, the Reverend George Millett. Edmund had spent the past year there, since leaving Charterhouse; Henry, just arrived, would remain a year, much of it after Edmund departed for Trinity College. The crucial task for both boys, less agreeable to Edmund than to Henry, was to acquire the grounding in mathematics so indispensable for success in competitive examinations at Cambridge. Millett had placed a competent fifteenth in the Cambridge Mathematical Tripos of 1814, while carrying off highest honors then obtainable in classics—the coveted Senior Chancellor's Medal, which Edmund would go on to capture in 1832.

Millett would long remember Edmund's "residence with me as the brightest spot in a laborious and often painful" twenty years of "tuition." Edmund's "proficiency . . . in Classical learning, the higher branches of composition, general reading, and especially the Greek language, was very uncommon for his age [seventeen]: his acquirements remarkably sound, and his mind clear and reasoning. His conduct was always gentlemanly and honourable, and I never had one occasion to reprove him."[3] Henry, too, Millett had described to Lushington as "indeed a very delightful young man" with "good temper," "unassuming character with companions very greatly his inferiors," and "accuracy of construction & perfect acquaintance with the idiom" of Greek and Latin "not inferior to his brother's." By December he had read through all of Thucydides, and was exhibiting "uncommon quickness & accuracy" in both Euclid and algebra. Henry, barely sixteen, was reciprocally delighted with Millett's amiability, a gratifying contrast to the overbearing Russell of Charterhouse. Along with the boys, Millett laughed at jokes, even those at his own expense. Henry found himself laughing "more than I have ever done in my life, tho' not as much as Edmund." When a boy like Henry sat reading past midnight, Millett would enter "looking gaunt and black in his plaid dressing gown" and hustle him off to bed.

Already in early summer, Edmund was impatient to obtain the books to be studied at Trinity College in the fall: Aeschylus with the notes of Scholefield, Regius Professor of Greek for the University; and the right edition of Virgil's *Georgics*. Would Lushington have his bookseller send those out to Bovingdon? Edmund's own books, packed for moving, might "be left packed up" for Cambridge: whatever few of his Greek volumes that were not already with him, and in Latin, "Cicero, Horace, Juvenal, Persius, Livy, Sallust, Tacitus, & perhaps Ovid." Millett was recommending "Mitchell's English Translation & notes of 4 plays of Aristophanes," which the bookseller should send. Books Edmund was reading with Millett included Aristophanes' *Wasps*, Plato's *Politics*, Bentley's *Phalaris*, and Woodhouse's *Plane Geometry*. "If any other book of Plato is read more than the Pol. I should like to know," since it seemed "so very easy that I can hardly fancy anything set from it in a hard examination."

At Cambridge for a serious student like Edmund, expected by his father almost as a matter of course to carry off highest classical honors and at least acquit himself with distinction in mathematics (all, of course, as a prelude to going on to the Temple to qualify for the bar and distinguished public service), those periodically scheduled "hard" examinations, some set by the colleges and others by the university, would mean virtually everything. Trinity required two hours' daily attendance at college lectures, but these entailed no recitations or examinations. Beyond that the self-activating student set his own course of reading, doggedly performed day-by-day, while regularly consulting with a private tutor, whom he himself paid. During Edmund's first year, he "went to *two* Private Tutors every day," besides the two daily college lectures, and Scholefield's university Greek lectures "one hour in addition, every other day." But that program, he decided, had cut too drastically into his indispensable self-directed reading.

Though Lushington's own college had been Queen's, he was sending his sons to the college long proverbially preeminent in classical studies. Some of the smaller colleges had scarcely promoted the classics at all, since before 1824 the only route to university honors on graduation had been through the mathematical tripos examinations. When in 1821 the recently appointed master of Trinity, Christopher Wordsworth, brother of the poet, had pressed for a compulsory examination in classics and theology for all candidates for the bachelor of arts degree, he was suspected of seeking mainly to benefit his own prestigious college. A compromise, effective from 1824, provided a purely voluntary honors examination in classics (the new classical tripos) open only to men who had previously won university honors in mathematics.[4] During the next twenty-eight years, Trinity men would become the senior classics twenty times.[5] A recent historian has pictured "a society," in the latter 1820s, particularly at Trinity, "of earnest, industrious, religious undergraduates competing for the top places within the First Class of the Classical Tripos, all familiar with each other's talents and enthusiasms, meeting for meals, talking together on long daily walks round the countryside, worshipping together in the College Chapel, joining together to make pious resolutions."[6] Lushington was confidently expecting both his sons in their respective years to enter that circle and defeat all comers in the classical tripos after placing high also in the more prestigious mathematics.

Henry at Bovingdon had learned, and delightedly informed his father, of an early embarrassment Edmund sustained at Trinity. He had made "several calls" before "being greeted by a friend . . . on the street, with the agreeable intelligence that he was wearing his gown inside out." The friend declared, "I never saw a fellow look so green in my life." When Edmund himself wrote home, it was to expedite the arrival of a good Greek lexicon, and "also Aristotle's Ethics or Rhetoric for it is coming very much into the University Scholarship Examinations," scheduled for late January. On Sunday at St. Mary's, he had heard a sermon by William Whewell (scientist, mathematician, and future master of Trinity), "who is certainly the cleverest tutor in college, & I am inclined to think the best." Julius Charles Hare, the classical lecturer, had "taken 5 days to introduce us to the play, for we have not read a line yet. He is the best lecturer of his kind I hear."

What "kind" of lecturer was Hare's kind? Certainly hardly succinct, not necessarily most efficiently organized; but for young men willing and equipped, he could be gratifyingly stimulating, deliberately and intentionally so, aiming to fire their imagination, nurture their scholarly conscience, and send them away to seek new knowledge for themselves. (That year another Trinity freshman, Arthur Henry Hallam, was finding him "a man of great talent, but not, I think, of genius. His lectures are admirable, and so copious, I think, that they nearly exhaust the subject.")[7] Born in Italy in 1795, he had lived his first four years there, becoming fluent in Italian simultaneously with English; during a brief but mind-expanding residence in Germany in middle childhood, he had begun to study Goethe and Schiller, both of whom he had met during their visits to his dying mother's sickroom at Weimar.[8] Evidently he was a natural linguist, adept from boyhood in four modern tongues, while diligently acquiring Latin and Greek.[9] At Charterhouse from 1806 to 1812, he was schoolfellow of two boys destined to become more eminent than he—Connop Thirlwall, later his collaborator in translating Niebuhr's *History of Rome*, and the Greek historian George Grote. (Thirlwall too, of whom we will hear more later, lectured at Trinity during the Lushington brothers' years there.) By his freshman year at Trinity, Hare was considered unique among Englishmen his age for his command of German language and thought. In 1827 Edmund was finding in Hare, then thirty-two, a man of prodigious reading, a proselytizing proponent of the tireless philological scholarship that flowed from the German universities, a merciless prosecutor of shallow, pretentious scholarship, and, no less signficantly, a devout if discriminating disciple, intimate friend, and fierce defender of Samuel Taylor Coleridge.[10] Probably no other mentor did more than Hare to broaden Edmund's interests and shape his scholarly ideals.

The Lushington boys would be studying at Cambridge during the very years when, decidedly more than at Oxford, the impact of Continental, and especially German, scholarship upon English thought would reach its most dynamic momentum. In comparative philology the first three decades of the new century, under the leadership of scholars such as Rasmus Rask (1787–1832), Jacob Grimm (1785–1863), and Franz Bopp (1791–1867), had been an exciting time of consolidating and ordering a great mass of data accumulated by various scholars during the previous century. Of even more interest to Cambridge men seeking classical honors was the branch of study labeled classical philology. Here the giants were men like Christian Heyne (1729–1812), F. A. Wolf (1759–1824), Gottfried Hermann (1722–1848), Wilhelm von Humboldt (1767–1835), and August Boeckh (1785–1867). In their most expansive moments, these men aspired to the collecting, apprehending, and interrelating of all the multiform manifestations of the ancient human spirit, everything already uncovered but not yet contextually recombined by previous historians and archaeologists—in social, political, and economic institutions, in architecture and the plastic arts, in mythology, as well as in literary works. Such diverse philological activity assumed certain philosophical axioms concerning the human spirit. Supposedly the soul of a human community, millennia later, can converse with sympathetically imaginative listeners through all of that community's multitudinous activities, utterances, and artifacts. Like ourselves individually in our microcosmic lifespans, each "nation" develops and declines organically in the course of generations. And for specialists who have learned how to penetrate such mysteries and empathetically expound them, each individual language, in its unique morphological and syntactical structure as well as the constantly developing semantic content of its vocabulary, will at every stage of its own organic existence subtly reveal the successive stages of its corresponding national soul. For a boy like Edmund, already enthralled by traditional language study, such recently imported ideas at Cambridge could only add an exotic new dimension, potent for diverting him still farther from the stolid English goals so cherished by his father.

Indeed, was not even the most diluted infusion of those enticing "new ideas" into the regime at Cambridge, though benignly intended, almost an act of subversiveness, undermining the expectations of the ambitious parents who sent their boys there? Even when language study had seemed relatively static, it would have been inconsiderate enough to expect a retiring boy like Edmund to devote fifteen years of life, jeopardizing his health through unremitting toil, grimly perfecting an all-demanding, specialized philological game, only to triumph briefly, take his unconvertible trophies, then resolutely turn and stoically proceed to an entirely dissimilar arena and a hitherto unpracticed combat like the bar for the remainder of his life against temperamentally superior competitors. But was it not downright heartless to compound the offense by introducing him gratuitously to the seductions of a scholarly life for which the national economy offered virtually no openings?

As it turned out, Edmund would not publish research; but throughout his often sorrow-distracted life, his studying the research of others would remain a delight and consolation. Those metaphysical concepts of the philologists, on a less ambitious scale, remained a vantage point for countless practical observations concerning a particular language, like the Greek, and its literature. In general, the scholarly approaches of the classical philologists moved relatively unaltered across the divide to shape the early working assumptions of modern language departments in German, British, and American universities. And in the realm of literary theory the philosophies, metaphysical and aesthetic, of the German idealists—Kant, Fichte, Schelling, and others—mediated largely for the English-speaking world through the seminal mind of Samuel Taylor Coleridge, became the nucleus of a transformation in criticism that, although at no time universally accepted, was predominant until at least the 1960s if not, indeed, numerically prevailing even now.

One of the privileges of being at Trinity during Edmund's years was to breathe an air so charged with the ideas of Coleridge. It is a truism of intellectual history that while Oxford in those years was logically Aristotelian in its approach to knowledge, Cambridge was idealistically Platonic, Kantian, and Coleridgean. Probably Edmund never met Coleridge, but he was much in the company of at least two men who knew him firsthand. Apparently Edmund's closest friend among Trinity undergraduates came to be Robert Tennant, respected by his college contemporaries as one who on at least several occasions had conversed with the great man.[11] Hare, who cherished Coleridge as a friend, was not only intimately familiar with everything he had published, and himself steeped in many of the writings—German, classical, and others—that had furnished Coleridge's wonderful mind, but had spent hours in his company, experiencing the artesian flow of his celebrated conversation. Hare would have found occasions in his lectures to refer, if only briefly, to the poet's insights on various points pertaining to language and literature. Emerson Marks, in an exemplary recent monograph, writes that Coleridge's "own lifelong interest in language went far beyond its use as an artistic medium, ranging from the most complex issues of its status as an index of human consciousness to the minutest details of grammar, syntax, and vocabulary. . . . No linguist today could lay greater stress on the centrality of speech generally to the nature of man and specifically to his aesthetic creativity."[12] The subject is vast and multifaceted with much not yet worked out by really qualified scholars.[13] Our present purpose is simply to suggest the richness of thought to which Edmund (with Henry soon to follow) was so rapidly being introduced. Even before he would leave Trinity, the two finest expositors would have preceded him, Hare departing in 1832 and Thirlwall in 1834, the year that Coleridge died.

At Cambridge the scholarly reputation of a promising freshman often arrived ahead of him. By early December, Henry at Bovingdon was assuring

Lushington, "Edmund is already very famous at Cambridge." In late January, three days into the university scholarship examination, a fellow freshman, Arthur Henry Hallam, was correctly predicting that Christopher Wordsworth (1807–85, future headmaster of Harrow and bishop of Lincoln), a third-year student, would probably win first: "I don't think Lushington can beat him, but he will be near."[14] Pessimistically, Edmund had professed to believe he would be "lucky to place with 'a single digit,' " to which Henry retorted, "A single digit certainly it will be—1—." Edmund was concentrating almost entirely on Greek, rationalizing that his lesser command of Latin was unlikely to be greatly improved in so short a time. In the Greek language, "everything tells. I consider that by reading Aristotle I am gaining knowledge not only of the particular author, but of the language." He would be "much more enabled to translate Plato or Polybius from having read Aristotle, than Livy or Tacitus from having read Cicero." Of course, he uneasily conceded, another reason was his "superior admiration of the Greek language and authors." His reading, such as it was, in Cicero was "more . . . to assist my composition, than to improve my knowledge of the words and phrases."

Fortunately, Arthur Hallam's letters reveal the contents of that scholarship examination. The first day's composition was a theme in Latin concerning Greek and Latin historians. Required translations were from "three bits of Greek prose; one from *Lysias*; the second from *Polybius*; & the third from *Lucian*. We were all very indignant at being supposed to deal with anything but *classical* Greek." Next day, after being "annihilated" by a passage from Aristophanes' *Women at the Assembly*, they faced "a passage from *Eubulus*!! five, or six scrap questions," and "a part of Lady Macbeth's sleeping scene to be translated into Greek Trochaics." The third day brought "some lines in Thomson's Liberty to put into Latin Hexameters; a page of Hume into Latin prose; and an awful page of Scholefield's containing a chorus from the Hercules Furens to construe which," Hallam thought, "would have been superhuman." The final three days required "sharper work every day": "to translate a chorus in the Iphig. Taur. into Latin Alcaics, as well as English prose; also some Juvenal. Friday, Latin Prose Translation from Hume, & original Hexameters on Skaiting [*sic*]: also three bits of Latin Prose—Cicero, Tacitus, & Livy. Saturday, some Bolingbroke to put into Greek prose; & some Herodotus, Plato, & Thucydides to construe."[15]

Edmund's place turned out to be fourth in the field, first in his own year. "Next time," he consoled himself, he would have "only one of those who have beaten me, to contend with." But that one, a year later, the phenomenal Charles Rann Kennedy (1808–67), would prove too formidable, although Edmund placed second. He never did succeed in receiving any of the coveted university scholarships,[16] although he easily became a scholar of Trinity College, and in his senior year (1832) would follow both Wordsworth (1830) and Kennedy (1831) in becoming the university's senior classic.

Beyond doubt Edmund was enviably fortunate in the private tutor he secured at once for himself, and the next year for himself and Henry. James Prince Lee (1804–69), who would become famed as one of the most successful classical teachers of the century, was available for those two years only, before accepting an assistant mastership at Rugby under Dr. Thomas Arnold. Eight years later Arnold would "feel it almost presumptuous" to speak of Lee's scholarship, "because it is much superior to my own." Surely there was "no man employed in education in England at this moment, whether at the Universities or elsewhere," who could "in this respect surpass" him. In Lee's later headmastership of King Edward's School, Birmingham, his pedagogical reputation would soar. In nine and a half years, he would send to Cambridge five chancellor's medallists and eight others in first class. The most eminent of his boys would be Brooke Foss Westcott, New Testament scholar and bishop of Durham; Joseph Barber Lightfoot, theologian and Westcott's predecessor at Durham; and Edward White Benson, archbishop of Canterbury. Unfortunately for Lee's ultimate reputation, he was temperamentally unsuited, tragically so, for the bishopric of Manchester, to which he was elevated in 1848. But at St. Edward's School, he was admired by his boys to the brink of idolatry.[17] During Edmund's first years at Trinity, Lee's perfectionistic supervision combined with the broadly stimulating scholarly lectures of Hare and Thirlwall to solidify his dedication to Greek. Ironically, the more heartily he would gratify his father's expectations as a scholar, the more alienated he would become from the father's prescription for his career.

At Bovingdon that spring Henry was cheerfully progressing with mathematics while reading six plays of Sophocles, two books of Livy, and four of Herodotus. Predictably, he was also finding time to read about contemporary "politics," including several of Cobbett's papers, finding them "very clever but full of lies." Was there "any foundation," he asked his father, for the "assertions" that the "Church of England has, for its numbers, produced less learned than any other such an establishment; that one simple Benedictine Abbey has produced more learned men than our church from its' establishment"? Obviously, that could not be true, but was there "any foundation for it"? Was not the opposite true—that "the English church has . . . produced 10 times as many specimens of useful learning, likely to benefit the world in general than any other body"? (Unhappily, Lushington's judicial verdict is lost!) Edmund was at home, ill, for two months that spring immediately preceding the annual college examination, but still placed first class. Returning, he remained at Trinity to read during the "long vacation" that summer and warned his parents in mid-August that he could not join them during late summer vacation at Dover unless left alone for "uninterrupted reading . . . from breakfast to dinner, or 2 o'clock."

Henry joined Edmund at Trinity in the fall of 1829. As his fellow freshman and closest friend, George Venables, remembered it years later, Henry's "singularly attractive appearance and manners" made him immediately popular, and "he entered with keen enjoyment both into the society" and his studies. He was already "an excellent classical scholar," had naturally "a remarkable aptitude for mathematical studies, and his memory" was always "extraordinarily tenacious." He seemed "always at leisure for social amusement and occupation, without interrupting the rapid progress of his studies." During that year, "which he always regarded with fond regret as the happiest of his life, he learnt more perhaps from intercourse with the friends by whom he was constantly surrounded than from lectures, books, or examinations."[18]

In mid-January 1830 Edmund and Henry were invited to take some "good tea & good advice" with the amiable old professor of modern history, William Smyth (1765–1849). The tea, Henry found, was excellent, but he was less certain about the advice: "an exhortation to us not to read too hard, not to endanger our health, etc, of which he seems to think us in more danger than we ever have been, & probably shall be." But Smyth had observed numerous ambitious boys in his nearly forty years at Cambridge. The previous year, as he may have recalled, Edmund had lost two months from illness following the scholarship examination. And in less than a year, Henry, from whatever cause, would suffer devastating illness and never fully recover.

In the 1830 university scholarship examination, where Edmund placed second after Kennedy, Henry placed fifth or sixth, more than respectable for a freshman. A "person who had conversed with two of the examiners" advised Lee that Edmund "ought to read with attention much of what" he had read before, should practice Latin composition, and never let his "classical knowledge be stagnant," lest he drop behind. Edmund grimly agreed: "I must certainly use best precautions & most vigorous exertions, & it may be a matter of considerable importance what I do during my next long vacation."

Plans for that summer posed a troublesome problem since George Peacock, the college tutor, had decreed that, unlike the previous year, only the appointed scholars of Trinity might stay on. Edmund hoped to qualify in the forthcoming Trinity scholarship examinations, and did so; but Henry, as a freshman, was ineligible. Resolved to avoid being separated, the boys cast about for alternatives, but found none, unless Peacock could be persuaded to relent. "Reading at home to any extent," Edmund considered "impossible, at least incompatible with enjoyment." Some Cambridge men "went out" (away from Cambridge, perhaps even to the Continent) with a tutor. But the "expense" was "pretty considerable; besides that there are hardly any tutors, except the very best, whom I should be willing to read with after Lee, & these are seldom to be got." Anticlimactically, after all the fretful suspense, Peacock yielded, persuaded perhaps by Henry's scoring the highest in both mathematics and classics as well as the total Trinity College examination that spring.[19] The brothers remained at Cambridge, but shared their father's dissatisfaction with the amount of reading they managed at first to accomplish. Before August they revised their daily schedule, rising by half past six and reading some two hours before breakfast. The "chains of idleness," Edmund announced, "are a good deal slackened, & will shortly be quite broken." But even then, Henry reported, Lee seemed "considerably troubled about our common indisposition, if I may use the word, to Latin prose."

Political developments that summer in both England and France provided distractions that Edmund would find hard to resist while Henry, always tugged toward current events, was with him. The death of George IV on 25 June and ceremonies in the Cambridge Senate House on the thirtieth proclaiming the new king were only the beginning of excitements. "After a good deal of much ado about nothing," as Edmund watched from the "tolerably filled" galleries, "the vice chancellor proclaimed King William IV" and then startled everyone by doffing his cap, and "with a God save the King hurra!! gave the signal for three times three." Then nearly everybody trooped outside "to read it in three different places," while some of "the snobs" (Cambridge townspeople) from the gallery rushed down to the vacated tables and "set to work vigorously upon the remaining cake & wine." In late July the overthrow of the Bourbon monarchy in three days of Parisian street fighting created a new sensation at Cambridge, where nearly all the undergraduates, Tories included, cheered the revolution. George Peacock was in Paris and falsely rumored to have been accidentally shot. He had been, truly enough, surrounded by the carnage, soon writing back that in walking from one street to another he had counted 150 dead bodies. Irreverently, Henry wondered "how often he had exclaimed '*shocking!*' while counting the bodies." In mid-August the county election speeches cost the brothers more study time. Edmund was astonished by "the orators, & the style of mob oratory," and "the way in which the crowd of common people were affected & expressed their sentiments." The "chairing" of successful candidates was "very amazing; every 10 (?) yards they lift the chair up rapidly . . . to a considerable height, so that an unpractised member has great difficulty some times to hold his seat." Henry dryly added, "Contrary to my hopes, the quantity of damage was decidedly small," Cambridgeshire oxen having been "the principal sufferers . . . as some *barrels* of beef were consumed by each party diurnally, not to mention ale and pudding." Before the end of the month, the mathematical tutor had concluded his summer instruction, Lee was tapering off and preparing to depart for his new duties at Rugby, and Lushington's old friend, John Whishaw—surely not without his prior approval—had invited Edmund and Henry to join him for a holiday at Brighton and the southern coast. Obviously eager to accept but uneasy about the summer's accomplishments, Edmund resolved to "make up as well as we can by tremendous reading" for the few remaining days.

The excursion, evidently the first view of Brighton for Edmund and Henry, began auspiciously enough. Through the window of an inn, they glimpsed the new king "robed . . . in a white great coat, & sitting in an open carriage of plain & handsome appearance, with two outriders," but were even more impressed by the lights of Brighton and the coast adjoining, with all the "long shades of light, streaming in furrows along the surface of the sea"—a "glorious panorama" from the end of the great pier. They proceeded to Arundel and its castle recently rebuilt by the Duke of Norfolk, where Edmund found the library "scantily supplied with books" and complained that "foolishly" the really picturesque "fine turret of the old castle" was not shown. The planned itinerary, weather permitting, included Chichester, Portsmouth, the Isle of Wight, Salisbury, and then back through London.

Most unluckily, "in the uttermost parts of the Isle of Wight," as Edmund described it, Henry suffered an attack of severe intestinal pain. It was the initial episode of a tenacious disorder (perhaps a tubercular peritonitis) from which Henry would never really recover. He "renounced" the eating of fruit, and began his second year at Trinity. Another attack came swiftly, blamed at first on a piece of pastry eaten in hall. Discouraged, "far from well," he wrote Tom, who would soon depart for India: it was "not agreeable to be in such a state of body that the slightest want of care may lay you up for 2 or 3 days." Perhaps the underlying cause had been "irregular hours for the last year." Following a third attack, in early December, Dr. John Haviland, professor of medicine, worried about the recurrences, prescribed "some very strong medicines" and advised him to return to Maidstone in a hired post chaise, and to further avoid fatigue by traveling two days instead of one. Almost two years would pass before he again saw Cambridge. Venables, nearly thirty years later, with Henry then four years dead, called his December 1830 illness "an attack of internal inflammation, which, after a few days of severe illness, produced a permanently deleterious effect on his health and strength." Although, as Venables thought, "perfectly free from constitutional disease" (a doubtful opinion, at least), he had ever afterward been "obliged in some respects to adopt the habits of an invalid," never being "able to walk two or three miles, or to ride ten or twelve, without inconvenient fatigue."[20]

In the family, long after Henry and his father were dead, it remained legendary how Lushington ceaselessly had nursed him, "personally waiting upon" him "with the gentleness of a woman. . . . All considerations of expense or inconvenience" were "set aside with a view to his improvement in health."[21] As months dragged on, with the family for his sake sojourning by the sea, at Dover or Eastbourne or Hastings, Henry seemed to them at times more well than he himself thought. Doctors prescribed warm baths, or replaced baths by showers. Unmistakable relapses brought "feverish nights," "general weakness," and "depression of spirits." By late March 1832 he finally felt sufficiently hopeful to resume writing letters to Tom, no longer likely "to add pain" to his "exile" by betraying his own despair. Yet within two weeks he suffered one of his worst relapses, with "violent pain in the stomach—sickness [vomiting] & stoppage of the bowels," and a physician by his bedside throughout three successive nights. That attack seems to have been some kind of crisis, both physical and emotional. Before the end of April, he was busily composing Greek iambics for the Porson Prize at Cambridge, which he would win, and writing Tom, "I think I shall very soon recover all the strength I lost in the last attack, and, I hope, proceed in an onward course." If his doctor would allow him to return to Cambridge in October, he would be "satisfied."

Return in October he did, but with modified goals. No longer would he feel impelled by pressures internal or parental to emulate Edmund's single-minded devotion to the classics, perhaps even to match him honor for honor. His memoir by Venables asserts he "resumed his social habits," but took no "active interest in the objects of University ambition." (His Greek verses did, however, capture the Porson Prize again, in 1833.) He "seldom looked at a book" except to acquire an "amount of knowledge" in mathematics "precisely sufficient to ensure a tolerable degree." With the "stock of acquirements . . . accumulated at the age of eighteen," before his illness, he would succeed in becoming a Fellow of Trinity College, "the highest object of Cambridge ambition."[22] He would henceforth be consciously a survivor, determined so long as possible to remain alive and stave off another collapse. Yet fifteen years later the time would come when, in sheer frustration at inactivity and underutilized abilities, he would take a desperate risk, intuitively suspecting that it would eventually cost him his life, as in eight more years it did.

Contrary to assumptions occasionally published as fact, it was not at Cambridge that either Edmund or Henry began their close friendships with Alfred Tennyson. Not even is it certifiable that Henry ever spoke to Tennyson, or so much as saw him, during the year (1829–30) when both were at Trinity. By mid-December 1830 Henry's illness sent him home, and in March 1831, long before Henry returned, Tennyson left Cambridge permanently when his father died. By an unaccountable inaccuracy, Venables dated as late as 1841 the fulfillment of Henry's "long-cherished wish, by forming the acquaintance" of Tennyson,"[23] although we shall find that they had become friends in London by early 1839. Edmund himself, writing in old age, tentatively placed his own first known "sight" of Tennyson on the occasion of Arthur Hallam's reading of his prize declamation in Trinity College Chapel, which occurred on 16 December 1831. On a bench just below Hallam sat Tennyson, "listening intently to the spoken words."[24] (He had come from Somersby for the occasion.) It was "a year or two later, Edmund thought, before he and Tennyson were introduced by Robert Tennant at a breakfast given by James Spedding "in the course of the long vacation." Spedding and his four guests—Edmund, Tennant, Tennyson, and Hallam—had "various talk about Shelley and Keats"; and Tennyson recited "some lines of Virgil" and his own sonnet, "Mine be the strength of spirit," which would appear "in his next volume." (The summer meeting, then, would have been in 1832, after Edmund had received his bachelor of arts degree.) The breakfast finished, Spedding stayed in his rooms while the others went walking—"A. T. in front with Hallam, Tennant behind with me."[25] If it seems hardly credible that during more than two years together in the same college two students like Edmund and Alfred would not have known one another by sight, even after Alfred had captured the Chancellor's Gold Medal for English verse with his innovative "Timbuctoo," we should note that Edmund's rooms were at college, Alfred's lodgings in town, and that Edmund's obsessive studying habitually filled his time. But, indeed, it seems that several months elapsed between the arrival at Trinity of the less studious Arthur Hallam and the beginning of his now famed assocation with Tennyson.[26]

Edmund had arrived in 1828 with conservative tastes in English poetry and apparently little knowledge of recent poets other than Byron. Almost immediately, he informed his father, he found the prevailing university taste "to my idea . . . horrible." Understandably he had scorned the pretentious Etonians who pronounced all the plays of Aeschylus "bad" or condemned "the style of Addison," and he loyally winced at hearing a man from his own Charterhouse "prefer Southey's Roderick to the Iliad or Paradise Lost,—indeed such instances of good taste & improved criticism are not uncommon." But he was hardly less discomfited by the Cantabridgian admiration of Shelley (preposterously, he felt, considered the equal of Milton) and of Wordsworth (deplorably placed above Byron). Soon, though, he too was participating in the admiration of these English Romantics: in August 1830 desiring the one-volume collection of Coleridge, Shelley, and Keats, and by that November delighted with a debate at the Union that by a 10-to-1 vote supported "Wordsworth's claim to be a great Poet," despite "several speeches of illiberal sophistry, gross & petulant ignorance, against him." Hare had pleased him by relaying Wordsworth's opinion that although he still preferred Milton's "Lycidas" to Shelley's "Adonais," he "could not consider Shelley's genius inferior to Milton's." By May 1831 Edmund was allowing himself a nightly "half hour of recreation . . . just before bedtime" in "reperusing" Shelley's tragedy *The Cenci*, esteeming it "indeed a glorious work." For once, Shelley had freed himself "from the passion for good & the sympathy with human suffering which were continually churning within" his mind. Of course, "the sickly taste" of the present age "wd object to the subject, in a tragedy, wh however it would very probably endure and admire in a novel." Throughout his life Edmund would continue to admire Shelley and Keats, and particularly their classical poems, perhaps Keats's "Hyperion" most of all.

In January 1831 he was attempting to collect his thoughts concerning Tennyson's *Poems, Chiefly Lyrical*. A reviewer in the *Westminster*—evidently "a man heart & soul in what would be usually denominated the Cambridge School of Taste in Poetry"—had praised the book vehemently.[27] Edmund felt it "rather too much to give to so young an author on his first appearance," but remained unsure "in what respects it exceeds the deserts of its object." By 1832, or sooner, Tennyson's poems were being "widely circulated about Cambridge in MS," with Edmund one of the network of recipients.[28] On one occasion Tennant copied out the entire "Palace of Art" expressly for Edmund to study on a journey by coach to Bath.[29] In April 1832 Henry was disappointed by Edmund's absentmindedly leaving at Cambridge "some very beautiful poems of Alfred Tennyson which he intends to read to us when he can get them." In early June he had copies at Park House to read to his sisters, who greatly admired them. During his first meeting with Tennyson, at Spedding's breakfast later that summer, he may have told the poet of the sisters' admiration. For whatever reason, on 21 December 1832, Tennyson inscribed a copy of his *Poems*, fresh from the press, to "Maria Catharine Lushington/ Emily Lushington,"[30] although not until after another seven years would he actually meet the Lushingtons, aside from Edmund and Henry.

Before Henry took ill in 1830, Edmund had grumbled his way through the "torture" of composing a required declamation to be delivered in Latin, a tongue he had always merely endured. Henry was amused at his "intense disgust" with Latin composition and gleeful when he contrived to smuggle in "several Greek quotations & some phrases." In February followed Edmund's English declamation upon "a very good, though difficult & extensive, subject, the character of Swift," chosen on the recommendation of Connop Thirlwall during a convivial four-hour conference over a bottle of wine. Thirlwall then loaned him some books and "recommended . . . what to read."

Increasingly during the next three years, Thirlwall would influence the configuration of Edmund's scholarly interests, already inspired and nurtured by Hare. Thirlwall had been a child prodigy, reading Latin at the age of three and Greek at four. After winning the Chancellor's Medal for classics at Cambridge in 1818 and becoming a Fellow of Trinity, he had reluctantly entered Lincoln's Inn in 1820 and practiced for several years as a barrister, all the while fervently hating the work. "It can never be anything but loathesome to me," he wrote; "my aversion to the law has not increased, as it scarcely could, from the first day of my initiation into its mysteries."[31] No doubt knowing of Thirlwall's earned disdain for the bar only deepened Edmund's reluctance to attempt it, no less so since Thirlwall was a forceful public speaker, a thing Edmund was not. Thirlwall had returned to Trinity in 1827, taken holy orders, and entered vigorously into academic work. With Hare, his long-time friend and fellow enthusiast for German scholarship, he set about to broaden classical study at Trinity from a myopic preoccupation with textual criticism and composition to a sympathetic comprehension of ancient history and thought. He did not achieve a revolution. But despite the relative brevity of his academic career—only seven years before his pamphlet indiscreetly attacking compulsory chapel attendance and the exclusion of dissenters from degrees offended Christopher Wordsworth, who asked him to resign—Thirlwall is still credited by historians of classical studies in Britain with being the leading innovator in the liberalizing of his discipline.[32] Even Alfred Tennyson, not a systematic scholar, was no doubt benefited in at least one respect by the presence of Hare and Thirlwall. Both those innovational men were among the four examiner-judges who awarded the Chancellor's Medal for English verse in 1829 to Tennyson's "Timbuctoo," the first blank verse poem ever to win that prize.[33]

Entering his senior year, 1831–32, Edmund had not yet attained any substantial academic triumphs. He had won no prizes, or perhaps not tried for any. Despite his placing high in two university scholarship examinations, the scholarships had eluded him. Although he disliked mathematics, to compete at all for the classical tripos he had first to qualify at least nominally in the mathematical tripos. And to compete next for the coveted Chancellor's First Classical Medal, which three of his great uncles (one, the bishop of Bath and Wells, still alive) had carried away in their time, he would have to finish among the mathematical senior optimes, the second rank, just beneath the wranglers. But even in the classics, it was no foregone conclusion that he would capture highest honors. His competitors included two men, Richard Shilleto and William Hepworth Thompson, who would come to be ranked among the most famed Greek scholars of their century in England: Shilleto the most respected of Cambridge private tutors, Thompson the Regius Professor of Greek and later master of Trinity College.

The family would scarcely permit Edmund a moment of peace until after the mathematical tripos, in January, was completed. In answering his first letter from Cambridge that fall, as Henry informed Tom, "Mama & myself . . . exhorted him warmly to obtain *considerable honours* in Math. In fact he has been so lectured & objurgated on this score, that I hope the continued dropping of our good advice will wear out at last, not his patience, which is great, but his hatred of curves which is greater." As the examination began, he wrote "almost in despair about his mathematical rank—but in good spirits generally." He finished quite respectably: not up among the wranglers but fourth senior optime, "far beyond my hopes," five places above Thompson and much above Shilleto, who dropped to the bottom of the junior optimes, thus becoming ineligible for the medal examination and barely eligible for the classical tripos. Lushington, knowing how formidable Cambridge mathematical examinations could be, was presumably satisfied; but Mrs. Lushington thought it "sadly *too low* for what he *might & ought to* have been, if he had exerted himself *in time.*" The septuaginarian bishop of Bath and Wells chimed in that all the family ought to feel "considerably disappointed."

In the classical tripos Edmund more than redeemed himself by finishing first, although as Henry reported, "in the translations only one piece was set which he had seen within the past year, & hardly anything . . . he had read for the last two." Shilleto was second, Thompson only fourth, with William Dobson, Edmund's Charterhouse friend, at third and Venables at fifth. Thirlwall invited Edmund to breakfast and "very kindly told" him "several things about the examination." He had apparently finished first in all parts except Latin prose, where "no one at all" was "otherwise than brutally ignorant." Even in Latin hexameters he had been "far first," rumored to have received "more marks" than the originally intended maximum. Thirlwall asked him for a copy of his Greek iambics, "if I ever corrected them." Another of the examiners, Benjamin Hall Kennedy, had helped teach Shilleto at Shrewsbury and privately tutored him at Cambridge. Kennedy's obituary of Shilleto in 1877, after conceding that his social life had retarded his studies, confidently affirmed that "the hardest reading would not have availed to place him at that time" above Edmund, "whose papers in every subject were more finished and faultless than any which have come under my observation during a long life of teaching and examining."[34]

With bolstered self-confidence Edmund awaited the Medal examination. Thirlwall had persuaded him to set Greek aside and "read nothing but

Latin . . . particularly Plautus," and loaned him a commentary on some of the plays. "He is so sure of the medal," Henry wrote to Tom, "that you may consider that he has got it. His own modesty even will hardly make him express any doubt on the subject." The first medal went to him and the second to Thompson.

The parents celebrated their twenty-third anniversary by relaying the joyful news to Tom. The Greek professor, James Scholefield, "who seldom ventures upon a word of praise to any man[,] could not withold one" from Edmund. People were saying that except for B. H. Kennedy (in 1827) "no such exercises had been shewn up for many years." Lushington, visiting Edmund at Trinity, talked with "some of the first rate men & exulted in the terms in which they spoke of him to me," their praising his "good disposition of the head & heart" as well as his scholarship. Had his mother been there, she would undoubtedly "have felt them stronger than myself." The bishop of Bath and Wells lost no time in fulfilling his promise to send Edmund one hundred pounds if he won the medal, magnanimously assuring his grandnephew that "few persons could receive a £100-0-0 with greater pleasure than he paid it." The family nurse, when informed, was not excessively impressed: "Well, it's a good thing that he has remembered it for he seems to forget so often that I fear'd he'd never think more about it, but it's a sad thing that he never gave poor Tom a present before he left us."

Henry's return to Trinity that fall was almost anticlimactic for the family. Their anxiety when he approached examinations would center less upon his ranking than upon his health, which they urged him not to jeopardize. While out walking early in 1833, he "felt a sudden weakness," as his father told Tom, "in one of his thighs, which he took for a sprain"; and though his physician found nothing "really wrong," he would always thereafter be unable to walk any substantial distance. That spring he wrote the Trinity scholarship examination, with no further physical setback, but may not have obtained a scholarship. He would have pleased his father by postponing his tripos examinations from 1834 to 1835, but elected otherwise, possibly afraid that another illness might preclude his ever taking them. In the mathematical tripos he placed only fortieth among the senior optimes, but thereby remained eligible for the classical tripos, in which he disappointed himself by placing only sixth in the first class. He proceeded to the medal examination but, as he expected, did not overtake the leading men above him. In the tripos, he told his father, there "certainly were many things which I either did wrong or left undone, that other men knew perfectly." He hoped the family would "not be much disappointed and still more, that you will not be distressed at the thought of my being so; for I, besides my other good qualities, am or shall be a philosopher." Edmund found

Henry's placement "quite unintelligible," but was consoled by the rumor that "all the first seven were very close together."

Edmund himself since his triumphant year had experienced an academic set-back. Unlike other Cambridge colleges, Trinity was choosing its fellows by imposing still another competitive examination in mathematics, classics, and metaphysics. Even a senior classic and first medalist such as Edmund was not exempted. Although the examination, if fairly evaluated, might be a hedge against arbitrary favoritism, it occasioned controversy. In December 1832, as Henry wrote Tom, the reactionary old Professor Smyth was talking "as usual in impartial abuse of German metaphysics and the Trinity regulations for making men sit to be examined for fellowships after their degrees." When the new Fellows were announced in October 1833, Edmund was not among them. His father's unhappiness was directed at the college rather than at him: all informants agreed there had been "a most extraordinary preference of inferior men. The principle that they ought to have been chosen because this was their last opportunity, & because this last year there were only two vacancies & there will be many more before the next election may be good in itself—but then it ought not to be professed, that the choice is to be determined by the attainments of the candidates." Edmund's own explanation was divergent and simpler: "Very foolishly indeed I had not read any metaphysics, at least next to nothing with a view to the examination & had not got up any maths." Peacock had declared that cutting "so entirely two out of three subjects . . . it would have been almost impossible for anyone to be successful."

Further, Edmund admitted to Tom, he was not greatly dissatisfied with the outcome: "Being forced for at least another year to confine myself to Academical Studies, I consider it a great advantage, as the later I commence the law, within moderate bounds, the better in my opinion." And the "very necessity of studying Metaphysics hard" would be "more than sufficient to counterbalance the slight mortification to my vanity." One suspects that his failure may have contained a dollop of wish fulfillment. More than a year earlier, Henry had written that Edmund was "by no means disposed to attempt the study of the law at present. I have instructed him to exert himself in speaking at Cambridge, but I fear he will be too lazy and too diffident." In the next fellowship examination, however, he would eminently succeed, evidently doing satisfactorily in mathematics and metaphysics, and in classics, as Peacock later testified, being "equally remarkable for . . . finished elegance, and for . . . profound knowledge of nearly the whole range of Greek and Latin literature."[35] And that year's forced study of metaphysics initiated him into a field that, second only to Greek, would become his lifelong interest.

Both Edmund and Henry became members of the exclusive Cambridge

Conversazione Society, more frequently called the Cambridge Apostles, now most famous for having earlier encircled Arthur Henry Hallam and Alfred Tennyson. Edmund, contrary to the tradition that no man the society elected, after laborious deliberations among themselves, ever refused,[36] had declined his first invitation in March 1832, when enveloped in reading for the classical tripos. Henry, naturally enough, had urged him to broaden his interests by accepting; but William Dobson, not an Apostle, had advised him otherwise. Even Tennant, himself an Apostle, agreed that Edmund was "right, though he very much regretted my not joining them." Two years later Edmund accepted a second invitation. For Henry, who had joined the group in May 1833 ("a glorious fellow," one Apostle assured another),[37] the society was the ideal outlet for his skill in persuasive writing and his broad ethical and political orientation. When the Apostles assembled each Saturday evening, a designated member would read a newly composed essay upon a subject of his own choosing, thereby launching a lively discussion in which all the members participated. The Apostles prided themselves most on their openness of mind to diverse viewpoints, including opinions opposite to their own. Tennyson would immortalize these salutary interchanges in his *In Memoriam* (87):

> Where once we held debate, a band
>   Of youthful friends, on mind and art,
>   And labour, and the changing mart,
> And all the framework of the land;

> When one would aim an arrow fair,
>   But sent it slackly from the string,
>   And one would pierce an outer ring,
> And one an inner, here and there.

In the poem, of course, it was Hallam, "the master bowman," whose arrow would finally "cleave the mark," while all "hung to hear / The rapt oration flowing free / From point to point, with power and grace / And music in the bounds of law, / To those conclusions when we saw / The God within him light his face." The whole described proceeding, with the unerring archer invariably the same, though generically appropriate for an elegy, seems a bit too uniform for real life. (But before the first of the Lushington members, Henry, actually joined the Apostles, both Tennyson and Hallam had left Cambridge, and four months later Hallam would die in Vienna.) Honorary membership for those who desired it continued after they resigned and ceased attending regularly. For decades annual dinners brought together the Apostles of several generations. Venables's journals show him frequently attending these reunions, at times with one or both of the Lushingtons.

At Park House during the older brothers' early years at Cambridge, a lively troupe of five young sisters and one brother were happily growing up under the benign surveillance of Lushington and Sophia. When Edmund won his medal in 1832, Maria was sixteen, Emily almost fifteen, Rosa about thirteen, Ellen eleven, Franklin nine, and Louy eight. Two letters to Tom that spring described typical domestic hilarities. Rosa, as Henry described it, was "playing on the old piano—N.B. it is considered so old" that when visitors came it was "carefully kept in the background." Maria and Emily were out walking, "Ellen doing nothing except turning over Miss Carveth's drawing books, and impeding every body—a dear little creature, however, she is, and has just devoured the hugest tea (bread at tea, I mean) that I ever beheld." "Mama" was reading, and "Papa employed, as he ever is, in something for the good of others—the present subject being, I think the Maidstone Dispensary report." Why didn't those "girls strike up? There—there they are off; at full gallop: Rosa & Maria—stopped again—they are terribly lazy, all except the latter, who is becoming a! vigorous girl." Emily had "just been trying to cheat" him by "imposing some other airs" for a song, but he "knew it too well, and her malice" had "failed of its purpose. She has just read this sentence and rewarded my fidelity of record with a thump that will retard my recovery for a month." Some six weeks later Tom's informant was Emily. The piano had just been tuned, and she would try what she could "do in singing, I shall endeavour to persuade Rosa to try with me, & I hope I shall succeed; I am almost sure she would sing very well with a little instruction [and] practice." Rosa and Ellen delighted the family with two songs—"one is the imitation of the psalm singing at Heston, in which not only Ellen's voice, but also her face, screwed into the shape of an old woman's is very good; and Rosa's is equally so in the character of an old man." But the other song was "universally allowed to be the best": "a fragment of a satirical song upon the Duke of Wellington which they heard repeated by a man in the streets of Hastings." They had "completely composed the tune themselves, and as Rosa makes additions, & changes it every time she performs, Ellen's attempts to keep up with her are excessively amusing." It was "impossible to describe . . . how good their songs are."

Sadly, though, a year later, in the summer of 1833, the family would lose its comedienne, when Rosa died in London after a brief illness, where the parents had taken her to be nearer to medical superintendence. It is doubtful that poor Ellen, Rosa's partner in those comic duets, ever really recovered from the shock of her closest playmate's death. It would be Ellen whose nerves gave way when others in the family died or seemed threatened with death. From late May until mid-July, when Rosa died, Henry, home between terms from Trinity, was the surrogate squire of Park House, relaying almost daily reports to London concerning the business of the estate. Edmund had been traveling on the Continent, including Germany, where he had begun the mastering of the German language so indispensable for a student of philology in those decades. From Edmund's letters after his return, it is clear that Henry was still far from well. "Harry [Henry]," Edmund wrote his father on 12 July, "has not yet decided whether he shall come up to London" for Rosa's funeral, "and says he must be guided by circumstances. I hope and think you will approve of this resolution."

Edmund and Henry remained together at Cambridge until 1837, receiving their respective master of arts degrees in 1835 and 1837, Henry having become a Fellow of Trinity College in 1836. Both had performed some private tutoring, until Edmund in 1835 was appointed an assistant tutor and classical lecturer, giving daily lectures upon subjects in classical literature, holding the same title that Thirlwall and Hare had held. Indeed, in the absence of those two luminaries, his models, he seems to have been considered the best of the remaining classical lecturers among the Fellows at Trinity.[38] Self-conditioned to systematic study, and emancipated after 1834 from preparing for examinations, he had steadily and efficiently concentrated upon perfecting his German, reading extensively in German philology and philosophy, and reinforcing his expanding knowledge by incorporating it into his lectures. For one entire summer and parts of two others, he studied in Germany, where, as his friend Dobson reported, he had selected especially the cities "in which the lectures of the most distinguished professors might advance his knowledge."[39] His testimonials for Glasgow in 1838 would include letters from three eminent scholars at Bonn University—Christian Lassen, who had introduced the study of Indian archaeology into Germany; Friedrich Gottlieb Welcker, formerly closely associated with Wilhelm von Humboldt, and librarian and director of the Museum of Ancient Art at Bonn; and Friedrich Dietz, acclaimed as the founder of Romance philology.[40]

Most unfortunately, retaining an assistant tutorship was dependent upon remaining a Fellow of Trinity, which status in turn carried two conditions Edmund was unwilling to accept: taking holy orders within a brief specified time and remaining unmarried. Not only did he have no vocation for the priesthood but, more important, he desired to have a family. University professors, of course, could be married; but to take orders and await a professorship could be extremely risky. Indeed, Thompson would replace Edmund as assistant tutor in 1837, take orders, and eventually become Regius Professor of Greek, but only after waiting, unmarried, for sixteen years. (Then, and promptly, he was married, to the widow of George Peacock, and went on to become master of Trinity College.) Shilleto, on the other hand, had married too soon to become a Fellow at all; but he took orders and remained at Cambridge, only to drudge on as a private coach for thirty years until, finally, Peterhouse altered its rules and made him a Fellow and an assistant tutor, only nine years before his death.

Although Edmund intensely disliked the prospect of entering the law, he was resigned to doing so eventually, since he seemed to have no other practical option. Peacock in 1838 would declare flatly, "There is no appointment in this place [the University] which a layman can fill, which is worthy of Mr. Lushington's acceptance."[41]

As early as May 1833, Edmund had begun going through the formalities of preparing for the bar, taking his obligatory three dinners that year at the Temple, before hurrying off to travel and study on the Continent. According to the *Alumni Cantabrigiensis*, his actual call to the bar came on 20 November 1835, probable enough, since a call was attainable three years after the receipt of a bachelor of arts degree from Cambridge or Oxford. A letter to his father from Trinity in the spring of 1835 mentions his having suspended his legal studies ("laid aside Blackstone") temporarily, and "consequently . . . not advanced much this term." That was written before he received his assistant tutorship, but while he was eagerly, if not very hopefully, wishing his father would approve of another possibility that, had it materialized, might have become the great adventure of his life.

The most eminent of all royal hydrographers, Captain (later Admiral Sir Francis) Beaufort, believed in taking along "savants," researchers in various scientific and other scholarly fields, to conduct onshore researches while his hydrographic survey vessels crept along offshore. He it was who in 1831 had arranged the fateful meeting between Commander Robert Fitzroy of the *HMS Beagle* and the young biologist Charles Darwin, before they sailed toward the coast of South America.[42] In 1833, Robert Pashley, a Fellow of Trinity, had enjoyed free passage on a voyage to Crete, before exploring the interior of the island, with its ancient cities, and gathering material for two distinguished volumes, *Travels in Crete*, to be published in 1837 by Cambridge University Press. Now Beaufort desired to take another classicist to examine ancient sites on a forthcoming survey along the coast of Asia Minor, and Pashley had recommended Edmund.

In four earnest letters by Edmund between 11 February and 25 March, two with addenda by Henry, the brothers implored their father to realize the potentialities of such a venture and give his consent. The expenses would be slight, the fare and passage free of charge, and the savant welcome at the officers' mess. The ship would land him at any place, and likewise pick him up, providing meanwhile a bodyguard of a dozen sailors to assist him while ashore. The work, while "utterly delightful," would be no "mere idle enjoyment," but "laborious as well as useful," and a "possible opening to reputation" for him. In preparation he was already studying modern Greek and various books about Asia Minor and could soon begin with architecture and the Turkish language. Two years abroad would not unduly retard his progress in the law. He was

younger than most of his Cambridge "cotemporaries." Certainly the proposed venture could not possibly make the law "more disagreable & uninteresting than it appears at present." In fact, two years of "such a steady invigorating
occupation" might be a "relief and support under the drudgery of the law,"
leaving him "better equipped in mental energy" than he would be "with the
annoying recollection constantly at hand, how great & rarely granted an opportunity I had past by." After "filling" his "mind in such a manner, the struggle to
bend it to utterly distasteful pursuits would be less irksome & less difficult."

The more rhetorically gifted Henry, who had himself been admitted to the
Inner Temple to begin his three-year wait for the call to the bar, did not "altogether" share Edmund's distaste for the law, but felt he had "not at all . . .
overstated the advantages" of Beaufort's plan. True, Edmund was "not
ambitious—but I am, as much for him as for myself; and I would not encourage
his present wish" unless it seemed to offer "a prospect not only of enlarging his
views & powers, but of attaining high distinction." With his "enthusiastic
love" of his subject "joined to eminent talents," Edmund "might obtain at once
a name on his return from the East, among the distinguished men of his country." Did not that "prospect . . . deserve to be set against being two years
forward in the study of a profession to which he cannot, at present, look with
satisfaction"? "Ambition" was, indeed, "a strong spur to many minds; but it is,
you know, an infirmity of noble minds, and not that which makes them noble:
to one like him, the wish of doing good would be stronger: the desire of self-
improvement stronger still." He would not pass his two years "in indolence
. . . but in active occupation, and the collection and comparison of interesting
and important facts." It would not be like setting up in England "for being a
literary man only . . . thinking & writing instead of a profession," but "a
practical employment, a daily call upon his energies, which will . . . altogether produce a most favourable effect upon his mind, and fit him better for
any station." In truth, if Edmund were "a German, which thank heavens he is
not, this course which he proposes would be the first step, I perceive, towards
becoming a minister." It would not work so in England just then; "yet it is to be
expected that, as every year makes the English better acquainted with Germany, their pursuits & this class of knowledge will have a higher reputation
among us than they have hitherto borne." Then maybe a little too conscious of
his own supple rhetoric, of his role as a pleader for the plaintiff at the bar, young
Henry could not quite forgo taking two or three steps backward and modestly
calling attention to his performance: "I hope you will think there is something
in all these arguments (I trust they are such) which I have written just as they
occurred to me."

Of course, Edmund did not go to Asia Minor, and we hear nothing more about the matter. Perhaps the position did not materialize, for him or anyone, or perhaps the assistant tutorship he accepted a few weeks later seemed anti-climactically fortuitous to his father after all the daunting unknowns in the other scheme. It may have been more than coincidental that Edmund remained at his new position for the same two years he might have expended on the voyage. Even so, the two-year postponement of the bar occasioned consterna-tion in the Park House family, echoed from afar by Tom out in India: "I cannot disguise my fears that Edmund . . . is likely to become a regular University resident, & would prefer the honour of a classical annotator high in repute among scholars, though useless to all other persons, to entering upon the dry study of the law, the profession for which he was intended." Such would be a pity, for his talents well qualified him for "a career of greater usefulness, & on a higher stage of action."

Only the pragmatic and enormously wealthy uncle, Sir George Philips, on 14 August 1835, ventured to place his weight on Edmund's side. "The more I think of Edmund's love of letters, & particularly of Greek literature . . . the more I am led to the conclusion that he would be happier, & possibly even more suc-cessful in a college, than in a life of contest at the bar." If Henry had better "health for the bar, it would, in my judgment, be the proper theatre for him. Perhaps I ought not in this manner to volunteer my opinion." Yet it proceeded "only from my affection for them, & my desire that 2 young men, so distin-guished for their talents, & attainments, should be placed in the profession best suited for them; & that as Sydney Smith says, the round man should not be put into the square hole, & the square man into the round hole. Love to all." Of course, not even the manufacturing genius of a Sir George Philips could run ahead of fate in producing an appropriate permanent opportunity for Edmund "in a college" in those years. But perhaps the seed thought, planted in Lushing-ton's mind, peeped above ground in 1838 when the Glasgow Greek professor-ship suddenly materialized just as Edmund had at last settled into the study of law.

In May of 1837 Edmund finally bowed to the inevitable and resigned his assistant tutorship. Even then, he postponed the ordeal by going off again to Germany and, inevitably, toward the intellectual attractions of Bonn, trans-gressing against Henry's fraternal admonitions to forget Bonn now, and go out in society, see the theaters, and become more aware of international politics. Writing from Bonn, Edmund did not conceal his melancholy. Although Hen-ry's "war against Bonn," his "prejudice against the innocent place," proceeded solely from his "kindness & anxious affection" for a brother whose "powers" he feared might become "crippled" there, Edmund could not admit the danger. "At least" it was "no new trait in me to find consolation for the want of theatres & parties in a most beautiful country & interesting studies." As for small talk about public affairs, "I used to hope that you at least acquitted me of utter absence of interest upon subjects on which I forbore from often speaking because I hardly ever hear anyone else speak without trifling words." He was "fully conscious of not having the universality of sympathies" that Henry possessed, "but this is a boon granted to very few." Surely he there at Bonn once again was "not wrong in gratifying a strong devotion in a more particular direction." He would have "little" to "look forward to in the long course of misery which lies before me" if he took to "what is called my profession" a stunting of the powers given him apparently, it seemed then, "but to be thwarted." But he would "not dwell longer" on that "cheerless prospect."

Temporarily, Henry, then twenty-five, was still residing at Trinity, as its Fellows were entitled to do, although in the following year he would move to London to study law. While legal studies would not be to his liking (he spoke sarcastically of "the unthankful profession to which I have devoted my golden youth, in return for which it holds out, at the best, a doubtful promise of making my age golden"), he would expend no sighs over laying aside the classics. Latin and Greek had enriched his mind, provided contexts for understanding the world, rewarded him with recognition of his talents; but for him, unlike Edmund, they did not constitute the definition of his identity. With his uncannily retentive memory, he could retain the fund of classical learning he had, and add to it if he pleased; but the center of his interests lay elsewhere—in the consideration of national and international affairs, always viewed from the perspectives of justice, morality, and ethics according to his concepts of these. He relished argumentation, not excluding the weapons of irony cheerfully aimed at himself as well as others. "I made a long oration last week," he wrote his father in 1835, "yea, an opening speech of 1/2 an hour, and also a reply, wherein I exposed sundry fallacies, detected various impositions, and advanced as far as can be expected towards the regeneration of the world, & putting things in general, on their proper footing."

He read extensively, though not always intensively, in history, political commentary (he relished, among others, Carlyle), and modern literature, especially poetry, keenly studying the possibilities of prosody. Venables reported that he "scarcely ever read a book through, but while he was dressing, or resting, or in an interval of conversation, he turned over the pages of miscellaneous volumes; and it always appeared that he afterwards knew better than others the material part of their contents." But "his intellect was thoroughly scholar-like or mathematical in its accuracy, and promiscuous knowledge at once arranged itself into a symmetrical form in his unfailing memory."[43]

Henry was feeling ready to test his rhetorical pinions by issuing a pamphlet.

Residing at Cambridge, he selected a target near at hand, an institutionalized preferential treatment of students on the basis of distinctions founded on birth or wealth. Membership in a category of undergraduates called "fellow commoners," from their special privilege of dining at tables with the Fellows in their commons hall, was obtainable to any man willing to pay the requisite fees. Most were younger sons of noblemen or sons of wealthy gentry. Their academic gowns were more dignified and ornamental than others wore, and they sat in preferred seats in chapel. In addition, noblemen or presumptive heirs of noble titles, or any men who could trace royal descent, could receive their degrees after fewer required terms of residency, and sit for the classical tripos without qualifying for honors in the mathematical tripos.

Henry's thirty-one-page pamphlet *Fellow-Commoners and Honorary Degrees*, by a Resident Fellow,[44] attacked the system as unfair and alike injurious to recipients and nonrecipients. Recipients were injured when separated from other students by both dress and manner of living. The system deprived them "alone, among all our youthful community, of the inestimable advantage—the greatest, perhaps, after all which any public place of education can afford,—the free mixture in society of their own age, and the free choice of congenial friends." It virtually assured "that they shall never forget their eminence in rank or riches; we have set a permanent mark upon them, as if it were our object to remind them that they were above the need of exerting themselves, whether for profit or honour." The university was "betraying" these young men "with kisses, inflicting deep injury, under pretence of granting privileges."

The statistical records of both the university and its colleges plainly established the inferior academic performance of the fellow commoners. "They are not an intellectual class; they do not exercise over fellow students an intellectual influence proportionate even to their numbers, far less to their opportunities and station: the atmosphere in which they move is not favourable to the development of energetic thought or elevated feeling." The fault was not their own: "No shadow of blame can be fairly imputed to individuals for results so directly traceable to institutions." They had been "exposed to ten-fold trials." Fellow commoners entered Trinity College annually in a ratio of 1 to 10 of fellow students; they attained first class in the annual first-year examination at a ratio of 1 to 32. Far worse, in the senior honors examinations "the odds against a fellow-commoner, matched with an average pensioner for distinction in degree" were "just 12 to 1."

Turning to the reduced residency requirement for honorary degrees, Henry ironically professed to speculate concerning the university's real motives. Was she considering "the residence of these gentlemen fraught with danger to her usefulness, or liberties, and . . . only anxious to get rid of them as soon as she could with decency?" Or was she confessing "that her studies are not adapted to assist in the formation of that character which should belong to well-born and influential Englishmen?" Whatever her motive, in the fourteen years from 1824 to 1837, of the sixty-four noblemen who had taken honorary degrees only eight had qualified for either mathematical or classical honors. Statistics for the various prizes were even more dismaying: of 587 prizes awarded in the previous eighty or ninety years, the titled students had won exactly four. "Thus," wrote Henry, "does the University, an unkind mother to these her spoiled children alone, bribe them to indolence with playthings, and cramp their youthful strength under the weight of gilded chains."

Even less forgivable was the practice of giving these titled students "equality with, or precedence over, their superiors . . . both in University rank, and in age, importance, and learning. It is, to say the least, unseemly to see the venerable head of a Noble College cautiously abstaining from leaving the chapel in advance of one stripling among the hundreds possibly committed to his charge."

The minds of the "mass of unprivileged students" were hardly less injured. Those already disposed to overrate rank and wealth were "led to exchange nobler aims for the desire of sharing" those distinctions—"deeply injured—*debased* is the right word." Those already disposed to "underrate such claims to respect are shortly provoked to scorn them, and are thus exposed . . . to the corrupting influence of jealous pride." Those avoiding both extremes were in no way benefited. Nobody was.

Finally, the university was very possibly injuring herself by increasing "the indifference, the slight regard shown by wealthy and noble legislators, when the interests of the University become matter of national deliberation." When "did the flattered ever esteem the flatterer? or who respects those who will not respect themselves?" Of course, one slight pamphlet by an anonymous Resident Fellow produced no repeal of such long-established, though long-outmoded, practices. Only time would do that.

In 1838 the "Apostle" J. M. Kemble's *British and Foreign Review* carried Henry's review of two books of poems by his and Kemble's friend and fellow Apostle Richard Monckton Milnes.[45] Henry's treatment of his friend's generally competent but undistinguished poems, though remaining on the safe side of puffery, was predictably lenient. More interesting now, coming as they do from the man whom Alfred Tennyson would later call "the best critic he had ever known,"[46] are his theoretical generalizations, filling nearly the first half of the review.

The prevailing English poetry of the later 1830s, Henry declared, was the "Poetry of Reflection." It stood at the end of a phenomenal "revival of English poetry," to which, "for extent, originality, and beauty, any age and any nation might refer with pride; inventive, not imitative, one of those outbreaks which mark an aera . . . distinguished . . . by genuine vigour . . . unparalleled width and variety." It was a "privilege to live under the immediate influence of a time from which posterity" would "date the revival of English Poetry." At first, naturally enough, it had included an element of anarchy—"the ephemeral . . . struggling with the permanent, often successful as such upon the many, and vexing with doubts even the judgment of the few." But the general tendency of that "singular revolution" early in the century was showing itself at present in the poetry that had developed from it. The new "Poetry of Reflection," "thoughtful and meditative," had derived much more from Wordsworth than from the once phenomenally popular Byron, of whom hardly any traces remained. "Those who delight in Byronism must seek it at the fountainhead; but the gentler influence of his great contemporary is everywhere."

Yet even Wordsworth's influence, though pervasive, appeared more crucial than it was: "The genius of no single man could have created the intellectual circumstances which, in making such a school of poetry possible, made its rise sooner or later almost necessary." In the "progress of the human mind towards maturity," the "world of inward" had naturally come to "encroach upon the world of outward action," until finally "thought itself"—the act of reflecting or the result of reflecting—had become "an object of contemplation." Every "time, like every writer, will exhibit a character of its own"—necessarily, "so long as poetry is not a thing separate from our daily life, but rather the expression of what is highest and best in it. . . . What many men are thinking of, one will be found to write of."

Unfortunately, however, the "reflective element" in poetry, "at once the symbol and the cause of much good," had introduced "a dangerous heresy" into the "poetic faith," leaving too much poetry essentially unpoetical. Poets needed to remember that "though reflections may furnish us with the proper materials for poetry," not every reflection "put in verse" necessarily becomes poetry. The beauty essential for lifting reflection above mere "Thoughts in Verse" must be "conveyed . . . in one of three ways": by dramatic "subservience . . . to the development of character," through an "inherent beauty" of the concept itself, or through being "embodied in action or expressed in imagery." Too many gifted poets of the time had fallen into the error of didacticism, beguiled "by their very reverence" for their art and their "sense of its deep responsibilities." They had pursued what they thought "the only worthy aim," but with "an exclusiveness" that deprived them "of the means of attaining it." They should "consider whether the first requisite for everything is not, that it be what it professes to be."

Like most of his Cambridge contemporaries, Henry had adopted aesthetic principles from Coleridge. Though the "poet be an instructor," Henry insisted in explicitly Coleridgean terms, "the immediate end which poetry proposes to itself is not instruction, but the production of beauty; and the writer who forgets this, throws off his nearest allegiance, and ceases to be a poet." However instructive, a poem deficient in beauty "is but a sermon which has condescended to a useless disguise; it is something which might have been said as well, and therefore better, in prose." Readers are "entitled to expect from a true poet that he should have faith in his art, faith in the good which is inseparable from its genuine exercise, in its essentially noble and elevating tendencies."

Henry's lengthy introduction concluded with an apt quotation from "the great poet" A. Tennyson, "whose intuition pierces and whose practice realizes the harmonious co-operation of the presiding genii" of poetry:

> That Beauty, Good, and Knowledge are three sisters,
> That dote upon each other, friends to man,
> Living together under the same roof,
> And never can be sundered without tears.

The lines, of course, are from Tennyson's piece addressed to Richard Trench, introducing "The Palace of Art." Henry had subtly turned back upon itself the commonly oversimplified moral drawn from those lines—that poetry should dutifully incorporate Good and Knowledge into its Beauty. True, Henry is saying, but not true enough: Good and Knowledge, unaccompanied by Beauty, will not be poetry at all.

Later, as Tennyson's favorite critical adviser, Henry would be at hand to encourage his friend's sound instinct to position his poetic pedagogy, as in *The Princess*, along the path of some kind of "diagonal," though not obligatorily a "strange" one. *The Princess* would ultimately be dedicated to Henry, who as we shall see, had been in close proximity to Tennyson during much of its composition. No doubt with some consciousness of exaggeration, Venables, after Henry died, claimed that if "all Mr. Tennyson's writings had by some strange accident been destroyed, Henry Lushington's wonderful memory could, I believe, have reproduced the whole."[47]

IV

The Glasgow Professorship

1838-1875

E DMUND'S "LONG COURSE OF MISERY" toward undesired political honor by way of the uncongenial bar soon would be terminated. At Glasgow University, on 4 February 1838, the much-acclaimed Greek professor Sir Daniel Keyte Sandford, only forty, died after a week of typhus fever. In many respects the vacant professorship was enviable, despite certain drawbacks from Edmund's standpoint. Its holder was numbered with the elite "faculty of the college"—the principal and thirteen professors with chairs predating 1761— who virtually ruled the university. When one of the thirteen died or resigned, the survivors on "the faculty" elected his successor (the principalship and less-favored chairs were filled by the crown).[1]

Edmund's friend and fellow Apostle Robert Monteith had studied at Glasgow before going up to Cambridge. Now returned to Carstairs, the family estate near Glasgow, he was well known in the area, where his wealthy manufacturer father had twice been the city's lord rector (chief magistrate). When Sandford died, Monteith could have written immediately to urge Edmund to try for the chair.

Whatever discussions may have passed between Edmund and his father, what pleading of the case by Henry, before Lushington assented, little time was lost. Within two weeks of Sandford's death, at least one testimonial for Edmund (dated on 17 February by the younger Christopher Wordsworth, headmaster of Harrow and future bishop of Lincoln) was moving toward Glasgow. Numerous others would rapidly follow.

Edmund's strongest motive was the permanent return to his cherished Greek. The material rewards also were substantial. Most of the income was fees handed directly from student to professor; and the Greek classes, taken by nearly all first-year men and required of every aspirant to the Scottish clergy, were the university's largest. No other professor, or even the principal, earned more.[2] Sandford had begun in 1821 with about four hundred students, eventually increased to about five hundred. Between 1824 and 1828 he averaged £1,663 annually and on the best year received £1,843.[3] Although less self-promoting, Edmund in 1856 would still have "about 300 students" in three sections, and reportedly still earn "above £1,000"—for less than a half-year, summer holidays extending from early May into mid-October.[4] The professors also had comfortable, if relatively small, houses rent-free. A Glasgow history professor, writing recently, viewed the situation wistfully: "Established in their fine houses and enriched by the fees which flowed from the rapidly increasing classes, the Professors were happily placed."[5] To these houses, fine or not, the students came trooping at the start of each term, their fees in their hands.

As D. H. Boyd, in *Fraser's Magazine*, described the scene, the professor might briefly interview the student before taking the fee and giving a "ticket of admission to the classroom." Some "more civilized" lads would quietly lay the exact amount on the table, but others would "hand their money to the professor and demand the change in regular shop-fashion." Some professors would give the money no more than a sidelong glance. Others would "count it over, and pocket it with a bow, saying 'Thank you, sir; much obliged to you, sir.' "[6]

Unlike the typical young gentlemen at Oxford or Cambridge, most Glasgow men were of the middle or lower classes, "characteristically and essentially," as one writer put it, "plebeian; plebeian in their population, plebeian in their standard, plebeian in their reward." They lived with parents, or friends, or may have "tended sheep or worked in the fields all summer . . . to save enough to pay for a garret in Glasgow and a barrel of herrings or oatmeal."[7] A motley crowd they were, some boys of eleven or twelve, others "men with gray hair, up to the age of fifty or sixty; great stout fellows from the plough; men . . . from the North of Ireland; lads from counting houses in town," coming to take a logic class; English dissenters not admitted to English universities; "young men with high scholarship from the best public schools; and others not knowing a letter of Greek and hardly a word of Latin."[8] But almost to a boy or man, so say their historians, they were willing to work hard to make the most of their hard-purchased opportunities.

Curricular offerings were wider than at Oxford or Cambridge, including vigorous instruction in logic, philosophy, theology, and the natural sciences.

Most students did best in logic and, being poorly prepared, worst in classical languages, especially Greek. But, prepared or not, nearly every student was obliged to do a year of Greek. And one professor, alone, instructed the entire lot, collecting all the fees, doing all the work, enduring the attendant frustrations.

It had long been recognized that Greek professors in Scotland, with two or three hundred students, faced virtually impossible expectations. In 1819 J. G. Lockhart, a Glasgow alumnus, denied that "in any proper meaning of the term," the professors were enabled to teach "the principles of language." They were reduced to "schoolmasters in the strictest sense," compelled to lay "the very lowest part of the foundation." Although some were "profound and accomplished" scholars, neither "depth" nor "elegance" was required.[9] In 1821, before the election of Sandford, the Glasgow faculty voted to appoint a separate professor of elementary Greek, to be reimbursed by student fees; but the vote was soon rescinded: too little money would have remained for the professor.[10] As years passed, would-be reformers, influenced by German higher education, hammered away at the theme. "The Scotch," claimed one, had "manifestly failed in one great mission of a university. For what is called academic learning in other countries, they merely give an elementary school drill." But a "good school is always better for boys than a university toned down to the level of a school." The classics professor needed to "metamorphose himself into a schoolmaster," and could do so "the more readily the further he is removed naturally and by culture from the massive intellectual proportions of a Hermann and a Boeckh."[11] By then, 1855, Edmund, vastly overtrained, temperamentally untuned to such a role, had been at Glasgow eighteen years, repeatedly dispensing the kind of rudimentary material he had in some fashion taught as a twelve-year-old Charterhouse praepositus. Fortunately for his sanity, he would also have a small "senior" class for the select few with enough Greek to follow him.

Fortunately, also, prize contests in both Latin and Greek, called the Blackstone Examinations (from the large black marble-seated armchair where the examinees sat), motivated the better prepared, or more venturesome, students to supplement set assignments with as much of the classics as they could contrive to read. Although every man was examined, the prizes rewarded the largest quantity of self-assigned reading substantiated by oral translations of passages selected by the professor. Some candidates, legends say, came to be examined with wheelbarrow loads of books.[12] Another legend has it that Edmund as examiner once handed "his own Aeschylus to a spectator" and examined "without book, calling the competitors' attention to such grammatical expressions and turns of phrase as he thought desirable."[13] In its rougher way the Blackstone gave Glasgow students some of that broadening which the Classical Tripos and Chancellor's Medal competitions provided the most ambitious at Cambridge. A recent scholar has claimed that when honors examinations were introduced at Glasgow in 1861, the Blackstone "was already producing a width of reading and accuracy of knowledge which probably only the best undergraduates of contemporary Oxford and Cambridge could rival."[14]

Most unfortunate in those years was the location of the university, its buildings, including the professors' houses, all huddled along a notoriously deteriorated section of High Street. The Scottish Universities Commission of 1858 officially deplored the New Vennel slum-district neighbors, the nearby "chemical and other nuisance-creating manufactories," and the consequent "atmosphere impregnated with the affluvia arising from the filth," all in a city where "the sewerage" was notoriously unsatisfactory.[15] A journalist in 1856 pictured the alleys, the "flood of poverty, disease, and crime," "drifts of stifling and noisome smoke" trailing "slowly all day over the College gardens," and "the very filthiest lane in Glasgow" paralleling the quadrangle within sixty feet of the professors' houses.[16]

Such surroundings, such air, would have been discomfiting enough for Edmund, although as a schoolboy he had weathered the Charterhouse neighborhood. To his wife after 1842, the highly-strung hypochondriac Cecilia Tennyson, reared in the clean air of the Lincolnshire wolds and acclimated to pleasant places like High Beech, Tunbridge Wells, and rural Boxley near Maidstone, Glasgow would prove unendurable, even when she and Edmund moved farther from the slums.

Inevitably, Edmund, quiet and undemonstrative, would be compared disadvantageously with the two famed classroom performers who had successively held the Greek chair for sixty-four years. For his oratorical presence John Young (1750?–1820), forty-six years in the chair, had been compared to Edmund Burke. His histrionic reading of the *Iliad* gave "life to every line," and he overflowed with laughter along with his students at Lucian or Aristophanes.[17] Lockhart praised him lavishly. His "lynx-like intellectual glance" left listeners "quite thunderstruck" with "his transport[s] of sheer verbal ecstasy" about the Greek particle or "the deep pathetic beauty" in Homer. Tears "gushed" from his fervently sparkling eyes, kindling "answering flames" in the eyes of his students.[18]

In 1821 the twenty-three-year-old Sandford (1798–1838), son of the bishop of Edinburgh and an Oxford graduate with a first-class B.A. (M.A., 1825; D.C.L., 1833), had launched into his professorial duties with brave, though perhaps excessively self-conscious, enthusiasm. In his inaugural lecture, after dutifully eulogizing Young, he announced, "I should not discharge my duty toward yourselves, nor [to those] who have raised me to this important office," unless he attempted to improve upon his predecessor's work. He would prudently strive for "a greater closeness and vigour" in pedagogy and a "higher elegance and accuracy" in student scholarship. His oration unveiled a florid English that Edmund could never have hoped, even had he improbably wished, to equal. He roundly forswore all pedantry, mere "etymological refinements, and the edge and eagerness of philological acumen." His aims, it seems, were more practical: he would help his students turn into euphonious orators. Euphony had been the very controlling principle of Greek grammar. Beyond broadest generalities the lecture said little about Greek literature. (Indeed, in at least two passages, Sandford displayed a preference for Latin literature.) Plato, it would seem, was better avoided than cultivated: "With intellectual powers which compel us to rank his name as second to none but that of BACON among the sons of men, he yields the most signal example the world ever witnessed of the perils to which a warm imagination must expose the speculative reasoner." Aristotle, "whose genius was formed of colder, though as subtle elements," would furnish more "instruction." Anyhow, why belabor all these points? Glasgow had long excelled in Greek.[19]

Sandford started his seventh year at Glasgow with a "preliminary lecture" outlining the plan of instruction he had evolved.[20] Edmund would continue the general structure with significant differences (stressing greater precision of grammar, and in the advanced class more of the philological and philosophical). Sandford had innovatively divided his first-year students into two levels. Those who knew some Greek would soon start reading a book of the *Iliad* and a tragedy, and begin Greek composition. The sheer beginners would receive "a brief but necessary survey of the most usual inflections of verb and noun," then "proceed to the translation of some easy author." He from the chair would provide "a *spoken* version" and elucidate "every difficult passage." They would faithfully employ their lexicon and the "simple notes" in the book of extracts.[21] This process, with systematic review and constant diligence, would assuredly enable a man after attending the class five hours a week for six months to "read by himself the poetry of Homer, and the simplest works of Attic and Hellenic Greek—to understand and to apply the preliminary canons of Greek construction," and prepare himself "by the unassisted studies of vacation, for his further progress within the walls of this or another university." But there would be no "working of miracles without any trouble on your part." (Of course if any laggard failed to achieve those improbable results within those few weeks and under those conditions, while studying several other subjects, to say nothing of earning money by labor during the summer, the fault would be solely his own! Conveniently, the majority of men would not attempt a second year.)

Sandford proposed to guide his second-year class across an ambitious expanse of Homer, Sophocles, Euripides, Xenophon, Herodotus, Aeschylus, Aristophanes, and "a portion of Thucydides," attempting to "instill the elements of critical learning and to create such familiarity with the finest models in the different branches of the Grecian tongue as will smooth the path to future attainments." (Although necessarily superficial, such a survey with such an enthusiastic lecturer would no doubt have been quite stimulating.) In his private "advanced class," he lectured, or praelicted, "upon the choicest works of Grecian criticism," and the more difficult poetry, as well as "upon the origin and structure of the Greek tongue, because I know how essential it is to the student's private researches in philology" to have a firm foundation for a science that would "whet the curiosity . . . expand the intellectual range, and . . . clear and simplify our knowledge not only of *words*, but of *things*, not only of the rules of *grammar*, but of the constitution of *mind*."

Although some critics charged him with inferior scholarship, Sandford with his dramatic presence was widely perceived as successful. His advanced classes greatly expanded, increasing his income. (They were thematically expansive too, where Edmund's would be purposefully concentrated and demanding.) His sketch in the *DNB* asserts that he "succeeded in awakening a love for Greek literature far beyond the bounds of his university." In some years, reportedly, he had as many as five hundred students, including Glasgow clergymen, lawyers, and merchants who came to hear his "eloquent and enthusiastic praelictions."[22] He had become a sort of local phenomenon.

But early 1829 brought a turning point in Sandford's life, when he sped all the long journey from Glasgow to Oxford just to cast his vote for the reelection of Sir Robert Peel as M.P. for his university. Peel, as home secretary in the duke of Wellington's government, had felt honor-bound to resign his seat after, amazingly, yielding to overwhelming circumstances and leading the historic successful fight in the Commons for the Roman Catholic emancipation he had always before so adamantly opposed. Peel lost the election, 609–755 (though he soon returned to the Commons with a different constituency).[23] Sandford for his extraordinary effort was knighted. After that, as the *DNB* puts it, he virtually "abandoned Greek for politics." He made numerous speeches favoring the 1832 Reform Bill; then he stood for Glasgow city in the 1832 election, was defeated, but in 1834 was elected M.P. for Paisley. He stayed in Parliament less than four months. In applying to the Glasgow faculty for permission to "terminate his professional labours" early, in mid-April, he had pledged himself, "in deference to" their "general opinion," to "resign his Professorship" before September or "withdraw himself from all engagements inconsistent with the personal discharge of its duties."[24]

The *DNB* declares flatly that Sanford's "appearances in the House of Commons were failures, his rhetoric, which had won admiration at the university, exciting only derision there." Actually, *Hansards* reveals that he could be factual and concise when speaking briefly about Scottish matters. But in two longer speeches, one on 15 May supporting a bill introduced by Alfred Tennyson's uncle Charles (later Tennyson d'Eyncourt) for repealing the Septennial Act and requiring more frequent parliamentary elections, and another on 21 June opposing the bill to enfranchise Jews, he ridiculously belabored his sometimes specious arguments in elongated, mellifluous sentences. His anti-Jewish posturing exposed him at his worst, as he undertook immoderately and recklessly to demolish every argument favoring the Jews. Such a "monstrous novelty" as Jewish enfranchisement would forever destroy the harmony and "unanimity of feeling" of a Christian parliament. The "glow of a high and just enthusiasm, if for a moment it lighted up the countenances of that assembly, must be slackened by the contemptuous sneer of Jewish unbelief." Only two brief statements followed after Sandford sat down. A Catholic member stated simply that he would vote to give the Jews the franchise. Robert Grant, introducer of the measure, believed that nothing more needed to be said: "All that had been said on the opposite . . . had done very little harm to the measure." But he profoundly and sincerely thought "that such arguments as had been advanced against the Bill did no good to the cause of Christianity." The bill passed by a majority of 91 votes, but subsequently lost in the House of Lords. Jews remained without franchise until 1858.

Before his September deadline, Sandford, pathetically dispirited, gave his decision to the Glasgow faculty. He would have preferred to continue in Parliament, where "with such degree of popularity as still belongs to me," he might have been a "bold and zealous advocate" for measures benefiting the college. But ill health had left him no choice: "the irregular hours, the severe labours, & the trying anxieties of a Parliamentary career" had been too much for his "health and strength to support." A "great shock" to his "nervous system" had led to "very serious symptoms" digestively. His physicians agreed that his persevering in "the fatigues and cares of political life must have a steady & fatal termination."[25] It is uncertain how much he recovered his health. In a little more than three years, he would be dead.

The printed *Testimonials in behalf of Edmund Law Lushington, M.A., Fellow of Trinity College, Cambridge, Candidate for the Office of Greek Professor in the University of Glasgow* was a formidable array of twenty-eight letters, including three from professors at Bonn. The first letter, with twenty-two signatures from "the Master, Vice-Master, Tutors and Resident Fellows of Trinity College," detailed his years of achievement at Trinity, asserting that his interest in "all subjects connected with Greek history, philosophy and philology . . .

amounting to a lively and well-regulated enthusiasm," had "led him to investigate and make himself master of all the researches of the most eminent scholars of modern times, whether at home or on the continent." George Peacock, Lowndes Professor of Astronomy in the University, testified that Edmund's classical lectures as an assistant tutor had equaled if not surpassed "the most distinguished of his predecessors." He was a "gentleman of singularly pleasing appearance and address, of great sweetness and evenness of temper, and of the utmost purity of life and conduct." Regrettably, no position at Cambridge "worthy of Mr. Lushington's acceptance" was open to a layman. Julius Charles Hare, formerly Edmund's tutor, was "convinced that, with the single exception of Thirlwall, there is hardly a better scholar in England, and very few so good." Edmund's private tutor, James Prince Lee, assistant master under Dr. Arnold at Rugby and future bishop of Manchester, attested to his "habit of thinking and feeling . . . in the Greek and Latin languages, especially the former. . . . It was impossible to read or converse with him, without being strongly possessed with the existence of this faculty in him."

Edmund's own contemporaries, mindful of Scottish commonsense conservatism, carefully balanced their laudations with assurances of his soundness. J. M. Heath testified to the "pure and unfeigned love of knowledge, which has induced him, since he took his degree, to devote more hours to study than most of our students do even under the strongest stimulus of ambition," and to his mastery of "all that is valuable in modern German literature and criticism," but assured the electors that he was "by no means one who will take up with a view merely from its novelty, but exercises a strong and sober judgment upon all that he reads." William Hepworth Thompson, future master of Trinity College, would have it understood that "the scrupulous deliberation with which his opinions have been formed, and his powers of clear and luminous argumentation" were "equalled by the candid and tolerant spirit in which he has regarded the sentiments differing from his own." William Dobson, future headmaster of Cheltenham College, reported that Edmund's "most extraordinary assiduity" in classical studies sprang more "from natural inclination," than from desire for "honours and emoluments." George Venables, too, stressed Edmund's love of learning for its own sake, producing both "a profound and critical acquaintance" with Greek literature and antiquities and "a mastery over the idiom of the language which amounts almost to colloquial familiarity." Yet his "moral character is pure and faultless, his disposition and manners such that I believe he never made an enemy, and his feelings are in every respect those of a gentleman and honourable man."

In mid-March, Edmund made the customary personal "canvas" in Scotland among those who might influence the faculty electors. By then the one aspirant who would almost certainly have beaten him had withdrawn. Archibald Campbell Tait (1811–92), future archbishop of Canterbury, was a Scotsman, a former student of Sandford's, being graduated from Glasgow before going to Balliol College, Oxford. Taking a first class in classics, he became an M.A., a Fellow, and a well-esteemed tutor. He had converted from the Scottish Kirk and become an Anglican clergyman. Even before Sandford's illness, he had written the Glasgow principal, Duncan Macfarlan, asking whether an Anglican minister would be eligible for a Scottish university professorship, where all professors must subscribe to the creed of the Kirk. Five days after Sandford died, Tait wrote again. He would do nothing to subvert the Church of Scotland, providing he could "conscientiously" reserve "liberty of conscience" and freely exercise his "own mode of worship as a clergyman of the Church of England." Considering Macfarlan's reply unsatisfactory, Tait withdrew on 15 February with regret that "in days when opinions are carried out into extremes on all hands," he would not have the opportunity to help "unite in closer bonds two communities of Christians, which, however differing in externals, are, I verily believe, one in heart." Tait's own difficulties with the Scottish confession lay with "those very strong Ultra-Calvinistical and Supra-Lapsarian statements, which I am now led to suppose that a great many of your clerical body explain away in an inoffensive sense."[26] Tait's disgruntled uncle, Sir Archibald Campbell, asked Macfarlan "whether you go to the length of holding that no Episcopalian *Lay* or *Clerical*" could be a professor at Glasgow. If so, something had gone wrong when Sandford, whom he knew to be Episcopalian, was employed. It was rumored, but could hardly be accurate, "that Sandford did not sign the Confession of Faith & that his not doing this was *winked at* purposely." Would Macfarlan please inform him what candidates seemed best qualified and when the election would occur? He would "be nearby to attend at any time you fix."[27]

Another rival candidate, destined like Tait to become internationally eminent, was Robert Lowe (1811–92), who would be chancellor of the exchequer under Gladstone from 1868 to 1873, and in 1880 become Lord Sherbrooke. Reportedly Tait after withdrawing had recommended Lowe, a well-regarded private tutor who had resigned his Oxford fellowship upon his marriage. Though physically powerful, he had the complexion and weak eyes of an albino; and that, as one story has it, brought about his rejection at Glasgow. David Murray quotes the recollection of William Fleming, then professor of oriental languages and later of moral philosophy:

We thocht a great deal o'[Lowe] . . . he had a testimonial from Tait, he was a fine scholar, a good lecturer and an active and capable man; but ye see, Sir, he had white hair and red een and we werna' quite sure hoo he wad git on wi' the students, and jist as we were on the swither Mr. Lushington cam' doon wi' a letter from Sir Robert Peel who was our Rector, in which he gave a very high character for scholarship and ability, and hoch, Sir, after thinking owre we jist gied the chair to Mr. Lushington and he has dune very weel.[28]

Lowe himself, for whatever it may be worth, had a decidedly different explanation for his defeat; and, fascinatingly, Lowe's version chiefly involves none other than the reminiscent Professor Fleming. Lowe's recent biographer, James Winter, quotes from a letter of his to a friend at Oxford, claiming he would have been elected had not Fleming, who was Lowe's chief supporter, been aspiring just then to be translated from his oriental lanuages chair to the more prized chair of moral philosophy. Allegedly Edmund's mere three supporters, who represented landowning interests that opposed all radicals (and Lowe was perceived, with some reason, as radical), intimidated Lowe's seven supporters (with the faculty consisting of twelve since Sandford's death, that leaves two unaccounted for, three if the principal had a vote) by threatening to oppose Fleming's forthcoming candidacy. Lowe peevishly claimed that Edmund's being "so objectionable in every way, and my being so universally popular made it more of a punishment to bring in Lushington." It was all the fault of that "miserable system of translation."[29] One does not know how much to credit Lowe's story. Winter's balanced biography establishes that Lowe, with all his formidable talents and energy, tended through much of his life to be testily pugnacious and perhaps something of a sour loser.

One part at least of Fleming's story is verifiable: Peel had assuredly lent a hand, at least indirectly. In mid-May, Macfarlan received a "Private" letter from Sir George Clerk, Peel's close friend, who had served as undersecretary in the Home Office and later as secretary to the treasurer. Clerk's wife was a daughter of Ewan Law, a great-uncle of Edmund. Peel had instructed Clerk to tell Macfarlan what he knew about Edmund's "Political Sentiments." Surely there had "existed some great misapprehension on this point," a confusing of Edmund with "Mr. Charles Lushington or Dr. Lushington who are distant relations of his." Edmund himself was disinclined "to take any active or ostensible part in Politics" and "unwilling to make any public declaration of his Political opinions." But Clerk knew that "his opinions are decidedly conservative and have always been so, & that on all the great questions which at present agitate & divide the country" he would "always . . . support our National Institutions in Church & State." Devoted to "Literary Pursuits," Edmund was "not likely officiously or unnecessarily to obtrude his private opinions on . . . other persons." Clerk hoped Macfarlan could "remove any prejudice against E. Lushington." Certainly "his testimonials & character as a Scholar are infinitely superior to those of any other candidate." For its own sake the university should elect him. Again Clerk stressed that it was Peel who, knowing Clerk's "relationship & acquaintance" with Edmund, had expressly commissioned him to write.[30]

Coming from Sir Robert Peel, even such a proxy recommendation would have been a potent force at Glasgow in 1838. Most if not every one of the professors would have seconded Peel's recently enunciated conservative principles. Early that year he had been installed as the university's lord rector, delivering an inspiring hour-long rectorial address. Two nights later he had been fêted at a giant banquet in a spacious temporary structure erected at Glasgow for the occasion. As his biographer, Norman Gash, relates, the dinner started at five o'clock. For two hours Peel delighted more than 3,400 guests with one of his greatest political speeches, urging support of the growing conservative party he had fashioned since 1832 on the middle ground between Whiggism and ultra-Toryism. Then "speaker after speaker . . . peers, gentry, clergy, professors, lawyers, and politicians ranging from the Marquess of Tweeddale and the Moderator of the General Assembly to the Principal of Glasgow University and Mr. W. E. Gladstone, M.P.," praised Peel and his principles until half-past one, "by which time only the nineteenth toast had been reached of the thirty-seven heroically listed in the program."[31]

Edmund, beginning his "canvas," had been dismayed by an absurd rumor among the professors that he was politically radical and had "two radical uncles." In mid-March he had interviewed Tait's uncle, Campbell, who seemed encouraging but "asked a question or two about politics." Edmund returned honest conservative answers. A month later he went to see Campbell at his estate but found he was in Glasgow "talking with my friend [William] Hamilton [the metaphysician] about my doubtful politics & connexions." Monteith, who as an aspirant to Parliament had spoken at the Peel dinner,[32] had written to reassure the professors; and Edmund himself had talked with some of them. Afterward, although professing hope, he was uncharacteristically bitter about "the jobbing knavery of the race whether of Scotchmen or Professors," and the "Scotch wormspawn that writhes in my way & coils itself outward & upward to dragon sides."

But he had supporters who were positioned to recruit more influential ones. Someone had enlisted the cooperation of two other eminent conservatives, Lord Lyndhurst (formerly lord chancellor under both Wellington and Peel) and Henry Goulburn (formerly Wellington's and Peel's chancellor of the exchequer).[33] Lyndhurst was not intimate with Peel, but nobody endorsed by him (famed as the indefatigable scourger of Whiggism in the House of Lords) could be suspected of radicalism. Goulburn's son, like Edmund a recent classical medalist from Trinity College, and one of the twenty-two signers of Edmund's Trinity recommendation, may have asked his father to do something for Edmund. The senior Goulburn for many years had been Peel's closest friend: a word from Goulburn was like one from Peel himself. Twelve years later when Peel died after a fall from his horse, Goulburn and Sir George Clerk were two of the six pallbearers at the strictly private funeral.[34]

Should Edmund's election be written off as strictly political? Better to call it a happy irony. A nonpolitical scholar had initially presented nothing except impressive professional qualifications. Then an absurd political rumor had begged to be refuted, and the political prestige of the refuters bestowed an advantage no materialistic considerations could have bought.

The election on 1 August seems anticlimactic: Edmund was chosen with only one dissenting vote—from the staunch Calvinist professor of theology Stevenson MacGill (1765-1849).[35] Edmund had met with the faculty on the previous evening, when the real decision was formed. (I cannot discover what other candidates, if any, appeared.) In at least three letters, all now unhappily lost, Edmund related details of his "struggle up to the point of victory." Tired and pensive, at two in the morning on 2 August, he wrote his feelings to Henry: "Neither Monteith nor I know exactly how to feel, now that all is over." He was not "very triumphant, rather somewhat quietly content, looking to a serious life of responsibility, material & tangible." Would it be "ignoble? or effective of good? Time may prove—but no desponding now." At least the news would "give my father & all of you a great pleasure, & that is itself a pure gratification—stimulus & earnest, of other more solid satisfying ones."

He still faced some routine initiation rituals: a Latin discourse "Optimum historicis examplar Thucydides" (Edmund revered Thucydides but hated to discourse in Latin); some Greek iambics translating Milton's *Samson Agonistes*, ll. 710-31, ushering in the dissolute Dalila, from "Who is this, what thing of sea or land" to "But now again she makes address to speak" (did the eyes of Edmund or his grave examiners subliminally twinkle?);[36] and finally, the mandatory signing of the Confession of Faith of the Church of Scotland.

Would his signature be incompatible with his liberal Anglicanism? As Tait had interpreted Macfarlan's interpretation, it would. But Macfarlan, when pointedly queried, had said what his position as the official upholder of an outmoded regulation seemed to require. Recent practice was against him. Sandford had been an Episcopalian whose bishop father outlived him. The current Latin professor, William Ramsay, was an Episcopalian. Glasgow had elected non-Presbyterian lord rectors, like the current one, Peel, to the nominal headship of the university, and installed them with no reference to the subscription. The Scottish Church officials designated to witness a new professor's signature and issue a certificate of subscription had no authority to investigate the subscriber's present or future good faith. As a *North British Review* writer later put it, the existing form of the test was actually "insulting" to the Scottish Church, and "admitted on all hands" to be of no kind of benefit.[37] In 1853, after more than a decade of intermittent agitation against it, the test was finally abolished, replaced by a simple pledge not to oppose the doctrines of the Scottish Church or otherwise seek to subvert it.[38]

As David Murray (who had not been present) wrote the story, Edmund presented himself before the Presbytery. Macfarlan, suspecting "he would know little regarding the Confession of Faith," had deliberately arrived early and "inquired, 'Have you read the Confession of Faith?' "The law requires that I shall subscribe, not that I shall read, the Confession of Faith,' and before the astonished Principal could reply, the signature 'E. L. Lushington' had been added to the roll and the ceremony was at an end."[39]

It may have all happened just so, but it would be wrong to consider it a show of insouciance. Edmund, given the opportunity, was deftly but soberly divesting his position of as much of its falseness as possible. A majority of the faculty, all of them previous subscribers, had knowingly elected still one more Episcopalian. Both Macfarlan's question and Edmund's reply would further expose the emptiness of an anachronistic ritual.

Sixty-four years earlier, in 1774, Edmund's latitudinarian great-grandfather, Edmund Law, later bishop of Carlisle, had published a trenchant pamphlet opposing all required subscriptions to articles of faith. Such articles, Law argued, had developed only after the "very plain and practical" Christianity, "level to all capacities," had swerved "into the subtleties of metaphysical debate" and become an "ingenious system of speculative science." Such creeds departed from the true protestant personal transaction between each man's conscience and his God, "there being no third person commissioned to determine it for him; no sect or society on earth, how respectable soever upon whose authority he can depend." Subscribers were being relieved from thinking for themselves and were merely giving "credit to those wise and learned persons, who have taken so much pains to remove all difficulties for us." God had not given any "teacher of the Gospel" the right "so far to abridge his *Christian liberty* as to entangle himself with new *yokes*, or tie himself up from impartially examining the Word of God." All such obligations to subscribe leave persons "oftentimes violently tempted" to profess what they do not believe, thus "leading them into all the labyrinths of loose and perfidious casuistry; more especially when it is considered conscience, once strained, seldom contracts again to its first position."[40] The bishop's namesake descendant had, at least, detoured around those labyrinths.

Edmund's inaugural lecture, delivered on 8 November, some 12,000 words long, must have taken ninety minutes or more to read.[41] Although it began

FIG. III. Edmund Law Lushington. Circa 1865. Photograph by Cruttenden. Courtesy of the Tennyson Research Centre, Lincoln, by permission of Lincoln Library Service.

haltingly, and remained always meditative, never declamatory, it was sufficiently eloquent throughout and, in places, loftily, almost ecstatically, beautiful. The first person "I" occurs fewer than a dozen times, but the statement was
intensely personal, articulating the wider, deeper significance of the studies
that had engaged Edmund's imagination since his eighth year of life. Now,
without deviating from the unique configuration of his inner being, he could
live in the present as a scholar-educator, rather than struggling to turn into a
future jurist or statesman. The service for humankind would be no less valuable, the power he could wield might be higher. The lecture is his *apologia pro
vita sua*. First of all, he was addressing his father, too physically infirm to journey to Glasgow—a beloved man whom he had hitherto to some degree
disappointed.

The "moving principle" of education itself, Edmund declared, is an "unceasing process, whose consequences stretch beyond time and space." We should
"speak of it with cautious and awful reverence." To "educate a man, is to
educe or draw forth from the soul all that is potentially in it; to call up into
power and action the mighty faculties with which he is gifted; and to temper
their energies, disorderly and bewildered at their first waking, into that harmonious union wherein alone is strength." In "each man, as man" is some
personal "something greater and higher" than needed for the practical manag-
ing and controlling of the world outside himself. With "profound earnestness
and tender anxiety" educators are "bound to endeavour that he may learn to
feel, comprehend, and make his own this individual excellence to which he is
entitled, cultivating the entire fulness and richness of the spirit that is in him."

At a time when expanding physical science was increasing man's mastery
over his environment, he was in danger of forgetting that his "higher work,"
the object of his "noblest faculties and aspirations," was "to obtain right and
clear conceptions." Education must help us remember that "what we can least
do without, is not our highest need; that man cannot live by bread alone."
Through studying history and literature, the student could become conversant
with the "speech, feelings, and actions" of "other men and nations," learning
to "comprehend his own nature—say rather *our* nature—by beholding its
common humanity mirrored in the thousand glasses of other minds, in other
climes and ages."

Each particular nation was also "like a man, having a fixt individual stamp of
character, by which it is something different from any other nation." We may
study that character "manifested in all that it is destined to endure and achieve,
growing firmer and more distinct from the time of its half conscious infancy,
till it attain the maturity of the powers implanted in it by the Creator."

Moving into the lengthy and poetic central portion of his lecture, Edmund
lovingly traced the rise and decline of Grecian uniqueness as displayed in Greek

history, Greek literature, and the expanding vocabulary and syntax of the Greek language. Though only twice overtly referring to Coleridge, this section is permeated with his conceptions and those of the German thinkers he admired, whom Edmund had begun to study in their own language. Coleridgean organicism emerges in Edmund's dwelling upon the inward and its becoming outward, and through such phrases as "the unfolding and ripening of the blossoms of genius that were implanted in the national heart"; "quickened the seeds of an imperishable growth in man"; a nation's distinctive peculiarities "fused" in its literature "with a higher originality of their own"; "the quintessence and symbol"; the "whole Attic drama, with its harmonious fusion of elements that seem so difficult to blend, mingling the stir of action and life with the deep melody of lyric passion" (Coleridge's "reconciliation of opposites"); "the bewitching graces" of Plato's "style," which his "consummate skill makes appear but as the ethereal and transparent body from which the living soul of his ideas looks forth." We will feel Coleridge and the Germans equally in Edmund's presentation of philological study toward the end of his lecture.

We must be contented with a modest sampling of this richly complex discourse. There is the contrast between the two historians Herodotus and Thucydides. Herodotus "feels as one of a people, gifted with a peculiar fineness of intellect, before which intellectual triumphs are already beginning to expand." History may "unfold pages of splendour, on which his country's name may not unworthily stand. Yet he is far from regarding other nations with contemptuous self-complacency." Although revering "the high part which heaven has allotted to his own," he does not seek "to take the measure of its comparative rank and importance; satisfied that the world is wide enough to afford ample scope of greatness to all." With "thrilling sympathy" he dwells on the "noble devotedness" of Greece to the "sacred cause of her independence; on her sublime efforts that seemed so frantic and hopeless, that proved so triumphant."

In the "sombre and awful colours" of Thucydides, after a succession of devastating wars, we encounter the "shock of adverse interests and prejudices," "the unquenched ardour and the devoted hostility with which each party maintained" the conflict; "the machinery employed, and the spirit that regulated its intricate motions; the convulsive hopes, the slowly overshadowing despondency, and the protracted agony of the long death-struggle." He "probed" it all "to the bottom," and exhibited it with a "severe clearness, remote alike from hasty emotion, and from the cold quiet of insensibility." Thucydides' feelings are "condensed and embodied with the long and profound meditation of the man who had endured much, wandered far, and learned the cities and minds of many men: they are woven into the frame of his whole intellect, and pervade the entire tone of his contemplation and description."

Plato, whose supposed instability Sandford had viewed with such confident apprehensiveness, was to Edmund a "wonderful genius" who had framed "of his gorgeous fancies and rich melodies a robe for Truth that is worthy of her, freely displaying the divine vigour and loveliness of her proportions." His was a "boundless wit and humour," a "profound and luminous insight that has scarcely left a speculative depth unsounded." As though "by divination," he could "discern some peak" on "every distant eminence of knowledge," making it a "landmark for succeeding thinkers, till the intervening obstacles be hewn away by slow successive labour, and the height itself be reached at last."

One hopes that even Dr. MacGill, the septuagenarian theologian who had cast his lone vote against Edmund, was content with his reverence for Christianity. Of Greek religion he had said: "All modes of presenting religion objectively to mankind are necessarily anthropomorphic, and before men had a human form revealed to their view, containing in itself the fulness of godhead," their gods naturally displayed both the "frailer as well as the nobler parts of manhood." But in the Greek language it was that the Gospel was finally revealed: "in a remote province of the [Roman] empire, the Hellenic language, glorified in its ruins, was selected to be the vehicle of a holier inspiration and sublimer truths than ever haunted the dreams of bard or seer in ancient Hellas."

Turning to the philological study of the Greek language itself, Edmund gave a rationale for the emphasis that through the following years would so mark his teaching effort. Language in its "constructions and forms" carries symbols, the "outward expression" of "some of the fundamental laws of human thought." With "preseumptuous and shallow metaphysical systems, we shall have narrow and short-sighted views of the scope of language," whereas "a more searching analysis of thought will go hand in hand with sounder conceptions of the law and essence of language." There is a "boundless diversity" of phenomena between different languages in the way that they grow, "varying with all the influences which conspire to affect a nation's character—the soil, the climate, the physical obstacles it has to overcome, its relations with foreigners, its domestic history, and the pregnant ideas struck out by great original minds which sway the thoughts and speech of unborn generations." The Greek is "the most perfect specimen we have" of a language whose "frames were determined from within, by a principle of spontaneous growth." Its "progression from the sensuous and epic, to the reflective and logical period" demonstrates how "successive touches of historians and philosophers have fully drawn forth its unexplored virtues 'from the deep gold-mines of thought;' feature after feature emerging from potential to actual existence, with a clearness and symmetry from which much has been learnt, and probably much more remains to learn."

Then, too, it is a "lofty privilege" to be able to commune with the Greeks in their own tongue: "expanding our sympathies beyond our time, to possess a community of consciousness with men who spoke three thousand years ago," perceiving the "unbroken continuity which links generation to remotest generation, in the thoughts which live in them and actuate them." The experience combines "the freshness and delight of novelty with the sacredness which attaches to every thing old," and illustrates "the brotherhood which comprehends all mankind." Their "struggles in the lot of humanity, their triumphs and glories, belong to us: we can clasp the hand of antiquity with an enlarged affection, akin to that of Dante's friend, when in Purgatory he clasped the hand of Virgil, and exclaimed, 'O Mantuan, I am of thy land!' "

At least one young man, John Campbell Shairp (1819–85), future principal of the United College at St. Andrews and later professor of poetry at Oxford, enjoyed telling "with the utmost enthusiasm until the end of his life" how enchanted he had been by Edmund's lecture. He had walked away repeating to himself a great line from Milton's "Lycidas": "That strain I heard was of a higher mood."[42] For us, since Edmund did not publish any classical scholarship of his own, this lecture, long out-of-print, must stand as the fullest embodiment of Tennyson's gracefully compact characterization of its author, his new brother-in-law:

> And thou art worthy, full of power;
> As gentle; liberal-minded, great,
> Consistent, wearing all that weight
> Of learning lightly like a flower.[43]

In Edmund's earliest Glasgow years, before completion of the railroads, the journey between London and Glasgow required four days by coach or post chaises.[44] Edmund, perhaps accompanied by a sister or two, later by his wife, then by wife and small children, and after 1850 too often alone, would leave Park House in mid-October, returning in early May. After the laying of the railroads, they might, but did not always, return to England for the Christmas holidays.

At Glasgow a busy teacher's life fell into a routine. The hour-long classes, including Greek, began at 7:30, in comparative darkness during much of the term, and often in severe weather. The hundred or more students, sleepy and cold, sat on benches, like church pews.[45] Edmund would come out of his house fifty yards away, walking as Murray describes it, "hurriedly along, his head bent, his eyes turned toward the ground, his left hand clutching his gown at the neck as if it were in danger of being blown away." By the 1850s, when Murray knew him, he had a beard, it and his hair seeming "somewhat unkempt and his face had a startled look." At his pulpit-desk he would rise, repeat a collect from the Morning Service in the Book of Common Prayer, then losing no time begin the instructional routine. In the large elementary classes, the method included much recitation, calling upon the students to construe, questioning and commenting by the professor, or asking other students to correct the first one's mistakes.[46] Yet so large were the classes that any one student might rarely be called upon.[47]

Edmund was remembered for his habitual courteous mildness, his never stooping to scolding or ridicule, though he might murmur, "Pray be accurate," or, "Do you think, Mr. Robertson, that is quite accurate?" Murray, who had found him "reticent and undemonstrative," though "singularly courteous, considerate and fair-minded," wondered at his "marvellous" control of such large classes. Though he never raised his "soft, sweet voice," and sat straight and erect without gesticulation, or even at times held a new book in his lap, cutting it as his eyes followed the textbook on the desk, he seemed always to have total attention. "There was an extraordinary fascination in the man; it seemed as if his own gentle spirit took possession of his students while they were in his presence."[48]

Others, unfortunately, though perhaps admiring or loving the man, found him an unstimulating teacher. James Thomson, Glasgow professor of mathematics, father of the future physicist William Thomson, Lord Kelvin, frankly placed Lushington in 1846 among the Oxford and Cambridge graduates who had "not given satisfaction" at Glasgow. He urged his son, returning to Glasgow from Cambridge as professor of natural philosophy, to forestall such dissatisfaction by writing "out some lectures of as simple and elementary kind as possible." Kelvin himself, who as a boy had studied under Lushington, always delighted in praising him, but confessed that his youthful mind had "wandered from the Greek class to natural philosophy."[49] Another Glasgow professor's son, John Nichol, who became Glasgow's dynamic first professor of English literature and one of Edmund's lifelong friends, declared flatly in a memoir that he had been unable to make any progress in Greek under him. Any that he made was owing to private tutors and not to Lushington's "sleepy class." It "grieved" him that "the professor whom above all others I liked" was the only one with whom he had no success. Lushington was "at once one of the best, and one of the worst, teachers I ever knew"; even his "most zealous . . . advocates" would admit "that he was not made to teach the rudiments."[50]

Edmund's muted performance suffered by comparison with his more robust Latin colleague and closest Glasgow friend, William Ramsay. Five years older than Edmund, Ramsay had been at Trinity College with him, taking B.A. only one year before him, in 1831, being promptly elected to the Chair of Humanity (Latin) at Glasgow, where he had been graduated before going on to Cambridge. He was an admirable scholar, though perhaps a less finished philologist than Edmund; with interests extending to all aspects of ancient life, he projected a contagious enthusiasm. Nichol insisted that as an expositor of untrained boys, Ramsay, "with his clear, resonant voice, with his vigilance, activity, and precision, would have been at home where Lushington was at sea. . . . the very man to drill boys just passing into men." He would announce "that his hair stood on end when we made a false quantity," and would count "the errors in our verse on his fingers." He was a "shrewd man, with sharp little eyes . . . a vein of dry humour," and a flair for histrionics: "His renderings of *Aulularia* and *Miles Gloriosus* were inimitable."[51]

Fordyce, however, in his recent essay concerning classical study at Glasgow, although seconding Ramsay's reputation as teacher and scholar, stops short of ranking him, even as a teacher, above Lushington. The two men complemented each other, Ramsay bestowing "a wide view of the whole field of antiquity," Lushington the "patient exegesis of a text" and "a sensitivity to the value of words, an awareness of idiom as a reflexion of thought." With the two, Glasgow "at last . . . had a school in which scholars could be made. And they were made." Fordyce mentions, among others, Charles Badham, the first professor of Greek in Australia; W. Y. Sellar, classics professor at St. Andrews and Edinburgh; Lewis Campbell, Sellar's successor at St. Andrews; D. B. Monro, provost of Oriel; and Sir James Frazer, "who declared that his life work was determined by the influence of William Ramsay."[52] Fordyce might also have mentioned John Campbell Shairp, principal of St. Andrews; Edward Caird, master of Balliol College; and James Bryce, whom Fordyce does mention in another connection—all of whom were lifelong admirers of Lushington.

Unfortunately, we know so little of how Edmund conducted his important advanced class that we may too easily reach wrong conclusions. The only detailed description comes from Edmund's obituary by his old student and friend, Lewis Campbell:

> He 'prelected' on the author to be studied,—the attention of the students being tested at the end of the course by a searching written examination. . . . The Professor first read a passage in the Greek, then construed it word by word, repeating each phrase in the Greek before the English for it was given. Then he would proceed to support and illustrate his interpretation, chiefly by the aid of parallel passages, for which he had jotted down the references in pencil on a strip of note-paper. At the same time various readings and alternative renderings would be discussed. Conjectural emendations, with their grounds, would be clearly set forth and the objections to them fully stated,—the net result in corrupt passages being often one of blank uncertainty. The metre of lyric passages was always ex-

plained. Together with great beauty of enunciation, he had a certain peculiarity of utterance, that made the words seem to come from him reluctantly, producing an effect, not of hesitation, but of deliberate choice,
which made his language more impressive.[53]

Obviously, the emphasis was primarily upon close reading of the poem itself,
not a mere quarrying of the poem for sake of morphological or syntactical
analysis. The analysis, it may be contended, was for sake of the poem. Even so,
it may still sound arid—all that quibbling over minutiae when the professor
might have been germinally descanting on the history of literature, or reinforcing its ineffable beauties with his own poetic observations. But we should reflect that students in this kind of class were there by their own choice. Looking
forward to competing for prizes at Oxford or Cambridge, or otherwise ambitious to increase their mastery over the language itself in an age when such
mastery still carried rewards, they might be eager to receive the very kind of
specialized information that Edmund was so superbly equipped to give. With
eyes and ears opened through Edmund's observations, to the kinds of details to
watch or listen for, they might begin to develop a thing not easily extracted
from books—the existential feeling for doing close reading of their own, or
venturing into specialized articles in philological journals.

Nor should we assume that the formal structure of a classroom hour is the full
measure of what the teacher imparts or the students acquire. Where teacher
and students are closely attuned, insight can emerge through brief offhand remarks, asides as it were, dropped between the more formal sentences of a lecture or demonstration, in relaxed chats after the lecture, or through written
comments on papers returned to students. Shairp, who took the advanced class
early in Edmund's tenure, went on to Oxford, where he would quote to friends
"happy translations of lines or half-lines of Sophocles, & pregnant bits of criticism" from Edmund's lectures. Shairp's prize-winning essay was a comparison
of the *Ajax* of Sophocles and Shakespeare's *Coriolanus*, and he proudly remembered that Edmund, "who though warm in his appreciation of merit, was habitually temperate in the expression of praise, spoke in terms of more than
common appreciation."[54] Bryce, who obtained a gold medal in Greek from
Edmund in 1855, remembered the advanced class, where Edmund "took us
through the Agamemnon, translating it himself and commenting as he went
along, the comments almost entirely on the language, but now and then helping
us to appreciate the poetry." But Edmund also "encouraged" the students, and
Bryce considered it "excellent training," to translate some of the choruses into
English verse. He gave out "English pieces to be turned into Homeric hexameters. This is the only kind of classical verse composition I ever enjoyed or attained any facility in, perhaps because Homer appealed to me more than any of

the ancient poets had yet done, and I could remember the verses better." Bryce began voluntarily memorizing long Homeric passages: "I remember a good deal of it to this day, and how delightful it all is."[55]

For Edmund himself Glasgow would never be all delightful. For thirty-seven years he would spend half his time in comparative loneliness away from the home he loved. One constant at Park House was the annual departure of the head of its closely interdependent family for a six-month absence. Never would he be enabled to give the fullest attention to his work. His wife was almost constantly ill, often after 1850 not coming to Scotland with him, and usually living away in Edinburgh when she did. He was in Glasgow when his father died; en route from Glasgow to Park House when his mother died; and had rushed home for his second daughter's death on a cheerless Christmas day in 1868. In 1856 he was back at his Glasgow post only a few weeks after the lingering death of his only son. Though he made warm friends in Scotland, he was never an easy mixer anywhere. He remained aloof from faculty politics; the faculty meeting minutes show him frequently absent. Life in general would deal him more than a common portion of heartbreak—a marriage comparatively unhappy or worse, the agony of three loved children's deaths, the loss, finally, of all his siblings but one—three during the Glasgow years.

One may suspect that, as year followed year, with his griefs expanding and his vigor diminishing (he suffered recurrently from rheumatism or gout), he may have become too disposed to repeat himself rather than seeking new methods for altered times. The greatest needs of his Greek students in the late 1860s may no longer have quite coincided with those of the early 1840s. Thirty-seven years were more than one-third of the dynamic nineteenth century. His successors, R. C. Jebb and Gilbert Murray, would justly become more eminent than he.

Yet during his years at Glasgow, his reputation and quiet influence steadily grew. Typical students regarded him "with a holy awe, as a sort of Olympian Jove."[56] Sir Henry Craik, his student during the early 1860s, would memorialize his "consummate dignity . . . absolute simplicity of manner . . . voice rich and melodious . . . massive head and features of almost ideal beauty . . . diction graceful and harmonious but never studied or artificial . . . calm and reverent enthusiasm for all that was noblest in thought and language." He had "offered no ready intimacy, and sought to form no following. But his words, few and well chosen, made themselves felt as pure gold, and a sentence of praise or sympathy sank into the heart . . . stirred reverence and enthusiasm." "Only slowly did that absolute modesty, linked with unassailable dignity, make itself felt as a power, radiating into the hearts of others his own illuminating enthusiasm for the ideals of noblest literature."[57]

When the university finally moved to its present location in 1870, Edmund was selected to deliver the celebratory address. When he retired in 1875, the university gave him an honorary LL.D. And in 1884 he received the highest honor that the university could bestow, unanimous election to the lord rectorship that Sir Robert Peel had held when he helped Edmund secure the professorship. And even in 1889, after his brilliant successor Jebb had held the chair for fourteen years and gone on to the Greek professorship at Cambridge, young Gilbert Murray was scorned in a Glasgow newspaper as "the young fool who now sits in Lushington's chair"![58]

V

The Old Order Changeth

1839–1841

W HILE EDMUND was settling into his Glasgow professorship and Henry studying law at the Inner Temple, their father's life was waning. The brief memorial privately published more than forty years afterward (1881) by his daughter Ellen Eliza gives only scant detail.[1] Late one summer he had gone with some of his family on a "long" journey, returned to the seaside at Eastbourne, and fallen "very ill with an attack from which he never entirely recovered." Thereafter he was "always very much of an invalid, though his powers of mind and the beauty of his nature were quite unaltered." Approaching his birthday, 11 July 1838, he thought only of the "72 years of . . . happiness" granted by his "Creator" and all "those dear relatives."

He lived to read Edmund's published Glasgow inaugural. Previously he had gone over the manuscript, suggesting various alterations, most of which Edmund, although "with infinite trouble," as he wrote his father, had dutifully made. "I own to you," Lushington wrote on 3 March 1839, "I am more pleased seeing the whole than when I examined it only piece by piece." Its "general views" were "elevated and just," though possibly too hopeful about the "height of excellence" humanly attainable through education. It might have had "something more of quotation to illustrate and prove the *peculiar* spirit and excellencies ascribed to the different Grecian authors," but Edmund could provide such illustrations in "future lectures." Meanwhile all the family was looking forward to "the happy period" of Edmund's long summer holidays. His own health recently had "rather varied." Apparently he was becoming reconciled to Edmund's new employment: "God bless you," he concluded, "and make your earnest and high-minded exertions a source of advantage to the world and to yourself."

Within two weeks, without again seeing Edmund, Lushington quietly died. On the blank page of a book, his adoring widow described his final evening, 26 March. Seeming "quite well," he had walked with her "round the yard, before dinner," talking and joking as usual "with the workmen whom he met." After dinner he "conversed, and with his usual delightful affectionate manner, contributed to the enjoyment and comfort of our family circle. At half-past nine o'clock, read our evening prayer; kissed and wished his dear Girls good night; by twelve o'clock the Lord took his angelic spirit to Himself!" On 4 April "the mortal remains of one of the best and most deservedly beloved of husbands and fathers, were followed to the grave by a deeply mourning family."

Although never to be lavishly wealthy, the family was left comfortably secure. Besides Park House and about five hundred acres of adjoining or surrounding land, Lushington left another substantial house near Maidstone with about two hundred fifty-two acres; perhaps still another manor house in Kent with lands and surrounding woods totaling about two hundred thirty acres; a house and four hundred seventy-nine acres (although mortgaged) in Essex; and perhaps two houses in the Poultry in the City of London.[2]

Ellen's 1881 memoir idyllically describes Lushington's last decade at Park House. Though a newcomer to Maidstone, he had soon become "known and revered as a kind and experienced magistrate, as a man who was ever ready to forward every scheme for the good of his fellows, as a gentleman before whom nothing unjust or mean could be allowed to exist." He had helped promote the founding of "a large Hospital" and a "public Lunatic asylum." Before "the purity and gentleness of his mind . . . those of a lower standard of excellence were unconsciously elevated . . . and shrank from expressing anything unworthy in his presence." He could calmly discuss political or religious differences without giving offense, and was always a kind and courteous host to the friends of his sons and daughters.

All the laborers and cottagers on his lands he knew "in their histories, in their cottages, in their family life." He "would stop to chat with the old half-blind hedger, or watch the work of the sturdy woodman with his axe, or speak kindly to the little bird boy in his hut of hop-bines, yelling and shaking his rattle to frighten away the crows." He was always courteous "whether he asked the direction of a road from a laboring man in the fields, or spoke to a beggar in real want." To the "faithful nurse," who had cared for all the children "from the eldest to the youngest," and "spent her whole life in the family . . . 'Master's order' was . . . an unquestioned law." She declared that "if any bad person tried to kill Papa, I would shoot him with my own hand!" The gardener, delighted with glimpses of Park House family life, "exclaimed, 'It reminded me of the Kingdom of Heaven!' "

In the long evening after an early dinner, the father would assemble the family and the governess and read aloud from Shakespeare, Scott, Milton, or Southey. "When the elder sons were at home, they would perhaps introduce literature of a later period, but he always returned to Shakespeare with never failing interest." During journeys, or sojournings at the seaside, he would take the children for walks and

> open their minds to the wonders of the shore, to the beautiful mysteries of fossil or spar hidden in the boulder like flint stones, to the many changing hues of the sea or the South Downs, to the high white wall of cliff studded with its black lines, with the clouds hurrying along in the blue overhead; filling their minds with pictures which remained vivid and fresh through their lives.

With Lushington's death the Park House property passed to the scholarly Edmund, an otherworldly man of twenty-nine whose energies since his eighth year had been concentrated on classical or philological studies, and who would live in distant Scotland for half of every year. Not until thirty-six years later would the new master of Park House reside there the year round.

Henry had grieved deeply at the death of the father, with whom he had been more than commonly close. Venables recalled that he could never afterward mention his father's name "without a change in his tone of voice" that expressed "undying affection and regret."[3]

That summer Henry wrote Milnes from Sandgate on the Kentish coast, where he was staying several weeks "gradually recovering" from a cold that had "nearly killed me." He had been skimming through miscellaneous novels in a local library and reflecting upon the unintended farcicality of the forthcoming Eglinton tournament.[4] "The Iron Age, a farce by performers of distinction," Henry dubbed it. Lord Eglinton had gravely assured the sheriff that "no one could by any possibility be hurt" under the conditions of safety he was imposing. "Much cry and little wool," Henry dryly commented, "or rather perhaps much wool (sawdust at least to make the lists soft) and little cry. Is the troop of horse to be shod by felt, also, that nobody be hurt by a kick? O brave new world that has such men in it!" Some clergyman ought to "discourse" against the "impious sin of mocking our ancestors and bringing them into contempt." But Henry feared that if he said more Milnes would "throw your Troubadour lyre at me, and I do not wish it to be broken." Henry was scornful

FIG. IV. Henry Lushington. Circa 1840 (?). Chalk portrait by E. U. Eddis. Private collection. Photograph courtesy of Courtauld Institute of Art.

too of the prosecution of minor Chartist agitators then taking place: "The law has indeed power to bind and to loose; and it exercises the power rather impressively: it is a net which breaks with large fishes but holds the little ones tight." One "wise" judge had defined sedition as "the speaking with disrespect of the Government and laws in public," a definition, Henry remarked, which would condemn "every speech made on either side at an election."[5] A month later, back at Park House, he was commenting upon Carlyle's recently published *Occasional and Miscellaneous Essays.* Perhaps people would read Carlyle "now that he has a name." If so they would "surely find one or two things to astonish them. The phenomenon of an English writer, and in his way a religious one, assuming the mythical nature of all Old and New Testament wonders as long since demonstrated, would be portentous to many, and is certainly new."[6]

Burdened as always by poor health, Henry had entered the nine-year period of greatest interest to posterity, his years of association with Tennyson.[7] Actually, that friendship had begun no later than March 1839, when Henry wrote to his father that the "girls will be interested to know that I have the great poet in my room at this moment, smoking with the shortest & blackest of pipes." Henry, who thought it "only provoking" that Tennyson would not publish, had been "settling with him that he is to come down with me sometime or other. Which of her rooms will Maria [the eldest sister] give up for smoking?"

No doubt the mourning period after Lushington's death later that month delayed Tennyson's projected visit. Edmund, writing shortly before his own death in 1893, believed that "the first time Tennyson visited me in my own house was in the summer of 1840 when he came to stay a few days."[8] There is no record that Henry had brought him to Park House before then.

By the summer of 1839, Henry had access to various of Tennyson's unpublished poems. On 8 July he repeated to Venables "parts of 'Locksley Hall,' which is very beautiful, & might be very popular. The freshness & vigour of Tennyson is wonderful." And on 7 February 1840, Henry recited "parts of Tennyson's new poems, which seem to be more tending to comedy, & less ornate." After March 1840, when Henry and Venables began sharing chambers at the Temple, both were seeing Tennyson occasionally, and during some periods frequently.

For Henry the nine years between 1839 and his departure in November 1847 to begin his chief secretaryship of the British government of Malta would be a period of unsettlement and consciousness of underutilized talents. Although admitted to the bar on 20 November 1840 and equipped with gown and wig by the end of the year, he never really practiced the profession. As Venables carefully wrote, "The experiment of his profession was a failure, or rather, it was never seriously tried. . . . With the exception of a few briefs in criminal prosecutions at assizes and sessions, he had no opportunity of cultivating or displaying the legal abilities which he possessed in an eminent degree." His ill health, Venables believed, "would probably have prevented him from profiting from opportunities of practice"; and it certainly "disinclined" him from enduring the physical discomforts of "resolute attendance on courts and circuits," which too often failed to bring even a persistent new barrister any profit.[9]

Milnes, however, had discounted Henry's physical infirmity, considering it rather like "a normal condition which with due care would give him the same chances of life that any of us possessed." Such an "intense vitality" had appeared "in all he said, and did, and even looked. There was no languour in his feebleness, no apathy in his enforced quiet; he was less like a weak man than like a strong man tired." His mind, certainly, "was eminently apt to perceive, and his imagination to illustrate, the strong points" of any court case. Milnes suspected that the "real cause" of Henry's not succeeding at the bar was "his own want of interest in legal employment."[10] For these suspicions Milnes had grounds. Henry's epistolary references to the bar had been too laboriously facetious, exposing rather than cloaking his aversion. Did not Milnes "know that this is term time, and that the whole mystery of iniquity is going on at Westminster as hard as it can all day, & for a month to come? Into which mystery, more mysterious even than iniquitous, it is really time for me to get some small insight." And again, "For the next few days my time will be very agreeably spent in sitting in court with a wig on, and hearing other people insinuate perfectly groundless suspicions against the character and veracities of perfectly honest witnesses: with no better hope than that I may at some future time be myself called upon to practice similar iniquity."[11]

An aversion to such an "iniquitous" vocation would have been natural in a man so determined, as Venables later celebrated him, to be straightforwardly truthful in nuance as well as word:

> From his infancy to his death, I believe he never uttered a wilful inaccuracy, and so strong was his instinctive love of verbal truth, that his language, even when it was most free and playful, scarcely ever took the form of exaggeration and irony. . . . He maintained, in seriousness and in jest, a single-minded directness which was not less distinctly expressed in the tones of his voice, and in the play of his expressive countenance, than in the substance of his conversation.[12]

In our more vocationally diversified century, given his imaginative absorption in politics and international affairs, such an articulate and personally winsome man might, with adequate health, have disregarded the bar, and risen in the BBC, become a correspondent for a London daily, held a professorship in political science or international relations in one of numerous British universities, administered a philanthropic foundation, or done any number of other things.

Yet from our present standpoint, his abandoning the bar may seem fortuitous. A busy young barrister, ambitiously pursuing political honors, would have lacked the leisure to spend weeks from time to time as confidant and practical critic to Tennyson. A certain shared rootlessness was necessary to that relationship, so important to Tennyson just then.

Another simple fact ought not to be overlooked. Even before Henry was called to the bar in 1840, a competing occupation was beckoning him back to Park House. With his father dead and his elder brother preoccupied in Scotland, he had an aging mother, four young sisters, and a teen-aged brother who needed a readily accessible, able-minded man, a surrogate head of family. The need would become even greater after the levelheaded mother died in 1841. Henry performed that new role until his departure for Malta, by which time the boy Franklin was a man of twenty-four and graduated from Cambridge with his own highest classical honors.

Between periods of illness and despite family responsibilities and all the random distractions that beset people not regularly employed, Henry also managed during those nine years to produce and publish a respectable amount of writing, including three substantial pamphlets and an admirable 303-page book. We have no certain way of knowing how much anonymous writing he may have done for periodicals. From Venables's journals we can identify one or two articles previously unattributed. There may have been others, although the systematic Venables, with his constant regard for Henry, probably recorded most if not all.

Undoubtedly Henry's best-remembered achievement has been the impression he left upon Tennyson as a practical literary critic. Venables reported Tennyson's "frequent remark" that Henry was the "most suggestive" of "all the critics with whom he had discussed his own poems";[13] and Hallam Tennyson's *Memoir* of the poet immortalized a pithier piece of Tennysonian praise: "Others may find faults in a poem, but Harry finds *the* fault and tells you how to mend it."[14] Finally, in *Tennyson and His Friends*, Hallam declared that his father had "pronounced" Henry to be "the best critic he had ever known."[15] (We must more thoroughly explore this poet/critic relationship in later chapters.)

Early in 1840 Henry began to share chambers at Mitre Court in the Inner Temple with Venables, who had resigned his tutorship at Jesus College, Cambridge, and moved into London to study law. Venables's journals demonstrate that his strongest motive for moving was to live nearer his friend. On 25 March,

Henry vacated his own rooms, moved in with Venables, and with frequent extended absences lived there until 1847.

The room quickly became a resort for Tennyson, for Edmund when he was in town, and for various of the Cambridge Apostles and their friends. "A. Tennyson came," Venables wrote on 3 April, "and sat all day, repeated the Gardener's Daughter, which is improved in point of unity. With him & Spedding dinner at Ireland's in Leicester Square—afterwards to Spedding's—B.L.C. [Benedict Lawrence Chapman, Chancery barrister, close friend of both Venables and Henry], R.M. [Milnes or Monteith], & D. Heath. Repeated the Vision, Dora & the picnic eclogue ["Audley Court"]—all good." The next day, Saturday, Tennyson was back with Chapman for breakfast: "Again idled all morning talking with him." And then on Sunday, "B.L.C. to breakfast, afterwards A.T." (But Tennyson was away from London during frequent stretches of weeks or months.)

Often in the years that followed, Venables would wonder if his move from Cambridge had been wise. His progress at the bar was painfully slow (though in later years the profession made him wealthy), Henry was too frequently absent, and so many other friends popped in and out that he could hardly do his own work. On 11 May 1841 he wrote: "Attempted at night to continue the Fichte translation, but interrupted by Pollock, &c. It is not to be expected that one can have company when it is wanted without taking the chance of its interfering with other matters. The debate still goes on."

A biography of Venables might be obliged to speculate in depth concerning the configurations of that totally conscientious man's feeling about Henry. Even a biography of Henry cannot simply ignore the topic, since he could hardly have escaped being affected by some of its ambiguities. Almost all of the documentation comes filtered through the single consciousness of Venables. Apparently only two letters survive from the hundreds that Henry wrote Venables during the twenty-seven years of their friendship, but during the final seventeen, Venables in his journals set down frequent, no doubt often too hastily scrawled, takings of his own pulse. More than anything else, it seems, he introspectively needed to define for himself the meaning of the relationship: not only what it was not but more precisely what it was. The journals when carefully studied, not merely skimmed, afford sufficiently numerous indications that during the half-decade before Henry died, Venables was beginning to articulate his long-needed perspective.

Professor Peter Allen, near the end of his admirable book about the early Cambridge Apostles (1978), inserts an untypically febrile paragraph about Venables and the "one-sided love affair," the "single overwhelming passion—his unrequited love for Henry Lushington," that "dominated his life."[16] True, there was a dominating feeling. But is it not rather too sweeping to announce that "Venables' cultivated exterior, his extensive social life, the insatiable round of work to which he submitted himself, were all masks to hide his deep unhappiness"? Every one of those three? Masks and nothing else? Nor have I found anything at all in the more than twenty-eight years of journals after Henry's death, or in any other documents, to support Allen's other inherently unprovable declaration that Venables was left with "nothing but bitter memories." At the risk of sounding sentimental, I suggest that "tender, belatedly reconciled, memories" would better accord with the documentary evidence. Bitterness, if latent after 1855, lay unexpressed, though frequent expressions of discontent had been recorded during earlier years.

Venables had long recognized that his preoccupation with Henry created an imbalance, that he consumed more time thinking about the friendship than Henry did. Therein for him lay much of the gall. Allen seems accurate concerning Venables's journalized feelings when he applies the term "emotional life." The sole wish specified in the journals (not intended for publication) was for more constant comradeship and a more equitably reciprocated regard. The journals indicate a commitment to a conservative moral code for both himself and others. His biographical sketch of Henry celebrated an idealist whose "purity and simplicity of . . . nature repelled every form of vice without any apparent effort."[17] When Henry and Venables were together, there had always been much hearty day-by-day enjoyment, much intellectual communion. Loneliness and melancholia descended for Venables when he and his friend were apart, or in the days immediately preceding a parting. But in time, as we shall later see, Venables came to recognize that Henry had indeed valued him too, genuinely in the way of truehearted friendship.

An additional, and ironical, circumstance must not be disregarded if one would see Venables whole. His journals reveal unmistakably that both during and after Henry's lifetime—at least from 1847—Venables came to be emotionally preoccupied, often painfully so, with another Lushington, Henry's sister Emily (born in 1817, the same year as Cecilia Tennyson Lushington). During stretches of his journals, including one period when Henry was present in England, home from Malta, Venables seems considerably more absorbed with Emily than with Henry. There are more than sufficient indications that Emily loved him. Unfortunately, Venables, with or without good reason, feared marriage. It may be that, in the end, the unfulfilled relationship with Emily was the real tragedy of Venables's life. It was almost unquestionably so for Emily.

Tennyson, making his first visit to Park House some time in the summer of 1840, would have met Mrs. Lushington, unless she was staying at the seaside, as various family members often did during summers. Earlier that spring or summer,[18] Mrs. Tennyson with Alfred and her daughters had moved from High Beech to Tunbridge Wells. Most probably Tennyson came to Park House in late summer after Edmund returned from his visit of "some months in various parts of Germany." Edmund later recalled that already the Tennysons had found their new residence "not healthy for all of the family, and they were wishing to meet with some other place to settle in." After "a day or two" Edmund returned with Tennyson to Tunbridge Wells for "a short visit to his mother's house," where Edmund would have first met his future wife. "Not long after this first visit" (whatever that phrase means), Tennyson brought his mother and "two younger sisters" (it would have been Cecilia's first sight of her future home) "to stay some days," while they looked "round the neighbouring country" for a house.[19] If that visit occurred any time during 1840, Edmund's mother and Cecilia's mother—admirable, near-saintly women both—could have become fleetingly acquainted.

Soon sorrow struck again. After an apparently brief illness, Mrs. Lushington died at the age of sixty-one-and-a-half on 10 January 1841, Edmund's thirtieth birthday. She had been seriously ill before Edmund, home for Christmas holidays, had been forced to return to Glasgow. On 5 January, Maria wrote that although "very languid," their mother seemed improved, more "cheerful & comfortable," taking an interest in reading and asking to be wheeled about in her chair. But soon she was worsening, and Edmund began speeding southward. Snow delayed the mail coach between Glasgow and Lancaster. At the Birmingham railway station, he received a letter from eighteen-year-old Franklin: "May God grant you strength and comfort under the painful news I have to give you. Our dearest Mother passed from this life about 4 o'clock this afternoon, with very little pain as we hope and believe." After receiving the Sacrament, she had lain "quite tranquilly and easily . . . perfectly conscious" until almost the end. Another letter, from Henry, awaited Edmund at London. "The girls continue more calm, more free from agitation of any kind, than any could believe who did not know the strength as well as the tenderness of their minds." Their "steady unfaltering resolution" in nursing their mother had "brought tears" to Henry's eyes "oftener almost than anything else, in recollecting it." Edmund reached London, hours behind schedule, between two and three in the morning, rested an hour at Henry's and Venables's chambers, and then started for Park House by chaise, arriving on the fourth day after the death.

In London, Venables had written that the mother's death would be "far worse in its consequences for the family" than the father's had been, and that so "great a shock coming after the first may affect the feelings and character of some of them for many years, or for life." After "having known deep sorrow," there might never again be "cheerfulness of the same kind as before. If any other blow should come it will be of a still heavier kind." Fortunately, another thirteen years would pass before the next family loss in 1854 would introduce a terrible train of four premature deaths in less than five years.

Even so, with Sophia's death the old order at Park House had irrevocably passed, yielding place to a not very enviable new. The most steadying hand was gone. Not again during the nineteenth century would any one woman be the center around whom a generally happy Park House would unambiguously revolve. Cecilia Tennyson, who in less than two years would become the nominal mistress of the place, would possess neither the uninterrupted tenancy nor the physical and emotional endowments requisite to the role. During long stretches she would be necessarily away with Edmund in Scotland, or else would reside in various places at the seaside. Even when in residence she would be weighed down by chronically poor health.

Four Lushington sisters, not without health problems of their own, survived from the seven daughters born to Lushington and Sophia. For the next fifty-two years, until the last one (Emily) died only three months before Edmund, one or more of the sisters would, except for brief intervals, reside at Park House. Ten days after the mother's death, the eldest, Maria Catherine, became twenty-five. Born with, or soon developing, cataracts in both eyes, she had sustained two ophthalmic surgical operations before the age of three, but her sight was never normal. Her letters indicate a fine intelligence, and temperamentally she appears the most serene of the four, a steadying influence, perhaps the one most like her mother. Emily, twenty-three, herself often ill, seems to have been the most comely of the four, extraordinarily appealing, the one with whom men fell in love; yet she was consistently self-effacing, devoted to caring for children, nursing the sick, visiting the needy. Ellen Eliza, nineteen, was highstrung, the one whom the others sought to shield from nervous excitement. She became the literary one, writer of inspirational verses and creditable though undistinguished moral stories peopled with good and simple characters and adorned with admirable descriptions of the countryside, especially her beloved South Downs. She had frequent illnesses, early and late, and in her final years was unable to walk. Louisa Sophia ("Louy"), not yet seventeen, was apparently vivacious and admired for her mental accomplishments and breadth of interests. She seems to have been relatively healthy but would die, probably from dysentery, when barely thirty. Perhaps it should be stipulated that the greater part of all we know about the sisters must be extracted from one source, Venables's journals, not entirely unbiased since he was devoted to them all; and had he ever married, he would have married Emily.

Meanwhile Edmund, like his former tutor Julius Hare, and Hare's revered master, Coleridge, had been developing into a Germanophile and something of a metaphysician. Before 1841 he had traveled for study in Germany at least three times. As early as 1838 Professor Christian Lassen, of Bonn University, had testified that Edmund understood German "perfectly, and speaks it with correctness and fluency," besides having "acquired an extraordinary knowledge of German literature, especially the portion of it relating to philology and philosophy."[20] In German metaphysics Edmund was finding a second field of study to complement his dedication to Greek. Since boyhood he had practiced precise concentration, analyzing a given text, determining just what it was or was not saying, what those particular words in the uniquely functioning syntax of that particular language seemed to denote and connote. He would continue to put himself sternly through that kind of finding out before embracing or rejecting philosophical ideas, or venturing into speculations of his own.

His openness to German higher criticism of the Scriptures had occasioned raised eyebrows among the Apostolic set. To Milnes, Henry had written light-heartedly on 2 January 1837:

> Notwithstanding your good wishes for his orthodoxy, [Edmund] is deep in Strauss, having gotten to the end of one volume not less thick than impious, and being preserved from the abyss of skepticism only by the accident of having left the second at Cambridge. His fate cannot therefore be deferred beyond February. My ignorance of German, which however I intend to remove, may preserve me a little longer.[21]

With more apparent seriousness, Monteith, who within a few years would become a Roman Catholic, wrote to Milnes in October 1839:

> Lushington gave me some pleasant days here—great talk about all the secret troubles of theology—they are mere mental perplexities with him—his lymphatic, xanthous temperament never permits these things to be really grievous to him. It is curious inquiry, as about Greek roots, & his intellectual ambition to be a man of insights & a truth-proclaimer maybe mortified—but he pineth not at heart, & will die of gout like his fathers for 4 generations hale & happy & fresh of spirit, all riddles unread, & God's statutes unexpounded.[22]

Venables in July 1839 recorded "various discussions with ELL on philosophical questions connected with Kant, Fichte, & philosophy in general." Venables too had learned German, was writing reviews of German works, and later occupied himself by working on (but did not publish) translations of Fichte. Edmund's obituary writer in 1893, his former Glasgow pupil the Greek scholar Lewis Campbell, remembered him in middle life, sitting "in summer days

. . . under the stately 'immemorial elms' " at Park House, "holding a classic volume or some book of German philosophy in his hand." In philosophy "he leaned rather to Kant than to Hegel. An idealist to the core, he was at the same time a lover of close and accurate reasoning."[23]

Out of Edmund's absorption in German thought and his indignant intolerance of whatever seemed superficial or shoddy scholarship grew the only anonymous periodical article known to be his. From Venables's journals we know that Edmund wrote the article in his friend J. M. Kemble's *British and Foreign Review* that mercilessly examined a small book entitled *Observations on the attempted application of pantheistic principles to the theory and historic criticism of the Gospel. Part I. On the theoretic application, being the Christian Advocate's publication for 1840,* by Dr. William Hodge Mill (1792–1853).[24] Mill, a former Fellow of Trinity College respected for his work in oriental studies, including Arabic and Sanskrit, had been the founding principal of Bishop's College in Calcutta until forced by ill health to return to Britain. In 1838 he became chaplain to the Archbishop of Canterbury and Christian Advocate on the Hulse Foundation at Cambridge. In 1843 he would stand unsuccessfully for the Regius Professorship of Divinity, being distrusted for supposed Tractarian leanings; finally, in 1848, he would become Regius Professor of Hebrew.[25]

Mill's 1840 book was the first of five annual installments of a work intended to demolish D. F. Strauss's *Leben Jesu.* The part that Edmund reviewed attempted broadly to link Strauss with recent German philosophy, all of which Mill denounced as generally "pantheistic" and therefore patently anti-Christian. With his eighteen years in India and his background in Indian languages and thought, Mill felt prepared to expose all the impious enormities of pantheism. But apparently he commanded less of German than of several other languages, and would not recognize possible differences between Indian pantheism and its current German counterparts, or between degrees of pantheism in different German writers. To him, pantheism was pantheism, and most if not all contemporary German philosophers were pantheists. Their philosophy had already "begun to visit us." It regarded "God and nature in a light utterly irreconcilable with Christianity," rejected "all notion of a Creator, Redeemer, and Sanctifier, above and beyond ourselves," and discarded "all faith in the unseen, all hope of an *individual* immortality of being." The Idea was God, "and mankind at large is the Christ." Sacred records were mere "dreamy visions and legends." The "only reality admitted in any system of traditional religion" was the "identity of our highest reason with the essence that is all-pervaded and indestructible. Those to whom the Hegels and the Schellings are exhibited as restorers of philosophy should at least know what is the kind of doctrine they are called upon to admire."

Edmund finished his review in mid-April, then sent it to Venables in London, who read it at first "with a good deal of disappointment," unable to "see how Edmund's answer [to Mill] can be an answer." After Edmund arrived from Glasgow in May, he conferred with Venables, then made some "alterations" before sending the piece to Kemble.

Mill erred, Edmund argued, in linking Strauss's *mytho-historical* criticism with German *philosophical* speculation: there was no "obvious or immediate connexion." Essentially, Strauss was following a prevalent German *historical* trend that thoroughly examined *all* unsubstantiated narratives "from any nation"— "Greek, Asiatic (including Jewish), and Teutonic." But even when Strauss did introduce certain "philosophical principles," Mill erred again in trying to answer Strauss in particular by broadly assaulting "Hegel and other philosophers":

> No writer is entitled to consider it as a light matter to speak hastily and on insufficient knowledge, of the combined labours in thought of men who have earnestly devoted their lives to subjects on which he has bestowed but a passing glance; or to endanger the success of what is well done in his undertaking by mixing it up with what is ill done, and perhaps need not have been attempted at all. In the first-mentioned defect he is unjust to his adversaries, in the latter to himself.

Furthermore, Mill's basic rhetorical method, ostensibly expositing a whole philosophical system by displaying a few isolated excerpts, was irredeemably defective. It was doubtful that the "essence" of any system could be "fairly conveyed to an uninitiated reader by a few prominent sentences, without the slightest sketch of the process of reasoning by which this essence has been obtained from the first data." The difficulty increases in proportion to the complexity of the system. The "several parts of the system" must always "keep each other in check, and occupy their place in virtue of something else than mere juxtaposition." To have "anything beyond dead mass in building" requires "interwoven conceptions to make the law which binds stone to stone." If that rule was true of "matter symbolizing mind," it was much more so "of the immediate products of mind itself." Words alone "do not form sentences; and thought too has to be spelt out, not singly and apart, but along with and by the aid of conceptions which lead to it step by step, and which mutally lend and borrow meaning."

"If I know not how Plato or Hegel thought up to this principle," inquired Edmund, "how can I feel certain what he thought *in* it? Am I not exposing myself to the error of fancying that from words alone I can legitimately derive a comprehension and knowledge of things?"

But if such a caveat applied to the delicate task of tracing "a train of speculation in a single mind," it was "more pointedly" applicable to the philosophy of
an entire nation like Germany, which had "wandered its own way for fifty
years, with few lookers on and yet fewer attendants, toiling to find the light by
steps painful and slow." Each "successive development" had involved much of
the "preceding." All historians of German philosophy agreed that "the prominent speakers, Kant, Fichte, Schelling, Hegel, are relatively to each other necessary points of transition." Each formed part of "the existence and ground of
the comprehensibility" of his successors. All these thinkers had "emphatically"
asserted that "their predecessors have more truth in what they assert than in
what they deny." Each had attempted to "include, and by reconciling explain
and verify, other systems."

It was particularly "dangerous and deceptive" to characterize such a com-
plexly "various, yet interdependent, national philosophy" with one basically
meaningless term like "pantheistic." That unfortunate adjective had been
"rarely equalled" for "vagueness of application" and "frequent unmeaning-
ness." If ever used at all, it "should be carefully fenced round by rigorous
definition" to avoid "misunderstanding or misapplication." When misused,
such an epithet "tempts those to judge rashly who perhaps might never be
qualified to judge at all." It "fosters ill-will and contempt, both in the one party
who complains that he is not understood, and the other who will not take the
trouble to seek to understand him, or believe that he may be worth
understanding."

After exposing miscellaneous defects in Mill's arguments and assumptions,
and supplying a three-page listing of his mistranslations from the German, Edmund urged British scholars to step forth and lead out in attempting to understand the Germans, "presenting in a true undistorted light to the independent
minds of England the career which German thought has opened for itself in the
last and the present generation." Incompatibilities between English and German beliefs would inevitably persist for many years. The "leading thinkers of
the nation which produced Luther" were not likely to "regard any subject
whatever as guarded within a sacred pale from scrutinizing glances of pure
thought" or to "acquiesce in holding a religious creed" that does not harmonize
with reason. But a study of the Germans "carried on more in the spirit of love
than of distrust," with "the aim of finding, not errors to repel, but rather
concurrent truths to attract," despite differences in their clothing, would
"draw to light points of contact and community now hidden from the general
view." And it might "tend to the purifying of faith and the illumination of
reason alike" in both nations.

Apart from his Glasgow inaugural, this review is the longest and fullest surviving exposition of Edmund's scholarly ideals. It reflects with distinction the rigorous, fair-minded spirit of his best mentors—Hare and Thirlwall and the men at Bonn—and the open-minded receptivity of his namesake ancestor Bishop Edmund Law. It was probably his only venture into writing for the reviews. Neither his Glasgow position nor his own self-esteem was contingent upon publication, and by ordinary standards he was apparently deficient in ambitiousness for reputation. For him study was its own reward. But if this article is unique, so was the occasion for his intellectual outrage: a wrong-headed attack upon a field of study he had recently begun to love, made by a professed fellow-philologist who ought to have known better, offending Edmund's most cherished ideals of scholarly integrity and responsible use of language.

In mid-March of 1841 Edmund, back in Glasgow after the burial of his mother, had been dropped into close friendship with a remarkable man only six years her junior. The aging and infirm "Opium Eater" Thomas De Quincey (born 1785), had escaped with a few books and a great bundle of treasured papers one night from Edinburgh, after hiding out for nine years to avoid debtor's prison, and turned up at the door of John Nichol, professor of astronomy at Glasgow and a close colleague-friend of Edmund.[26] When a bulky shipment of new astronomical instruments for the Glasgow observatory elbowed poor De Quincey out of Nichol's house, Edmund, alone in his own house nearby, took in the fugitive until he could locate other quarters, as he did about three weeks later. Those weeks of association between the specialized but open-minded young linguist and the versatile old journalist, with his encyclopedic reading and assimilative mind—a man who had intimately known the Wordsworths and Edmund's ideal, Coleridge—held promise of enjoyment and instruction for both. Both were good listeners, and De Quincey, given a receptive audience, was a fascinating talker hardly less prodigious than Coleridge himself. But De Quincey's biographer relates that "on the very first evening, as Professor Lushington and De Quincey were sitting down to dinner, De Quincey was seized with a violent affliction, inflammatory and connected with strong delirium, which for many subsequent days prostrated him in an infant state of helplessness."[27] He remained at Glasgow, living near the college, for about three years, almost continuously ill. Edmund assisted as he could, bringing books from the college library. De Quincey had long been proud of his proficiency in Greek, doing his own translating for his articles; and his interests extended to the German metaphysicians and philologists, into whom Edmund had more recently delved. The friendship continued after De Quincey returned to Edinburgh, where Edmund frequently came to cheer him when he was depressed. Some of the best, most confidential letters De Quincey ever wrote, priceless sources for his biographers, were addressed to his young professor friend. Edmund was one of the last to visit him before he died in 1859. And surviving the old man's death, until the end of Edmund's own life in 1893, was a mutually sustaining platonic friendship between Edmund and De Quincey's youngest daughter, Florence Bairdsmith (1827–1904), whose admirable husband, Colonel Richard Baird Smith, died on duty in India in 1861, leaving her with two small daughters. Highly intelligent and a sympathetic letter-writer, she will appear from time to time in our narrative.

The spring and later months of 1841 were a prospering time for the friendship between our Lushington brothers and Alfred Tennyson. For Tennyson it was a crucial year. Although he had not yet informed his friends he had finally committed himself in February to publishing his poems to forestall publication of the unrevised 1830 and 1832 versions in the United States.[28] In late fall his family would move from Tunbridge Wells to Boxley, near Park House. And he was continuing to endanger his inheritance by speculating in an ultimately disastrous wood-carving scheme of the High Beech lunatic asylum keeper, Dr. Matthew Allen.

Venables's journal records that Edmund arrived in London from Glasgow on 4 May, finding both W. H. Thompson and Tennyson at Venables's and Henry's chambers. Tennyson was "still occupied with the woodcarving speculation." The next day Edmund and Venables began going over Edmund's review of Mill, but were soon "interrupted by Tennyson, who staid all morning." When Venables went off to study at "the library," Edmund and Henry accompanied Tennyson to his quarters (probably at 7 Charlotte Street, where he wrote Dr. Allen a week later that he was "still living").[29] On the eighth, Henry and Edmund left for St. Leonards, but Henry returned on the eighteenth; and on the twentieth he and Venables called on Tennyson and "sat with him a long time—talking & looking over his M.S. book. Brought it away & dined late at the Club. Afterwards looked over some of the poems, as always with great admiration, particularly Locksley Hall & a new ballad, Ellen Adair ["Edward Gray"]. Succeeded apparently in persuading AT to take steps about money." On the next day they "read over more of the poems, principally the Hallam series, which are exquisitely true & touching, though perhaps few men, at least middleaged men will be able to feel their peculiar truth. A. Tennyson called & staid a very short time, leaving town to day." It remains unclear what Tennyson was persuaded to do about money; most of his finally fatal agreements with Allen seem already to have been sealed.

On 12 June, Venables and Henry went together down to Park House, where Tennyson was already staying with Edmund. On the night of the fifteenth, probably for all the party including the four Lushington sisters, Tennyson "repeated Lady Clara & some other poems, including The Picnic" ["Audley Court"]; and on the eighteenth, Venables's thirty-first birthday, "Tennyson repeated the Cock & Dora, the first admirable & less known. Not that these things are by any means unmixed pleasure." Obviously, Venables would have preferred more unshared time with Henry and the other Lushingtons. Both corporeally and vocally, Tennyson filled a lot of space.

On 8 July, while at home with his own family at Llysdinam in Wales, Venables learned through a letter from Chapman that Henry and some others in the family would probably go to Italy for almost a year. Franklin's physician had prescribed a warmer climate, and it soon appeared that the sister Emily needed it also. Another letter from Chapman received on 29 July contained another "strange piece of news," probably the decision of the Tennysons to move from Tunbridge Wells to Maidstone. A letter from Henry to Edmund, postmarked 8 July 1841, speaks of "Alfred's coming with or without Mr. [Charles Tennyson] Turner to look at the houses."

When Venables went down to Park House on 10 August, he found that Henry, Franklin, Ellen, and Louy were in "Tunbridge." Three days later they were all back "with the utterly unexpected addition of Alfred Tennyson." Tennyson departed on the fifteenth, probably bound for the Continent; he was in both Paris and Holland that month.[30] On the sixteenth Henry disconcerted Venables ("the most disagreeable result" of the Italian plan he had "yet thought of") by suggesting they give up their chambers at the Temple. (They were not given up.)

The seventeenth brought a young Oxford undergraduate, Franklin's former Rugbeian schoolfellow George Granville Bradley (1821–1903), future headmaster of Marlborough and dean of Westminster, who would also come to Park House in 1842. Although it has long been accepted that Bradley met Tennyson during this first visit, it seems improbable. Bradley's letter to Hallam Tennyson more than fifty years later says only, "I feel sure [less than positive] that I saw him during my first [1841] visit [to Park House].'"[31] But Tennyson had not appeared before Venables departed on the twenty-fourth; on the twenty-sixth Tennyson, back from the Continent, wrote from London to an American acquaintance;[32] and on 1 September, Henry and Franklin surprised Tennyson ("a Godsend I did not expect")[33] by visiting him at Dr. Allen's in High Beech. Bradley would always remember the contrast between the Lushington circle and the people he had known at Rugby and Oxford. If the Park House set even mentioned Newman or the Oxford Movement, it was only "as matters of secondary or remote interest"; but they "seemed as much at home in the language of the Greek dramatists as if it was their native tongue." Chapman had remarked to Bradley that Henry could at once "give the reference and the context" of almost any quoted Shakespearian line.[34] Bradley most vividly remembered Henry: "Ah! how his sweet and delicate face and kindly voice as mounted on a pony he joined us in our walks come back to me across the interval of more than fifty years."[35]

At Park House, after returning from High Beech, Henry ironically wrote Milnes that "the madmen" had seemed "little if anything better than ourselves. Dr. Allen's mania did not break out much—unless it were on the subject of wood carving." Alfred had been "very ill with sore throat, but otherwise very pleasant—as indeed he always is." Henry's party would be sailing for the Continent at the end of the week, and Henry was unreconciled. Two weeks earlier he had written Milnes that he "extremely" disliked the idea: "I am fully satisfied from all I have heard or read that the Continent is a humbug. . . . The Alps, perhaps—but I have no doubt that their height and grandeur have been scandalously exaggerated. The Rhine is well known to have been overpuffed." The Italian climate was notoriously "miserable and changeable." Even the physician who prescribed the journey admitted that Neopolitans were quite "subject to colds and catarrhal afflictions." Was it "for this that one is to leave one's native land, to change fires for stoves and the blessings of a pure and reformed Catholic church for an idolatrous polytheism? not even to get rid of colds? I have discovered in myself a new virtue of patriotism, at least a novel degree of it, since this scheme was resolved upon." To Milnes he pleaded—more than half-seriously, one feels: "Pray get me a sinecure before next May. I give up for the present my brilliant prospects at the bar—for at least a year and a half—by this exile, and my country ought to reward me."[36] On 1 October, Venables and Chapman met the Lushington party—Henry, Emily, Franklin, and Louy—in Switzerland, finding Franklin ill and Henry in a very "dispirited condition." As it turned out, illness would afflict the party for much of their time away from England; it is doubtful that anyone received much benefit, beyond the educational, from the displacement.

Before Venables reached London on 6 October, Edmund had passed through bound for Glasgow, taking Maria and Ellen for the winter, and emptying Park House of all its Lushingtons.[37] By 5 November the Tennyson family was settled at nearby Boxley Hall, close to the old churchyard where so many Lushingtons now lie.[38] Alfred was still living part of the time in London. On the seventh, in London, Venables "called on Alfred Tennyson, & sat with him a long time, talking mostly about Lushington matters, a kind of conversation of which one cannot tire." On that same evening Venables "heard for the first time that he was likely to publish." Two other times Venables found Tennyson "too ill to be seen." On 3 December, Venables and Monteith found him "with leeches on his arm, which was swelled, but not otherwise looking unwell or in very bad spir-

its." The three men had "very pleasant talk till about ten." It would be "difficult," Venables thought, "to meet two persons of so much originality & fulness
of matter in conversation."

Tennyson's health had improved somewhat by Christmas. Edmund, coming
down from Glasgow (with or without Maria and Ellen?), "spent the time
mostly at Boxley, [where] A.T. was now settled with his mother and sisters."
They all had "sometimes dance and song in the evening." (Could this have been
the time when Edmund, his own house nearly empty a mile away, began to fall
in love with the tall Cecilia? Or had the process already occurred?) The number
of *In Memoriam* poems "had rapidly increased since I had seen the poet [about
four months], his book containing many that were new to me." Edmund had
heard Tennyson "repeat" some of the elegies "before I had seen them in writing," and had read others "from the book itself which he kindly allowed me to
look through without stint." One night that December, when Edmund and
Alfred "were sitting up together in his bedroom," Alfred began to recite the
sixth poem, "One writes, that 'other friends remain.' " More than fifty years
later, with Alfred newly dead and his own death only a few months or weeks
away, Edmund would recall, "I do not know that the melodious thunder of his
voice ever imprest me more profoundly."[39]

Edmund returned to Glasgow, inevitably thinking of his sad journey from his
mother's bedside a year before. Some days later he had a letter from Alfred: "I
have been once into your grounds, the house looked very unhappy. Charles and
I went together: he admired the place very much, though everything was deep
in snow."[40]

VI

A Wife Ere Noon

1842

F AR FROM FINDING better healh, Henry and his party in Italy had been
suffering aggravated illness. During six weeks at Naples, he, with a prolonged
"sort of fever" and Emily with "cold and rheumatic fever," had been visited by
a physician twice daily: "Getting ill and getting well have been our sole occu-
pations." It was early January before they began recovering, and enjoying the
view of Vesuvius "half way down in white snow." If only the old volcano
would provide an eruption, or even merely "*flame*—the lighting up that snow
shroud with flashes of infernal fire—that would be worth seeing—but it will
only smoke as hard as Alfred Tennyson: wasting itself as he does himself in
cigars." But Tennyson's "promised volume" would soon, "if God wishes . . .
come out at last."[1]

The Deity evidently concurred. Soon Tennyson's "ten years' silence" would
finally be broken. When he wrote early in 1842 to acknowledge Edmund's
Greek translation of his "Oenone," he had "not yet taken my book to Moxon"
(his publisher), but intended to "get it out shortly." He had not been doing
"what you professors call 'working' at it, that indeed is not my way. I take my
pipe and the muse descends in a fume, not like your modern ladies who shriek at
a pipe as if they saw a 'Splacknuck.' "[2] With occasional assistance from Edward FitzGerald, Tennyson would work alone in James Spedding's rooms at 60
Lincoln's Inn Fields, Spedding having departed about 9 February for North

America as secretary to the Ashburton Commission to settle the U.S.–Canadian dispute over the Maine border.[3]

Down in Italy, Henry, later to be praised by Tennyson as his best practical critic, had lost the opportunity to watch his friend complete one of the century's greatest poem collections. He may have assisted with a few poems before leaving for Italy, but there is no good basis for supposing so. Most probably, his contributions to Tennyson's revisons were confined to *The Princess*, and possibly a few later alterations of the 1842 text.

By mid-April, Tennyson had settled into almost constant readying of his poems, continuing to alter some of them before returning the proof sheets to the printer a few poems at a time. He had turned for assistance to Venables, who like himself had won the Chancellor's Medal for English verse at Cambridge. On 8 April, Venables "called on Alfred Tennyson at Spedding's rooms, & found proof sheets lying about. Read several things, most of Morte d'Arthur, Locksley Hall, Talking Oak, &c. He thinks they do not look so well in print." Soon Frederick Pollock dropped by, and the three walked to "the printer's in Whitefriar," meeting with another Apostle, Stephen Spring Rice, in Fleet Street, "who joined us."

On 12 April, Tennyson came with proof sheets "of parts of the suicide ["The Two Voices"], & discussed some alterations." Venables thought the poem "in some places too long, in some obscure," but in "discussing particular passages I cannot trust my own judgment much." Tennyson stayed "rather late talking about it." On the next day Tennyson returned and "made the alterations proposed in The Two Voices." He had with him also "Godiva which I was not very familiar with. I should think the subject has never been nearly so well treated." Venables went back with Tennyson to his rooms: "Looked over the Daydream, read Lady Clara, & the Vision of Sin; which perhaps he is right in thinking the finest of all." On the fourteenth the two went over "the Envoi & Epilogue of the Daydream, Amphion, which is a good piece of criticism. St. Agnes & Sir Galahad." But there had been no "material alteration to consider since the passage in the Two Voices." On the fifteenth Tennyson had not "made up his mind about the Epilogue. . . . looked over the new version of the Miller's Daughter, the Lady of Shalott, Mariana, & one or two others which are on the whole improved. I do little good by this looking at his things, & it is burdensome for fear of being a burden." On the seventeenth "A.T. called at night with a new sheet"; on the eighteenth Venables went to "A.T. to discuss the choice of poems to be inserted"; on the nineteenth they "read the altered Oenone"; on the twentieth "Had the Vision of Sin printed. Liked the blackbird much better than before. Sat rather late." It was the twenty-ninth before Tennyson "called with Lady of Shalott & part of Mariana in the South"; on 2 May "A.T. called with the revise of the Lady of Shalott &c"; on the fifth, "reading Lotos Eaters &c." The poems came out in two volumes on 14 May.[4]

When Edmund arrived from Glasgow on 9 May, Venables found him "very agreeable"—naturally enough, since it appears he had already become engaged to marry Cecilia Tennyson. On the tenth, while together with Edmund and Tennyson, Venables "made a discovery by a few expressions used." Then three days later he went to "A.T.'s & heard account confirming previous guesses."

To say the least, Edmund and Cecilia seem to have had comparatively few opportunities to become closely acquainted. Had they met twice or only once during the summer of 1840? Edmund's chronology, in his reminiscences written in 1893, shortly before he died, remains tantalizingly ambiguous:

> I believe the first time [Tennyson] visited me in my own house was in the summer of 1840 when he came to stay a few days. . . . A day or two later I went over with him to pay a short visit . . . at Tunbridge Wells. . . . Not long after this visit [how long is "not long"—a few weeks later or the following summer?] he came over with his mother and two younger sisters to stay some days at Park House, which they partly spent in looking about the neighbouring country at . . . houses. . . . They eventually settled before long upon engaging a house . . . in Boxley Parish, to which they removed before the winter of 1841–42.[5]

It is a virtual certainty that at least some of the Tennysons were house-hunting around Maidstone in the summer of 1841,[6] and they did not move to Boxley until that fall. With Edmund invariably spending his winters at Glasgow, he and Cecilia may actually have met only twice before the Christmas holiday of 1841, when his family (possibly excepting Maria and Ellen, who may have come down with him from Glasgow) were all away from Park House.

No doubt there were exchanges of letters after that Christmas, and Edmund's proposal of marriage and Cecilia's acceptance could even have been exchanged by post. But courtship letters are seldom very reliable instruments for exploring ultimate compatibility, unless both correspondents are earnestly attempting to do just that; and Cecilia, by such indications as we have, was not a profound letter-writer, although she could be impulsively sympathetic, affectionate, and entertaining.

Cecilia, born on 10 October, 1817, was the eleventh of the twelve Tennyson children (the first-born had died in infancy). Her childhood had coincided with the stormiest years of her parents' troubled marriage. Her brilliant wreck of a clergyman father, Doctor George Clayton Tennyson, nursing grievances both real and imagined against his own father, was drinking heavily, behaving violently, and perhaps undergoing epileptic seizures. Alfred Tennyson's latest biographer declares that by 1820 (when he was only eleven and Cecilia was three), Alfred was "acting as virtual head of the family . . . his mother was loving but ineffectual, and his father was constantly aggravating his epilepsy by drink until his mind seemed to be cracking."[7] More plausibly for Alfred's purported role, Sir Charles Tennyson's account seems to place this stage in the Doctor's deterioration three or four years later, when Cecilia would have been six or seven.[8] She was barely ten when her mother wrote that "poor George's violence . . . I fear increases. We had a terrible evening on Sunday." He had forbidden her to take the children to visit his father, "nor will he let me have the Carriage unless I promise to stay from home half a year."[9] A few weeks later Alfred was matter-of-factly referring to his father's "unhinged state of mind."[10] When Cecilia was eleven, the parents both had decided upon a separation. He was determined that "the Children must not be under her care; I will . . . send all except my two elder daughters from under her superintendence."[11] (That was not done.) On her part she complained of his "ungovernable violence . . . I do not feel it safe either for myself or my children to remain any longer in the house with him." Wisely, she was fearing "the impression which his conduct," including "the perpetual . . . degrading epithets to myself and children," might "produce upon the minds of his family." He had flourished a loaded gun and a knife, threatening to stab his son Frederick "in the jugular vein and in the heart."[12] In the relatively small, overcrowded rectory, young Cecilia could not have remained unaffected by such scenes.

The father went off to the Continent to recover his health, returning the next year to resume the marriage, although his wife had "little hope of any permanent tranquillity. . . . You know . . . that when under the influence of liquor George is dreadfully violent."[13] But the end came otherwise: on 16 March 1831, at home, the unhappy Doctor died, purportedly of typhus fever but, as Martin argues, more probably of a cerebral hemorrhage.[14] He was about fifty-three. Cecilia, only thirteen, could have had few if any memories of her father at his best.

Across a narrow lane from the rectory and up a stubby path to the churchyard the body was taken for burial. Close by were other graves where, fleeing the Doctor's outbursts, the boy Alfred had "many a time," as his wife would tell her sons, "gone out in the dark and cast himself . . . nearby longing to be beneath."[15]

Meanwhile, stimulating occasions in the young country girl's life, out in those remote Lincolnshire wolds, would have been the periodic arrivals of her three brothers with news from Cambridge; their emergence, however obscurely, as published poets in 1827; Alfred's winning of the Chancellor's Medal at Cambridge for his patched-together visionary "Timbuctoo" in 1829; and the

FIG. V. Cecilia (Tennyson) Lushington. Circa 1865. Photograph by De Ath & Dunk, Maidstone. Courtesy of the Tennyson Research Centre, Lincoln, by permission of Lincoln Library Service.

publication of his memorable *Poems, Chiefly Lyrical* in 1830. Into adolescence Cecilia would go, carrying in her ears the melancholy melodies of Alfred's "Mariana" and "A spirit haunts the year's last hours," and perhaps puzzling over the disturbing introspections of his "Supposed Confessions of a Second-Rate Sensitive Mind."

The spring of 1830, when Cecilia was twelve, had brought the first visit to Somersby[16] of Alfred's ineffable confidant Arthur Henry Hallam, who would become the fiancée of her sister Emily, and be near-idolized by the family. When the terrible news of Arthur's sudden death from a cerebral hemorrhage in Vienna descended upon the already bereaved Somersby family in the autumn of 1833, Cecilia, then approaching sixteen, would share the grief that numbed them all for months. The previous year in the parsonage had been blighted by the final mental breakdown, never to be reversed, of the fifth son, Edward, four years older than she. Her world had early taken on its pattern of successive calamities, repeated shocks to the nerves, from which throughout her elongated life she would seldom for long be free.

By age sixteen she must have been strikingly beautiful and appealing. (Sir Henry Craik, Scottish educational official, twenty-nine years her junior, wrote that even "in later years," her "jet-black hair and brilliant clearness of complexion were still marvellously preserved," and her "fine contralto" singing voice had "something of the music that one felt in the Poet's rich tones.")[17] Edmund could have first become aware of her through entranced reports from his closest Cambridge friend, Robert Tennant, who had visited the Tennysons at Somersby in July 1834 and fallen for a time hopelessly in love with her. When Mrs. Tennyson opposed the courtship by an impecunious scholar seven years older, Tennant agreed to "bear my affliction in a proper spirit," so long as "the esteem of those whom next to herself I most love [the Tennyson family] does not even now fail me."[18]

We next encounter Cecilia in her twentieth year, immediately after the Tennysons had moved from Somersby to High Beech in Epping Forest near London. Sir Charles Tennyson tells us that she and at least two older sisters, Mary and Emily, had apparently by then "become the centre of a small group of young bluestockings called the 'Husks,' " who met in one another's homes to discuss the poems of their favorite Romantics, "Keats, Shelley, Wordsworth, Coleridge, and, of course, Alfred Tennyson."[19] From High Beech, and later Tunbridge Wells, during the next three years Cecilia wrote at least seven remarkably lively and affectionate letters (surviving at the Tennyson Research Centre at Lincoln and now published in the new edition of Alfred's letters) to a fellow Husk, Susan Haddlesey, back in the ancient wolds town of Caistor, where Cecilia's brother, Charles Tennyson Turner, and his wife Louisa were living. At their best, the letters, and another one of the same period to her cousin Lewis Fytche excerpted by Sir Charles,[20] display a terse descriptiveness coupled with lightness of phrasing and touches of apparently effortless irony unmatched in the letters of any of the other Tennysons. One sees here, as in nothing else anywhere in the pitifully few surviving letters from Cecilia, traces of the personality that might have captivated Edmund two or three years later.

Unfortunately, other characteristics already foreshadow ultimate incompatibility with a perfectionistic linguist like Edmund. Although Cecilia's spelling is generally accurate, her impetuous letters rush along in manuscript largely without benefit of punctuation:

> I ought to have answered before this thy very affectionate letter what wilt thou think of me surely not that I have forgotten thee which really is not the case I have only been idle that is all and thou must forgive me Mamma says I am to ask thee when thou canst best come and see us canst thou come and see us any time next month. Write and tell us I ride every day now Susan on a nice black pony we have bought so come and see us and thou shalt ride too we have given 9 pounds for it [et cetera]. . . . [21]

(Lang and Shannon blandly state that "in all of Cecilia Tennyson's letters . . . printed here most of the punctuation and capital letters have been supplied by the editors.")[22]

More ominous in light of what we know about Cecilia's later life are frequent vague reports of illnesses, including painful headaches, that she, perhaps with sufficient cause, mentions as reasons for not writing more regularly. From several of Edmund's letters in later years, it seems that some of her headaches were the extremely painful *tic douloureux* (spasmodic facial neuralgia). In late November 1837 she had been to London to consult

> Dr Marshall Hall (a famous physician) for my Headaches which I have had repeatedly lately. He is a very gentlemanlike man and has a kind manner which I like much in a medical man He has given me some medicine to take, but I was to continue it for a long time. These were his words to me "You must continue this medicine for years" (very pleasant to hear was it not) however there is no help for it, and anything is better than these headaches.[23]

Hall was probably the leading physician in England in the treatment of disorders of the nervous system. His ultimately voluminous medical writings already included *Lectures on the Nervous System and Its Diseases* (1836), and he would later publish several other neurological treatises.[24] But his writings, generally descriptive, stop short of reliably indicating what medicines he would have

prescribed for such long-continued use, or their possible undesirable effects.
Clearly, in any case, Edmund in 1842 would be marrying a person already
marked for a life of illness which in time (if not already by 1837) would include
more or less prolonged periods of lassitude and depression.

Off in Italy that spring, Henry with his family party had been thrown into
mental anguish by terrible news from India. The ill-considered British occupation of Afghanistan, begun more than three years earlier, had suddenly suffered
a nearly incredible catastrophe. British Army forces and miscellaneous camp
followers totaling some 16,500 persons had attempted a desperate mid-winter
retreat, and a week later all but a few were dead, killed by weather or ambush
or both. As Henry later wrote, "every mail brought intelligence of disasters so
new and so terrible, that it was difficult to replace the involuntary incredu-
lity . . . with a sense of their reality." "Greater numbers have perished in less
time; but no similar force of civilized men was ever so utterly overwhelmed."[25]
Venables declared that Henry's always delicate health was "seriously affected"
by the news. He had cherished an idealistic view of the British presence in
India, of which Lushington family members had been a part for nearly a
hundred years. One of his half-uncles had been governor of Madras, another the
chairman of the Indian Court of Directors when the Afghan war began, still
another a member of the Indian Council.[26] The governor general of India was
his father's first cousin, the second Lord Ellenborough. With an imaginative
compassion for human suffering Henry combined an extraordinary sensitivity
to immoral political action. It was "not indifferent whether all that had been
done so ineffectually, so disastrously, had also been done wickedly and
wrongly."[27] For the next two years, the Afghanistan question would never for
long be out of his mind; from extensive reading and intense brooding about the
subject would emerge the longest piece of writing, and possibly the best, that he
would ever do. That book will be discussed in our next chapter.

By mid-June he and his party were home from Italy. In coming weeks he
would be much in the company of Tennyson, who was living again at Boxley.
Even when Henry, looking "pale, thin & out of spirits," traveled to London for
a reunion with Venables, Tennyson was accompanying him. Only two days
later, Venables was obliged to go off on circuit, continuing a generally
wretched summer. He would receive so few briefs that he despaired of ever
succeeding at the bar. Just then Jesus College, Cambridge, was offering him
another tutorship, and he was going through a crisis of indecision. His discon-
tents were nourished by letters from the ever-excitable B. L. Chapman, apparently insinuating that Tennyson was supplanting Venables as Henry's best friend;
but by that time Venables, with Henry's advice, had turned down the tutorship
offer. After Henry in August, still looking "tired & on the whole unwell," had

come out to Wales, Venables felt more reassured that Chapman's intimations were groundless. He and Henry would go on sharing the Mitre Court chambers, at least when Henry was in town, for another five years.

At some point, probably in July or August, Henry bravely enough began to compose a review of Tennyson's two new volumes. On 15 August, during his visit with Venables in Wales, "H.L. did a very little of his review"—probably this one. The Lushington family papers have a fragmentary manuscript in Henry's hand that, before abruptly breaking off, has several substantial though inconclusive paragraphs interspersed with about a dozen unfilled blank areas. Ironically now, it is headed, "The Review which *must* be completed." It may have been intended for the Apostle J. M. Kemble's *British and Foreign Review*, which might have been expected to review Tennyson's book but for whatever reason never did. Not only was Henry physically ailing that summer but, along with other distractions, was perhaps spending too much time with Tennyson himself to spare the hours for writing about him. And then as he came to know the poet better, he may have grown the more reluctant to risk alienating a cherished friend who was always sensitive about his reviewers.

Apparently Henry was hoping to show that the newer, previously unpublished poems in Tennyson's second volume represented a definable advance in vision and technique over the more palpably captivating earlier poems in the first volume. But that would have been a formidable thesis to demonstrate, and Henry may ultimately have failed even to convince himself. His theoretical undergirding, in its leisurely nineteenth-century pace, is clear and sufficiently persuasive. An older poet, "thinking differently from the youth will write differently in proportion as his poetry is a genuine utterance of his state of mind (& no other poetry is worth much)." "He cannot write as he once could without imitating himself[,] one of the worst errors & worst failures possible for real genius—without producing the effect of falseness." A young writer's "original bent of mind . . . shows itself prominently in various exuberances, beautiful in themselves, but faulty in their connection"; later, that bent will "exhibit itself in the peculiarity & individuality of his manner, in all that constitutes style, all that makes it possible to distinguish one writer from another." The young poet's luxuriance too often obscures his thought; "the thing is beautiful but out of its place," like "a rose garland hung on the branches of an oak." With growing maturity he "leaves roses where they are" and "lets his oak speak or stand for itself," not wishing "to deck with flowers the beauty & strength of a tree of the forest." The supreme example of such development was Shakespeare, whose "profuse unbridled fancy" in his early poems and plays ripened into the tightly controlled language of the late tragedies, "where every word tells—if you change it you alter the meaning." Unfortunately, though, such salutary development had too rarely occurred. Most poets during the past half-century had written "their best books before 25, & . . . after 35 very few ever wrote anything worth reading." Not only did countless once-promising youngsters fail to develop at all ("a few years hardening and the sensitive poet steps forth the defaming reviewer"); but not even the giants of the age—Southey, Coleridge, Byron, Wordsworth—had surpassed their early achievements.

Tennyson, Henry wished to argue, was one of the few who had "victoriously" made that "necessary transition." But the manuscript hardly shows at all how that opinion would have been sustained. Henry mentions only three post-1833 poems—"Audley Court," a "proof" that the eclogue, "this very beautiful form of poetry[,] has greater capacities than we have been used to attribute to it, in relation to our own country & times"; another eclogue "Walking to the Mail," mentioned without comment; and "Dora," a "simple story told with a perfect and touching simplicity," although too prosy and sometimes imperfectly versified. We can only speculate how Henry would have treated such outstanding newly published poems as "Ulysses," "Morte d'Arthur," "Locksley Hall," and "The Vision of Sin." Or what feats of close reading he might have performed with a few well-controlled displays of Tennyson's revisions in "The Lotos Eaters" and "The Lady of Shalott."

The best thing in the manuscript—some might say the only solidly practical thing—is Henry's discussion of "Mariana." Tennyson's "distinguishing characteristic" had always been "a singular power of embodying states of mind & emotion in natural imagery."

> . . . With him images taken from external nature are not introduced merely as illustrations to explain the thought or heighten the emotion by combining with it the impression of some beautiful object—they are the very form in which the thought is embodied, not a separate aid to its forcible expression—an idea is transfused through the imagery, & the idea & the picture strike the mind as inseparably one.

So it was in the "beautiful & touching" "Mariana":

> Desolation, sadness, loneliness are the ideas which it is intended to convey & they are conveyed by the description of the old house in the middle of the dreary land more than by any full expression of the feelings of the deserted maiden. It is a picture of which every part every minute accessory aids in telling the story of the solitary and central figure—"She only said, my life is weary"—It is the entire reality which is given to this by the scenes around that make its simplicity so touching. Much might have been

said of her feelings, much would have been said by many writers—but it is better to convey those feelings through the medium of nature by making us see the scene as Mariana herself might have seen it.

Obviously no one can tell from such a fragment what the completed review would have contained, but nothing actually in it seems very auspicious for its success. Hindsight tells us now that the hour had hardly yet come for a review directly posing an older Tennyson against a younger. Henry himself would probably have known much of what we learn from Professor Christopher Ricks's edition of Tennyson, that nearly every notable poem in the 1842 volumes had been first composed within the five years following the appearance of the December 1832 collection, and several of the most memorable ones—"The Two Voices," "St Simeon Stylites," "Ulysses," "Morte d'Arthur," "Break, Break, Break," "Sir Galahad"—probably before 1835. Tennyson himself, for all his "ten years' silence," was not yet thirty-three when his 1842 volumes came out. Not yet written were most of the richly varied triumphs of his post-1840 style: much of *In Memoriam*; most if not all of *The Princess*, including its matchless songs; *Maud*; "The Holy Grail" and so much more of the *Idylls of the King*; the sermon, and the final lines of *Aylmer's Field*; the supremely perfected "Tithonus"; "In the Garden at Swainston" with its tribute to Henry ("Three dead men have I loved") along with Hallam and Simeon. Although the review remained unfinished, Henry's premonitory critical instinct would later be vindicated many times over. Tennyson was indeed "victoriously" making the "transition." But it saddens us to be left standing so close, yet so far, from a live demonstration of what with better direction, or firmer resoluteness, Tennyson's "best critic" might have been able to do.

On 6 July occurred the first of the year's two events centering around Park House that live on in poems by Tennyson. That summer day Edmund opened his grounds for the annual festival of the Maidstone Mechanics Institution. It was one of numerous such organizations flourishing in England since the latter 1830s, encouraged by Owenist and other Socialist elements, and dedicated to the educational and moral improvement of the laboring classes. At a typical festival the people participated in games, heard music, joined in group dancing, and saw educational demonstrations of electrical and other scientific innovations. The *Maidstone and Kentish Advertiser* described the goings-on at Park House: two bands, "one for quadrille, and one for country dancing"; "cricketing, trap bat and ball," and other games; a "cannon . . . occasionally fired off, ignited by a spark from an Electrical Machine about 20 yards away"; "a model of a steam engine . . . turning a circular saw with great rapidity, and . . . of a steam boat plying round a light house"; a table displaying such "philosophical instruments" as "telescopes, microscopes, etc. etc." A "capacious booth erected for the occasion" seated eight hundred persons for tea. Afterward "a large fire balloon ascended," and finally, in the evening, a bell summoned everyone to "assemble on the summit of the hill in front of the house," where they voted appreciation to Edmund for his hospitality and heard his "appropriate" expression of delight for "the interesting manner in which the company had amused themselves, and the decorum which had prevailed throughout the day."[28]

In well-honed blank verse, the Prologue to *The Princess*, published five years later, immortalized the day, apparently with few if any invented details:

> For all the sloping pasture murmured, sown
> With happy faces and with holiday.
> There moved the multitude, a thousand heads:
> The patient leaders of their Institute
> Taught them with facts. One reared a font of stone
> And drew, from butts of water on the slope,
> The fountain of the moment, playing, now
> A twisted snake, and now a rain of pearls,
> Or steep-up spout whereon the gilded ball
> Danced like a wisp: and somewhat lower down
> A man with knobs and wires and vials fired
> A cannon: Echo answered in her sleep
> From hollow fields: and here were telescopes
> For azure views; and there a group of girls
> In circle waited, whom the electric shock
> Dislinked with shrieks and laughter: round the lake
> A little clock-work steamer paddling plied
> And shook the lilies: perched about the knolls
> A dozen angry models jetted steam:
> A petty railway ran: a fire-balloon
> Rose gem-like up before the dusky groves
> And dropt a fairy parachute and past:
> And there through twenty posts of telegraph
> They flashed a saucy message to and fro
> Between the mimic stations; so that sport
> Went hand in hand with Science.

We can imagine a shyly smiling Edmund—along with a radiant Cecilia and other Tennysons, including Alfred, and various younger Lushingtons—moving with reserved cordiality (his father would have brought it off more heartily) among his motley guests. Imagine him we must, for Tennyson does not present

Edmund in the Prologue. Certainly he was not the middle-aged Sir Walter Vivian, stage stereotype of a titled landowner descending from a line of knights extending back to Agincourt and Ascalon. Nor does a thirty-one-year-old Greek professor meet the specifications for young Walter, home with six comrades from college. If any Lushington, this Walter would have been nineteen-year-old Franklin. And if so, then the "petulant" sister Lilia, "wild with sport, / Half child, half woman," would have been Louisa Sophia ("Louy"), a year younger and Franklin's sibling companion since their earliest childhood. From other indications, Louy seems to have been the sister most like her studious brothers, the one who would most have excelled if universities had admitted women. We can picture the two late adolescents, as in the poem, reclining on the grass comfortably close together at the picnic "feast" set out for the family and friends, including "lady friends from neighbouring seats" (the Tennyson sisters among others). If Franklin had ever patronizingly patted Louy's head while making a slighting remark about women, he would have been disappointed if she had not fired back:

> . . . 'There are thousands now
> Such women, but convention beats them down:
> It is but bringing up; no more than that:
> You men have done it: how I hate you all!
> Ah, were I something great! I wish I were
> Some mighty poetess, I would shame you then,
> That love to keep us children! O I wish
> That I were some great princess, I would build
> Far off from men a college like a man's,
> And I would teach them all that men are taught;
> We are twice as quick!' And here she shook aside
> The hand that played the patron with her curls.

Lilia's role in the Prologue was to motivate the framing device for the succeeding seven books, whereby the seven college boys would successively extemporize a tale of a preposterous "female university" ruled rigidly by the larger-than-life Princess Ida. Ida is not Lilia (or Louy), but only what Tennyson's seven romanticists contrive to make of the "great princess" of Lilia's dreams.

On 14 October—not the tenth as sometimes incorrectly stated[29]—came the wedding in Boxley Church of Edmund and Cecilia, four days after her twenty-fifth birthday. The Epilogue to *In Memoriam*, addressed to Edmund, ecstatically describes the event, and releases Alfred's delight: "Nor have I felt so much of bliss / Since first he [Hallam] told me that he loved / A daughter of our house."

The poet, who had "danced" his infant sister "on my knee," "watched her on her nurse's arms," and "shielded" her "all her life" from danger, now succinctly eulogizes her bridegroom:

And thou art worthy; full of power;
    As gentle; liberal-minded, great,
    Consistent; wearing all that weight
Of learning lightly like a flower.

The bride "enters, glowing like the moon / Of Eden on its bridal bower." Her "blissful eyes" see first Alfred, then Edmund, and brighten "like the star that shook / Betwixt the palms of paradise." Standing before the altar, "Her feet, my darling, on the dead; / Their pensive tablets round her head" (one of these at Boxley memorializes the poet, travel writer, and Virginian colonist George Sandys; another the family of Sir Thomas Wyatt, poet and reputed lover of Anne Boleyn), Cecilia exchanges vows with Edmund and joins him in signing the register. The bells overhead begin

. . . the clash and clang that tells
    The joy to every wandering breeze;
    The blind wall rocks, and on the trees
The dead leaf trembles to the bells.

On the porch the "maidens of the place" (these would include Mary and Matilda Tennyson and the four Lushington sisters) "pelt" the party with flowers. But "white-favoured horses wait" for the newlyweds, who exchange farewell kisses with loved ones, "and they are gone." There is more—the subsequent "feast, the speech, the glee."

Then Tennyson reaches, or overreaches, for a prophetic climax to *In Memoriam*, an epitomizing of the optimistic postulates of his sections 106 to 131, that would justify his resolution to end with the aparently irrelevant wedding. A son born to Edmund and Cecilia might pick up the mantle of the fallen Hallam and help advance the race along a divinely directed evolutionary scale toward ultimate moral perfection ("the Christ that is to be").[30]

A soul shall draw from out the vast
And strike his being into bounds,

And, moved through life of lower phase,
    Result in man, be born and think,
    And act and love, a closer link
Betwixt us and the crowning race

. . . .

No longer half-akin to brute,
  For all we thought and loved and did,
  And hoped, and suffered, is but seed
Of what in them is flower and fruit;

Whereof the man [Hallam] that with me trod
  This planet, was a nobler type
  Appearing ere the times were ripe,
That friend of mine who lives in God,

That God, which ever lives and loves
  One God, one law, one element,
  And one far-off divine event,
To which the whole creation moves

In retrospect the unanticipated irony of these visionary lines is almost unendurably bitter. Fourteen years and six days after that wedding day, on 20 October 1856, the only son of Edmund and Cecilia, a sweet-tempered boy not yet thirteen, would finally die from a terrible lingering illness. One wishes the stanzas had not been written. Indeed, interesting as the entire Epilogue is to a biography of the Lushingtons, Tennyson's masterpiece might have been a more unified work without it.

Even with a joyous wedding and with his poems selling gratifyingly, these were unhappy months for Tennyson himself. By the summer of 1842, Dr. Allen's wood-carving speculation, in which Tennyson had sunk his patrimony, was facing imminent collapse.[31] Tennyson wrote at least two heated letters (one now lost) to the doctor attempting to disengage his mother and sisters from the risk.[32] Lawyers had advised the family that after Cecilia's marriage Edmund might be "liable to the debts of his wife" if she was involved in a failed enterprise. Mary Tennyson wrote Mrs. Allen on 21 July that the Tennysons had heard "strange and dismal accounts" of the speculation lately from several quarters, "and the anxiety it creates amongst the house circle is painful." Alfred "fidgets himself to death"; she feared he might relapse into a "complaint" he had recently suffered which might endanger his heart.[33] On 15 October, the day following the wedding, Tennyson wrote Mrs. Allen demanding that she stop her husband from borrowing £1000 from Septimus Tennyson, then staying in the asylum, who probably did not have "another thousand in the world." Allen had "already at different times received from our family about £8000," so that Mrs. Tennyson and the daughters were now "living upon my brother Charles" and Alfred himself was "a penniless beggar and deeply in debt besides."[34]

How nearly penniless he actually was remains a matter of conjecture. Robert

Bernard Martin, not very confidently, estimates a comparatively comfortable £500 to £600 for his income in 1843.[35] But half or more of that total is £300 a year that Martin believes FitzGerald gave him between 1843 and 1845. Martin's source is a statement by Carlyle in his old age to Charles Eliot Norton—a story rejected, with Lang and Shannon "emphatically" concurring, by the editors of FitzGerald's correspondence.[36]

By the final weeks of 1843, Tennyson's health had become so deranged by nearly "two years" of "perpetual panic and horror" that he was nearing total nervous exhaustion. Having to "write a letter on that accursed business threw me into a kind of convulsion."[37] It must have been very early in December that he voluntarily entered a water-cure establishment at Prestbury near Cheltenham, where he would remain for more than six months. (He wrote to Fitz-Gerald on 2 February, "I have been here already upwards of two months."[38] The *OED* defines *upwards of* as "rather more than.")

The letter that induced the convulsion was almost undoubtedly one now recently published for the first time. Tennyson wrote it from Cheltenham, where his family had moved from Boxley, and dated it on 30 November, no more than a day or two before he began the water cure. It should materially alter our perception of what Edmund did when he paid for an insurance policy payable on the death of Dr. Matthew Allen. Tennyson wrote to a London solicitor, Joshua Julian Allen (apparently the doctor's solicitor, probably not a relative), informing him that "Mr. Edmund Lushington of the College, Glasgow will this year advance the money to be paid on the life assurance in case it is *impossible* to procure it from the right quarter."[39] The right quarter would have been the doctor himself, who three years earlier (23 November 1840) had given Tennyson "the Policy of my life for two thousand pounds as security . . . for the sum of nine hundred pounds and the sum remaining to be paid over to Mrs. Allen, unless a further sum be lent me, then to receive the amount of such further sum as may have been advanced."[40] Since Hallam Tennyson's *Memoir*, Tennyson biography has known that Edmund "in 1844 [apparently in 1843] generously insured Dr. Allen's life for part of the debt."[41] But the transaction has seemed faintly surreptitious, if not downright shady (Christopher Ricks carefully calls it "a shrewd act of kindness"),[42] not less so for Cecilia's declaration on 11 December 1844 that "Old Allen still lives—it is a sad thing one is obliged to wish for the death of any man—I suppose thou knowest that Alfred will get most of his money back when that desirable event takes place—to secure this Edmund pays some eighty pounds a year for him."[43] Surely Ricks was not the first to reflect that such a letter "might have attracted the attention of the police"! But now we can be assured that Edmund was quite openly maintaining a policy that the doctor himself had taken out for Tennyson and renewed two times. Unexpectedly, the doctor died in early January 1845, and Tennyson regained his £2,000. The protection had cost Edmund £160.

From cryptic entries in Venables's journal, it appears that the marriage at Boxley may not have come off without creating tensions in the Lushington family. Having been away from London for four months, Venables returned in late October to find a mass of letters including some from Chapman "containing most of the curious episode of the past six weeks. His intent for writing is such that I think if it was known it would be generally admired." Possibly, but not necessarily so. Chapman seems to have been less than squeamish about casting unflattering reflections or imposing extreme interpretations. Yet he was a recurrent visitor at Park House, being closer to Henry and probably also to the sisters than to Edmund, and would later be, if not already, in love with Emily Lushington. He would be keenly sensitive concerning the younger Lushingtons' prerogatives. Venables himself, whom Tennyson had informed of the engagement in mid-May, had been disappointed by Edmund's prolonged secretiveness. Not even Henry had mentioned the engagement until late August. "Probably one ought to be glad" about the marriage, Venables then wrote, "& I can hardly say I am sorry, but how unwise it is in such cases not to enlist those who will be losers, in the cause, by a little confidence & appeal to their sympathy." He may have been recording personal worries only, no longer so assured of ready welcome to Park House, under a new mistress he had not met. Or his potential "losers" might have included other Lushingtons. At the least, there were latent strains that would soon enough become actual. It could hardly be otherwise when the mistress, absent along with the master half of each year, would for the other half be sharing her home with four sisters-in-law of her own generation who had lived there since childhood and would still do so the year around. Although varying from year to year, at times with two of the sisters at Malta, at others with Cecilia and her children not returning with Edmund to Glasgow, the situation would remain trying to the nerves of all. And Cecilia's nerves were never strong.

VII

An Ill-Fated Heir and a Stillborn Book

1843–1844

<hr>

T HE BEST SURVIVING SPECIMEN of Henry's practical criticism of poetry—a twenty-six-page review of Thomas Babington Macaulay's *Lays of Ancient Rome*—appeared in February 1843 in the Anglo-Catholic *Christian Remembrancer*, edited by the "Apostle" Francis Garden.[1] The final nineteen pages closely examine lines, stanzas, and passages Henry considered superb, merely good, or downright bad. Macaulay had tried in English verses to embody his conception of the long-lost primitive ballads, ultimate sources, he believed, for the early chroniclers, who in turn were sources for Livy's Roman history. Henry welcomed Macaulay's attempt, having himself since childhood possessed an enthusiasm for Roman history and Latin poetry that complemented Edmund's for the Greek. He was a keen student of prosody, and would always be attracted to the spirit and sound of ballads and other martial poems. Independently of Macaulay he was convinced that Livy's prose displayed vestiges of much older poems, with accentual rather than quantitative metres, faint traces of occasional rhyme, and "strong indications of the systematic use of alliteration," all presumably closer to modern European than to classical verse.

But Henry thought that Macaulay had too indistinctly perceived the "peculiar difficulties of his task": his battle poems should have tried not for "an ideal *battle*, but an ideal *poem*." Since it was innately impossible to create "a perfect illusion"—a faithful replica of a primitive Roman ballad—the poet should have aimed at aiding us "to reduce into form" our "own vague conceptions of those forgotten poems." He should have strictly avoided "anything decidedly incongruous," such as his overly obvious echoes of Sir Walter Scott. In his best passages Macaulay had kept his mind "imbued with the characteristic colouring of his original, altogether renouncing Scott, and following, if any one, Livy." Through a "high and successful effort of imagination," he had "caught . . . the very tone and spirit of the old legend. . . . The imagination of the poet has given life and reality to the knowledge of the antiquarian, and the two are harmoniously combined."

Straightforward, unadorned, uncluttered narration with just a hint of the teller's wonder was what Henry most commended when he found it in Macaulay—that "which reminds us sufficiently of Livy, not too much of our own ballads":

> And with a mighty following,
> To join the muster came,
> The Tusculan Mamilius,
> Prince of the Latian name.

Henry's favorite stanzas in the book— "decidedly and far the best passage"— were two coming near the end:

> They gave him of the corn land,
> That was of public right,
> As much as two strong oxen
> Could plough from morn till night
> And they made a molten image,
> And set it up on high,
> *And there it stands unto this day,*
> *To witness if I lie.*
>
> It stands in the Comitium,
> Plain for all folk to see,
> Horatius in his harness,
> Halting upon one knee
> And underneath is written,
> In letters all of gold,
> How valiantly he kept the bridge
> In the brave days of old.

Through their simplicity the stanzas had triumphed:

> By simply stating the traditional fact, but by stating it in the right tone and right spirit, by the sudden emphatic reference to the daily experience of

the poet's hearers, by the use of earnest, simple, antique, yet unaffected diction (we are but giving prosaically the means which it required a high effect of imagination to combine into the result,) Mr. Macaulay has in these two plain grave stanzas attained his object. . . .

Macaulay's great fault, Henry felt, was hasty diffusiveness. Eight shorter ballads instead of the four long ones would have been preferable. Macaulay had gratuitously begotten and christened too many extraneous characters, rigging them out with irrelevant histories simply to redeem them "from the reproach of being merely First Etruscan, Second Etruscan, and so on." There was too much pseudo-Homeric heaping on of details in descriptions of combat, too much ineffective elaboration in some of the speeches. "The consul Aulus answers in a 'bitter jest,' which might have been bitterer if it had been briefer." "Icilius rushes forward and 'Poured thick and fast the burning words which tyrants quake to hear'—that is, makes a long speech which, if here correctly reported, might have been heard by the most timid of tyrants without causing them to quake. . . . "

Seven "alarmingly raw-head-and-bloody-bone lines," probably the "worst Mr. Macaulay has ever written, or ever will write," were these:

And from the ghastly entrance
  Where those bold Romans stood,
All shrank like boys who, unaware, (!)
  Ranging the woods to start a hare, (!!)
Came to the mouth of the dark lair (!!!)
  Where, growling low, a fierce old bear (!!!!)
Lies amid bones and blood.

The unintentional absurdity of the lines seemed almost beyond belief:

There is something perfectly irresistible in the long-continued scale, ever rising with the rhyme, from the tranquil "unaware" to the comparative animation of "hare," thence to the truculent "dark lair," culminating in the growl of the "fierce old bear," and sinking down, under cover of that fearful crash, into its bed of bones and blood. The temptation, moreover, to transpose the two quadrupeds, "a fierce old hare," is one of which, Mr. Macaulay may be sure, the many boys, full grown or not, who read these poems will not be "unaware." We should doubt the goodness of that man's heart who could read the passage aloud, from the boys to the bear, without laughing.

The criticism was not inordinately cruel, considering its target. Macaulay's own excoriating of other writers, most notoriously of the hapless poetaster

Robert Montgomery, had earned him an immunity from critical clemency. But Henry also accorded Macaulay's better works high and particularized praise. Of his speeches: "sentences of noble and perfect eloquence . . . each like a medal of enduring metal, stamped with a high thought at once and forever." Of his prose essays: "the well-known, unmistakeable hand—the epigrammatic turns, the short, sharp sentences, the sparkling illustrations, the antithesis, always lively, and often (not always) just." Of his work in general: "Brilliant" was "the very word," although his reviews were occasionally marred by the "sacrifice of truth to point . . . the substitution of flashing cleverness for serious thought . . . the risks and temptations" of a writer who possesses "imagination, wit, and a dazzling power of language."

More than the typical early Victorian review, Henry's article exemplifies the merits of systematic normative criticism. It clearly enunciates and applies its criteria for a single genre—a cleanly imagined ancient Roman lay. It finds praiseworthy lines in generally dispraised passages, and inept ones in passages generally praised. Surely it must afford some intimations of Henry's critical acuity, so lauded by Tennyson, concerning particular lines or phrases. But necessarily it lacks the best of what Tennyson gratefully received: the tentativeness, the lowered voice and genuine smile that disarm constructive suggestion, all the pleasant informal exchanges between poet and trusted friend bending over a manuscript together.

Henry himself was growing increasingly discouraged from having no regular employment and no visible prospects. He had imbibed of his father's never-satisfied ideals of lastingly serving humanity, of leaving the world better for one's having lived. But now his life seemed permanently becalmed, an unpainted ship upon a faintly daubed ocean. Venables, lonely in a hotel room on circuit at Gloucester in early March, seeing no professional future for himself, felt that, even so, Henry's sense of failure was sadder than his: "I think with still more pain of H compelled as he is to adopt altogether a life as repugnant to his taste as this, which only occupies a short time, is to mine. He too has all my susceptibility to disgust, & fewer resources." (Henry's "taste" would have been for the public arena; the "resources" he lacked were vigor and bodily health.) Again on 24 June, Venables would record, "H . . . feeling very dissatisfied with the unmarked progress of time."

But for two or three months that spring, Henry did find urgent work—crucial, he believed, no less for Britain than for himself. Out of indignation against the rash perpetrators of the Afghanistan war and compassion for its victims he would construct two long articles for the *Christian Remembrancer*, exposing the war's indefensible beginnings and vividly recreating its inexorable course.[2] "We cannot undo the past [,]" he believed, "but a clear and just judgment on the past is the best and only preparation against the difficulties of the future." These would not be ordinary review articles, tediously scratched out to support some built-for-the-occasion thesis or to extract payment from a publisher. They would enshrine his most encompassing convictions. How else could he hope just then to rise from physical debility and galling obscurity to help redeem his beloved nation from mortal sin? "Impolicy, error, want of judgment,—these are calm terms which trouble and shock no one; but the charge of shedding blood without just cause, is felt at once to be no trifle. Let it be felt so more and more."[3] Several primary documents, eyewitness accounts by participants, had by then been published but inadequately evaluated. Henry would synthesize these and strike.

On 1 March, soon to leave on circuit, Venables recorded, "Looked at the beginning of H's India review, which seems good." Back from circuit on 14 April, he found "H occupied all day with his interminable article on Afghanistan"; the next day "H again working hard at his review"; on the seventeenth "H sent off part of his review"; on the eighteenth "H at last finished & sent his article." But that was only the first article. On the twentieth he began the second, which he finished in about three weeks. The two together were a *tour de force* of seventy-five gripping pages, approximately forty-thousand words. On 13 June he read the proofsheets. Ten days later, as we have seen, he was feeling let down, naturally enough, "very little satisfied with the unmarked progress of time."

That summer he briefly attempted to be a barrister without risking illness from the rigors of a circuit. At least twice in June, he held briefs in the county court at Maidstone, less than a mile from Park House; but in early July he experienced opposition to his holding Maidstone briefs (to the presumed disadvantage of others faithfully enduring the circuit?), and this seems to have closed that episode.

Edmund and Cecilia returned from Glasgow on 3 May. More than fifty years later, Edmund, probably working from a diary, recalled that journey, with the number of travel hours each day. "In those days little help was afforded to travellers in the north by railways. Our journeys were generally performed in coach or postchaises." They consumed three days going from Glasgow to Lancaster, and on the fourth day reached London, "part at least no doubt by railway."[4] It would be Venables's first glimpse of Cecilia, but he found her so unwell that it was "difficult to judge of her looks. . . . I scarcely conversed with her." We know now that she was in the early months of pregnancy. And she, who never before had lived in a town larger than Tunbridge Wells, had suffered her first dismal winter on the slum-enveloped campus at Glasgow, which later she would describe: "black houses and thick fog is my almost daily view made more hellish often by a red glow through it all—proceeding from the numerous fires in and about this city of dirt and dumps."[5] When she returned with Edmund to London on the twenty-ninth, Venables joined them at tea, where "she talked more than before"; but on the next day, he was still fretting: "There seems little chance of ever having an opportunity of becoming acquainted with" her. And, indeed, although he would see her frequently over the next forty-five years, his journal seldom indicates his ever trying very hard to understand her.

Tennyson would be seeing the Lushingtons through most of the summer and fall. His mother and her family moved away from Boxley to Cheltenham no later than September,[6] but he did not join them immediately. Two Lushington family letters provide vivid glimpses of their poet visitor. On 26 September, Edmund and Cecilia gave "their first great dinner party." On the day before, as Emily described it, the house was a hubbub. A child, "little Poddy,"[7] was "hammering away on the piano, making double the noise that she would if I wanted her to play Fortissimo." Ellen, "for once," was "talking hard & energetically, appealing to everybody against Edmund's shabbiness in having cheated her out of riding to make a call with him, & sent her instead in the carriage with Cissy [Cecilia]." Henry was "calling out every five minutes to come with him to shoot." The butler was "demanding an answer to some questions about new dishes." Edmund was "affecting great eagerness about shooting, solely to get rid of" Henry's calling. Emily herself was sitting "at the table writing . . . and answering . . . innumerable questions that everybody keeps putting to me & each other." But there sat "the poet at one corner of the sofa the only one perfectly quiet, deep in a book."

A week or two earlier,[8] several of the family had been at the seaside at St. Leonards (near Hastings). As Louy related it, they had sent "a sort of invitation" to "the poet" to join them, but "did not much expect him to come." One day looking down from Hastings Castle, "on the road below we half recognized two persons walking up the hill . . . at a very quick pace." Louy, "looking through a crevice in the wall, remarked to myself and Ellen 'That man walks very much like the poet!' 'Yes,' says Ellen, 'and he looks about just in the same way.'" The other man, in "white trousers—cap," was "rather like Edmund," who was not expected at all. The girls hurried down the hill and "found we were right. The old fellow [Edmund] and the poet had walked 9 miles from Maidstone to meet a coach, and come to spend a day or two with us." (Edmund fifty years later would single out that experience, how he and Alfred "walked the first 10 miles of the road carrying a bag between us, and then found the help of a coach for the remainder of our journey.")[9] But some of the greatest hilarity (again described by Louy) came after Edmund's return to

Park House. The cliff at Beachy Head drops five hundred sheer feet to the sea. "The poet," not very seriously we may hope, expressed "a strong desire that we should all get into the phaeton and drive right over the most perpendicular part of the cliff and we have just been agreeing that when we are all tired of life we will set out perfectly coolly and all drive over."[10] Two of the sisters that day had "donkeys which went at a marvellous slow pace in spite of Ellen's and our belabouring them, till when we returned home Ellen leapt on the laziest with astonishing energy and set it off trotting in a way which nearly killed Harry [Henry] and kept the walkers at a pretty considerable pace for some time."

During late October and early November, Tennyson alternated between Park House and London. Sometimes he stayed with Venables and at times took a room in a Charlotte Street lodging house. On 1 November, Venables "looked over many of A.T.'s Hallam elegies, some of them new, & all beautiful & touching." It was probably this same manuscript that nine months later, following his half-year stay at a water-cure establishment, Tennyson instructed Venables to keep "till I see you." He supposed he himself had "slipt it behind your books to keep it out of people's way, for I scarcely liked everyone who came in to overhaul those poems and moreover the volume itself was not fit to be seen, foul with the rust dust and mildew of innumerable moons."[11]

Up in Scotland on the last day of the year, Cecilia gave birth to a son, much to the delight of all Lushingtons. Inevitably, he was named for his grandfather, Edmund Henry. Soon all the "working people" around Park House were calling him "the young squire." Edmund wrote: "It's very odd but I certainly get to care for that little wee baa, and to like him rather, and to think him less of a brute than most children. He coos and oos at his mama as if he were a bullfrog, where as he is but a human tiny absurdity." Cecilia declared simply that "his smile is quite beautiful." Returning from Glasgow in early May, both he and his mother "stood the journey capitally." Edmund was relieved that Cecilia, breathing again the fresh Kentish air so unlike the nauseous fumes of Glasgow, had "not been so well for many weeks, months I might perhaps say." At his christening in Boxley church, where in the churchyard twelve and half years later he would be buried, little Eddy "behaved decently, save that he laughed at the parson, which greatly scandalized the curate's eldest daughter, aged 4; she said it was very wrong of him indeed."

The early months of 1844 found Henry back at his desk, diligently readying his Afghanistan material for book publication. The publisher, John W. Parker, West Strand, felt—all too correctly, and even then too hopefully—that the peak of interest in the question had passed, but that a book might sell if it included a treatment of British India's more recent annexation of Sinde, which from Henry's viewpoint was no less iniquitous than the proceedings in Afghanistan. The discussion of Sinde, with appendix and notes, fills the last 136 pages of a 301-page volume that appeared at the end of May: *A Great Country's Little Wars; or, England, Afghanistan, and Sinde; Being a Sketch with Reference to Their Morality and Policy, of Recent Transactions on the North-Western Frontier of India.*

All the devious negotiations and mutual tergiversations of the Sinde conflict, ending in two brief bloody battles in 1843, have long ago been faithfully processed and prudently filed away in histories of the Empire, together with the more appalling accounts of the Afghanistan horrors. What matters here is the way Henry's book preserves the spirit of this almost forgotten young man. Here is a descriptive passage from the second Afghanistan section:

> The third morning found them at the mouth of the Khoord Cabool Pass, a disorganized multitude of from fourteen to sixteen thousand human beings, having as yet suffered comparatively little loss from the direct attacks of the enemy. But the two dreadful nights of frost had already paralyzed them. "Only a few hundred serviceable fighting men remained." At this point they were assailed in force by the savage Ghilzies. Losing men by their fire at each step, the column pressed on through the terrible defile. At the top of the pass they halted, leaving in it, according to Lieutenant Eyre, 3000 men, having in three days completed fifteen miles, and ascended to a still colder climate than they had left behind. . . . The next day, the fourth since leaving Cabool, was spent on the top of the Khoord Cabool, in negotiation and delay. Under the circumstances, this seems to have been sheer madness. One march more might have carried them clear of the snow. . . . [The delay] sealed the fate of the army, who must with the followers even now have amounted to more than 10,000 men, but most of them helpless, hopeless, and disabled; utterly without shelter, food, or fire; remaining day and night on the snow. The unfortunate natives of Hindostan suffered, of course, more than the English: hundreds of them were seen sitting on the snow, not sunk in the apathy of despair, but howling with pain.

On some pages the condemnation of Britain's international outlawry is ironic and epigrammatic. Defenses of wrongdoing often rest "upon the general but transparent error, that a good man in private life is incapable of injustice as a ruler. A man may be good and amiable towards Englishmen, and yet be unjust toward Affghans and Belooches." Of the British ministers ultimately responsible: "The blood was shed far off,—[their] hands were never stained with it,— why should it be required at [their] hands?" "Since vice first paid to virtue the homage of hypocrisy, the conqueror has never wanted a pretext sufficient for all who chose to find it so." "The Indian Government, however, were apparently well satisfied with their own conduct towards Dost Mohamed; they wiped their mouth, and said they had done no evil." "A conqueror, who re-nounces the harmlessness of the dove, should at least try to have a little more of the wisdom of the serpent." "Surely, surely, we were not set up in India for this only; to teach its hundred nations once again the one lesson which it seems the world in six thousand years has perfectly learnt, that strength is strong."

Other pages depend upon the building up and gentling down of rhetorical tension:

> Many a worthy friend of civil liberty, who follows up with virtuous indig-nation the case of a drunken man, unjustly knocked down in the next street by a policeman, cares little whether it is with justice or injustice that we have slain our tens of thousands in Asia. Many a subscriber to Bible Socie-ties, many a zealot in the cause of converting the heathen, hears with coldness, and considers with indifference, the recital of actions which may turn the hearts of countless millions against the very name of Christianity. This indifference is the cause, but it is part also the consequence, of ignor-ance, and of ignorance which is to a great sense unavoidable. . . .
>
> A few words written in the Cabinet of England are like the sudden removal of a tiny bolt, setting free the complex forces of a great engine. The vast machinery of Oriental war stirs and works; armies march, ar-tillery rolls, lands are wasted, cities are stormed, the thrones of Asia go down, half the human race is shaken with alarm. And for all this—the nation does not care. It must learn to care, if it would keep the right to be proud of its empire. . . .
>
> It is an every-day remark, that the first step in wrong is often all. The man who has freely taken it finds himself no longer free. A second step must be taken, and then a third, each enforced by an increasing penalty. Nearly such is the progress of nations in a course of injustice; but with this difference, that to retract a criminal step is far more possible for an indi-vidual than for a statesman. At every stage of international transactions new interests spring up, new duties are contracted; and even if the right and wrong do not actually change sides, the result often is, that the nation cannot right its original wrong without wronging others whom it is bound to protect. This is part, and an appropriate part, of the penalty for national wrongs.

Paradoxically, we may think it now, all these apparently anticolonial sen-tences came from a man who still fervently believed in the idealist defense of colonialism, being convinced that even with "every drawback that can be named, with all their faults, national and individual," the English represented to the Indian people "a something above . . . and better than themselves[,]" something to be respected and imitated, but "not if we place obstacles in the way; not if we teach them to make the significant distinction, '*We know* that you are powerful; *you say* that you are just.'" England's "real mission" in India was "not to crush, but raise." Every "broken word, every gratuitous war, every unjust acquisition, not only stains the present indelibly, but retards or destroys some part of the promise of the future." All English persons indifferent to those considerations were "so far indifferent to their duties as English citizens"; persons in authority who failed to correct such abuses were "so far unfit to guide the destinies of England"; and those who deliberately abused their power were "false to the best hopes of mankind, and ten times false to the highest glory of their country."

Henry had given his rhetorical all, and with no mere rhetoric. It was sufficient, but too late. The book sold scarcely at all. As Venables later recalled, "Henry Lushington's name was unknown, and he had allowed the height of flood to pass."[12] The loss most regretted by Henry would not have been money. He never would have hoped for torrential sales, only for an audience fit though few. The theater, alas, was empty. Attention had shifted to other concerns, other sensations.

Fortunately in that summer of Henry's disappointed hope, Edmund as usual was present at Park House with Cecilia and the new child. Even more fortuitously, the beloved younger brother Tom returned in July on furlough from India after nearly thirteen years. Franklin, aged twenty-one, was home too; he had been only eight when Tom last saw him.

Additionally, a near-brother, Alfred Tennyson, would be around for much of the summer and fall. He had taken leave of the water-cure, saying he would return, but did not. By 29 July, after a jaunt into Wales, he was back in London, staying in Henry's and Venables's empty rooms in Mitre Court. About 15 August he abruptly turned up at Park House, visiting, among others, his sister and new nephew. On 19 September, Henry wrote Milnes that Alfred had come "down here one afternoon . . . bringing with him things for a day or so; and he is now entering the fifth week of his sojourn, with (I hope) every prospect of indefinite prolongation thereof." He seemed to have benefited "from the water treatment, or its concomitants. Yet he has been very unwell during the last three days." He would not exercise physically. "Indeed if one of the *earlier* set of Apostles were to heal him for the time ever so completely, he would not continue well—as long as he paid so little attention to the words of healing: '*arise and walk*.' How can a man with such great natural strength of body live so indolently, & be well?"[13] Henry, having himself almost no bodily strength, may not have intuited what we may surmise: that his large-framed friend was undergoing some of the lassitude of depression, a condition periodically experienced by most if not all of Dr. Tennyson's offspring—Edward the most grievously, but also indisputably Septimus and Arthur, as well as Cecilia Lushington.

Tennyson's stay at Park House would not have extended much behond mid-October. Cecilia and Edmund left early in the month. By 21 October, Henry had gone to visit Milnes at Fryston. Tennyson twice visited the Carlyles, in the early and middle parts of the month, while again staying in the Mitre Court rooms.[14]

One would enjoy speculating that during those nearly two months at Park House, Tennyson had begun to write parts of *The Princess*, discussing them with Henry. Possibly, barely so, but evidence is lacking and probability seems poor. Park House was more than usually crowded just then, and Tennyson seems to have required relative solitude for composing, although afterward he could discuss revisions with those whose judgment he trusted. Martin, probably correctly, considers Tennyson's health too poor during those weeks to produce much if any poetry.[15] What he and Henry just then had in common, though not necessarily discussing it, was battered self-assurance. For six months Tennyson had shut himself away, much of the time proscripted from writing or reading, and had still not substantially recovered from his ailments. Henry had reached out to his fellow-Britons and had personally encountered that national deafness which his book had so forcefully condemned. Tennyson could give courage as well as receive. That had been his comradely way with Arthur Henry Hallam, who almost as much as Tennyson during their great four years of friendship had needed, and been accorded, a quality of reassurance that he was simultaneously reciprocating.

VIII

The Princess *and a Maltese Appointment*

1845–1847

T ENNYSON HAD NOT PUBLISHED any poem longer than his 462-line "The Two Voices," although since 1833 he had been accumulating the individual lyrics for his eventual masterpiece *In Memoriam*, published finally in 1850. Now, early in 1845, or slightly sooner, he began another book-length work, eventually entitled *The Princess*, apparently in the back of his mind since about 1839. Through a semi-farcical fantasy involving a female university ruled by a despotically zealous feminist princess, the poem attempts to suggest the ideally relative roles of women and men in a properly balanced society. The first edition, December 1847, was followed early in 1848 with a somewhat revised second edition dedicated to Henry. Perhaps the dedication was an afterthought, a belated, inexplicit reward for Henry's encouragement and practical assistance during Alfred's nearly three years of composition. Such an elongated experimental work would have provided numerous opportunities for practical suggestions. Throughout its composition Henry was at hand in England, seeing the poet at frequent, well-spaced intervals. It must have been mainly with this poem that he merited Tennyson's later praise for his critical acumen.

If Henry did substantially help perfect *The Princess*, when and where did Tennyson write it and when could he and Henry have seen the manuscript together? This chapter will suggest a tentative chronology.

Tennyson was staying with his mother and family in Cheltenham in January

1845 when he received the news of Dr. Matthew Allen's death,[1] after which he would recover £2,000 through the life insurance Edmund had kept valid for him. He departed for London to visit FitzGerald (Venables saw him there on 17 January), but returned to Cheltenham by the first week in February.[2]

In London he and Henry were two of seven men at a dinner party given by the wealthy old poet Samuel Rogers. An eighth guest, arriving late, was Richard Brinsley Sheridan's daughter, the Honorable Mrs. Caroline Norton, a writer and feminist with a notorious reputation since her estranged husband had accused her of immorality with Lord Melbourne. Although a court trial had vindicated her, Tennyson squeamishly shunned her at dinner, afterward compared her to a serpent, and declared he had "shuddered sitting at her side."[3] John Killham's book about *The Princess* suggests she had been in Tennyson's thoughts back in 1839 when he was first mulling over the idea for such a poem. Killham even speculates that a known conversation with fellow Apostle John Kemble, who despised Mrs. Norton and railed against feminist innovations, including female colleges, may have partially stimulated Tennyson's initial plans for his poem. Killham refrains from claiming that Caroline Norton was "the model for the Princess in the poem."[4] But if his other conjectures are correct, Tennyson's unexpectedly encountering her six years later may have regenerated an interest in the project. In early March at Cheltenham, he would be reading to Venables from his new manuscript.

Decades afterward, in 1885, Edmund disputed an account that seemed to dissociate Park House from the fashioning of *The Princess*. Thackeray's daughter, Anne Ritchie, had asserted in an article that the poem "was born in London." What did "born mean?" Edmund demanded of Hallam Tennyson. If it merely denoted "published, so were all his poems; if it has any other sense, I dispute its correctness—certainly it was mainly written in his Boxley period (which extended from Autumn 1841 to 1846-47)." But Edmund's full statement shows that the time, terminating in 1843, when the Tennyson family actually resided at Boxley, was not that of *The Princess*. Edmund recalled first seeing and hearing "the first book, beyond which not much was written at that time . . . in the summer of 1845," when Tennyson was "staying at Eastbourne and I went down to him. But many a time after that I remember parts of it being read or talked about at Park House."[5] Since Edmund lived at Glasgow from October through April, those "many" times at Park House would have been limited to early fall of 1845 and the summers and falls of 1846 and 1847. Although Edmund did not place the actual composing at Park House, Lushington family tradition has it that Tennyson wrote at least some of *The Princess* in a now-demolished little garden house there. In any case, until Henry left for Malta in 1847, Tennyson visited so frequently and sometimes so extendedly that the Lushingtons could have felt that his "Boxley period" was continuing. Edmund was ending it with Henry's departure for Malta.

Furthermore, in common justice, Edmund might have reflected, wherever some of Tennyson's scribbling might have chanced to occur, *The Princess* was essentially a Park House, and in no sense a London, poem. Its real world setting, in its framing situation, as opposed to its contrived fantasy, was Park House through and through, in the Prologue indisputably and hardly less so in the Epilogue—a Park House idealized there forever, high on its Kentish hill, contemplatively looking out and down upon the world below:

> . . . we climbed
> The slope . . . and turning saw
> The happy valleys, half in light, and half
> Far-shadowing from the west, a land of peace;
> Trim hamlets; here and there a rustic tower
> Half-lost in belts of hop and breadths of wheat;
> The shimmering glimpses of a stream; the seas,
> A red sail, or a white; and far beyond,
> Imagined more than seen, the skirts of France.

More puzzling is Hallam Tennyson's highly questionable assertion in the *Memoir*, which fortunately Edmund did not live to read, that *The Princess* was "mostly written in Lincoln's Inn Fields."[6] That would have meant while stopping with James Spedding, but no other biographical sources seem to indicate that Tennyson stayed with Spedding for any substantial time during 1845 to 1847. Hallam, of course, could have queried his father where the poem was written. If so, could Tennyson have misunderstood the question, or forgotten earlier circumstances, or Hallam have wrongly remembered the answer? Or was Hallam attempting to minimize the participation of Henry Lushington? But if so, why?

Actually, it seems almost certain that considerable portions of *The Princess* first came to life neither at Park House nor in London, but at Mother Tennyson's house at Cheltenham. There in "a little room at the top of the house in St. James' Square," remembered by Dr. Buchanan Ker, brother of Mary Tennyson's husband, as "not kept in very orderly fashion," with books and papers "quite as much on the floor and the chairs as upon the table," Tennyson, "pipe in mouth, discoursed to his friends more unconstrainedly than anywhere else on men and things and what death means."[7] There too, in an ideal kind of solitude, both away from and close to persons who loved him, he could perhaps unconstrainedly write. There, at least, as we shall see, he stayed during some ten weeks of 1845 between early February and mid-April, crucial weeks for the

early shaping of the poem. And he stayed there during other crucial periods in
its composition.

He had returned from London to Cheltenham around the first of February.
Venables, on circuit, visited him there a month later on 7 and 8 March. On the
eighth, "called again on A.T. & sat with him a couple of hours. He read to me
the part which he has written on the Female University—part of which I like, &
the story is amusing, but I am afraid the language is often too trivial."

The previous evening's entry should interest any old-fashioned Tennyson-
ians still speculating about Tennyson's "sources": "went up to A.T.'s room, &
sat a good while, he reading out passages from [Shakespeare's] Pericles &
Love's Labours Lost. He is a very fine critic." Scholars have long remarked
upon situational similarities between *The Princess*, where young females at a
college are forbidden by their royal headmistress to look upon any males, and
Love's Labours Lost, where a young king and three male companions in "a little
academe" futilely swear to see no females.[8] And as Killham notes, both *Pericles*
and *The Princess* present joustings for the hand of a princess. If Tennyson actually was remembering *Pericles*, the "mention in the Prologue of the Shakespearian precedent for a winter's tale would . . . gain rather more point."[9] Well,
whatever such genetic considerations may be worth critically, Tennyson was
indeed deliberately reading both these plays—a comedy and a romance—while
settling into the composition of his own comico-romantic "medley." Probably
at least one motive for turning to Shakespeare was to feel the Bard's matchless
blank verse—its pacing, its overtones, its exquisitely achieved adaptation to the
unique spirit of particular subgenres or kinds of plot situations. His wife's journals during the 1850s show him laying aside his pen and reading aloud from
Shakespeare's plays and from Milton during periods while deep in his making of
various Arthurian idylls.[10] Nonplagiaristically he was wooing the Longinian
"effluences" that wait to pass from master artists to receptive successors.

By 15 April, manuscripts in hand, Tennyson was back in London, where
Venables saw him at his publisher, Moxon's, house. Two days later Aubrey de
Vere found him "at first much out of spirits" but he "cheered up soon," and in
two sessions of reading "'crooned' out his magnificent elegies [parts of *In Memoriam*] until one in the morning." The next evening de Vere heard some of
"the University of Women" [*The Princess*].[11]

On the twentieth Tennyson went down to Park House, almost certainly (as
usual) taking along his manuscript, and stayed a week. It would have been the
first opportunity for him and Henry to consider the poem together. The two
returned to London on the twenty-eighth. For the next week, every day and
evening often until past midnight, the Mitre Court chambers were so crowded
with Tennysons (Alfred and Horatio), Lushingtons (Henry and Tom), and assorted friends that Venables despaired of getting his own writing done.

Then after 4 May, Tennyson abruptly disappears for several weeks from Venables's journals, although de Vere saw him on the tenth and again heard more from *The Princess* manuscript.[12] Soon thereafter Tennyson went to the seaside at Eastbourne to stay several weeks. One letter by FitzGerald indicates that he may have gone on or near the twelfth, although Elizabeth Barrett wrote on 22 May, "Tennyson is still here" (but he may have left without her knowing it).[13] Certainly he was in Eastbourne during June, for Venables records his return from there on the twenty-second.

On 15 June, while Tennyson was at Eastbourne, Venables made an overnight visit to Park House, arriving by one route shortly before another party came by another: Cecilia, her mother, Franklin Lushington, and "a Miss Sellwood." Obviously the Sellwood name meant nothing to Venables; but he was meeting Emily, Tennyson's former fiancée and future wife. She and Tennyson were pledged not to meet, and did not do so until they accidentally did at Park House two years later. So closemouthed had Tennyson and the family been concerning the engagement and its termination that more than one of his close friends besides Venables had never heard of it.

More than two decades later, Emily, as Tennyson's wife, would set down for her sons some idyllic memories of Edmund and Cecilia at Park House in those early years of their marriage. Cecilia "reigned as a queen to whom all did homage. It was pretty to see that daily tribute from her husband, the nosegay so chivalrously given. Student as he has always been . . . he had never the manner of a student, but one of graceful, though shy charm."[14] The nosegays, readily procurable from the extensive flowerbeds of Park House, would have looked pretty indeed to Emily, who in those years had given up hope of marriage. Edmund would never lose all his shy charm nor his love, or sympathy, for Cecilia. But as we shall find, and as Emily Tennyson knew well enough by the time she penned her lines, Cecilia's tenure as undisputed queen of Park House had never been very secure, and by then was long ago past.

During late June through at least the first week in August, Tennyson was back in the London area. Henry too was there for part of the time. But by mid-August (as verified by a letter posted on the twenty-third), Tennyson was sojourning again at Eastbourne.[15] There, "during the hottest part of the summer," Edmund, as he recalled forty-eight years later, found his poet brother-in-law "lodging in one of two cottages prettily grouped together, bearing the well-deserved name of Mount Pleasant." He had "completed many of the cantos in 'In Memoriam' and was engaged on 'The Princess,' of which I heard nothing before." Edmund's ambiguous "of which" probably means *from* rather than *concerning*, for surely he would not have been unaware of a new work that Henry would certainly have heard, and told him about. *The Princess*,

Edmund recalled, had "hardly advanced" beyond the first book.[16] Edmund was remembering accurately. Before leaving London, Tennyson had shown Fitz-Gerald "two hundred lines of a new poem in a butcher's book."[17] Part one in its present form has 245 lines, of which about forty were added after 1847. By the time Edmund came, Tennyson may have proceeded somewhat into part two. One day Tennyson gave Edmund "a perfectly novel surprise": "I have brought in your marriage at the end of 'In Memoriam,'" showing him the stanzas of the Epilogue.[18]

Tennyson's letters and Venables's journals continue to reveal Tennyson's movements from place to place. Lang and Shannon convincingly locate him in London until late September.[19] On the twenty-ninth he wrote from Chelten-ham to Sir Robert Peel to accept a Civil List pension of £200 awarded for literary merit. At the beginning of October, he gave Henry's London chambers as his address, but by mid-month was back in Cheltenham,[20] apparently for the remainder of that year. He was planning to visit Henry Hallam, historian father of Arthur Henry, near Bristol at the end of the month, and declared that he would "not be in London in November." Edmund and Cecilia and little Eddy had visited the family at Cheltenham: "the little one looks like a young Jupiter with his head full of Greek: but she poor thing, was out of health and dreaded the winter in Glasgow, which does not agree with her."[21] During that dreaded Glasgow winter, Cecilia's fourth, she would be carrying her second child. Ve-nables was in London from November until late December, and his journal does not mention Tennyson.

On 9 January 1846 Venables dropped in at Cheltenham, having learned from Charles Tennyson Turner that Alfred was "very unwell." Apparently he had some kind of internal infection. Venables sat with Tennyson for an hour in his room. He was "tolerably cheerful," but described "his pain as very formida-ble." Soon afterward Venables talked of Tennyson with George G. Barrett, Elizabeth's brother and leader of Venables's circuit, who told his sister, prompting her often-quoted remark to Browning that, ill or not, Tennyson was writing a new poem. He had "finished the second book of it—and it is in blank verse and a fairy tale, and called the 'University,' the university members being all females. . . . I don't know what to think—it makes me open my eyes. Now isn't the world too old and fond of steam for blank verse poems, in ever so many books, to be written on the fairies?"[22]

Again, as in 1845, Tennyson remained at Cheltenham through the winter until early April. Venables, instead of going on circuit, stayed in London all winter, practicing his profession before parliamentary committees—his initia-tion into the branch of law that eventually made him wealthy. He recorded Tennyson's arrival from Cheltenham about 9 April, no more than a week earlier than the previous year. There seems no way of telling how much of *The Princess* he had written since January, but in the relative quietness of Cheltenham, the opportunity had been present. Venables saw Tennyson on the twenty-fourth and the twenty-ninth, when Henry was also in London, and several times in early May.

By 16 May, Edmund had returned from Glasgow, looking "paler and thinner." Henry and Tennyson were not together often during that month, since Henry was working hard on a pamphlet (of which we shall hear more later). During early June, Tennyson visited friends on the Isle of Wight. On the twentieth Venables went to Park House for the weekend, finding Cecilia "very ill & languid," but little Eddy "looking very well." Four days later Cecilia gave birth to a daughter, who in her turn was named Cecilia but would be called by the uneuphonious nickname of Zilly, which in later life would increasingly ill-match her earnest, understated dignity. She alone of her parents' four children would attain full adulthood, finally inheriting Edmund's properties and dying in 1921 in her seventy-fifth year.

In the final days of June, Tennyson was back in London, where he spent four days together with Henry. Then, apparently, he went down to Park House for the better part of a month, Henry being there too, except for one period of less than a week. Edmund wrote to Frederick Tennyson on 5 August that Tennyson had stayed with them "two or three weeks."[23] Venables's journal shows that Tennyson left Park House on 21 July. Henry had gone from London to Park House on 1 July, but not in company with Tennyson, who could have already arrived there or would come a day or two later. Either reckoning allows about three weeks at London and Park House during which Tennyson and Henry together could again have carefully examined *The Princess*. By then the poem had grown substantially. At Park House on 20 July, Tennyson read to Venables "the Female University, of which I heard the beginning in the spring of /45 at Cheltenham. It improves greatly as it goes on, & I think very good, showing considerable power of construction in addition to other merits." (One suspects the composing had proceeded at least well into book three, if not beyond. Although the second book, more than twice the length of the first, displays constructional power, the plotting decidedly picks up pace in the third.) The next day Tennyson and Venables returned together to London, where Tennyson began preparing for a journey with Moxon to Switzerland, begun on the first day of August and concluded on the last.[24]

With Venables out of London during September and October, Tennyson's movements are more difficult to follow. Venables saw him at Cheltenham on 20 October, and letters show him there until late in November.[25] From about the twenty-fifth until late December, he was back in London, as also was Henry much of the time. If any more of *The Princess* had been composed during the weeks at Cheltenham, Henry again could have read it with him. On 22 December, Tennyson was at Cambridge for the three-hundredth anniversary of the founding of Trinity, as were also Henry and Venables and a troop of Apostolic and other brilliant friends. The talk must have been electrically heart-warming. But by 4 Janury 1847, Tennyson was settled again in Cheltenham, where for the third successive winter he remained through most of March. By then *The Princess* was substantially finished.

Henry was now well into his thirties, ever chafing beneath a galling sense of underutilized talents. Constantly less than robust and seldom far from ill, he could scarcely anticipate even normal longevity. Although never wealthy, he was less in need of money than of self-fulfilment. Months were ticking away into years. If he died, it would be to the world, and almost to himself, as if he had not lived. Such frustration can breed desperation. If any opportunity emerged for significant service, he might imprudently risk premature death. With his sense of impending mortality, Henry, like Tennyson's Ulysses, might decide it futile "to store and hoard" himself when he might yet do "something near the end,/ Some work of noble note." But what?

Meanwhile humbler opportunities for voluntary service might materialize now and again. One such appeared to beckon during a week in the spring of 1845. For neither the first nor the last time, the moderate Tory prime minister Sir Robert Peel had placed public interest above partisan expediency and supported a parliamentary bill widely unpopular in his own party. His proposal to increase the grant to the Maynooth Seminary in Ireland, which educated Roman Catholic priests, aimed to treat the Irish majority religion more equably, and to reduce nationalist agitation. But in England the issue united diverse anti-Catholic elements, and might then and there have overthrown Peel's government. The bill passed, but only through heavy support from the opposition Whigs: Peel's own party rejected it 149 to 148. Peel had forecast the result: "This Bill will pass but our party is destroyed." Within little more than a year, but only after he had courageously acted to repeal the Corn Laws, a combination of his natural opponents, the Whigs, and his old High Tory enemies within his own party would bring him down.[26]

Henry, ever more liberal than Tory, approved of the Maynooth grant. But at Cambridge as well as Oxford, the measure had numerous opposers, along with nuclei of dedicated supporters. As the final vote approached, opposers in the Cambridge Senate drew up a petition urging the bill's defeat; then its supporters at Cambridge dispatched a petition of their own. In London it was Henry who rallied a cluster of friends to compose a petition and track down favorable signatures from Cambridge men scattered around the metropolis. For eight bustling days the work went on from the Mitre Court chambers, men going and returning with hand-delivered signatures. Finally on the afternoon of 1 June, Henry, Venables, James Spedding, and one other carried the petitions with exactly three hundred signatures to the two M.P.'s from Cambridge.[27] One of these, Henry Goulburn, Peel's chancellor of the exchequer and closest friend, would as a foregone conclusion vote "Aye"; the other, Charles Ewan Law, the late Chief Justice Ellenborough's second son and hence a cousin of Henry's, would almost as predictably vote "Nay." The petition changed nothing; but Henry and the others had meant it primarily to endorse Peel's high-principled stand. They were less than edified when the amiable Goulburn, miscalculating that they were all zealous Peelites anxious to preserve the Ministry, gravely tried to reassure them: "You will be glad to hear, gentlemen, that our friends on the other side are not seriously hostile. They take it up *only as a matter of principle.*" Henry, "though he fully appreciated the unconscious humour," was "disposed to grudge" the trouble he had taken.[28]

Not so entirely altruistic, perhaps, was Henry's publishing in 1846 of two trenchant pamphlets concerning railways.[29] The issues discussed affected all of the British public, but the chief immediate beneficiary would have been a single company, the Great Western Railway, in which, as it happened, Henry was a stockholder. In fact, he finally put out his pamphlets in collaboration with Great Western officials.[30]

Historians of British railways call the years 1845 to 1847 "the Great Railway Mania." Schemes by the hundreds burst out for financing and establishing new railways or extending existing ones. Even after various wilder projects were eliminated, 217 railway bills came before Parliament in 1845, 435 in 1846, and 257 in 1847, until finally 330 bills had been passed authorizing capitalization in excess of 167 million pounds.[31] The demand for legal counsel to represent both the railway promoters and their various opponents before parliamentary committees created a boom in parliamentary law practice. Venables, who in later decades would rise to the top of the parliamentary bar, received his first such case in March 1846, followed swiftly by several others, paying him generously throughout the session. Henry too, during most of that May, between his two periods of pamphlet writing, worked hard on a parliamentary case. His purse might have become fatter and his life longer if instead of pamphleteering that year he had concentrated upon solidifying a parliamentary practice. But the question is imponderable, since the extraordinary demand for parliamentary barristers seems to have leveled off abruptly soon after 1847.

Henry's pamphlets undertook to discredit the report of a three-man royal commission appointed in the summer of 1845 to settle "the Battle of the Gauges," a complex of problems and conflicting claims resulting from the unfortunate coexistence in one small country of two rival widths (gauges) of railway tracks.[32] On the Great Western line from London to Bristol and on certain other lines in the south, the distance between the insides of the rails was 7 feet, a radical departure from the earlier 4 feet 8½ inches prevailing on the majority of lines. With existing locomotives the broader gauge facilitated greater speeds and more passengers; but at junctures (called "breaks") where the two gauges intersected there were various inconveniences. The commissioners conceded the superior capabilities of the broad gauge but recommended "entire uniformity" based upon the narrow. Broad gauge lines should convert to narrow; at the least, an equitable way should be found to "admit of the Narrow Gauge carriages passing, without interruption or danger, along the Broad Gauge lines."

These sensible-sounding recommendations teetered upon a foundation of refutable misstatements and illogical opinions elicited from biased witnesses who had not been cross-examined. Promptly, the Great Western published a long prosaic reply,[33] which Henry probably found invaluable when he penned his livelier attack. But he was already becoming knowledgeable about railways, having in the previous autumn become a director of a proposed Kent Atmospheric Railway, finally not constructed, one of several short-lived projects in those years for propelling the cars through pneumatic pressure created by stationary external engines.[34]

Aside from challenging the perspicacity of the commissioners and exposing the obvious bias of their witnesses, Henry's keenest rhetoric was leveled at two vulnerable targets: exaggerations of the evils of the break of gauges, and disingenuous testimony that the speeds then attainable on the narrow gauge were quite sufficient and, indeed, that the broad gauge speeds ought to be outlawed as excessive and unsafe.

The commissioners conjectured that a break might be deleterious to rapid transport of troops and equipment, especially when "little or no notice can be previously given." Henry feigned surprise that "our scientific Commissioners" had not heard of the telegraph: "In the course of their experiments on railways, their attention devoted to a comparison of their watches and the milestones, was never attracted by those curious wires, trained from post to post, along the lines." Transferring troops and their equipment would involve simply "walking from one side of a station to another." Offsetting such occasional disadvantage, the larger carriages and engines of the broad gauge could always, "carry something like double" the soldiers and "at least half as much weight again" as their narrow-gauge counterparts. The worst imaginable "breaks" were those already simply taken for granted: the ones between the various terminals around London. Eventually the problem might be remedied, but "in the meantime we bear it with as much philosophy as we can command, and do not talk of applying to Parliament for twenty millions to aid in removing it." A set piece in the commissioners' case was their description of a break: "The change of carriages, horse-boxes, and trucks, and the transference of luggage of an entire train of much extent must, even in the daytime, be an inconvenience of a very serious nature, but at night it would be an intolerable evil; and we think legislative interference is called for to remove or mitigate such an evil." Henry responded:

> The first sentence, massing carriages, horse-boxes, trucks, and luggage into one vast heap of confusion is indeed enough to weigh down the most elastic imagination. The Commissioners present us a lively picture of enormous mountains of portmanteaus,—every portmanteau we presume requiring a fresh reference to its owner as to its place of ultimate destination, not at once, and as a matter of course, transferred from Partition A in one train to Partition C in another; wandering passengers; distracted porters; kicking horses; all this limbo of the world in the darkness of night, and all exposed, unsheltered, in the rigours of winter; it being a thing impossible and unheard of to build an extensive station with an acre of zinc or iron roof, and to make some hundreds of gas lights supply the place of day.

Surely it would be within the limits of "the mind of man" to devise "some means of approaching one horse-box to another, in such a manner that the horse may be led from the first to the second with less risk than was originally incurred by placing him into the first." Nothing was "easier than to exaggerate a partial evil: nothing more unwise than to relinquish a great gain for a little inconvenience."

Greater speed was a blessing, and to deny the fact, much less to insinuate that demonstrably safe speed was undesirable, was downright dishonest. "Experience" had "proved that traffic grows with the means and facilities of traffic. Mere common sense shows that it is better to choose the system which is still beyond our growth, in preference to that which is within it." Yet three commissioners were presuming to decree for a nation that the possibilities of speed be deliberately turned backward. Surely speed was "after all . . . _the_ advantage of railways. They have others, but all secondary and dependent on this." Time was "equally lost, whether unnecessarily spent in moving boxes from carriage to carriage, or in sitting longer than is necessary on a train. . . . Men pay heavily for time, and time is gained by speed." Why was "delay so destructive, when the gain of time is so unimportant? Why are ten minutes lost between Bristol and Birmingham to outweigh two hours gained between Exeter and London?" (Obviously, neither Henry nor his narrow-gauge opponents had envisioned the greatly increased speeds potentially obtainable quite independently of gauge width, through improvements in locomotive engineering and the strengthening of tracks by methods including the conversion from iron to steel.)

Ironically, in the summer of 1846, Parliament ostensibly endorsed the commissioners' report but in effect emasculated it by allowable exceptions, so that the problem of the coexisting gauges was not finally solved until decades later, by which time Britain had more than thirty "breaks."[35] It is doubtful that Henry's pamphlets had any effect upon Parliament's action. Not inconceivably, however, they may have called new attention to his talents and thus to some degree shaped his future.

Except for the birth of Zilly, the most memorable incident in the Park House family during 1846 was Franklin's graduation from Cambridge that spring at the top of the Classical Tripos, a repetition of Edmund's achievement fourteen years earlier. In early December, as we learn from Venables's journal, Henry had made some sort of arrangement with the *Morning Herald*, possibly to write regularly for it. But we hear no more about that. In his thirty-fifth year, Henry was still reaching out in apparent futility for something significant to do with his life. So ended 1846, and 1847 began.

Then suddenly on 23 January, apparently without the slightest intimation of such a possibility, Henry received a letter from Lord Grey, colonial secretary in the new Whig government of Lord John Russell, offering him the chief secretaryship of the British government on the island of Malta. I have not succeeded in finding out what persons had recommended him for the post. The position ranked second only to the governor's in the civilian administration of the island, and under Lord Grey's plans to liberalize the Maltese government, gave promise of acquiring additional importance. But for Henry, particularly, there were two obvious disadvantages. Not only would it exile a no-longer-young unmarried man from family and friends but the humid Mediterranean heat might worsen his always precarious health. (The less-obvious drawbacks—the frustrations of coping with human recalcitrance in a notoriously complicated sociological and political situation—would make their appearances later.) The problem of loneliness would be partially solved by Henry's sisters, one or two of whom would always reside at Malta with him. The climate would ever be a hazard.

Henry's decision, traceable step-by-step through Venables's journal, proved quite literally agonizing. Clearly he desired, yet deeply feared, to go. He consulted physicians, including John (later Sir John) Liddell, who had directed the hospital on Malta, and Sir James Clark, leading authority on climate and chronic diseases. Apparently neither forbade his going, and another doctor recommended it. Other persons who knew Malta urged him to accept. But three of the ones who knew him best—Tom, Frank, and Venables—remained afraid. With him they spent the fourth day of deliberating, "rather in melancholy anxiety than in discussion," until late afternoon, when Henry wrote a refusal. Then almost immediately he became "much depressed." Venables, remorsefully convicting himself of having given biased advice, feared that Henry would "never be what he was before." Two days later, with Venables's reluctant encouragement, Henry wrote again conditionally "reopening the business," and soon afterward retracted his refusal. On 3 February, Lord Grey accepted the retraction.

But significantly, with the agreement sealed at last, Henry almost at once became again "very unwell," physically and emotionally. Venables had not anticipated "the gloomy view which he now takes of the business. It infects me." Throughout the next three weeks Henry would remain "in bad spirits," "seriously unwell," in a "very painful state of despondency." The worried family summoned Edmund, who petitioned the Glasgow faculty to be absent on "urgent business."[36] and arrived at Park House on 24 February. Henry, after five days with Edmund, was still "certainly not looking well," but had "recovered his spirits in an extraordinary degree." The need for self-fulfillment had prevailed over the premonition of death. He would take the risk, a very real one. Malta, seven years later, would claim the life of his sister Louy and, the following year, his own.

On 11 February, during Henry's deepest despondency, Venables, invited by Frank to Park House, was annoyed to find the place at that troubled time half-filled with assorted Tennysons: "Mary Tennyson and a Miss Hamilton, a Scotch old maid . . . also of course Horatio & Matilda Tennyson, which is a great nuisance." The next day Venables "found no opportunity of speaking to H, all day from the crowd in the house." Alfred, still at Cheltenham, would arrive some time before 20 March, when Venables, going down at Henry's invitation, found the poet there. That evening Henry gave Venables "an explanation" for not having written or invited him sooner. Most probably, Tennyson and Henry had been going over the newly completed *Princess*. On the twenty-ninth at London, Tennyson was ready to lend the manuscript to Venables, who on a railway journey to Hereford "read the greater part of the New University with pleasure and admiration." In court all day on the thirty-first, "without a symptom of a brief," he finished the poem, liking the end less than the rest, but pronounced it "a noble poem." Back at Park House on 4 April, before returning to the circuit, Venables left the manuscript for Tennyson, who "was expected."

By the sixteenth Tennyson had returned, intending, as he wrote to T. H.

Rawnsley, to "see the last" of his "brother-in-law's brother," who would soon be off for Malta and, "being a man of feeble stamina," was "afraid of the climate and altogether down in the mouth about it." Tennyson would "do my best to set him up, though I am very unwell myself." The Malta position would pay "(I believe) about £1500 a year."[37] Tennyson would remain at Park House until at least 25 April. By the first week in May, he was back in London; but before the month's end, he entered a hydropathic establishment at Umberslade, near Birmingham, where he would read proofs of *The Princess* and remain a month or more.[38] The poem would come off the presses at Christmas time.

Evidently Henry had not told Tennyson of a more immediate reason than the Maltese climate for his being "down in the mouth" just then. Early in April, as he informed Venables, the Colonial Office discovered it had carelessly overstated his authorized salary: the true amount was £1,000, not £1,500.[39] Again he became nearly ill from worry and suspense. As he later wrote the Colonial Office, he had "had some Parliamentary practice last year and expected some more this year, from which I have of course been precluded from what has occurred." But having not accepted their appointment from pecuniary motives, he would not refuse from such. Still he would appreciate being considered for a future salary increase. But Lord Grey agreed with his undersecretary that Henry "must accept the office at the present salary & without any consideration or understanding as to the future. Any future alteration of salary must stand upon different grounds."[40] In immediate compensation Grey granted Henry a leave, presumably on salary, by extending the sailing date until autumn.

Park House during those singularly unsettling months had perhaps seen more than its normal quota of visiting Tennysons, especially when we consider that Cecilia, the resident Tennyson, was away in Glasgow. In general, were Alfred and his siblings sometimes less welcome at Park House than they may have supposed? Plausibly so. But the only documentary evidence is a questionable paraphrase of some statements reportedly made that spring by Franklin Lushington to Arthur Henry Hallam's surviving brother Harry.[41] More heavyhandedly than lightheartedly, young Hallam wrote his cousin Jane Elton Brookfield that at dinner after "some guarded fencing, and preliminary beating about the bush," he had drawn from Franklin "the grand fact that the Tennyson habit of coming unwashed and staying unbidden was, is, and will be the great burthen and calamity of the Lushington existence, socially considered." The Lushingtons "actually groan under M. [Mary or Matilda?], who they expect will stay to keep up the establishment, when the original family retires to Malta." The last statement was an absurdity (more likely Harry Hallam's than Franklin's), since there never were any plans for more than two of the four

Lushington sisters to accompany Henry to Malta. Neither Hallam nor Mrs. Brookfield had forgiven Emily Tennyson, Arthur Hallam's bereaved fiance, for being supposedly unfaithful to his memory by marrying Richard Jesse, much less for subsequently retaining an annual allowance from Arthur's father. Harry Hallam's real target surfaces in his next sentence: "I did not venture to touch upon the delicate ground of E., but I expect they labour under undefined but not ungrounded alarms that Mr. J. may be a permanent fixture."[42] In short, Franklin had said nothing at all about the Jesses, but it was obligatory that Harry do so to Jane. Whatever Franklin may have said, Hallam had mischievously pumped from him. Anyhow, it would be a mistake to draw long-term inferences from the uniquely unnerving situation at Park House during that one spring.

Sir Charles Tennyson informs us that "Park House, under Cecilia's sway, always remained a haven of refuge for the rootless" Tennyson brothers and sisters.[43] No doubt that is to some degree true; but we would best take it cautiously. How frequent and during how many years was "always"? Actually, year in and year out during the decades after Cecilia married Edmund, there was relatively little visiting of Park House by the Tennyson brothers and sisters, especially after Henry departed for Malta. Matilda, the Tennyson spinster, is the exception since in the latter half of her long life and Cecilia's they were nearly inseparable companions. Most significantly, through the years, it is surprising how little total time even Cecilia herself, nominal mistress of the house, really spent there, even when not in Scotland with Edmund. These facts will emerge as our story proceeds.

Tennyson's own most momentous visit there was probably the one when he accidentally encountered Emily Sellwood, having almost certainly not seen her during the approximately seven years since the end of their engagement. In her epitomized journal Emily recounts that believing him gone to Italy she visited Cecilia, "who was very dear to me & faithful thro' all." He "appeared unexpectedly before breakfast. I returned home to Hale as soon after as I could."[44] But the awkward encounter led to Tennyson's renewing the courtship and finally in 1850 to resumed engagement and marriage.[45]

Sir Charles Tennyson does not attempt to date the meeting, and Martin places it only roughly as "early 1848"[46]—impossible because in 1848 until late spring Cecilia was in Scotland. But now at last Venables's journal provides an approximate date. Arriving at Park House from Wales on Friday, 17 September 1847, Venables found among several visitors "Miss Sellwood and A.T." On Monday, after a mid-day dinner, Tennyson surprised Venables by departing for London. Thus it was Alfred, not Emily, who first relieved the awkwardness. She "returned home" on Saturday, the twenty-fifth; significantly, as though on signal,

on that evening "A.T. appeared, to me most unexpectedly." Venables remained another week until Monday, 4 October, when he and Tennyson departed together. On Sunday, the tenth, Venables returned to Park House,
without Tennyson. Meantime, Emily Sellwood had come back; on Tuesday,
the twelfth, Venables records that "Miss Sellwood went." Quietly, she and
Alfred had avoided another meeting by alternating their visits.

Finally, after various delays, Henry would soon be off for Malta. While
waiting he had been perfecting his Italian, with instruction from one Bucca-
lussi, "a good-natured little" Italian master. Italian was indispensable for success in Malta, being the official language of the establishment. (Ironically, most
of the common people on the three English-ruled islands spoke neither Italian
nor English, but only their native Maltese.) On 2 October a doctor came to
examine Henry and his sisters Emily and Louy, who would go to Malta with
him. On the twentieth Edmund, Cecilia, and the two children said farewells
and departed for Glasgow. On the twenty-first Henry went to London for his
first meeting with the new governor of Malta, Richard More O'Ferrall
(1797–1880), under whom, as it turned out, he would serve for the next four
years. On the thirtieth he would at last be on his way.

Beyond broadest outlines, we will not be attempting to follow the details of
Henry's service on Malta during the final seven and one-half years of his life.
But his and O'Ferrall's assignment was plainly intended from the first to be no
mere continuation of status quo rule but a consciously bold, although carefully
controlled, innovation. As explained in Grey's 26 November 1847 dispatch to
O'Ferrall, two immediate innovations would facilitate "such amendments and
improvements as time and altered circumstances may render necessary, in concurrence with the feelings and opinions of the people for whose benefit they are
intended." First, responding to "a very general feeling expressed in Malta,"
O'Ferrall would be Malta's first "Civil Governor," free from the military responsibilities of commanding the garrison. Second, the overwhelmingly
Roman Catholic population would at last have a Catholic governor: "a
practical proof that religious opinions are no disqualification from offices of
great trust and importance under the Crown, and that loyalty to the Sovereign
and attachment to British interests will ensure to all classes of Her Majesty's
subjects, in every part of Her Dominion, an equal share of consideration and
confidence." O'Ferrall was charged ever to "bear in mind that an additional
responsibility attaches to the Government of an unrepresented people, and
renders it more incumbent on those who administer their affairs, to supply so
far as possible the advantages to be derived from direct representation by an
attentive observation of public opinion."[47]

One possibility for reform Grey and O'Ferrall were considering was the setting up of some sort of local municipal government. They asked Henry to proceed to Malta by way of Italy (instead of the usual shorter sea route from a port in southern France), investigating as he went the differing municipal systems in the several Italian states. The more arduous, if more interesting, route would keep Henry and his sisters in transit for more than two months, from 30 October to early January.

At the Colonial Office for his meeting with O'Ferrall, Henry sat nervously "waiting in this appropriately called Waiting Room," composing a letter to Milnes, then in Spain. More than half bantering, he recorded his worries. The papist O'Ferrall would be "my head—the head whose thoughts I am to think, especially on all points of doctrinal subtlety, and whose volition I am to execute." Milnes might soon "hear that I am, in the strict performance of duty, officiating as chief candlebearer at St. John's, and betraying the island into the hands of the infidel yet Papist infidel French, out of those of the equally infidel but Protestant infidel English." What "line" would he have to take between the Romanist governor and the notoriously Protestant Anglican bishop on Malta? "Shall I mediate? or shall I be ground to pieces in their collision? the one point on which they agree being that of burning the heretical secretary?" He was "writing such stupid nonsense" partially because "rather sicker at heart than usual," having "just seen Edmund and his set,—all of whom I do dearly love, including the most original of year-old babies [Zilly]—off for Newcastle— when & where next to meet them?—what a senseless, natural, inevitable question—put with the usual chance of answer to any really interesting question." Here the letter broke off as Governor O'Ferrall came in. Henry finished it at Park House a week later, two days before departing. He had liked "what I have seen of the governor." After leaving Paris he would "pick up . . . as much knowledge as I can with reference to the Italian municipal systems, & have letters to the embassies at Turin, Florence, & Naples," but would not remain long at any one place.[48]

It seems to have been during those final days before the departure that the longstanding friendship between Venables and Emily Lushington began to acquire a new dimension, a deepening of affection that would remain unfulfilled, bringing them, and to some extent the entire Park House family, long years of anxiety and mutual frustration. On 27 October he cryptically recorded, "Long talk with E., pleasant but not perhaps wholly so." On the twenty-ninth, after "Emily, Ellen, and Louisa each planted a pine by the clump to the S.W. of the house, & I an oak by the reservoir," Emily presented Venables with a rug she had "worked" for him. Next morning the party, Venables included, took to the road in the Lushington family carriage, which would convey them to Paris. Tom boarded a train, but the others "remained with the carriage—I outside with E. all the way to Folkestone. In other company I should not much have liked it on the rail, as the wind was high and the bridges rather near one's head." "Jesse and his wife [Emily Tennyson]" joined the party at Folkestone—in Venables's opinion "a great bore." The channel crossing to Boulogne was relatively calm. At the hotel during the evening Emily and Louy "persuaded" Venables to "come on to Paris." After the Jesses next day took the English coach for Paris, the Lushington party started "with four horses in the usual foreign fashion"—and with Venables still "on the box with E." The more than eight-hour journey through "driving showers" and generally drab landscape "was no doubt very tedious to every one else, but I enjoyed it as might have been expected." The next day was "bright and beautiful," the country more picturesque, and "the party to my infinite satisfaction arranged as yesterday." They reached Paris by evening but next morning, anticlimactically, Emily was "very unwell" and remained so, although not bedridden, for the next three days, causing a delay in the travel schedule. (Had she caught cold riding on the box through rain?) During the wait there was much walking about in Paris, and two visits to the Louvre. At last on 5 November "the parting came." "So ends," wrote Venables, "all the first part of my life—to be renewed?" Tom, "after innumerable changes of mind and grumblings," accompanied Venables by railway back to Boulogne and thence to England.

Henry and the others arrived at Malta early in January 1848. Finding no place for his sisters and himself to live within the capital city of Valletta, he rented a capacious villa at San Giuseppe, about two miles away, which he later purchased. As Venables later reported, the Governor "had, with a characteristic appetite for business, already provided abundant employment" for Henry as well as for himself. Henry "commenced his new duties with an energy" that injuriously affected his health. He had "never sufficiently acquired the power of passing lightly from one subject to another, or of dealing in a perfunctory manner with trifling affairs; and his rapidity, both of apprehension and of execution, was in some degree counteracted by an excessive solicitude for finish and accuracy."[49] Our twentieth century would have branded him tritely as "a perfectionist."

Not the least of his tasks at first was to compose his report—more than 17,000 words—describing, contrasting, and analyzing the municipal governments he had inquired about in Piedmont, Tuscany, the Papal States, and the Continental Neapolitan dominions. His conclusion suggested that his entire project had probably been a waste of strength. It would be easy enough "to adopt the forms or names of one or the other of the Italian systems, or form a modified system based upon all, and to give plausible reasons for introducing it into Malta." But Henry doubted whether "any such system or any municipal system at all, would work to the advantage of the people in the present state of Malta." All those Italian systems had "hitherto become a machinery for Government rather than a means of protection for popular rights." In Malta there were "so many points at which municipal and, so to speak, State purposes cross and are intermingled," that they would be difficult and disadvantageous to separate. Constructing a municipal system "would be working not with, but against, the tendencies of things; in other states, men have constructed a great many separate units into one political body; in Malta we should be breaking up a natural unity into artificial divisions."[50]

As we shall see, the restructuring that soon took place on Malta was by a quite different plan, although itself never very successful. In the new colonial edifice, Henry would occupy a cornerstone position.

IX

A Precarious Stability

1848–1853

T HE NEW YEAR, 1848, found only two Lushingtons, Maria and Ellen, residing at Park House. Tom frequently dropped down from his London rooms, but would return in November to India. Edmund and Cecilia with their two children had routinely begun their sixth dreary winter in his faculty house at Glasgow College. For him its notorious location, however much it offended the nostrils, had the advantage of proximity to his classroom. For her the place was an ordeal unmitigated, conducing to despair.

At last, in mid-January, he obtained a house in a better neighborhood; but Venables, visiting in the following November, found the "new house . . . small & uncomfortable," and the "whole impression of Glasgow depressing." When he walked with Edmund still farther "outside the smoke," the "day was very fine & the sunset beautiful." Edmund was "very well," Cecilia "looking ill," and both "hospitable as usual." Eddy by then was almost six, Zilly between two and three. A cramped house would amplify their childish noisiness. Their father every morning would start out, often through cold fog, in semi-darkness toward an underheated roomful of sleepy, mostly ill-prepared Greek students. He soon wrote Tom that the "children's row distracts every corner of one's brain." He was sleeping again "in college, & shall probably for 10 weeks except on holidays." This nightly separation from his family foreshadowed separations more radical during his remaining twenty-six years at Glasgow. In

October 1849, after subjecting her children to the perils of a cholera epidemic during the previous winter at Glasgow, and giving birth that summer to a third child (Emily, later called Emmy), Cecilia did not go north with Edmund. Nine years would pass before they again wintered together in Scotland; and even after that, she usually lived in Edinburgh, seeing Edmund only on weekends.

When Henry reached Malta in early January 1848, he was travel-weary, ill—by his own accounting "very nearly dead." Then, as he informed Milnes some ten days later, he had imprudently "plunged into work at once," risking "very serious illness." Although "not good for much yet, hardly round the corner," he felt hopeful concerning his work. His "Papist employer," Governor O'Ferrall, seemed "a good & kind man. I hope we shall agree very well. I would write more; but my head will hardly let me bend over to paper for five minutes together."[1]

Unfortunately, Henry and his earnest Irish Catholic governor would not long enjoy uninterrupted tranquility. Both were men of good will, each idealistic according to his values. But the revolutionary years of 1848 and 1849, with their violent upheavals in nearby Italy, were not auspicious for harmony between men of such divergent convictions. Henry eagerly sympathized with the Italian nationalist movement that broke out in Piedmont and soon affected most of Italy. Before the end of November, the well-intentioned but muddled Pope Pius IX, overwhelmed by developments in that revolution he had once seemed to be encouraging, had fled in disguise from the Vatican to the Kingdom of Naples. O'Ferrall, never disloyal to Britain but a dedicated Roman Catholic, felt mostly antipathy for Henry's admired Italian liberals, especially disliking their schismatic harrowing of the pontiff. After French troops dispatched from Paris, more or less at the pope's invitation, occupied Rome in July of 1849 and overthrew the new republican government, numerous refugees fled from inevitable prosecution carrying questionable passports issued by the British consul, reportedly with the tacit consent of the French. O'Ferrall's reluctance to admit the fugitives offended the humanitarian sensibilities of Henry, who saw no need to require a passport. Although the two men managed to carry on despite disharmonies, Henry would feel relief when O'Ferrall resigned in 1851. Venables would later claim that O'Ferrall was "the only person with whom, during his whole stay in Malta, or, I might say, in the whole course of his life, [Henry] had any unpleasant relations."[2]

Henry, then, in 1848 was beginning a career—the final seven and one-half years of his life—that would be sufficiently free of boredom but frequently replete with tensions. The last three and one-half years, under a new governor, would be less unpleasant; but by then Henry's health, precarious from the outset, would be further deteriorating. "On the whole," Venables wrote, "his strength diminished slowly from year to year." Perhaps physical inactivity, "his languid habits in the intervals of occupation and of social excitement . . . increased the debility which they indicated." It was "difficult to ascertain the effect" of the Maltese climate on Henry's "constitution, although he always himself considered it pernicious." He would sum up his feelings about the place: "We are tolerably well—barring that in Malta, to get up from your chair is, summer and winter alike, as great an effort of will as to walk a quarter of a mile in England; that nothing ever tastes like anything; that one does not sleep, and is sometime bothered; barring these and similar trifles, I am myself very well off at present."[3]

During January 1848 Venables was preparing for the private printing of four lengthy poems (including a dedicatory one) that he and Henry had made together over a span of several years. The single-paragraph introduction to the 90-page book, *Joint Compositions*,[4] printed anonymously in early March, explained that the poems had been "produced in conversation; a line suggested by one of the writers in his turn was often completed by the other; and there is scarcely a passage . . . which either could recognise as his own." The dedicatees, indicated only by four spaced asterisks above the thirty-quatrain "Dedication," were the four Lushington sisters,[5] who had been constantly ready "To catch our meaning at a word, / And, best of all, to listen." The three other poems were reflections upon persons or incidents in the contemporary pursuit of justice. If their high-intentioned verses failed, the authors would not be the first who "at morn have schemed / What noon dissolves in vapour: / 'Tis not so easy as it seemed / To put the world on paper."

The earliest of the poems, "Swing, at Cambridge," was written some time between December 1830, when its described events occurred, and January 1839, when Venables's journals begin. (The journals record the composing of the other poems, but not of this.) Peter Allen's *The Cambridge Apostles: The Early Years* (1978) reproduces nearly half of it.[6] Its forty-four lively six-line stanzas recreate the response of Cambridge students, including, as we know, Tennyson and some other Apostles, to a nearby rick-burning during the agricultural workers' agitation.[7] Students rushed out, joined bucket lines, and afterward talked themselves into readiness to defend the university from a rumored, but never materializing, attack. When their oracular "poet wise" (Tennyson) was mock-gravely consulted whether " 'any law of battle' " would be broken by " ' pouring from afar / Water or oil, or melted lead?' / The poet raised his massive head— / 'Confound the laws of war.' " A final section, omitted by Allen, condemns the subsequent hanging of one of the rick-burners: "A sight of bitter woe and shame, / A sight that brought man's wisdom blame, / A mournful tragedy." Following a perfunctory trial, the jury foreman pronounced " 'Guilty,' in easy tone." A market-day crowd jostled about the gallows. Surely that era of railroad building, an "age of boasted power, / Of conquered land and sea," might be expected to find a "worthier remedy" for crime. By a "gentlier kindlier spell, / Must greater works be done":

> When rich and poor in mutual trust
> Shall know each other and be just,
> Not bound by laws severe:
> And a true mother commonwealth
> Lead back sick children into health
> With love and gentle fear.

The most ambitious and least poetically successful of the compositions was "The Coronation," finished in April 1840. Its 513 lines in various meters and rhyming patterns describe London on Victoria's coronation day and evaluate the constitutional monarchy from several viewpoints: two Americans, a rabid and a more moderate British radical, a philosophical and a more conventionally patriotic conservative, a pragmatical Whig, a German metaphysician, an Anglican clergyman, and the mediating Spectator, who speaks for the two authors—the cautious, pessimistic Venables moderating Henry's quick indignation. All the varying positions had pieces of the truth: "Turning to each a different side, / The changeless truth is multiplied." Yet all positions were not equally true. History was displaying a pattern. In the previous century the men of the Enlightenment, growing "tired of home and ancient ways," the close walls and low roofs, had impetuously broken out, pursuing a "phantom hope." Tiring now of wandering, "some would fain / Rest in their old content again." Such reversion was impossible: "Our course lies onward, change and strife / Are better than self-blinded life. The "conscious march" must proceed to new conquest, not boastfully, ever mindful of the ancient virtues of Loyalty, Faith, and Love.

Less than a week after completing "The Coronation," the two friends began their best poem, "A Rural Ride," a 425-line tribute to the radical journalist William Cobbett. Alone the sturdy Cobbett departed from London one early summer morning:

> A labourer's son, 'mid squires and lords
> Strong on his own stout legs he stood;
> Well-armed in bold and trenchant wit;
> And well they learned that tempted it,
> That his was English blood.

Through pleasant farming country Cobbett would ride his horse southward toward "the prettiest town I know," which Venables's journal identifies as

Maidstone, and minutes earlier would pass a place we learn was Park House. As he rode along, he would see much to approve, and other things to disapprove. A mower was sweeping from right to left, his "thin sharp blade" cutting "cleanly through":

> With understanding critic eye,
> The rider watched each motion lithe;
> The length of stroke; the steady swing;
> And stopped to hear the whet-stone ring
> Against the upright scythe.

> But if he saw them droop and flag,
> He said: "They want their fathers' beer;
> "And much I dread, that tea and slops,
> "Supplanting honest malt and hops,
> "Have done the mischief here—"

The hostess of a small roadside inn "poured forth the troubles of her mind," how the agent "raised the rent, / And took the tithes in kind," and their horses were commandeered for highway work when most needed to stack hay, and the poor themselves were taxed poorer by the "poor rates." But when she piously consoled herself that life was short and heaven would be sweet, Cobbett would have none of that kind of passive millennial dreaming. The "lazy Methodists" were much at fault for the decline of rural England: " 'That barn with stucco plastered o'er, / 'And *Ebenezer* on the door— / 'I knew it boded harm.' "

With loving descriptions of the English landscape, the duo-poets escorted the old radical along his way: "thick planted trees and hedges rank," an old church tower "framed in deepest blue."

> Trembling with heat, the crystal air
> Quivered and glistened, as it were
> A silver woven veil.
> . . . .
> The light oats trembled on the slope,
> The rich wheat clothed the loamy plain—
> Red poppies blushed, and charlock bright
> With sunny steaks of yellow light
> Gleamed through the taller grain.

And then Park House, the best contemporary description we have of it:

> Before him rose the well-known mark,
> Where from the fir-toll in the park
> The walls of elm ran down,

Relieving with their depth of shade
The light grey walls of tinted stone—
Gay creepers decked with lavish growth
The goodly front that toward the South
Bowed out to catch the sun.

Dim openings in the laurel screen
Winding through light acacia bowers
Led to the pleasant walks behind;
To smooth plots safe from every wind,
And rich with tended flowers.

When a small child of a laborer, "big with his errands from the farm," became
frightened by some cows and the dogs herding them, one of the daughters of the
house tenderly came to his rescue. Cobbett "raised his hat and bowed his praise,
/ There was no man who all his days / Had honoured woman more."

Down the hill at the Kent County Hall, a milling crowd of working people
waited to greet their champion. A scornful baronet uttered a "gentlemanly
sneer": " 'See whom the thinking people's choice / 'Delights to honour with its
voice— / 'They love a charlatan.' " But another gentleman, more astute, demurred: he cared little for "clamourings of the crowd" who judged men and
laws "off-hand," but he wished " 'that their quick applause / 'Were never
worse bestowed.' " In Cobbett the people saw a British strength like their
own, mixing evil with good but making " ' our sullen island blood / 'Lead on
the march of Time.' "

"I know him well—on every side,
"Walled round with wilful prejudice:
"A self-taught peasant, rough of speech,
"Self-taught, and confident to teach,
"In blame not over-nice.

"What matter, if an honest thought
"Sometimes a homely phrase require?
"Let those who fear the bracing air
"Look for a milder sky elsewhere:
"Or stay beside the fire.

"There are worse things in this bad world
"Than bitter jests and bearing free—
"I hail thee, genuine English born—
"Not yet the lineage is outworn
"That owns a man like thee."

Cobbett's apologist was modeled from Henry's late father and Venables's friend, Squire Edmund Henry Lushington, known through his latter years at Maidstone as a liberal friend of the poor, one who in his capacity of magistrate was not above putting off dinner with his family to go down to the gaol and sign a release order for a prisoner, since " . . . if I wait till later in the day, the poor fellow might not have time to reach his home and friends tonight."[8]

The book was printed solely "for the amusement of some of those who may be acquainted with either or both of the writers." Venables sent off copies to various family members and friends, including Emily Sellwood, whom he had twice met at Park House. The British Library copy, used in this study, was that of B. L. Chapman, in 1848 an intimate friend of both the authors.

The summer and fall of 1848 brought the zenith of the uneasy attraction between the then thirty-eight-year-old Venables and the thirty-one-year-old Emily Lushington. She had returned in poor health from Malta, Maria having gone out to join Henry and Louy. Venables from the first was both eager and dreading to see her, fearful of the outcome of a more intensified friendship. For whatever reasons, never spelled out to himself (and gratuitous conjectures are no adequate substitute for fact), he obviously considered it untenable to consider marriage. If she should so come to love him as to wish for marriage the situation would become distressing for them both. And an estrangement from her family, one that he cherished as if his own, would have constituted emotional death for him and sorrow for them all.

On 1 September, lonely in London and frustrated at the collapse of half-formed plans to visit Henry and his sisters at Malta and Naples, Venables went down to visit the Lushingtons at the seaside at Eastbourne. Met by Edmund, and finding a room at a nearby inn, he began three weeks of near-idyllic enjoyment not to be equaled again in his life. His most satisfying times with Emily thereafter would seem "not as in 1848." Edmund and Cecilia and the children, as well as Tom, Emily, and Ellen, were there. Daily routines included walks and talks with all, bathing in the ocean with Edmund, rides by horse, excursions by boat and once "in a carriage to Pevensey, fine old ruins, such as one has often seen, though not in such company. Returning we walked over a desert of shingle to the sea, & by the fort home. Another day snatched from the burning." On 6 September: "I never was happier for the moment, but afterwards there come grave regrets." On the tenth: "In the middle of the day heavy rain came on with a gale. At night the sea was very grand. Out at it with E. & got wet." On the thirteenth, after a walk with Emily & Tom: "Ed. & E. E. [Ellen Eliza] met us. More personal talk than usual or formerly." On the sixteenth, after a rough boat ride with Emily, Ellen, and two others: "I read out some of Plato's Banquet, & a good many passages from Shakespeare—to my own pleasure &

theirs"; then "At night a most communicative talk, & I begin almost to think that the result is come that I have so long hoped & feared." On the seventeenth: "After dinner read Comus & Paradise Regained to E. & E. E. on the beach, & walked with them to Holywell, where we climbed down a steep path in the cliff. Back in fine starlight. One thought incessantly occupying me in many forms." On the eighteenth: "Read part of Hamlet & of Julius Caesar to Emily & Ellen under the cliff. They appeared to like it. . . . More talk of the same kind, but with a screw loose, as if I had been mistaken, which ought to content me & does not. I wish it was over." On the nineteenth (the day of his departure): " . . . out with E. & E. E., who were finishing pictures for me. . . . I am quite surprised at their kindness, which relieves my complicated regrets." Persons of strictest integrity, neither would deviate from Victorian propriety; but they would continue to be drawn to one another, and both suffer. The story is not irrelevant to a biographical study of Henry. We will later encounter the persuasive probability that Henry on his deathbed in 1855 intimated, at the least, to both Emily and Venables his wish that they would marry.

In late November, when Tom left at last for India after an extended furlough of more than four years, Venables accompanied him to Southampton. Afterward Venables took advantage of the occasion to write "for the first time a note to E.L."(He had first met her twenty years earlier.) Three days later came "a kind friendly note from E.L. with nothing particular in it but valuable as the only one I ever received." During the nearly forty remaining years of his life, and of their friendship, he would record the receipt of numerous others, but only a very few survive.

Henry's responsibilities on Malta acquired a new dimension after 11 May 1849, when letters patent from the queen's government reconstituted the Maltese Council of Government. Previously it had included no elected members; now it would have eight elected by popular vote, to serve together with ten official members, half of whom were Maltese. The new arrangement was a compromise between the desire of the Maltese spokesmen for a fully elected legislature and the opposition of Lord Grey and O'Ferrall to going that far. The governor would be president of the council with veto power. When it was in session, Henry as chief secretary would be heavily involved with its day-by-day operations, and would deliver frequent speeches defending the government's position on various proposals.[9] From the first he was skeptical concerning the council, and wanted to believe that the Maltese themselves were indifferent to the reform, since "a constitution is neither a church procession, nor bellringing, nor fireworks, and these are the real excitements of the Maltesian mind."[10] Evidently he was partially mistaken: of the 3,767 men qualified by education and property to vote, more than eighty-eight percent turned out for the first election on 16 August. Significantly for future controversies, no Liberal Maltese were elected, and three of the eight new members were Roman Catholic priests (one of them a titular bishop); eventually the priestly membership would reach five (sixty-two percent of the elected contingent).[11] The most heated debates, those in which Henry as a fervent believer in complete religious equality would become most deeply involved, would be occasioned by Catholic attempts to legislate preferential treatment for their religion.[12]

In mid-August 1849 Venables left for Malta to visit Henry and the sisters. Before he departed, Cecilia kindly presented him with "a pretty ring with the children's hair." Southward from Paris the weather was already "becoming greatly hotter" and would be worse at Malta. Henry's villa there had large "lofty rooms & a garden full of flowers." But Henry himself, looking "thin, pale, & ill," although "rather the better for extravagantly long hair and whiskers," soon fell severely ill, in pain every night for more than a week. Later Henry, on an extended holiday with his sisters and Venables in Italy, wrote that Venables "joined me . . . at Malta; became acquainted with the meaning of the term caloric, & the influence exerted by that mysterious force in cosmological arrangements; nursed me through an illness, and otherwise enjoyed himself; & finally left Malta in company with us on Oct. 2." The beauty of Italy was "really excessive," but as for Malta, "people all whose small wits have been gradually evaporated from them in that wretched little oven, do not recover them by a few weeks freedom."[13]

The Italian sojourn provided its politically instructive ironies. A fellow passenger on the flea-infested ship from Malta was the aging Neapolitan patriot General Gulielmo Pepe (1783–1855), who had unsuccessfully led troops against the Austrians as early as 1821; became for two decades a refugee; returned to Naples in 1848 to oppose the Austrians again, only to have his king call off the campaign; then led two thousand volunteers to Venetia, where he became the commanding general, and was again overcome by Austrians; escaped to Malta and was now bound for Genoa. While the ship was anchored for several hours in the Bay of Naples, "within sight," as Venables wrote, "of the dungeons in which the old soldier would have perished if he had stirred three yards from the ship," his "humbler and plainer spoken comrades" shouted "an edifying volley of abuse" at the Neapolitan "policemen and quarantine officers who lay alongside in their boat."[14] Henry's party too, although ultimately bound for Naples, was unable to put ashore there, since the kingdom of Naples was refusing to admit visitors from France, or from Malta, which was in "free communication with France." Persons from Malta had first to spend two weeks in the Roman States; but, of course, as Henry pointed out, the Roman States, then actually being occupied by French troops, were "in the freest & most constantly possible communication with France."[15] The fortnight of sightseeing in Rome, including inspection of damage from the recent summer's resistance to the French, passed rapidly. The travelers were off by carriage to the Neapolitan frontier and thence by train to Sorrento. They found Naples "full of anecdotes of royal ferocity," and although Englishmen were safe enough, all were pained by so much evidence of "the destruction of Italian liberty."[16] General Pepe had estimated no fewer than forty thousand political prisoners in Naples and Sicily. Henry had begun writing a spirited historical summary of the last two years' Italian wars; more than a year later the *Edinburgh Review* would published it in two installments. During most of November, Henry kept comparatively well; but Louy was alarmingly ill with a fever, visited by physicians daily or oftener. In early December they all returned to Malta, where Venables remained until mid-January.

Soon would begin the first session of the new Council of Government. Venables judged from a letter that Henry was "interested and pleased with his council work." On 4 April, came "some Malta papers with an admirable speech of HL's" about the Roman Catholic "question." The twenty-second brought another Malta paper, with a "long & able article" by Henry about Piedmont, which Venables inserted in the *Daily News.* "His energies," Venables felt, "are remarkable."

In the life story of Alfred Tennyson, the year 1850 is proverbially his "*annus mirabilis,*" when he published *In Memoriam,* finally married Emily Sellwood, and became poet laureate. The Park House circle, as we shall see, was actively involved in all three of those events.

Between 5 and 13 March at London, the proof sheets for *In Memoriam* had, as a friendly service for Tennyson, been read and corrected by Venables. The book appeared in late May. The two lengthiest sections of the elegy—85 and the epithalamial Epilogue—seem addressed directly to Edmund. The Epilogue indisputably is; and the similar phrasing in the two salutations—"O true in word and tried in deed" (85) and "O true and tried, so well and long" (Epilogue)—would hardly have been a mere coincidence. True, parts of 85 predate Tennyson's friendship with Edmund; nothing survives in documents to link Edmund to that poem; and Hallam Tennyson in 1913 dropped an earlier note that had identified Edmund as the poem's addressee.[17] Yet within the poem the addressee, a tactful friend, earnestly but gracefully concerned with Tennyson's welfare, resembles the Edmund Lushington of numerous later letters to the poet. He questions Tennyson, "to bring relief / To this which is our common grief, / What kind of life is that I lead." Was Tennyson's "trust in things above / . . . dimmed of sorrow, or sustained"? Had his love for Hallam "drained" his "capabilities of love"? The interrogator's words, lightly reproachful, "half

exprest," had "virtue such as draws / A faithful answer from the breast."
Reasssuringly, Tennyson replies that his "pulses . . . beat again" for "other
friends" and for the "mighty hopes that make us men." The "widowed" heart
"may not rest / Quite in the love of what is gone, / But seeks to beat in time
with one / That warms another living breast." That other heartbeat could have
belonged to any or all of several intimate friends, not necessarily as Hallam
Tennyson claimed, to Emily Sellwood, Tennyson's fiancée,[18] nor just to the
interrogator. Tennyson's closest friendship with Edmund postdated the broken
engagement with Emily, but before the poem was finally published, the engagement had been resumed. At best, such biographical speculations have only
limited value. Aesthetically considered, 85 as finally patched together is one of
the least satisfactory sections, barely achieving coherence; but in the total argument of *In Memoriam*, it marks an important turning from despair toward
regeneration. If Edmund, as still seems probable, is addressed in 85, Tennyson
was deliberately associating him with the hope of a happier life, as he certainly
does do in the Epilogue.

In the resumption of Alfred's and Emily's engagement, Edmund and Cecilia
had been centrally involved. As Emily would tell her sons, she and Alfred had
met at Park House at least once after that unintentional first reunion there.
Edmund "with loving generosity" offered to sell his carriage horses for money
to help them marry, but they did not allow it.[19]

At the quiet wedding on 13 June at Shiplake-on-Thames, Edmund and Cecilia were among only seven adults present, not including even Tennyson's
mother.[20] Martin says it was Edmund who "produced the ring, which he had
rightly guessed Tennyson would forget."[21] Edmund later quipped to John For-
ster that the secretive Alfred would "gladly give 7/6 . . . to every penny-a-
liner" who would keep the wedding story "*out of the papers.*"[22] Even so close a
friend of Tennyson's as Venables, upon hearing about the wedding, could only
pronounce it "a strange piece of news," having been unaware that the newlyweds had ever been more than casual friends.

It was perhaps the wedding, culminating a courtship begun in the Lincolnshire wolds some twenty years before, that inspired Cecilia to return there that
summer to her own childhood haunts. For her, as with any of her sisters or
brothers, the memories must have been mixed with sadness. Edmund, on his
first visit, was unabashedly entranced. They went first to Mablethorpe, of old
the favorite seaside resort of Cecilia's family. Edmund, as he wrote to Tennyson, so loved the place—so "grand and vast"—that he could "hardly bear to
leave it." In mid-July they had "winter fires every day, great comfort in the
hospitable inn—generally fair weather with keen west wind." Cecilia had
taken "her 3 walks every day with great spirit, today for the first time one was

helped by a donkey." They "wandered at low water ever farther seaward" while a mirage played "wild work with airy banks & sham waves." Then they proceeded inland for a twenty-four-hour stay at Cecilia's native Somersby. The Burtons at the old parsonage could not spare a bed in the house but provided a room "sedulously polished" in a house nearby. Cecilia and Edmund could walk about "with as much privacy" as they wished, reviving memories with Dr. Tennyson's old parishoners. Edmund found it "very touching to see their fondness for Miss Cecilia & delight at seeing her." "Even apart from all its interest," he found Somersby "beautiful thorough English *laneland*, with rare richness of trees all along."

But, as with so much—one feels tempted to say "virtually everything"—in Cecilia's life, even this glad nostalgic holiday led ironically to sorrow. The "week's excitement & exertion . . . brought on a very early miscarriage." Although "a good deal distrest," she was remaining cheerful "when not opprest by faintness."[23] No doubt so, at the time. But what of the years that lay ahead, when in 1856 and 1868 and 1874 three of her four beloved children died? Did she bitterly reflect in her times of dark depression that the child perhaps unnecessarily lost at Somersby (was the place accursed for Tennysons?) might have been one who would have survived to comfort her, perhaps a manchild to outlive his ill-starred brother and carry on his parents' line?

For the Park House family, it was a summer of varied coming and going, including the customary sojourning by the seaside at Eastbourne. Toward the end of July, Henry and his sisters Maria and Louy returned for a visit from Malta, the first homecoming for all three, although Maria's absence had been shorter, only since the summer of 1848. While the Alfred Tennysons were honeymooning at Tent Lodge, on Coniston Water in the Lake District, Franklin and Ellen and, at another time, Edmund went up to visit them. Emily Tennyson recalled that during Edmund's stay a stormy wind one night broke a window, driving her and Alfred into another room.[24]

On 23 October the Tennyson newlyweds arrived at Park House for a stay of almost three months, while Alfred searched for a house to lease. Between househunting trips, he and Henry could again be together, the last times that they would ever see much of each other.

On the twenty-fourth, Venables came down and, except for two or three very short returns to London, remained continuously until early January—one of the lengthiest views we have of Park House life. A typical day was uneventful yet varied—an almost ritualistic round of companionable walks in frequently changing groupings around the park and into the countryside surrounding, of boat rides on the river, rides on horses, and of evening conversation circles. On Sunday the twenty-seventh, Edmund departed in the afternoon for

Glasgow. But that morning Venables "walked a short distance" with Maria and Louy, walked in the afternoon with Maria, Louy, and Henry, then met Emily and another guest "coming from church." That evening "after talking upstairs with A.T., we came down & had a long pleasant talk with Mrs. L[ushington]," Maria, Ellen, Frank, and Henry. "Ghoststories & others." The next day, "walked a short distance" with Emily and Ellen, and later "Rode Oddo with" Henry and Frank "by Maidstone, Barming, & Aylesford." And so the record had typically gone through the ten earlier years of Venables's recorded visits, and would continue, with inevitable changes of person and circumstances, for three decades more. Tennyson that autumn of 1850, besides househunting, was busily "correcting his three books," as his wife wrote a friend on 26 December, "for new editions."[25] Tennyson could, if he wished, again seek Henry's advice concerning specific alterations.

On 9 November a letter came from Windsor Castle offering Tennyson the poet laureateship.[26] His son long afterward wrote, "He took the whole day to consider and at the last wrote two letters, one accepting, one refusing, and determined to make up his mind after a consultation with his friends at dinner." Afterward he "would joke and say, 'In the end I accepted the honour, because during dinner Venables told me, that, if I became Poet Laureate, I should always when I dined be offered the liver-wing of a fowl.' "[27] Actually, we find from the journals of both his wife and Venables, he hesitated not one day but four, accepting on the thirteenth.[28]

The wide approval of *In Memoriam*, mourning Arthur Henry Hallam, had helped bring the appointment after the eighty-seven-year-old Samuel Rogers had declined it because of advanced age. Ironically, Park House had just learned of the death at Siena on 25 October of Hallam's younger brother Harry, a close friend of Frank's.[29] By a grim coincidence, Harry like his brother seventeen years before, had died during a Continental journey with their historian father.

As fall turned to early winter, Tennyson was still periodically going out and returning from househunting. Henry, often less than well, was preoccupied with problems concerning Malta. Cecilia's health, never good, remained variable, doubtless not bettered by separation from Edmund nor by the additional activity at home. Shortly before the holiday season, she was driven to bed, Louy wrote to Edmund, by "a bad rheumatic headache," yet brightening somewhat when little Emmy was brought in to see her. Cecilia "talked, & baby examined with intense interest a medicine bottle."

By the twenty-third Cecilia was able to come downstairs for pleasant talk with Venables and Emily Tennyson. Christmas Eve brought "some indifferent fireworks," and after dinner "a magic lantern" which Venables thought "rather tiresome." Edmund did not arrive from Glasgow until late afternoon on Christmas day. After "a large Christmas dinner" came more magic lantern in the bow room. Henry next morning was "out of spirits, talking about Malta." Edmund remained to celebrate Eddy's seventh birthday, the thirty-first, with "a children's tea," then hurried off for Glasgow on New Year's morning, after being at home less than a week. Frank had decided to accompany Henry and the sisters Maria and Louy to Malta on the third. As the time neared, Henry was "in tolerable spirits, but languid." Cecilia was "much depressed." Henry sent his pony "to the dock," bound for Malta too. On the morning of departure, Frank's cheerful presence kept Henry "in comparatively good spirits"; but all the others—those going and those staying—were "very deeply depressed."

On 20 January the Tennysons left Park House for a picturesque old place Alfred had too impulsively leased at a gratifyingly rural location called Warninglid, near Horsham in Sussex. The house, as Emily described it, "had a lovely Copley Fielding view of the South Downs," and the birdsong outside enchanted Alfred with memories of Somersby. But a storm soon blew them "out of the diningroom & he was smoked out of his room & the rain went more than halfway thro' our bedroom and the storm was so loud we could not sleep so he got up and read some of the books we had unpacked the evening before." Furthermore, they soon "discovered that there was no post for the house, not even a carrier, and that we were five miles from a doctor." And Emily was expecting a child in April. On 2 February they abandoned the place, Alfred "with his accustomed tenderness" drawing Emily "in a garden chair some two miles over the rough road" to an inn, "guarding" her from "every jolt." They stopped several days with the Rawnsleys at Shiplake while Tennyson futilely searched for another house. On the twentieth, a month to the day after leaving Park House, they were back again staying with Cecilia. At a hotel on the way, Emily had stumbled against a step and fallen, spraining her foot and possibly injuring her unborn child, a boy, who two months later was born dead. By 11 March the Tennysons were at last settled in a secure house at Twickenham, having been assisted all the way by the Park House coachman. Alfred was soon taking his "walks before breakfast; short walks, not like the long Warninglid walks. Duty walks and alas! without pleasure."[30]

In July, Edmund and Cecilia joined Alfred and Emily for a few days together at Paris, before the Tennysons went on to Italy. Afterward, when Venables saw them at Park House, Edmund was "full of" his journey, "but she was much tired."

Tennyson had reached almost the exact midpoint of his life. Never again would he be homeless, a wanderer, or a recurrent visitor at Park House. He and his Emily would ever remain lovingly close to Edmund and Cecilia, but henceforth most of the visiting between their houses would be done by the Lushingtons, frequently by Edmund alone.

In January and March 1851 appeared Henry's two-part *Edinburgh Review* article,[31] approximately thirty thousand words, summarizing, describing, and evaluating "a series of events" in Italy during 1848 and 1849, "for magnitude, and strangeness, and rapidity perfectly unparalleled." A powerful sympathy with the Italian cause, an indignation and scorn against perverse authority and fumbling official ineptitude, permeate his pages. The prose is uneven, overelaborated in places. At his best Henry was, as always, a maker of phrases illuminating in their terseness, a cogent underliner of ironies. Concerning the Austrian position in Italian affairs: "The Austrian government [in Lombard], truly called by Mazzini, in 1845, the best in Italy, formed not the less the strength of the very worst. . . . the great insurance office for the otherwise dangerous speculations of tyranny." Of Pius IX: " . . . He will live in history as one more painful specimen of that commonest form of the irony of destiny,—the common-place blown into factitious greatness, at length brought face to face with great events, and ignominiously collapsing." Again: "He had come, so he flattered himself, to send peace on earth—he found that he had sent a sword. That is, he found the world was much more in earnest than he was or wished others to be."

One finds memorable character sketches of the principal actors in the drama. In the earlier battles the octogenarian General Radetsky, although the enemy, was "the one hero to admire . . . doing his duty, whoever else might fail in theirs, shaken as little by sedition in Vienna as by revolt at Milan, master of the ground he stood on, and resolved to hold that at least." But Henry's greatest fascination, combined with half-compassionate contempt, was for the vacillating Pius IX. His original liberal-seeming views "were probably as sincere as they were narrow." He knew that his temporal government of the Papal States was hated; "as a priest attached to his church, and a man not devoid of benevolence, he wished to abate this scandal," to attach his people "to his person." He had meant to work reforms, remove abuses, see that the "wolves should worry" his flock no longer. Lacking the wits to understand the near impossibility of what he was ostensibly attempting, he disregarded prudent advice to "declare at once what he would do, to do it, and to go no further." Too soon "an inclined plane of indefinite hopes and slack performances conducted" him with "almost unexampled rapidity to the point to which all such careers tend—the point where the roads *split*." Events pursued events, engulfing the hapless Pontiff, until he felt forced to declare against the Italian cause. The tragic farce had played itself out to a temporary apparent ending. As Mazzini wrote, Austria was again "the blade of the sword of which the Pope is the cross, and this sword hangs over all Italy." The "sole difference," Henry reflected, was "that the cross" of temporal sovereignty had "lost such sanctity as it once possessed, and the sword is sharper than ever."

The most eloquent set piece is Henry's description of Garibaldi's now famous retreat from Rome to Venice:

> If Song lives still in the Sabine mountains, many a future lay ought to tell how the outlaw of Italian liberty left the conquered city, foiled his French pursuers and gained the mountains;—how, threading the Apennines from Tivoli to Terni—from Terni to Arezzo . . . heard of here and there, repeatedly struck at by the Austrian pursuing columns, damaged but not crushed, evading through their lines when on the point of closing on him, he reached at last the Adriatic;—how, creeping along the shore with the relic of his band, his scanty flotilla was beset and scattered by the fire of an Austrian fort and gunboats,—how some were sunk, some taken; [his wife dying along the way]; and how at last, he reached Venice—worn out with toil, and almost alone—in time to accept a command in the last stronghold, and to see the last shot fired in the struggle which he had done and suffered so much to maintain. His story is a romance ready made.

Fortunately, the wars, although lost, had "tended to show the Italians what they are, and what their interests are." They were even less reconciled than before "to those great evils which some would persuade them to consider as blessings: bad government—priestly government—despotic government—foreign government." More solidly than before, they had "the idea of nationality in a bodily form," and with "many painful, but some proud recollections." The "idea of union" would remain more than "a dream. It is a spirit not yet laid; it walks in and out of Italy in many a thoughtful head and burning heart." Sooner or later it would once more find "an armed body to inhabit."

In the fall of 1851, Venables again joined Henry and his sisters for two weeks at Sorrento before returning with them to Malta. The island had a new governor and Henry a new employer, the Scottish soldier and meteorologist Colonel (later Major General) Sir William Reid, former governor of Bermuda and later of Barbados, who on Malta would be both governor and commander-in-chief. Henry arrived "unwell & depressed, but after seeing Sir W. Reid, with whom he eventually dined, he was a good deal better." There was the usual small colonial round of visits, balls, and other social events. On 18 December the new session of the council opened, "in the tapestry room, a long table with nine sitting on each side of the room." Governor Reid "read rather a stiff address. H. made two statements very clearly & pleasantly." On the twenty-seventh the Malta *Mail* "published a compliment to H. in the Report of the Malta Chamber of Commerce." On the year's last day, Henry and Venables walked on "the cavalier [fortification], where we saw the coast of Sicily plainly, & the white cone of Etna not so distinctly." The evening brought another ball: "a good house, & apparently a good ball. We were not back until 2.30. At midnight there was a country dance." Venables "asked Maria to join it, but she declined, so we sat together & talked the year out." He sailed for England near the end of January.

At Sorrento, Venables had found Henry hard at work on a new pamphlet, "as engrossing to him as usual." William Ewart Gladstone, after spending the winter of 1850–51 at Naples, had published a furious attack upon the Neapolitan government for throwing thousands of its political opposition into prisons and cruelly mistreating them there.[32] The Neapolitans had issued a flimsy pamphlet to refute Gladstone's charges, which had become an international sensation. The British embassy had influenced Henry to answer the defense. Documents he obtained included shorthand reports of disgraceful court proceedings convicting several prisoners, among them Carlo Poerio, recent minister of education and more recently leader of the opposition in the since-dissolved parliament, who had been sentenced to nineteen years in irons. (Gladstone had prominently discussed Poerio, whom he himself had seen in the dungeon chained to a murderer.)

Henry's pamphlet appeared in February 1852, anonymously—possibly because of his official position at Malta.[33] Combining factual refutations with scornful dismissal of illogical arguments, it assailed, one by one, the Neapolitan contentions. They had inanely blamed Gladstone for not coming to them for official information, rather than taking the word of convicts in prison and other traitorous informers. But, of course, Gladstone had "wished to see with the eyes which he might have had easily and pleasantly bandaged, even, if he had so desired it, by a sceptre-holding hand." The apologists had filled pages to prove that their laws protecting accused persons were just, none of which Gladstone had denied; his pamphlet had merely documented that they had shamelessly violated those laws. To the Government plea that priests, including the archbishop of Naples, had visited the prisoners, Henry replied: "Such is the honesty, such the logic, of this defense. Because the benevolent archbishop deigned to visit these wretched places, the descriptions of their miseries are false." Just as logically, "the presence of Howard in the horrible dungeons which he reformed, proved that they stood in no need of reform." Even if true, the Neapolitan denial of having tortured certain prisoners was no justification: "Savages kill an enemy with tortures; the slow death of years may suffice a Christian and civilized government." The Neapolitans would have been wiser to remain "absolutely silent," rather than revealing that they possessed no kind of rational defense.

At Park House young Eddy, in his ninth year, was getting on well with his

Latin, "very accurately" construing Ovid for Venables. Emily during March fell alarmingly ill, seeming for a day or two near death. Maria hurried home from Malta, happily finding Emily convalescent. On 13 July, Henry and Louy arrived on holiday from Malta. On 19 August, a week and a day after Hallam Tennyson's birth, Tennyson and Henry met for a brief visit in London; whether they met again that year is uncertain. Edmund, but not Henry, was present at Twickenham on 5 October, along with Arthur Hallam's father, Frederick D. Maurice, Browning, Thackeray, Venables, Jane Carlyle, and others, for little Hallam's christening.

Almost undoubtedly, Henry had mentioned to Tennyson the possibility that he might not be returning to Malta. It is clear enough that he and the family had been considering some alternative plan—as a rash conjecture, I think it may have been a marriage with some woman having money, but I have no idea whom. Whatever it was, Venables called it "a very uncomfortable plan in agitation." Even by 20 September the matter remained unsettled: Edmund wrote Tennyson, "Plans with regard to Malta are still uncertain but I think Malta seems most likely."[34]

Malta won. On 28 October, Henry departed, accompanied as always by Louy, but this time, untypically, also by Emily, and by Franklin and young Eddy. Within four years three of the group—Louy, Henry himself, and Eddy—would be dead. Also on the twenty-eighth, Edmund was off again alone for Glasgow, seeming to Venables "more out of spirits than I have ever seen him." Henry was still much depressed when he wrote Milnes from Folkestone before crossing the channel. Their mutual Apostolic friend Saville Morton, journalist, painter, and inveterate womanizer, had been stabbed to death at Paris by a jealous husband. Although "a sudden death has its recommendations," Henry reflected, "one cannot but transfer something of one's own horror" to the victim. No doubt it seemed all the sadder, not "because I find life as life more pleasant" than Milnes did, but "rather because I find it so much less pleasant, as indeed it is to me, I think." Consequently he "perpetually" felt that life "*owes* to me, and all other unlucky people, so much—which debt is repudiated by death." Persons who "have passed a life of happiness are much the readiest to die—putting aside, or supposing equal, all other considerations." In his party was "Edmund's little boy. Do you recollect him? A fellow with splendid long curls, he commences his travels thus early—let us hope he takes to foreign parts more kindly than I do. O for an honourable dismissal from Malta or an honourable tidewinter's place in England." Yet, if the winter in Malta should do "the good I hope, it will be a compensation for much, and I shall not regret having held the office for this year."[35]

Edmund too had ample basis for feeling out of spirits: he was facing another half-year of loneliness. His son might benefit educationally from travel and from tutoring by his accomplished uncles, but perhaps at indeterminate risk to his health. The possibility of delivering Henry from more of Malta had been abandoned or postponed. Emily was retreating not only from the harsh English winter, but also from her enervating emotional entanglement with Venables, an increasing preoccupation of the entire family.

Finally, Cecilia, seven months pregnant, had been progressively failing in health, emotionally as well as physically. Scattered statements regarding her health are brief, often allusive rather than explicit; but in aggregate they permit a tentative reconstruction. She was, and would be for long years to come, frequently more or less disablingly depressed; when agitated, she would occasionally become fractious, and to some degree hysterical. As early as February 1850, her first winter apart from Edmund, the Park House nurse had given Venables "a very unpleasant account." On 3 June 1852, he noted, "Mrs. L. with reasons for not going to Malvern," the location of Dr. James Manby Gully's hydropathic establishment, a refuge for the nervously afflicted, where Tennyson had stayed at the end of 1847.[36] In early July at Eastbourne, Venables found her "looking very ill." There again on 16 August, writing Emily Tennyson, he hoped the seaside had "done good as to its immediate object, & in general health she seems to be better; but how far the specific evil is touched I do not know." On the same day Edmund wrote Alfred, inquiring about Isle of Wight hotels: he and Cecilia were planning "a small trip," its duration depending partially upon "how far Cissy is able to enjoy it; she looks to it hopefully, & it is the kind of thing to do her more good than most others."[37] On 7 November, ten days after Edmund left for Glasgow, Venables found that "Mrs. L. has been nervously ill." Two weeks later she was not much recovered and kept to her room except for a few minutes daily. Edmund came at Christmas time, and drew her about in a chair. He came again briefly after she gave birth to a daughter, Lucy Maria, on 20 January. (Lucy would become her mother's inseparable companion, perhaps the one person in her life who most intuitively understood her, but would die at twenty-one of tuberculosis.) By February, Cecilia was looking "very well" again, but at the end of the month was suffering from severe facial pain. And so the record would continue until further illness in late summer led at last to an extended course of hydropathic treatment, but with doubtful results.

Living at Malta and several times sojourning in Italy, Henry, ever a quick learner, had become something of a master of the Italian language. Now in an article published in February 1853 in the nonconformist *British Quarterly Review*,[38] he emerged as a confident translator of verse from idiomatic Italian into stanzas of idiomatic English. The poetic voice of the Italian movement, the satirist Guiseppe Giusti, a Tuscan born near Florence, most of whose bitterly subversive poems had at first circulated in manuscript underground, had died in March 1850, two months short of forty-years-old. Henry had been fascinated by Guisti's poetry since at least the fall of 1847, when he and Venables had jointly translated some of it for a review by Venables. Henry's 1853 article reviewed Giusti's life and works, discriminatingly characterized his genius, and provided more than four hundred freely translated lines in various metres and stanza forms excerpted from about a dozen poems. To capsulize the peculiar flavor of Giusti's verses, their depth of feeling, passion, ironic force, and beauty, Henry suggested the term "lyrical satires." Giusti's "real master," Dante, had taught him the value of "the short description, which . . . emphatically outlives the object, the single line which brands, the single indelible epithet which recalls, and seems to comprise the character." In a verse "simple and even severe," Giusti used "the plainest and most popular expressions of the Tuscan dialect, condensed, vivid, familiar . . . in the strongest sense of the word, original," to tell "his countrymen how base, how hateful, was much of the life around them." In Coleridgean terms, Henry stressed that, as in "all poetry worth the name," nothing in Giusti is "ever put in for mere ornament; the exact words are used for the exact thought; thought and language are not separable; they are interfused and one."

"All earnest irony," Henry contended—and could do so from self-knowledge, being himself an earnest ironist, however minor—"is born of . . . conflict of deep feelings; the smile may in part express contempt perhaps, or a sense of the vanity of things, but the root of it is sadness and indignation which can find no adequate direct expression." Giusti, in "his own beautiful words," had sighed, "Ah me! the war of moods, the depth of sadness, / A soul in tears, a seeming smile of gladness." That "depth of feeling" had "at once sharpened the edge of that trenchant ridicule, and raised the poet into the element of true lyric passion."

In Giusti's most popular piece, "The Boot," poor boot-shaped Italy "relates how it has passed from leg to leg, through a series of larcenous wearers; how much misuse, patching, unprofitable wear and tear it has undergone in the service of these unrighteous owners." Priests, especially, had worn it, "spitefully and without discretion," and blockheaded poets had praised them for doing so. The boot needed "some fitting leg to wear me": "No German's leg or Frenchman's—understand— / I would be worn by one of my own land." Bonaparte might have been the proper wearer, but was bent on "rambling too far . . . until": "Alas! that snow-storm caught him far astray, / And froze his limbs, and stopped his walk midway." The poor boot—fragmented Italy— bemoans: "I'm a mere Harlequin of shreds and patches: / If you would really put me in repair, / Make me, with loving zeal and sense to aid, / All of one piece and one prevailing shade," then, perhaps, "the kick of the boot will be a serious matter to any insolent provoker." Another poem "of grave and sometimes grim humour, relieved with touches of melancholy beauty" was "La Terra Dei Morti" ("The Dead Man's Land"), where Italians, as Henry explains, lament that their "life, or rather this our present pseudo-life, is a mere intrusion among the living . . . yet from some things, one would almost think we were still living; who knows; perhaps it will turn out so":

> To us poor ghosts of Italy,
> Us, mummies from the womb,
> Our nurse is sexton, and our birth
> But opens up the tomb.
> On us the curates waste in vain
> The holy font's expenses,
> And charge our burial fees again
> On purely false pretences.
>
> Made up like Adam's sons
> In human likeness fair,
> True flesh you'd think us, yet we are
> Mere ribs and long shin bones,
> What do you here, poor souls misled,
> Strayed from your place of slumber?
> Oh, be resigned, go join the dead,
> The nation without number.
>
> For a departed nation
> There is no place in story,
> What is Liberty or Glory
> To this corpse generation?
> Garlands on graves? What good to them?
> They're just as well without it.
> Let's mumble off their requiem,
> And make less talk about it.

Henry translated nine more stanzas, still but a portion of the whole.

But Giusti's greatest work was his "*Gingillino*" (1844), a long poem offering instructions for the perfect education of a political scoundrel: "A satire more fiercely definite, alive in object and execution, was never penned." The making of the future arch-scoundrel would begin at infancy:

Hush, baby, don't cry,
　　You were naked when born;
Would you learn how to die
　　Not so bare and forlorn?

Come list to our maxims,
　　Which ever hold good,
And will float you like cork
　　To the top of the flood.

With a back early bent,
　　And a pliable marrow,
Cringe, crush yourself under
　　The pedagogue's harrow.

The candidate for scoundrelhood must forswear "the brilliant, the daring," keep head and heart undisturbed by heroic stories and "Weak dreams of honour, / Dim spectres of glory," reading only "What will keep you in earning." He must never weakly give way to conscience: "On the dirtiest fingers / Clean gloves can be worn; / Do this—or die naked / As when you were born." He must carry away from his university studies only that knowledge which will advance his sordid career:

What is left from all you've read,
Crudest studies, bump'd and hurried
In that nutshell of a head,
Urn in which the mind is buried?
Scantiest lore is yet enough
For that soul of coarsest stuff:
Yea, the slightest tincture of it
Will fit *you* for touching profit.

Don the gown of learned brother
Or attorney, which you will:
One name fits you like another
While it pays your baker's bill:
Born a hound and hireling wary,
Born Cossack or Janissary,
With bow'd neck and crooked shrinking
Making up for want of thinking.

Already adept in "the great art of omission," the apprentice scoundrel must also learn all the base things that must be positively done: "how to choose a patron; how to treat him when chosen; what services to render obtrusively, what inobtrusively; in short, the whole duty of a crawler, set forth with a calm and scientific accuracy, an absence of exaggeration, or obvious irony, in itself most ironical."

Taking Giusti's ideas and materials, Henry's thrilled ear and responsive mind had fashioned new poems in the quite different genius of his own native tongue. So it must be with any worthy verse translation of any poem that is really a poem. If Henry's own muse ever gave him a poem as good, it has not survived.

For Alfred and Emily Tennyson, the time was long overdue to escape from semi-urban Twickenham, too accessible to London, to a greater rural solitude more conducive to composing poetry. Except for two versions of his "Ode on the Death of the Duke of Wellington," Tennyson had written almost nothing in nearly three years. "Have you devised any means," Edmund inquired on 31 March 1853, "of getting away from that abominable Twickenham? I am very anxious to hear that you have, the sooner the better. While you are there, I am almost afraid to ask have you been doing any work for the future? but it is sad to think how the summers are slipping on." The manner was typical of Edmund's letters to Alfred: understated praise, quiet brotherly concern, occasionally cautious reservations concerning a poetic project, frequent gentle encouragement to write for sake of the world and his own reputation. "One begins at last," Edmund wistfully wrote, "to believe the day for setting off for home will sometime arrive."[39]

At Park House, Franklin had returned from Malta in early January. Early in June he and Venables, along with Edmund, who had come from Park House, met the ship bringing Emily and Eddy from Malta. Emily "looked ill & weatherbeaten after a bad voyage," Eddy "much improved in looks & very good company." At Park House "the meeting took place: such as I never saw, & in itself pure enjoyment." Between Emily and her nephew those seven months of almost constant companionship had sealed a bond for the remaining three and a half years of his life. At the lingering end it would be his Aunt Emily who tirelessly nursed him like a mother while his own mother, it seems, was incapacitated with illness and grief. On 20 August, Henry and Louy arrived from Malta, so that again for a few weeks all the family except Tom was together.

Earlier that August, William H. Allen and Company published a ninety-seven-page pamphlet by Henry, eloquently and cleverly done, *The Double Government, the Civil Service, and the India Reform Agitation*, defending against recent detractors the existing structure under which India was jointly governed by the crown and the directors of the East India Company.[40] Venables considered this book Henry's best piece of writing, which rhetorically it well may be, although more than a century later the central issues it discussed have died. But Henry himself lives audibly enough in many of its incidental touches. Through "a proper combination," he tells us, "of ignorance as to facts, recklessness as to assertions, and thoughtlessness as to consequences," the reformers had attempted to "stimulate the British community into one of those periodical states of high moral excitement" in which "something memorably disastrous and unwise is triumphantly attained." We share his scorn for specious, question-begging arguments. "Declamation is easy for those who have learned nothing of the India of to-day, and forgotten nothing of the India of Burke"; thus, "passages descriptive of the blunders of a young judicial civilian in 1853 are read side by side with passages descriptive of the crimes of perhaps his grandfather in 1763." Or the reformers irresponsibly generalize "in their single and sweeping dicta upon that congeries of not more than forty nations and languages which they are pleased to unify as the people of India."

Henry packages his insights in strikingly dramatic sentences. Having two governing boards obliged to exchange communications had distinct advantages: "You may, in a way more or less civil, pooh-pooh a gentleman across the table, or be conveniently deaf; but you must, unfortunately, attend to him if he writes you a letter which you are bound to answer." Again, "We use many words without even doubting that we understand them; and that we all and always understand them alike," until something "puts our phraseology to the test," and we "find that we are every day using the same word in twenty different senses as speakers, and . . . never understand it twice alike as hearers." For years the English had "been deaf as well as dumb on the subject of India," but now "we have got rid of one of the qualities. We have received the gift of speech, unhappily not as yet sufficiently accompanied by the counter-gift of hearing." He scores some good-natured points at the expense of his eminent kinsman, the Earl of Ellenborough, an accomplished Cambridge scholar who had contended that lack of literary education might be advantageous to a colonial administrator. "Like other men, Lord Ellenborough pines for the quality which he has not—deficiency in book-learning, freedom from the niceties of a cultivated intellect." Despite his learning, Ellenborough as governor-general of India was "undoubtedly an able administrator; and though he occasionally committed an escapade, which duller people would have avoided, yet there can be no greater error than to suppose that dulness is safe. Much duller men" than Ellenborough "have made much greater blunders." Surely the "blockheads have a fair inheritance already; the world, in how many senses, is practically theirs, and constructed for their benefit. Let not their indefeasible right to sit in its highest chairs of rule be theoretically conceded."

Decidedly more dated now is Henry's near-mystical belief in the supposed divine election of the British for morally educating the Indians: "Such a gift,

and with it such a duty—responsibilities so great, possibilities of good to ourselves and others so unlimited—the most wonderful, and what might be the
noblest page in the world's history, committed to us to make or mar." He skirts
perilously close to shrillness in disputing the contention of certain Indian agitators that Indians in general were equal in ability and morality with Europeans:
"If there is one lie more fatal to the hopes of India, and more monstrous in itself,
than those of their own religions, it surely is comprised in this,—'We are as
good as the English.' "Yet he readily concedes that in numerous points of local
administration the natives' "knowledge is more direct and greater than ours
. . . and their sagacity in devising appropriate and possible remedies is probably not less." He heartily advocates competitive examinations to qualify Indians for civil service positions formerly reserved for Britons. He despises the
resolute indifference that kept the English smugly ignorant of India's basic
needs. Actually it was "a poor country—poor essentially in itself and not
merely by former plundering. . . . a community, of which perhaps four-
fifths, some say nine-tenths, have been from time immemorial occupied in producing from the earth little beyond a sufficiency of food for themselves and for
the remaining fifth." India needed railroads, and irrigation—and money.
Available money had been squandered "by war after war": in recent years
most glaringly by the infamous "Affghan burglary," "the reason, more or less,
of every other war that has since tended to deprive India of irrigation and
railroads." Only when the English knew India well would they care about India
greatly.

The most memorable passage is Henry's tribute, modeled from his brother
Tom,[41] to scores of able young English civilians then serving in India—"English
boys of eighteen expanded into experienced Indians of thirty-two or thirty-
three." They displayed "that unmistakable mark . . . of the man who has
dealt with and ruled other men, blended with a kind of shy simplicity and
anxious correctness of manner," as they returned to English society. They were
"full of sense and confident knowledge on their own subjects; by no means
ashamed of them, but keeping them a little in the background." Men they were,
"wise as serpents, harmless as doves—men, with the mysteries of the finances
of half a dozen provinces, or the ravelled skeins of the intrigues of half a dozen
native Courts, clear and producible at a moment's notice, in their heads." Their
sympathy with the Indian people was real, as shown in "the tone in which they
speak of the natives . . . as a class; a genuine, not a canting tone: not compli-
mentary, often decidedly the reverse; but never sneering or contemptuous:
sympathetic, without sentimental falsehood; never other than calm, practical,
appreciating." These were "the rulers, in the main, of India[.] Eight hundred
men, most of them such as these."

At Park House the autumn brought new displacements. On 1 September, "a painful occasion for all," nine-year-old Eddy, accompanied by his father and Aunt Emily, went off to school at Shirley, near Southampton, for his first entire separation from his family, "unhappy," Venables wrote, "for the first time in his life." Characteristically, Venables worried about Emily's unhappiness at parting from the boy, but wrote nothing about possible effects upon his mother. She had been "ill in bed" on 27 August, but well enough to ride a pony to Boxley on the thirty-first. After that he mentions her not at all until 14 September, when she went away with Edmund to Ben Rhydding in Yorkshire to enter the hydropathic establishment of a Dr. MacLeod to begin the water cure. Just what kind of illness, other than her longstanding headaches, sent her away just then seems impossible to ascertain. Her infant, Lucy, left behind at Park House, was not quite eight months old. Edmund stayed with Cecilia about a month, returning to Park House before going to Glasgow on 25 October. She had visits from Louy and from Chapman, and still another from Edmund, who came down from Glasgow.

Edmund kept three of her letters, from early November, all chatty and cheerful: "I had a hilly walk today going with Louy up to the top of the garden past the bridge & up into that hilly field thou wast so fond of & going on to a cottage which thou mayst remember." She relays news from Park House about the children. The "Doctors here" were "going on very well & on the whole I am much stronger with much less headache." She was delighted at the "wonderful reason of the waiter this morning for bringing breakfast half an hour late—'The fact is mam that we have a gentleman staying in this house not quite in right mind.'" She tells Edmund, "I miss . . . thee much but still I feel comfort in the idea that I am getting real good here. I had a vapour this morning at half past eleven & a shallow after it which I liked." She worries over the expensiveness of the place: "Thou dost not say how many students thou hast this half year I hope it is good considering what I cost thee." When shortly afterward Edmund visited from Glasgow she was having "a good deal of headache again," but he wished to believe that she had been "getting a real good" that would "stay by her if she will only go on at home with trust & good habits."[42] (*What* good habits? Or bad ones? Dependence upon sedatives? Alcohol? Perhaps nothing more than neglect of physical exercise. We shall probably never know.) On 2 December, Franklin went to Ben Rhydding and brought her home. Three days later Eddy arrived, "very fat," Venables wrote, and "chattered away naturally about school." Edmund himself had been ill at Glasgow earlier in the month, and arrived for the holidays still looking unwell.

That year at Glasgow the Liberal student faction had rashly determined to violate a longstanding tradition and oppose the automatic second-year reelection of a lord rector. Against the Conservative incumbent, Lord Eglinton, whom they disdained as a sporting, rather than an academic, person, the Liberals entered the name of the new poet laureate. Tennyson, with Edmund sharing his feeling, demurred but did not flatly refuse to be supported. Tradition prevailed and Eglinton was reelected.[43] Afterward, Tennyson wrote to thank the Liberals for their support, then tactfully requested that they not sponsor him again:

> . . . I cannot but confess that I felt a kind of relief in learning that the College had adhered to its custom of re-electing the Rector of the former year; and though it may seem still stranger, I would fain request you (if I could hope that my wish as to this matter might have any weight among you) not to re-propose me next year, but to pass by one who is so essentially not a public man in character, whatever he may chance to be in name. . . . [44]

Twenty-seven years later, in 1880, there would be another semi-ambiguous effort—that time by the Conservatives—to make Tennyson the lord rector. Then, as we shall see, after first consenting he would finally firmly withdraw, much to Edmund's dissatisfaction.

Tennyson and Henry met briefly at Park House for a few hours on 10 November, when Tennyson came down with his brother Frederick. The two old friends had not quarreled, but with Alfred married and Henry preoccupied at Malta, the years of their closeness had passed.

International stresses along the Black Sea would lead before the end of March 1854 to the declaration by France and England of war against Russia. As early as October 1853, more than a month before the Russians sank the Turkish fleet at Sinope, Henry had announced to Milnes that he was, and intended to be, "thoroughly anti-Russia": "Having over you the advantage of untraveled ignorance, I have a strong and unshaken prejudice in favour of the side which is manifestly in the right, and against the side which is glaringly in the wrong."[45] The Crimean War in all its aspects would become for poor Henry his last all-encompassing preoccupation.

X

The Shadow Feared of Man

1854–1860

T O THE LUSHINGTON FAMILY the beginning of their six-year period of almost unremitting heartbreak and debilitating anxiety must have seemed if less than gladdening, at least uneventfully typical. On the first day of 1854, a Sunday, Emily and Venables walked to and from Boxley church "with rather pleasant & friendly talk." Henry was out skating on a nearby pond. Edmund departed for Glasgow on Monday, again without his family. Venables on the eighteenth found Eddy "very pleasant & in excellent spirits" as they traveled together to his school at Shirley. A day or two later, Henry departed for Malta, accompanied as always by his youngest sister, Louy, who was nearing her thirtieth birthday. (Edmund's Glasgow colleague, William Ramsay, would eulogize her as the most "remarkable" combination he had ever known, "of high intellect and varied accomplishments with extreme gentleness of temper and kindness of heart.") Never had Henry been on Malta without her. Maria, usually of their party, would join them again in the spring. Unfortunately Henry and his sister would experience "an uncomfortable journey," being for some reason obliged, as Venables learned, "to post all the way" from Boulogne to Avignon, "a great pity," and would reach Malta in "a very bad state."

Alfred and Emily Tennyson in late November had finally turned their backs upon Twickenham for their new residence, Farringford, on the Isle of Wight, where, as Emily recorded, she had been delighted immediately with the view from the drawing-room window, and soon with "the snowdrops & primroses in the plantation & by the cooing of the Stock-dove & the song of the Red-wings.[1] For the remainder of their lives, Farringford would be one of their homes.

Early in April, two days after Eddy returned from school, Edmund came down from Glasgow and took Cecilia back with him for his remaining month at the college, her first time there in five years. Eddy and his sisters remained at Park House. From there in mid-May, Edmund made his first visit to Farring-ford, where Emily Tennyson some two months earlier had given birth to another son, Lionel. Affectionately, Cecilia wrote her husband: "Thou hast been constantly in my thoughts since thou leftest me, & thy last kiss & parting look of love has filled my soul to overflowing. Get all the good thou canst with those dear creatures." She was delighted that "Alfred is bringing that poem up again 'Oh that twere possible.' I always loved it so much." (The poem, first published in 1837, was becoming the nucleus for *Maud*, to be published about a year later.) Baby Lucy was "jollier & better & chattering away on the sofa"; Emmy (soon to be five) "has come into the room and is kissing me so vehe-mently that I cannot go on . . . blessings on thee & those about thee."

Disconcerting news from Malta reached Park House in early July. Louy had been unwell (Venables later spoke of "an indisposition"),[2] and her doctors advised her to spend the summer in the Pyrenees. Frank and Ellen departed for the Continent to meet her ship and enjoy the Pyrenees with her. She sailed with a physician, Dr. Collings, and his wife, themselves quite ill during the voyage. A few hours out, as Frank wrote home on 19 July, Louy was "seized with violent diarrhhea," but the Collingses did not learn until reaching Marseilles "how seriously ill she was." That city being so "full of cholera," Collings thought it "absolutely necessary" to press on to Avignon, although Louy was "much pulled down by the voyage." The doctor was confident that she would soon recover but should change plans and return directly home "by easy jour-neys." That same day, after Frank mailed the letter, her condition abruptly worsened, "the pulse became gradually feebler, & the dear child sank about ½ past 10 . . . very peacefully & I trust quite painlessly." An immediate inter-ment was unavoidable, to be in the Protestant cemetery, although if Edmund and Emily wished, the remains could later be shipped home. (They remain at Avignon.) "God bless you all," Frank ended, with pitying thoughts for their "poor old nurse."

His next thought was of rushing as immediately as possible to Henry, know-ing "what a shock it will be to him." Frank would bring Ellen back to Paris, where someone would need to meet them to "look after her." (All knew that she broke down under strains.) The family sent the faithful Venables. No sequence of days in his forty-five years of journals carries more pathos than the record of his tender brotherly escorting of this near-prostrated woman back to her home. As she was coming with Frank from Avignon, between Lyons and Paris, her strength had given way. At Paris she lay in her hotel room in ninety-degree heat "almost like a skeleton . . . restless & feverish on the sofa," but "unrestrained in her feeling & very kind in the midst of her suffering." Next evening, she was "still hopelessly weak," but the three started by train. There was "much talk sad & yet not without sweetness. Her sorrow softened by illness. Frank grave, calm, indefatigable, in nursing her." On the boat from Boulogne, with Venables near, "Ellen lay on deck & was not ill, though there was a good deal of sea." At Folkestone they "got comfortable rooms at the Pavilion," and that evening "sat on the beach talking sadly but not unprofitably." He "read to her before she went to bed & then went out again. The charge of such an invalid, with her perfect reliance, strangely consoling." Henceforth between the two of them would remain a secure bond of sympathy until her death at sixty-four, two years before his own. At Park House, Emily was looking "hopelessly sad—even Edmund pale & depressed."

From Henry soon came "the most painful letter . . . I have ever read," written the day he had received the news, six days after the death. Venables had never known "such an expression of misery." The original is lost, but Venables preserved parts of it in his memoir of Henry: "Perhaps I ought to have thought of it as possible; but I did not; nor could I have been more surprised if I had heard that her ship had gone down in the middle of the sea." He could not "write much. I lay down my pen every minute. All one's more serious thoughts run in one direction, and from that I turn them away when I can." He could not "open the drawers in the room without seeing her handwriting. I can scarcely look round the room without expecting to see her." Of his own future, "Seeing nothing very promising in the way, either of utility or of happiness, I wish, as far as I can, to find out what is, under all the circumstances, right to be done." He was "far from sure that the most prudent thing would not be to turn this leaf of my life over decidedly"—leave Malta once and for all—" 'tis gone and let it go. It has brought little, yet not absolutely nothing; and it has cost much—how much more [than] it would have been worth, had it been tenfold what it was!" But, Venables explained, Henry finally decided to "remain at his post, at least during the continuance" of the Crimean War, since Malta was likely to become "the great depôt of the army."[3] It is hardly an exaggeration to say that he himself, a half-dead patriot, would become one more casualty of the dismal war in which he so passionately believed. Venables was convinced, finally, that "although he soon resumed his cheerfulness of manner," Henry "never entirely recovered the blow" of his sister's death.

At least four of the Tennyson family sent letters of condolence, each poignantly revealing of its writer's depths.[4] Alfred had thought Louy "almost, as far as humanity can be,—perfection." What could "be said in such a case?" what "comfort suggested? The blow must be borne." Edmund should "kiss dear Cissy [Cecilia] for me & tell her to be of good cheer: the mother of a family must not give way." Eloquently the poet's letter touches upon two of his lifelong preoccupations—his friendship with Hallam, and his willed determination to believe in a personal life beyond the grave. He had entertained hopes of visiting Louy, Ellen, and Frank in the Pyrenees, "in the same places where I spent some of the happiest days of my life with Arthur Hallam 25 years ago, but you see, that which rules over us will not have it to be." His wife, "Poor Emmy," was "writing & weeping at once. Who must not weep to miss for ever so sweet & gentle a creature? but it is exactly in & through these losses that the human expectation of another life for the individual in a nobler world rises into a passionate assurance that will not be gainsaid." They would meet Louy "again if we be worthy to meet her. Meantime we must bear." Now Henry might possibly quit Malta and "return to us which will be some gain in the midst of so vast a loss. I dread to think of the effect upon him & poor Maria, so far off from home." Ever "affectionately" theirs he was "in sorrow as in joy."

Through her tears Emily Tennyson began, "She was indeed a good angel and we cannot doubt she is still. There are few I love so well scarcely any I admire so much." Those that remained "must love each other all the more and her too for is she not with us still and in one way is she not nearer than ever and does she not bring us nearer to God. But indeed I cannot write. I beg of you to let us hear of you and especially tell us about Ellen. This seems all so sad and strange." A postscript added, "Cissy dearest kiss poor nurse for me."

Emily Tennyson Jesse had long mourned the sudden death of her first fiancé, Arthur Hallam, and was already inclining toward the mystical spiritism that would preoccupy her later years. "How earnestly & deeply do I sympathize with you all—how fully from fatal experience, independent of other feelings, can I enter into all suffering, and depths of anguish." Louy had been "excellent and almost beyond compare . . . we cannot mourn, except for the loss of her sweet, and loved society, for her pure spirit has passed those dark gates which have been opened upon all that is illimitable, and glorious, and blessed." The "dearest mother" of all the Tennysons was "well thank God, her eyes fill with tears a hundred times a day in thinking of you all."

In a letter of her own, Mother Tennyson, a devout believer in the imminent Second Coming of Christ, combined loving sympathy with zealous exhortation. Louy had "constantly endeavoured to imitate the meekness & gentleness of her Saviour & trusted in his merits alone for acceptance with her heavenly Father. I have no doubt she is happy forever." Meanwhile the "prize of everlasting life is worth contending for, all pains both bodily & mental to cease for ever & happiness unspeakable. . . . " "Oh dear Edmund," she wrote, "it is probable that you & Cissy & many of our dear relatives & friends will live to see our Blessed Saviour return." The "Clergymen at Richmond" were earnestly pointing out "that the signs of the times" were "very striking." Some prophetic interpreters had "prayed fervently on their knees for ten or eleven years" to be shown "the truth of the Prophecies, and we are told that the prayer of the righteous availeth much." All should be "preparing for that solemn that glorious time, may we be amongst the number of the sons & daughters of our Heavenly Father—& be gathered into our Blessed Saviour's Fold to see his Face & sing his love for ever & ever."

Henry, "pale & thin," arrived at Park House with Maria in early September. Little information survives concerning that visit, fated to be his last, no indication whether he saw Tennyson. Probably he was more or less ill for most of his stay, although it was probably during these months that he wrote, or finished writing, an article for the January *Edinburgh Review*, concerning "The Siege of Rhodes in 1480," now authoritatively identified as his by the *Wellesley Index to Victorian Periodicals*. Its vivid descriptions of the heroic defense of the island by the greatly outnumbered Knights of St. John against the Turkish attackers would have provided excitement for British readers during those early months of the Siege of Sevastopol. After he suffered a bilious attack at the end of November, his plans to sail for Malta on 12 December were postponed for a week by his physician. Even so, both he and Maria were ill when they departed on the eighteenth, with Frank going along to assist them. Ellen was "wretched," Emily "painfully anxious," and Venables gloomily reflecting, "It may have been the last time, as it was last year with Louy."

Cecilia with infant Lucy had gone up to Glasgow on 20 November to join Edmund, intending at last, after five years, to spend another winter with him. Unhappily, the experiment failed. As Edmund wrote Emily Tennyson on 11 January 1855, "Poor Cissy was made so ill with Glasgow that it was deplorable to see her." It was "very sad that she should be so knocked up after she had come so full of hopes & longing to help me." Nor did it seem to him "at all right not to have seen you & Alfred at Xmas, but I suppose as life goes on it grows harder to be as near to those we love . . . perhaps it is meant to be borne, if only we grow nearer to them in another way—as what has not to be borne?"[5]

At Malta, Henry and Frank had been composing poems celebrating English and French victories in the two famous Crimean battles of 1854, Frank writing about Alma, Henry about Inkerman. Decades later a historian would write that Inkerman "defies description";[6] Henry in 410 trochaic lines, tensely swift, attempted to recreate the furious action through the voice of a surviving British footsoldier:

Come listen, you newcomers,
You boys from the depôt;
You broke my tale of Alma
With many a loud bravo:—
But could I tell you truly
What Inkerman was like,
You'd clench your teeth in silence,
As men before they strike.

In "the dim dank morning, / O'er soppy ground and still," came the enemy:
"Thousands, thousands, thousands / . . . creeping round the hill."

Stealthy through the brushwood,
Hidden to the breast,
Crowds of points and helmets,
Up the hill they prest:
Misty columns looming
Far and near all round,
Cannon ready planted,
Sweeping all our ground.

The Russians' "great grey masses / Closed on our lines of red, / The rush, the
roar, the wrestling, / The growing heaps of dead." The fierce fighting
struggled backward and forward, leaving the men no time "for loading— /
One crashing musket peal: / The bullet for the foremost, / For the next the
steel." Still relentlessly came the enemy, vastly outnumbering the English:

Little then could aid us
Bugle or command;
Most was native manhood,
And your own right hand.
Back to back, each fighting
For himself and all,
Broken, yet together
Like a shattered wall,
In our ranks no bayonet
Lacked its stain of gore,
As through ten times our number
Our bloody path we tore.

Opportunely then arrived reinforcements, the Zouaves: "side by side with
Frenchmen / We met again the storm. / O battle-friends—oh brethren /

Across the chalky strait." The tide was turned, the Russians, though still stubborn, were doomed:

> Tens of theirs and twenties
> Are falling to our one:
> Yet they turn and struggle,
> Yet will not be gone;
> Yet their staggering masses
> Scarcely seem to thin,
> Though their corpses cumber
> Every step we win.

That night, with bitter thoughts, the English bivouacked "round the watch-fires." Next day burying parties searched out and buried their dead, digging "a mighty trench" and laying "them there like brethren / The English and the French." The Russian dead they buried too, and tended their wounded "as our own," although Henry's narrator claimed the Russians had earlier barbarously killed the English wounded. Yet the Russians had been good soldiers, "Men that did not blench." Their "serf-mothers" were mourning them. God alone "in mercy" would "Judge both us and them." By retaining its dramatic point of view "Inkerman" avoided the sentimentality and rhetorical stridency that marred the eight other war poems Henry published that year. Macmillan's in early February published "Inkerman" and "Alma" as a small book, *Two Battle Pieces*.[7] Venables "sent away a good many copies," including one for the Queen.

At Park House, Eddy, now eleven, had begun studying Greek, and recited to Venables from Homer. In early February, Chapman took him back to school at Shirley, where he soon reported his progress to Edmund: "I have really been trying to do my lessons as well as I can, and I have often thought of what I promised you." Resolved not to waste his father's money, he was really going "to try to please you by getting on." On 7 April, back at Park House perhaps on holiday, he wrote again, apparently (but perhaps not) healthy, and delighted by the signs of spring. "We went into the woods the other day, and we found a great many primroses, and light violets, and a few dark violets, but only one white one." With "a little more wind it would be beautiful weather for sailing the Arrow," which was "very dusty, for she has not been afloat for ever so long." The boys at school had begun cricket, "and if it keeps like this, I shall soon begin it here." He was pleased that Edmund was "able to come back sooner than usual and I hope I shall be at home long enough to see you."

In reality, Eddy may have already been brought back because of threatening illness. On the nineteenth Cecilia anxiously wrote Edmund: "Impatient I should think I am impatient for thee dearest but thou hast not yet told me on what day thou comest home. . . . Dearest my mind is very heavy about poor Eddy." She was "very much afraid of this swelling, more afraid than I dare to tell anybody because I have known the dangers of such things on the back. God bless him poor little loving fellow & spare him to us—he is a dear child—so amiable so clever, so loving, so brave & so good. My tears stop me dearest I cannot go on." Edmund did not arrive until the twenty-sixth, but by the twenty-first Horatio Tennyson had come to Cecilia, Eddy was alarmingly ill, and Emily Lushington took him to a physician in London. Although details are inconclusive, it seems that his condition soon evolved into what became a recurrent kidney infection,[8] bringing on his lingering death a year and a half later.

On Malta the health of Henry, also, was steadily waning. In a strangely beautiful letter to Edmund, on 20 March, he almost too casually mentioned having "been for some time in a very poor condition, but I think I am getting a turn now." His physician, Galland, was taking "infinite care of me, & manages his considerable medical business so as to give almost every afternoon at least two hours to going about with me, generally part in boat & part walking—he does not wish me to ride just now." Edmund's affectionate appreciation of his "Inkerman" had gratified him deeply. Even for Malta, which he had considered one of the world's few ugly places, his letter found mellow words: it was "wonderful how much beauty, with the help of sea & sky & the present bursting out spring green one can find to admire, even near these towns." He and Galland had "found, close to one of the harbours, one of the prettiest nooks of a ravine I ever saw: combining a foreground of gray rock, rough scrambling black green caruba trees, brilliant bright green almond trees, fresh springing grass, asphodels, barly &c, with a stretch of harbour shut in by high fortification masses." Altogether it was "well worth seeing—even to one disposed to say of it, as Carlyle said of the starry night in answer to Leigh Hunt's lively apostrophe, 'Eh, it's a sad sight.' " But most "nights—all perhaps here—are somewhat sad to me, still 'the blue sky bends over all,' & I sometimes hope, not without a meaning, though one which it will not explain." Meanwhile, "the world moves on, & its work is to be done." In the harbor was "a great steamer screwing out—where for? The Crimean; what has she aboard? Among other munitions of war an enormous gun: the biggest, it would seem, yet cast:—God speed her to her destination, & may they point her well when there." He had "no confidence in our rulers, but much in the spirit of the country: and I hardly think they dare make peace without something to show first. One wishes, in the meantime, that one could help more, but I can do little: it is all so purely military business."

"Did I not tell thee," Cecilia wrote to Edmund of this or another of Henry's

letters that spring, "how much I liked Harry's note to thee . . . full of deep &
true feeling, & brotherly love, which last Harry has in great perfection not only
in regard to thee & Frank & Tom but to mankind in general. Harry loves his
kind—& so dost thou I think great is thy love for all great thy sympathy for all
the greatest perhaps for the few which seems to me all right."

Henry's itch to be of greater help, the urgent impulse—perhaps under premonition of early death—to release his deepest convictions, and influence his
countrymen to stand firmly for right, was impelling him to compose too hastily
and publish summarily another set of war poems. As he wrote Venables, he
knew his "natural bent" was for prose, for speeches and articles, but at Malta
his prose had been expended chiefly "by writing letters calculated to aid the
transport of mules."[9] In that spring of 1855, after the death of Czar Nicholas
and during the course of a would-be peace conference at Vienna, zealous be-
lievers in the absolute righteousness of the fight feared premature peace almost
more than military defeat. Indeed, for them, to propagandize for "peace" before
Russia and all it stood for were soundly thrashed was tantamount to baseness, an
indication of mammonism, the lust for getting on again with business as usual.
The idea was more than implicit in an overwrought stanza from a poem published by Frank:

> Peace, peace, peace with the vain and silly song,
> That we do no sin ourselves, if we wink at others' wrong,
> That to turn the second cheek is *the* lesson of the Cross,
> To be proved by calculations of the profit and the loss:
> Go home, you idle teachers! You miserable creatures!
> The cannons are God's preachers, when the time is ripe for war.[10]

Henry's book was published by Macmillan in June, by which time the immediate peril of negotiated peace seemed passed. It contained nine poems by
Henry, including the republished "Inkerman," and five appended poems by
Frank, including "Alma." Henry's eloquent preface—he considered it a "sermon" on a text by Demosthenes—attempted a reasoned denunciation of compromise. England had no traitors, "except Indifference." Czarist Russia
represented

> Mental enslavement, consisting in the departure of ennobling thoughts,
> the growth of admiration for what is not admirable,—the passing of free
> institutions into a by-word with those who have them not, and a thing
> 'suspect' with those who have them,—an Europe, in short, in full march,
> with all its railroads and wealth, towards the condition of a larger and
> more civilized China—this will be sufficient for a generation which grew
> up with some hopes of the progress of man, some faith in their country.

The immediate danger was not a Russianized England but a largely Russianized Europe, specifically, a Russianized Germany. For the English the present danger was a diminished zeal for freedom, never ultimately a very strong urge in human beings. "The love of freedom has some analogy to what we call acquired tastes; it is not a mere instinct so much as a high capacity . . . capable of being checked, capable of being developed; capable of being, and often having been, utterly unlearned." The English had "a strong turn for it by nature; but what if we too found ourselves admitting the axiom affirmed even to-day by half-Europe—a free country cannot make war? It would be enough for one generation to be coerced or shamed into a lip-admission of that lie. Thank Heaven it is a lie!"

Henry's shorter poems included a dignified memorial to the Sicilian exile Pietro D'Allesandro, who had died at Malta in January; an address to King Victor Emmanuel of Sardinia, who had joined the English and French against Russia; "The Morn of Inkerman," in which an English soldier dreams of his dead wife, who assures him he will survive the battle; and the to-be-popular "The Road to the Trenches," with a dying soldier in the frozen Crimean wastes, bravely sending his comrades on ("So the soldier spoke, and staggering, / Fell amid the snow / And ever on the dreary heights / Down came the snow"). Three bitterly anti-Russian poems retain a shrillness that embarrasses now, and too little compensating merit. The 420-line "La Nation Boutiquière," filling nearly a third of Henry's pages, rang ironical variations upon Bonaparte's notorious taunt that England was a "nation of shopkeepers." They had shown that indeed they were:

'Traders, general merchants,
'So our title runs,
'Soft and hardware dealers,
'Firm, John Bull and Sons.
'Cottons and Colonials,
'Sugars, other trifles;
'Swords and spinning-engines,
'Howitzers and rifles.
'Ask your Spanish agents
'How our people there
'Recommend in handling,
'Certain of our ware.'

"Wellesley led their armies, / Watt and Arkwright paid, / And they quelled Napoleon / With their cotton trade." What kind of shopkeepers would the British of 1855 be? Would they need "Half a coward's faintness, / Half a worldling's sneer," whispering " 'English friends! give ear: / 'Peace is cheap and pleasant, / 'War how hard and dear' "? The mammon-worshiping propagandists for peace were chanting:

'Mammon, grown and glorious,
'Is no slave of Mars.

. . . .
'Talk of Thor and Vikings?
'You? and at your age?
'Are your Gods so many?
'Is there more than one?
'He is ours, whom all men
'Slander and enthrone.
'No half-hearted worship,
'No ideal scheme:
'Our GREAT FACT is Mammon,
'Finite,—but no dream.'

But England, great of old, would spurn such "euthanasia": "First the peace of baseness / Then the years of gains, / Last the foreign soldiers / Trampling English lanes." Mammon was indeed great: "Great but not the whole. / Nay, at times, in Mammon / Wakes the sleeping soul." Surely England would persist and win, then get on with her divine commission to civilize the world.

The Crimean poems of Henry and his brother, being finished during almost exactly the same weeks as Tennyson's *Maud*, may stimulate our imagination to restore a historical context for Tennyson's part three, where in only fifty-nine lines he too unceremoniously dispatches his barely recovered lunatic protagonist off to the Crimea to some sort of personal regeneration (if only, as A. Dwight Culler suggests, through endurance of honorable death—"the doom assigned" of the poem's final words), to match the national regeneration of England. Another of Culler's observations is no doubt also correct, that the notorious blunders of the war, "the state of the hospitals at Scutari, plus modern pacifism have effectively ruined Tennyson's symbol, and it is idle to say that anyone can now read the last scene of *Maud* and like it."[11] Well, if for no better reasons, the scene deserves to be disliked because it is too abruptly injected, too perfunctorily developed. But along with all else that it was not, its ideology in its time was, as Culler would no doubt agree, not in the least idiosyncratic, but rather, as the Lushington poems show, more nearly a commonplace among opposers of a "peace" that would have seemed to them no more than a craven cessation of hostilities. Like the Lushingtons and the idealized soldiers in their poems, *Maud's* protagonist "cleaved to a cause that I felt to be pure and true";

he too saw the war as a redemption of England from base mammonism, and was sarcastically intolerant of the idealization of "Peace" (" . . . love of a peace that was full of wrongs and shames, / Horrible, hateful, monstrous, not to be told"):

> Nor Britain's one sole God be the millionaire:
> No more shall commerce be all in all, and Peace
> Pipe on her pastoral hillock a languid note,
> And watch her harvest ripen, her herds increase,
> Nor the cannon-bullet rust on a slothful shore,
> And the cobweb woven across the cannon's throat
> Shake its threaded tears in the wind no more.

What we are observing is a jointly held conviction, not any kind of "influence" of the Lushingtons upon Tennyson. He and they, misguided or not, really did will to believe, along with countless other patriots, that the Crimean War offered a mammon-besotted English people a new salvation. Tennyson and Frank may have outlived the delusion. Henry did not. Nor would he ever read any part of *Maud*. Three days before its 28 July publication, he would be assisted, desperately ill, into the hotel in Paris where he would die on 11 August.

An ironical contretemps preceded the publication of his poems. He had concluded his preface with a joint dedication to "the friend of my life, George Stovin Venables,—and to an unnamed memory [Louy]. . . . The shadow of a wreath of lilies to the dead;—the shadow of a wreath of honour to the living." Venables saw the manuscript of the preface only after he had read the poems, disliked some of them, and sent off a letter to their physically depleted author, criticizing their workmanship. Venables, of course, was afterward filled with regret, Henry agitated because he had worked the hardest over some of the very parts that his dedicatee had liked least. In two lengthy letters he voiced his discouragement: "I suppose my taste is wearing out, *as other faculties* do." If "twenty-three instead of forty-three, if I had life & health before me, instead of a life which since eighteen has been one long failure behind me, I should care a good deal less for having written a few verses which I thought good and you thought bad—that is not much in itself." He was undecided about his future, but suspected that with all his recent poor health, he would soon "be *ordered away*" from Malta "if I did not volunteer it. Moreover I am in a condition that requires a good deal of consideration—not that I know that there is anything to be anxious about." Galland, his physician, had "repeatedly" told him "there is not: but my general health now was so shaken."[12]

On into the heat of summer he labored, growing weaker, waiting for the council to adjourn, which it finally did, "to the great disgust of the elective patriots, for whom seven months of sessions is not enough to concoct rubbish in." He did not know how "far, or how ever I shall get right, the moment I get out of this evil climate. . . . What I mean to say is this: think of me as fully intending to get well, and to not look *so* ill when I meet you."[13]

Before he and Maria finally left, his body and legs were badly swollen;[14] and he was requiring the daily attention of Dr. Galland, who stayed with them until after they reached Paris thirteen days later. When Venables met them at Arles on the eighteenth, Henry was so "alarmingly ill" and weak that Venables nearly despaired, "How we are to get over this journey I do not see." Next day, as they passed through Avignon, on the "exact anniversary" of Louy's death, Henry "pressed" Venables's "arm and pointed silently to the cemetery . . . adjacent to the railway."[15] After five days, through "exceptionally hot weather," a short distance each day, and one day not daring to move at all, they reached Paris, where Edmund met them. Almost all Henry's nights were "bad," and would continue so at Paris.

The end would not come until eighteen days later. The three English physicians who attended Henry are all in the *Dictionary of National Biography*. Sir Joseph Oliffe (1808–69), who practiced in Paris, a Fellow of the Anatomical Society of Paris, had served as president of the Paris Medical Society and was physician to the British embassy. Sir Philip Crampton (1777–1858), a famous surgeon, had been surgeon general to the forces in Ireland and surgeon in ordinary to the queen. Marshall Hall (1790–1857) was a respected, if somewhat controversial, physiologist, skilled in diagnosis, who ultimately authored twenty-seven medical works. As we have seen, Cecilia before her marriage had consulted him concerning her headaches. Nothing in Venables's accounts indicates that any of the three ever arrived at a clear diagnosis. Hall, especially, was at first encouraging, stating "there was no proof of organic disease"; but Henry could eat little, slept poorly, grew streadily weaker, and at the last developed constant diarrhea. From his twenty-five-year medical history, and the widespread prevalence of the disease during his century, it seems probable that he had some form of tuberculosis, but proof is lacking. His death certificate at Paris gives no cause of death.[16]

During Edmund's vigil in Paris, Cecilia at Eastbourne sent him an open-hearted, rambling letter. She would have written oftener, but had been having "almost without ceasing a pain in my back, & head, continuing all night in constant restlessness till from utter exhaustion I have fallen asleep toward morning." However, he should "not make thyself uncomfortable about me, keep thy thoughts on dear Harry & on sleep for thyself . . . tell Harry I can so well pity him for those nervous feelings at night, well I know the horror of them." She loved Edmund, was wanting him as never before, but "would not have thee leave Harry for worlds, but . . . want thee still more to get some sleep at night . . . for I am very anxious about it." It was not, she said pathetically, "as if thou hadst a healthy place to live in for the winter, & a good strong wife to take care of thee then, to fondle & comfort thee. Well dost thou deserve it dear kind husband & brother & father." Circularly, over and over again, she poured out the same sentiments—as if to reinforce them by persistent rehearsal—her love for him and for Henry, her anxiety that he get sleep, her sense of her inadequacies. "Thou knowest I am always trying to be well always selfishly looking after myself. . . . God ever help thee own darling & make thy wife a better wife to thee in the time to come. Ever thy very own, CL."

In an extraordinary manuscript document of nearly two thousand words, Venables described Henry's last hours, up to his death on Saturday afternoon, 11 August. Emily had arrived on Thursday evening. Franklin was coming from Corfu, where he had begun new duties as a judge of the Supreme Court of Appeals in the Ionian Islands, but Henry would be dead when he arrived. On Friday evening, all hope abandoned, Edmund informed Henry that he was dying. Incredulous, he argued with Edmund, gestured for Venables, who "leaned over him and told him that it was true and . . . would be very soon." Henry said something like " 'I did not wish to die, but if I must die I can bear it like any other man. . . . And if there is another life, which God grant' (then his voice sank)." He spoke farewells in turn to Edmund, to Maria, and then to Emily—motioning Venables away. Venables later "asked her what he said, & she said she could not tell me then. She told me something of it afterwards." (When she did, a month later, Venables wrote, "He meant something more; but her divine goodness made even what she said invaluable. I had partly guessed it before.") To Venables, Henry said that "no man ever had such a friend, and then he said that I had loved his family first for his sake", and then Venables "lost the thread of his speech, and I did not at that time fully understand his meaning." Edmund and Venables took a spoken last will: Henry's land to Franklin, his money and personal possessions equally to his brothers and sisters, his house at Malta with "the books & everything" to Venables. He was "much troubled with phlegm," laboring to breathe. Sometime before midnight "he said in a mournful tone, who will defend me against all the world? Edmund told him that we were all around him to defend him." Venables said, "That is not what he means, Emily speak to him. She leant forward . . . & told him in a few very simple sentences, that God would defend him & save him through Jesus Christ. Her words & her voice seemed to quiet him, but not quite to satisfy him." He looked appealingly to Venables, who said, "Listen to what Emily tells you." In the morning he whispered to Venables, "Is it impossible to do anything?" And another time "he said to me very earnestly something like—Matrimony—

proper condition of a man—my greatest mistake—then he spoke of India—alluding probably to Tom's happiness [since his marriage]—this also I did not at the time understand." (The inference seems clear that later, after talking with Emily, Venables did believe he then understood what Henry had meant in dying statements to each of them: that he wished they would unite in marriage.) Several hours later, when Henry ceased breathing, "Emily's arm was round his neck, & I hope he knew her to the end."[17]

Emily Tennyson recorded that when Alfred heard from Edmund that Henry had died, he read "Ecclesiastes" to her, "which he had once read to" Henry.[18] In early October, Venables wrote to assure her of Henry's deep regard for Alfred. If "all the poems had been lost he could have supplied a large portion of them from memory. Among thousands of admirers they had no more earnest or worthy admirer, & I do not think any other man exercised so strong an attraction upon him, though I was from circumstances nearer." Venables confessed that for years he had been "in some degree jealous & dissatisfied with a feeling less warm than my own;—but not of late," not since the dedication of the poems and "far more the wonderful & beautiful expression of feeling in his last hours." Edmund was not likely to tell them "how very sad a place that home [Park House] has become"—Ellen's despair, their anxiety about Frank's health when he returned to Corfu, Eddy's illness, "and Mrs L seems to get worse instead of better. Emily as usual takes charge of all & comforts all, but she had a peculiar affection for him & she grieves deeply for him." The Tennysons would be gratified at the comfort she had derived from *In Memoriam:* "If that poem had had no one else to appreciate it, it would have been worth writing." Venables hoped the Tennysons would not "blame me for once more dwelling on myself to you & on him."[19] Emily wrote back: "Blame you dear Mr Venables. No, trust me, I owe you real gratitude for speaking out to me if ever so little of what is in your heart." She would tell him what Maria had written of him since he went to Wales: "We feel a great blank without him the great gulph between the present & the past hardly seems so impassable while he is here. . . . There is no one with whom we have so much in common now." Emily Tennyson herself believed Venables's "irreparable loss has left you fresh a bond to Alfred in your memory of the past." They appreciated his "precious assurances" of Henry's "love and admiration" of Alfred. She supposed "we all must have our jealousies where there is much love and much separation also." They had "sometimes thought" Henry "did not care for" Alfred "as he used but what you say and what Maria says quite removes any such painful thought."[20]

During that fall Edmund had yearned to visit the Tennysons "to speak with you of Harry as one only longs to speak of the most dear to the most dear, I can hardly tell you what I miss in not coming"; but Cecilia's health—terrible boils on her face, constant pain—had allowed him neither to take her to Farringford nor leave her alone. Now, on 1 November, he was departing again for Glasgow.[21] More than a year later, Alfred admitted to Venables, "I have not yet written anything to his memory & perhaps never may, so it will be as well not to mention to any of the Ls that I ever spoke of such a thing but I do not suppose that you have mentioned it."[22] Long afterward, in 1870, he would to an extent memorialize Henry as one of the "three dead men" whose shadows walked with him "In the Garden at Swainston," the other two being Arthur Hallam and the recently deceased Sir John Simeon:

> Two dead men have I known
> In courtesy like to thee:
> Two dead men have I loved
> With a love that ever will be:
> Three dead men have I loved and thou art the last of the three.

During the months following Henry's death, Venables received several angry letters from B. L. Chapman, long his close friend and Henry's. His attempts to answer them were repulsed by Chapman. Although the two men met infrequently thereafter at Park House or in London together with mutual friends, their estrangement widened, and they would never become reconciled. A letter from Monteith to Milnes on 12 November carries a clue to Chapman's grievance. Edmund had paid Monteith "a flying visit"—"I am grieved by his account of that true hearted gauche Chapman. He seems unable to bear up after the loss of Harry following the, to him, still greater loss of Emily Lushington. When C. was here some time ago I was astonished at the crush he had got—& even before this account of L's feared he mt. never be the same man again."[23]

Monteith had also learned that Edmund was "not so pleased with Maud as the British public seems to be: & the same, he says, is the case with Alfred's wife & most of his friends." Edmund's classical reservations concerning so innovative a poem would continue. In the following July, after a visit to Farringford, he wrote to Tennyson, "You took my criticism on Maud like an angel, wh was very good indeed of you—I wish only you could be as glad whenever I thoroughly admire your poems as I am sorry whenever I cannot."[24]

Later Edmund would effectively influence Tennyson's handling of his Arthurian poems. By June 1857, having completed the idylls now entitled "Merlin and Vivien" and "Geraint and Enid," Tennyson had trial copies set up in type and was planning to publish. In one of these F. T. Palgrave wrote, " . . . Owing to a remark . . . which reached him, he at once recalled the copies out: giving me leave, however, to retain the present."[25] The "remark" (or remarks) was Edmund's. He was "much grieved," he wrote Alfred on 13 June, if anything in his recent letter to Emily Tennyson "distrest you. I said it all in love, & only my love could have prompted me to say it." His "tenderness" for Alfred's "fame will not let me be silent when I fear anything that may tend to cast a shade upon it, & few things can be more certain to me then that these 2 poems coming out by themselves would not receive their due of admiration." It would be "quite different if they were as I hope they will be supported by others of varied matter & interest, giving more completeness and beauty of circular grouping and relation." He wished Alfred to publish such a work, which "would surpass all you have written yet. Surely my speaking frankly is a proof how much I honour you if indeed any proof of that can be needed by you." If they could talk together, he would "be better able to say what I mean . . . in writing one may fail to touch the mood of a friend just as one ought."[26] Already, on the twelfth, Emily Tennyson had written in her journal, "A. resolved not to publish 'Nimue' ["Vivien"] & 'Enid' until he has a bigger book."[27] And Venables kept an undated note that Tennyson wrote him: "I have taken E.L.L.'s advice in the matter of the Poems: therefore I beg you to destroy my proofs which my wife sent. I shall wait till I have a bigger book."[28] But in 1859 Tennyson disregarded Edmund's philological objection to his calling the poems "Idylls"—"almost any title that could be given wd convey a truer notion. If Alfred wishes a Greek diminutive Epylls or little epics wd answer the case better—but it will be hard if for a subject so English an English name cannot be found."[29] Tennyson's incomparable ear for euphony could never have tolerated "Epylls of the King." Lexicographers of the future, although not the *OED*, were obliged to compose a definition of *idyll* that would embrace Tennyson's practice.

Poor Eddy was devastatingly ill, less so at times than others, but already by the end of 1855 Venables suspected that he was "probably dying." Through the early months of 1856, he could walk only painfully if at all, requiring to be drawn in a chair. He was better in late April, able to go to the woods, on ponyback at least. But by mid-July he was suffering from "dropsy" (edematous swelling) in the legs; by the end of August, family members and Venables were nursing him in relay around the clock, and an eminent physician who had examined him told Venables there was no hope. Other doctors confirmed the verdict. As October came with the boy still lingering, Edmund applied to the Glasgow faculty for permission to obtain a substitute teacher: "In the painful tendance on my dying son there are various things to be done both by day and by night which no one else could do so well as myself, and though he may linger on a few weeks more his weakness is so great that if I am to leave him at any time for a few days all might be over before I could return."[30]

"So one must go on in vague darkness," Edmund on 6 October agonized to the Tennysons, as perhaps he might have done to no one else, "doing what little, alas, one can do for his comfort." It seemed "almost cruel to feel a throb of joy when his sweet thankfulness tells one that we have given him some slight relief, but indeed at present one's heart seems strangely dull and narrow to compass the hugeness of such a life sorrow as lies near at hand before one." He reflected that the "roots of love and sorrow are verily twined together abysmally deep— there is something very awful and astounding in the vast loveliness of this little child's soul—and to see this glorious beauty slowly fading from our view, to whom it might have been so full of glory and blessing." To Alfred and Emily he cried out, "Oh, my dear brother and sister, may you be ever spared such a tearing away of life from life, and love from love."[31]

Eddy died on 20 October. Cecilia a week later was too ill from "head pain and depression" to leave for Park House for the funeral on the twenty-ninth, and did not appear, "depressed and quite silent," until three days later. There is no indication that during Eddy's final weeks she had been able to participate in nursing him. At the end her sister Matilda had been with her, the two of them probably living in a separate house. On the thirty-first Edmund informed the Tennysons that "her spirits fall & rise with wonderful rapidity." On the previous night she read aloud and talked about several poems of *In Memoriam*. "That book seems now dearer than ever."[32] Before the end of November, Edmund had returned to Glasgow, accompanied by Maria, and resumed his duties. Cecilia, who had "taken to" a new doctor at Eastbourne, returned with Matilda "to be under his care." The Tennysons having visited Park House, Emily Tennyson wrote Edward Lear, " . . . It is scarcely possible to express the sadness of the house . . . an almost hopeless sadness brooding over all things. I need not say this is hallowed and glorified by the divine light, and love in which they move and have their being."[33] At Christmastime Edmund returned, bringing Cecilia, but took her away again before going back to Glasgow.

Before the decade ended, the family would suffer yet another death and two alarming illnesses, one of which several doctors, fortunately mistaken, would predict to be almost certainly fatal.

In mid-May 1856 Tom with his wife, three sons, and a daughter arrived on furlough from Madras, his first visit in almost seven years. In 1850 he had married his half-cousin Mary, daughter of Charles May Lushington (1784–1841), who had been a judge and member of council at Madras. After the death of her father, she had remained in India, where her mother's family resided. (Interestingly, Mary's and Tom's descendants would carry double infusions not only of Lushington blood but of Christian family blood also, since both wives of their ancestor the Reverend James Stephen Lushington were descendants of that family.) In June 1857 Tom's wife gave birth to their fourth and last son, who would be christened in Boxley church. In early August, with mutiny sweeping through India, Tom was ordered to cut short his furlough and return; but by then, as Edmund told the Tennysons, he was "not at all as well as he should be. A great many things worry him & make him anxious in connexion with return to India, & this no doubt tells upon his health very much." His doctor had given "such a decided opinion that he ought not return yet"—he could hardly walk a mile without fatigue—that undoubtedly the court would not insist.[34] In early December, Venables saw him and his family off, watching the "ship swing round from the dock quays, & his kind cheerful face disappeared perhaps forever." By the end of March, the family learned that he had a fever. In the following weeks disturbing accounts arrived, including the news that he was returning to England by way of the Cape; but by the time that news reached England, he had already died on 17 July, and was buried in Ceylon. His death, the fourth in the melancholy succession, occurred just two days short of the fourth anniversary of Louy's.

By that time whooping cough had struck both twelve-year-old Zilly and nine-year-old Emmy. Zilly's case was alarming, with almost unceasing spasms of coughing recurring over a span of nearly four months. Not until late October was she able to talk again. During most of the summer and fall, Maria was also seriously ill. On 24 June she had received surgery on her eyes, which had been subject to cataracts since infancy. Recovery was not satisfactory, and then during the summer she developed another condition, probably gynecological,[35] which by the end of the year had brought her to the point of almost certain death. Neither she, her doctors, nor any of the family thought she could possibly survive. Edmund came down from Glasgow, she expressed her resignation to dying, and on 28 December dictated her last will to Venables. On 9 and 10 January she went into delirium, "speaking in a kind of rhyme, knowing us all & generally with a kind of intelligible meaning." The disease dragged on, with other crises including more delirium, until late March, when she gradually began to improve.

Through those years of crisis, Edmund's friendship with the Tennysons grew ever stronger. He went to Farringford when he could, with or without Cecilia, who too often lacked the will to travel. On 17 May 1856 he found them in the midst of remodeling the house, on the day they had nervously awaited a visit from Queen Victoria, who did not appear. The two boys wore "their rose-coloured dresses," and the family waited in the garden "to receive HM, not liking to go into the house tho' we did have rugs spread on the narrow path left between packages in the entrance hall." Probably "because of the stormy morning," the queen did not come. "Edmund comes to dinner."[36] Emily was "shocked," she wrote Venables, by Edmund's "worn look." He had consented to be a trustee for Alfred's will, and they were asking Sir John Simeon to be another—would Venables be a third?[37]

Edmund's letters to the Tennysons, while sharing his own worries and sorrows, were filled with concern for their welfare. Was Alfred getting enough "regular exercise, which Farringford is the last place in the world to excuse a man for not taking"? At Edinburgh recently Edmund had found that De Quincey (then in his seventies) "had not moved out of his house since Xmas day [more than two months], & his feet were becoming excessively painful—no doubt from this—but he took a walk of 4 or 5 miles with me & seemed rather the better for it."[38] After a visit to Farringford in July 1856, when Eddy's illness was worsening, he thanked them for the comfort they gave him: "Fifty things which I wanted to say & did not say generally come upon me after I have left you. . . . A day with you seems more than a week elsewhere."[39] He told them how much he had come to appreciate Charles and Louisa Turner (Alfred's brother and Emily's sister): " . . . Their going seems to make a great blank. I had not seen so much of Charles for years, & he grew more to me every day— nor had I ever seen so much of Louisa before, or felt so fully all there was to admire & love in her."[40] In 1859 he thought Alfred's "Maid of Astolat" ("Lancelot and Elaine") "most beautiful" but wished that "instead of 4 poems of the Cycle there were 8 or 10, to show more of what Arthur was, but perhaps that may come in time."[41]

Along with the deaths and near-fatal illnesses during that dismal half-decade came a sadly accelerated deterioration in Cecilia's emotional health. When Eddy died, she was barely thirty-nine, with an oppressively long life ahead. In 1856, added to her grief concerning Eddy, was the circumstance that never since her marriage had she known any really stable living arrangement. Although she was nominal mistress of Park House, actual circumstances blocked her becoming so. With her initial concurrence it had been projected that for half of each year she would be at Glasgow—a city she came to detest, one that intensified her illnesses. And then for much of the remaining time, following the custom of the Lushingtons, she would reside at Eastbourne or some other seaside place. At most she would be in her home perhaps four months of the year. Her sisters-in-law, four of them, none ever to marry, had lived in the house since early childhood, had the feeling of its rhythms, provided its continuity, and themselves had no other home. In a sense Cecilia had always been a supernumerary in her own house.

When in 1849 she began wintering there without Edmund, it housed only two Lushington sisters, with two at Malta. But after Henry died, even with Louy dead before him, there were three—three to Cecilia's one. Even with the best will all around, she no doubt felt hemmed in. Furthermore, the house had always had a schoolroom, where children of the family, and of the servants, and at times other children would learn reading, writing, and other accomplishments. (One young woman, Kate Morgan, who with her sister had spent most of her childhood at Park House after her Cambridge-educated father had died, would become the wife of Franklin Lushington.) The Lushington sisters were teachers in the school, so that Eddy's earliest schooling and all of Zilly's and Emmy's, would be under the capable tutelage of her aunts, or of persons assisting them. If Cecilia went to Glasgow or elsewhere, she left most or all of her children with the aunts. When the children fell ill, their aunts were their nurses. Zilly and Emmy would grow up being more the daughters of Park House than of Cecilia and Edmund. (Lucy, by contrast, would be first and last the child of Cecilia.) All the sisters-in-law seem to have been gracious persons, although admittedly almost everything knowable about them comes conveyed through their admirers, principally Venables, whose regard for Cecilia was slight. She herself would probably have seconded the general esteem for the sisters-in-law, and for much of the time would perhaps be, if not quite their peers under her roof and theirs, a fairly agreeable friend. But herself a victim of *tic douloureux* and recurrent depressions, she was also the daughter of Doctor Tennyson, carrying deep within her the childhood impress of him at his troubled worst.

Finally on 2 March 1856, with Eddy lame and already frighteningly ill and Edmund at Glasgow, Cecilia's tensions reached the point of eruption. Details, as always in the frequent outbursts of the future, are lacking. Venables, present, wrote, "A misfortune broke out which may have incalculable consequences"; the next day, "All very low this morning . . . I did not see Mrs. L., but another storm broke out"; and on the next, "The P.H. affair more & more grievous." When in early April Eddy's health seemed improved and Edmund came to take Cecilia for a month at Glasgow, Venables felt a "great relief as it was impossible to be sure that she would go." They returned in early May, and on 17 June, Tom gave "an account of new misfortunes. The effect may be terrible on all"; next day, Venables's forty-sixth birthday, was the "saddest birthday I have ever had with H. gone and Park House almost destroyed, C[hapman] alienated, and all things miserable. . . . Letter at night from Ellen with somewhat more of an account of the miserable state of things at P.H."

Devastated by Eddy's death, Cecilia as we recall, began 1857 at Eastbourne in her sister Matilda's company and under a doctor's care. As Franklin viewed her situation from Corfu: " . . . The good of a new doctor is generally transitory enough. I should be very glad to hear she was going up to spend the rest of the session with Edmund. The only thing to do her any real good is the being more constantly with him, and I believe, more constantly alone with him than she is at PH in the summer."[42] Whether she went to Scotland at all that spring is indeterminable. In May, Venables found her health "as usual," and again "still worse." Where she was from October 1857 to June 1858 is again undiscoverable, but for almost nine months she and her sisters-in-law did not meet at all. Not impossibly, she may have been with Edmund, but improbably so, since she did not reappear with him in May. Some sort of medical superintendence seems more probable. The sisters were "naturally very much oppressed by the arrival," which at last took place at Folkestone, where Zilly and Emmy were suffering from their whooping cough, Emily nursing one, Ellen the other. Cecilia, nearby, saw the ailing children frequently. In October she went with Edmund to spend a full winter, where she remained throughout Maria's prolonged, near-fatal illness at Park House.

Ironically, on the same day, 26 March 1859, that Venables first found Maria visibly convalescent, the sisters received some sort of epistolary ultimatum from Edmund that left them "all in distress." Later, in April, came "another of the wretched Glasgow letters." From subsequent happenings it is clear that Edmund was specifying at least that Cecilia would spend future winters at Park House, and perhaps also that hers would be the upper hand. The prospect, a patent impossibility considering her health and disposition, dismayed all the other Lushingtons, although the actual meeting, on 8 June, had as Venables "expected gone off quietly."

Edmund wrote Emily Tennyson on 11 June that Cecilia seemed "greatly comforted & cheered by seeing the children again." The delight of little Lucy, who had been at Glasgow with her mother, and her sisters at Park House "in seeing each other is very pleasant." Rather pathetically, Edmund professed "trust" that Cecilia was "wishing to do what is right and kindly."[43] Venables, going to Park House on 20 June, was "not ill received by Mrs. L.," but found the "state" of the sisters, "especially Ellen's, most pitiable," and feared that Maria was again "in a precarious state." On the twenty-fifth Cecilia was "civil enough," and the next day, "unwell, really so this time." On 13 August he saw her again "after several weeks, looking very ill."

On 21 October, Edmund was obliged to write the Glasgow faculty requesting a two-week leave because of his wife's "delicate state of health."[44] A week later Venables had "distressing letters from Maria, Ellen, & Frank. I can think of nothing else." On the twenty-ninth Edmund wrote the Tennysons that he was again off for his "lonely sulk at Glasgow," where he would welcome frequent cheering letters. Cecilia was "in the main no doubt better & stronger, but at times suffers pains wh bring terrible depressions. She strongly assures me that she will try not give way to this, but be as cheery & kindly as she can, & I fully believe she wishes this earnestly." (No doubt she did.) Emily Tennyson "must sometimes write her to keep her up to this." Her doctor had confidently declared that "there is nothing of disease about her nor any thing that may not come right under proper management—but she some times frightens herself with fancying she cannot have found out half her complaints."[45] On 19 November from Glasgow, he reported, "Cissy has been very low about the pains she suffers, & fancying there is some incurable evil, but this passes away, & she writes cheerfully & most lovingly. She is trying I am sure to take heart & do all I can wish her, & the tone of her letters is a true comfort."[46]

But in sad reality, on the day before at Park House Venables had recorded, "Old troubles broke out painfully." Soon came "fuller shocking details . . . confirmed by Frank." Edmund, informed, sadly telegraphed ahead for a room in London and rushed down, arriving on the twenty-sixth. On 2 December, after "apparently a crisis, which must be very painful," Edmund and Cecilia departed for Glasgow. Venables at Park House on the fourth found "A great relief compared with last time." In the decade to come, Cecilia would spend most (most probably all) of her winters in Scotland, but unhappily, her return to Park House in the spring would become an almost annual occasion for general apprehensiveness there. Possibly, fears of such intensity may have tended to become self-fulfilling.

XI

Middle Years, More Sorrow

1860–1874

F OR EDMUND AND CECILIA the early-December crisis at Park House was a turbulent prelude to nine years of relative calm, 1860–68, the least unstable they had known since 1849. At the end of 1859, Edmund had taken her, with Lucy, back to Scotland but not to Glasgow—installing them instead in a rented house in Edinburgh, where he joined them on weekends. His letters thereafter to the Tennysons show Cecilia often physically ailing but usually cheerful. Surrounded by a set of Edmund's intellectual Scottish friends, they attended frequent parties, and took their turns in giving them. Lucy studied under governesses, learned piano, lived always with her mother, whom she evidently came to understand and support emotionally. She must have been always a sober child, intuitively sympathetic, discerning beyond her years. Typically when the parents and Lucy returned to England in the spring, old tensions at Park House would soon be alleviated by Cecilia's and Lucy's going off to the seaside, where Edmund from time to time would come.

Late in April 1860 Edmund wrote the Tennysons that Cecilia had come to Glasgow a week before to help him pack for the move south, being "pretty well on the whole," although she had "suffered a good deal the last 2 days, she thinks from the closeness of the town."[1] On the way from Scotland, they visited Charles and Louisa Turner at Grasby in the remote Lincolnshire wolds, with a side trip to see Tom's widow, Mary, and "her little tribe" nearby. Cecilia had sat "before by the coachman," and afterward happily walked "thro' all the mud to the Vicarage at Grasby." At a dinner party there, she had sung two solos, including Emily Tennyson's setting of Henry's "The Road to the Trenches," which Edmund thought "people liked . . . very decidedly."[2] In February 1861 Cecilia was still "on the whole going on very well, having some times severe face ache, but in general keeping pretty strong & in good spirits." She "constantly" went out to dinner with him, or at least "comes in the evening. She has also sung once or twice in Edinburgh parties."[3] In April they visited William Sellar and his wife at St. Andrews, where Cecilia "had a great deal of terrible pain but was generally fresh enough in the evening to sing, & sing very well & admiredly."[4] In December, back at Edinburgh after a summer in England, Cecilia was "very well & in good spirits," the more so after going to hear Dickens read from some of his books. Their house that year was "roomy" and "comfortable . . . indeed too large; the upper story we do not touch." Lucy was "greatly delighted" with her little dog called Puck.[5] In early February 1862 Cecilia would have been "pretty well but for the damp wh is disposed to give her a great deal of tic—it kept her in bed all last Sunday, but she was better & took two walks with me on Monday."[6] The following Christmastime Cecilia was "very tolerably well, tho' sometimes face and back aching, & has been quite cheerful . . . for a long time." She liked their house and was looking forward to "a large party we have tomorrow."[7] Again in February 1863 Cecilia had been "much freer on the whole from head & back pains, & in general has been pretty cheerful." They had given another "dinner & evening party."[8] Next Christmastime she was suffering from a severe cold but "got up for a dinner party we had" and enjoyed it, singing although not in good voice.[9] A year later, as 1865 began, Edmund was reporting "a very pleasant Xmas in Edi, Cissy generally well & in good spirits, tho' rather tired with a party we gave (dinner 16, some 25 more in the evg, a very successful one all people said) & with going out to 3 or 4 other dinner & evg parties. She sings very well & practices by herself for it."[10]

Toward the end of January came the death of Mother Tennyson in her mid-eighties. Shortly afterward Cecilia went to visit her family at Hampstead, where Zilly, then eighteen, found her fairly well: "Mama talked a good deal, part of the time about Grandmama, and then cheerfully about other things. She seemed at the end especially glad to have had a sight of us." But in early May nearing a return to Park House, she "lapsed into abysmal gloom," so that Edmund thought "nothing can be made of her. She seems to think she wants to go to Hampstead, then she fancies the sea might do her good, but more often she speaks as if she was sure nothing in the world could possibly do her good."[11] But by January 1866 she was again "on the whole remarkably well."[12] In April, during Carlyle's visit to Edinburgh for his rectorial address at the university, Cecilia had sung "The Road to the Trenches" and another song for him, Edmund thinking "he liked her singing and talked with her very pleasantly."[13]

Not free of maliciousness is one impression of Cecilia during these years, published much later by William Sellar's wife, Eleanor. She found Cecilia an eccentric, "a constant source of astonishment, interest, and amusement," who had "inherited to the full the peculiarities of her family." She had something of a "morbidness, which showed itself in undue anxiety about her health—good enough, if she would only have let it alone." She was "dark, tall, and striking-looking of the Meg Merrilies type"—far from a flattering comparison. When she "stood at the open door, where she fancied she got more air, as indeed she did, and chanted to numbers of her own composing some of her brother's poems" and Henry's "Down Fell the Snow," it was "really very touching and fine, and never failed to draw tears from the eyes of her dear husband"; but it was "sometimes the cause of irreverent, if concealed, laughter to some of the audience, who could not get over the weird appearance of an ancient sybil singing in the doorway of a modern drawing room!" Yet "in spite of all her eccentricity there was something attractive in the genuineness and simplicity of her character, her sense of humour, and the originality of her expressions."[14] When Mrs. Sellar published these recollections in 1907, seventeen years after Sellar's death, Cecilia was still living, although senile, at age ninety.

Almost ritualistically, as each spring and summer came, Venables's journals noted discords, anticipated or actualized, between the year-round Park House residents and Cecilia. One such came in September 1861, just after Charles and Louisa Turner had departed from Park House for Grasby, when "in the course of the day a great storm" occurred, leaving the household next day in "a very uncomfortable state." In May 1863, it seems, she almost forcibly evicted her brother Arthur and his wife Harriet from Park House after he had offended by smoking inside. Greatly agitated, Arthur wrote Edmund: "I never say anything to you, leaving it in general all to Harriet," for fear of doing "more harm than good though the sorrowful state of things between you & Cissy has often made me fly to pen & paper" to comfort Edmund or "to say furiously honest passionate things to Cissy on your account until checked at once by the thought of the misery such would occasion you," and also by "my own conscience which tells me how capable I am of all hideousness were I not continuously hedged in" (protected from his tendency to alcoholism). But "if Cecilia is a responsible being for her sayings and doings sooner or later may she become widely awake first to the sufferings she gives you & then to the sufferings she gave Harriet who to this moment leaps from her bed nightmared by seeing Cissy standing over her." Harriet herself wrote that she could be reconciled only "if Cecilia

FIG. VI. (Left to right) Lucy Maria, Emily, and Cecilia, daughters of Edmund and Cecilia Lushington. Date and photographer unknown. By permission of Roger G. L. Lushington.

wrote kindly to me such a kind conciliatory message [as Edmund had done] & one word to show that she felt in any way the injury she had done us not only by cruel & false accusations but in actual *deed* violently turning us out of her house . . . but this must be *her* doing."

One source of galling discontent for Cecilia must have been how pitifully little she was seeing her two older daughters. Between the beginning of 1860 and the end of 1868, Zilly moved from thirteen to twenty-two, Emmy from ten to nineteen, separated regularly from both their parents and their sister from late October to early May. And then during stretches of the summers Cecilia and Lucy would often live at the seaside away from the Park House family. The few surviving letters from the two young Park House daughters reveal contrasting personalities—Zilly earnest, admirably thoughtful, often ill-at-ease; Emmy sparkling, eagerly responding to literature, fond of wordplay, developing early an easy writing style reminiscent of her Uncle Henry's.

We hear Zilly's typical voice at twenty-two when Lucy, sixteen, was confirmed: "It seems a long time since I heard from you, but do not infer from my saying that I do not think you have written well and frequently, for I am sure that you have." At the confirmation hour she would "think of you and pray for you . . . dear child, and trust that God will confirm and strengthen you in every good thing, and that you may be 'His for ever.'" All "the prayers in the short service of confirmation" were "very beautiful and those words 'Let thy Fatherly hand ever be over them,' speak of such an assurance of protection and care and Love." She hoped that Lucy would not "mind my writing this to you, dear; it is from no wish to teach, simply my own feeling about it and you." It sounded "strange to have Papa writing of his new house in Glasgow. They must have built the new College very quickly. . . . And what a piece of work the moving will be! Only think of all arrangements Papa's books will require!" "Well dear child," she ended, "I must leave off now; (I fear the word child offends you, but I cannot quite write 'dear young woman,' do you think I can?) . . . I shall hope to have a good account of Mama."

Emmy was about a month past her fourteenth birthday when she described an ordinary day at Park House: "This afternoon Mr Venables, Aunt Nelly [Ellen] & I, took a riding-walk, or a walking-ride, whichever you please, that is, we took Toby with us; and Aunt Nelly and I rode him by turns." They had gone "first to Boxley, then up the steep path to the top of the hill to the gate at the top, from which we could see the sea; and then we went down by the shorter zigzag and back again by Boxley. It was a beautiful afternoon, and being neither too hot nor too cold it was extremely pleasant walking." The flowers had been "growing very luxuriantly all along the sides of the hill and at the top of it, and the view at the top was clearer than we had expected." She

and Aunt Nelly had "just finished Rollin's [*sic*] History of Alexander the Great,
and Yesterday we began Goldsmith's History of Rome; which I think I shall like
very much indeed." In November 1864, then fifteen, she was full of exuberant
puns and other verbal pleasantries concerning her father's mislaying of one of
his boots. She had "supposed I should have to attempt some consolation however feeble," but was "glad to find that from your letter, consolation may be
changed to congratulation on its recovery. I hope the boot will be all the more
comfortable to make up for the dismay it has caused by its disappearance." Mr.
Venables had suggested "that it must be the spirit of Bhotan that has brought
back the wandering boot; if so I think it is a most obliging spirit, and had better
be employed about other missing things, that is unless it confines itself entirely
to boots." She appended a fanciful story of how "the Professor was unpacking
his portmanteau when he suddenly discovered that one of his boots was missing." Thinking that "Ann" might have the boot, he began "calling out, 'Boot,
Ann, Boot, Ann, Boot Ann,' " succeeding only in rousing a vision of "mighty
snowcapt mountains, with terrible passes, and rushing torrents, & frightful
precipices, and from the depth of the chasms came forth a husky and hollow
voice," identifying itself as "the spirit of Bhotan who am come at thy call."
The spirit instructed the Professor to dispatch his daughter to seek the priestess
oracle, who prophesied in punning jingle: "No prophet can tell thee the fate of
thy boot, / But seek thou what profit thou canst for thy foot / If thou take not
my proffer woe be to thee ever, / For the boot shall come back to thee never O
never." After "another awful pause," it turned out that the boot had "marched
forth for the tax of York":

> Tax me with no booty, but tax the great tax,
> Who taxed thee with trespassing known by thy tracks,
> He taxes thy boots for the sake of his pales,
> And makes up for his tacks in the boot's little nails.
> Puck may yet bear thy boot over hill, over dale,
> To apocryphal park and to non-extant pale,
> Gallic heads too have boots, from historical facts,
> And you'll need them to traverse East-lantian tracts.

Of course, Emmy may have had a collaborator in Mr. Venables, a circumstance
that Edmund could have readily divined. Venables had "been here all last week,
and he read King Lear to us, which I admire exceedingly. I think Kent's character so great and noble, and Cordelia's still more so; only the end is very sad."
Venables had taken "care to point out to us that there were a few slight defects
in Edmund's character, and that he was liable to making some mistakes." That
morning Venables had played billiards with her and Zilly, they "on one side,

and he on the other; of course he won, and it would not have been fair if we had won, for he gave us so many times back." She hoped "Mama is pretty well, and that she was not much tired by the party. Dearest love to her, and yourself and Lucy."

During most of his spring-to-fall stays in England, Edmund visited Farringford at least once, sometimes bringing Cecilia; or, less regularly, the Tennysons came to Park House. On 3 October 1860 Emily Tennyson recorded, "Edmund & A. have good walks."[15] Edmund's visit in late May and early June 1861 included an excursion with Alfred in the New Forest.[16] In late October 1862, his imminent return to Glasgow forced Edmund to cross from Farringford to the mainland during a storm that had caused two shipwrecks.[17] In July 1863 Tennyson, suffering from a painful infection in his leg, postponed a trip to London to consult a pathologist until after Edmund arrived. Cecilia and Lucy joined Edmund there but missed Alfred, by then in London. When the pathologist ordered Alfred to bed, Emily, Cecilia, and Edmund went back to London together.[18] In June 1864 Edmund arrived by sailing boat after the steamer that usually brought him had run aground.[19] No visit for 1865 is recorded; during parts of August and September, the Tennysons were on the Continent. In August 1866, after "a very sad parting" from twelve-year-old Lionel near his school at Hastings ("I watch the little face," Emily wrote, "& then the hand & then the top of his hat. A. T. walked twice back along the road with him to comfort him at parting."), the Tennysons consoled themselves with a week's visit to Park House. Emily found "as ever here a loving welcome. Pleasant drives and walks." They visited the Boxley house where Alfred had lived with his mother and sisters more than twenty years earlier. It was Emily's first time to see Alfred's "delightful" old room, "looking upon the bright garden with its fir trees & its crystal stream." Alfred and Edmund had long talks about metaphysics, a subject in which Tennyson, revolted by "the materialism of the day," had been taking new interest. During that visit, when Alfred learned of the death of his brother Septimus, Edmund "kindly" took him on short excursions. Emily wrote on departing, "How good they all have been. It is sad to leave them."[20]

When Edmund wrote the Tennysons, he was assiduous as ever in commenting upon Alfred's poems, transmitting the appreciations of others, and encouraging him to compose, particularly to get on with the *Idylls*, with more development of Arthur. "If the last 6 books of the Iliad had been lost," he argued in an undated fragment from a letter, "we shd not have seen Achilles in his full glory tho all that we hear of him in the other books might have told us that he was the first warrior of the past—& so I want to see an English hero in his full stature,—all himself & no excuse left for the criticism that other characters are drawn more vividly & powerfully than his."[21] In 1866 he inquired about Tennyson's forthcoming "Lucretius": "how long is it? any chance of seeing it in MS? & are there any more in progress? any of our Arthur? that's the true subject."[22] A friend of his had ranked "Guinevere" with *In Memoriam* as Tennyson's two greatest poems, neither likely ever to be surpassed by Tennyson "or anyone else."[23] The "truth & loftiness & tenderness" of Alfred's dedicatory poem to the queen after the prince consort died would "be felt," Edmund predicted, "in a hundred years as much as now." He had seen hardly any poem "addrest to a great person, in wh the poet was so true to himself, & so true, within truth without being niggardly of admiration, to the other party: This seems to me perfectly attained with exquisite grace."[24] Impatient with Alfred's English idylls for distracting their author from classical and Arthurian poems, he needled him: was "anything either of the Muses proper or the hardhanded Muses of the farm & plough going on"?[25]

Frequently Edmund asked Tennyson for "a signature" for the autograph collections of his friends, the poet's admirers. In 1866 he happily passed along a compliment from the eminent biologist Thomas Henry Huxley, who had "talked very pleasantly & exprest to me his unbounded admiration of Alfred's poems. 'We scientific men claim him as having quite the mind of a man of Science'—not that he put this as the highest point to praise—what he had said seemed to me on the whole sincerely and understandingly spoken."[26] In 1863 the bookshop windows in Glasgow were "teeming with side by side photographs of Alfred & Carlyle, done by Jeffries."[27] In December 1861, at Carstairs, when Monteith read "Guinevere to the assembled houseparty on Sunday," all had seemed "immensely moved except one oppressively fat honourable papist, who wonders what they saw to cry at, & avers rather triumphantly that he is not poetical." Several people had been "quite penetrated by Guinevere who never cared for anything of Alfred's before."[28] At Park House in 1864, B. L. Chapman had expressed a "most unqualified admiration of Enoch Arden, wh is not little from a man so qualified in his usual admiration. A like feeling has been exprest by several other persons I know."[29]

In January 1862 Edmund informed the Tennysons of "an overwhelming affliction" that had "befallen a very dear friend" of his, whom he had "known intimately for many years, & for whom" he had "the greatest regard & affection." It was De Quincey's youngest daughter, wife of Col. Baird Smith, "one of the best men in India," who had recently died there. In September his wife had left her two small daughters with her sister and departed from Gravesend—Edmund had seen her off—"to sail all the way by the cape to join her husband," knowing nothing of his broken health. Just before she arrived, he had been "ordered home as his only chance, not allowed to wait for her ship—

like poor Tom he was too much worn with labour to rally, & died before reaching Ceylon." To "the last minute" he was vainly hoping that the ships would meet. Now she would have heard of his death "just as she was landing in the glad hope of meeting him." Both of her sisters and Edmund were afraid that "the horror of the first shock" would "be too much for her to bear," since she was "so delicate and had so much illness while in England." If her "tender frame" did not "give way under it," she would no doubt "bear it with all the heroic patience that a woman can show," but he was "painfully anxious." He had talked with her "about In Memoriam, wh I gave her before she went out to India; and she told me she found an inspiration in it more like the inspiration of Scripture than anything she knew." In such a "painful world" one could "often do little enough to lighten the heaviest pain, where one wd give anything to be able to do it."[30]

Returning to England, Col. Baird Smith's widow (born 1827) combined his given and family names and lived as Florence Bairdsmith until her death in 1904. Smith (born 1818), a native of the Scottish village of Lasswade, where the De Quinceys lived, had met her on his furlough from India, and she had gone out and married him in early 1856. A distinguished engineer, he had specialized in canal works, studied and described the irrigation systems in northern Italy, and applied his knowledge to improving irrigation in India. During the 1857–58 mutiny he was wounded while leading the engineers in the siege and retaking of Delhi. Afterward he was master of the mint at Calcutta, and finally broke down while surveying and coordinating relief measures for the great famine of 1861.[31] De Quincey's biographer, the late Horace A. Eaton, who personally knew Florence Bairdsmith's daughters and had full access to her De Quincey family papers before they were auctioned and widely dispersed, referred to her as "obviously a brilliant and charming person," an impression amply reinforced by her few surviving letters to Edmund. To Eaton her portrait by Richmond displayed a "cultivated and even in her old age a singularly beautiful woman."[32] The same Eleanor Sellar whose recollections of Cecilia were scarcely better than patronizing could hardly contain her admiration of Florence. Eleanor had first met young Florence at the home of Alan Stevenson, uncle of Robert Louis Stevenson, finding "a lovely girl," even when "dressed in a pale-pink muslin, and . . . long black velvet ribbons hanging from the back of her head. This may not sound very elegant, but it was, and so was she, and 'the mind, the music breathing from her face,' made her a creature that once seen could never be forgotten." Later, in her widowhood, her letters, "written from her quiet homes first at St. Leonards and then at Bath, were among the most delightful I have ever received." With "tender grace and humour," she told of her children, the neighbors, the books she was reading, "while public questions roused an almost passionate interest." Her conversation had an "intensity and clearness of expression that made my husband—whose occasional difference of view only increased his admiration of her—liken her once to a 'beautiful bird of prey.' "[33] The professor's ornithological taxonomy seems unfortunately capricious, unless he intended more than his wife was willing to acknowledge. Freudians might clear their throats and claim that it inadvertently reveals something about Sellar himself.

When widowed, Florence was thirty-five, Edmund fifty-one. Across the next three decades, until he died at eighty-two in 1893, their friendship was deep and mutually sustaining. There seems no basis for supposing that it ever violated Platonic boundaries; but Edmund was an accomplished Platonist capable of realizing the subtle richness of a true Platonic relationship. Put bluntly, it appears that from Florence he received, and learned to reciprocate, a kind of emotional and intellectual sustenance that Cecilia had not been able to bring him.

But that is not to contend that he did not retain his love for Cecilia, although it had long since been forced to undergo substantial modifications, or even that the marriage, as a marriage, was in all respects unhappy. Evidently, on one side of her nature, Cecilia could be warmly affectionate. The amount that we do not know about her, including reasons she may have had on her part to be disappointed with Edmund, greatly exceeds what, in the comparative paucity of documents, we can possibly know. But at the least, the heartbreak she and Edmund ultimately shared in the loss of three children, the poignant memories of them at their happiest best, would remain as powerful ties. And for Edmund his marriage had sealed his friendship with Tennyson, the one friend he had come to value above all others in his life.

Among Edmund's close friends in Scotland were the Ramsays at Glasgow (the professor died in 1865): John Stuart Blackie, Greek professor at Edinburgh; the Sellars, first at St. Andrews and then at Edinburgh; another of Edmund's former students, Lewis Campbell, professor of Greek at St. Andrews (if Campbell's papers ever come to light, they may contain invaluable letters from Edmund); the much-beloved Dr. John Brown, the personal physician of the Lushingtons and author of *Rab and His Friends* and *Horae Subsecivae*; the respected theological writer Thomas Erskine, of Linlathen; and De Quincey until his death on 8 December 1859 (ironically, Florence, returning from India, reached England just after his death, even as on returning to India two years later she reached there immediately after her husband's death).

Another valued Scottish friend was the metaphysician James Frederick Ferrier (1808–64), professor of moral philosophy and political economy at St. Andrews, whose memoir Edmund wrote and published in 1866.[34] In 1852, before ever meeting Ferrier personally, Edmund had supported his unsuccessful candidacy for the chair of moral philosophy at Edinburgh. Presenting himself as a student of metaphysics, Edmund asserted, "There is hardly one philosophical author of the present day, whose writings so command my admiration." Another recommender of Ferrier had been De Quincey, who incidentally also endorsed Edmund's endorsement, ranking him in the fields of "German philosophy and German literature . . . not only the most extensively, but also the most accurately informed man that I happen to know next after Sir William Hamilton."[35] A recent literary critic, although not claiming that Ferrier had directly influenced Tennyson, who knew and admired the philosopher's work, has emphasized that "The Ancient Sage" and parts of *In Memoriam* have striking affinities with Ferrier's pronouncements concerning the unique potency of human self-consciousness.[36] It was probably Edmund who introduced Ferrier's thought to Tennyson. Twice in early 1855, Edmund asked the Tennysons for their reaction to Ferrier's *Institutes of Metaphysics*.[37] In her journal Emily had already recorded in December 1854 that they had been reading the book.[38] In July 1859 the philosopher with his daughter and son-in-law Sir Alexander Grant (later principal of Edinburgh University) visited the Tennysons at Farringford.[39] Two years later Ferrier suffered a violent attack of angina pectoris, followed by frequent recurrences that confined him largely to his home—his St. Andrews students came to him there—until his death in June 1864. Edmund had long since become his friend and learned to love him for "his tender thoughtfulness for others . . . characteristic touches of humour, frankness, beneficence, beautiful gratitude for any slight help or attention." Of his last years Edmund wrote in the memoir, "If ever a man was true to philosophy, or a man's philosophy true to him, it was so with Ferrier during all the time when he looked death in the face and possessed his soul with patience."[40] Edmund was articulating also a cherished ideal for himself, to possess his own soul patiently against whatever infliction of fate.

Of all the bereavements the Park House family was fated to endure, perhaps the greatest shock—certainly the one with the briefest forewarning (at least since Louy's death)—was the death from typhoid fever of the vivacious and adored Emmy, halfway through her twentieth year, on Christmas day, 1868. She had been with Ellen at the seaside, where both had been less than well. Venables was at Park House when they returned on 1 December, apparently not really ill then or during the next week. Back in London he first heard of her illness on the tenth; by the fourteenth the account was "very bad," and Franklin and his wife were trying to get a nurse for her; on the twenty-first Edmund, without Cecilia or Lucy, arrived at London from Scotland and rushed down directly to Park House. Emmy, as Zilly recalled in a letter to him an exact year later, "though only partly conscious gave you her loving smile and tried to stretch her hands out to you."

Something of the agonizing suspense that Cecilia and sixteen-year-old Lucy had suffered at Edinburgh was recorded, however artlessly, in a poem Lucy wrote then or soon afterward. It appears on the first page of a privately printed collection of her verses,[41] and is the first and least successful artistically of a group of fourteen poems concerning Emmy's death (an unpretentious effort by a grieving adolescent long immersed in her uncle's *In Memoriam*):

> Death near the darling of our hearts doth hover,
>   His presence dread is passing at our door;
> But the destroying angel may pass over,
>   And God bring back our gentle one once more.

They were clinging "with longing hearts and tender,/ To the fond hope that life may still be thine." They could not "sleep for thinking/ That thou art lying on a bed of pain,/ Beneath the heavy load of fever sinking,/ And that we may not see thy face again." In the second poem Lucy remembers how she had cried "to the Almighty to restore thee,/ With agony that none but He can know." She "would so willingly be dying for thee,/ But God hath will'd that it should not be so." A later poem in the sequence realizes the irony that "The church bells rang a joyous peal,/ The morn rose dim and grey,/ It was a Christmas morning when/ Our darling passed away." The heartbroken sister cries out:

> I would that I were dying,
>   Even as thou hast died;
> I would that I were lying,
>   My darling, at thy side.
>
> I would that I were sleeping,
>   Never to wake again
> To weariness, and weeping,
>   And misery, and pain.

The three final poems in Lucy's sequence attempt, as her uncle's great model attempted, to find some elegiac consolation. The twelfth: "What means this needless misery?/ I have but dreamed that she is dead,/ A troubled dream, and full of gloom,/ But now dispell'd, and I shall meet/ Her coming from some other room,/ Or at a corner of the street." The penultimate poem lyrically celebrates the ineffable sister:

> Thy smile was like unto a star
>   That shineth in the midnight gloom;

Thy face was like the snowy flower
That through the winter days doth bloom.

Bright star, whose beams have pass'd from us;
Fair flower, too frail for this bleak shore
Dear face, whose sweetness in my soul
Remains enshrined for evermore.

In the last of the group, Lucy reclaims the material gifts she had given her sister—the brooch, the chain, the "books wherein your mark I see/ At many a well-remembered line/ Which you would often read with me,/ And your heart found response in mine." It seemed so strange that where Emmy had gone, "No earthly gift could go with you,/ No little token of our love," all being only "memories to me alone." Yet there was one exception:

One gift I gave you, O my sweet,
    Love,—tender, passionate, and true;
Keep *that* till we again shall meet;
    It pass'd thro' death's dark gates with you:
I take not back *that* gift again
    Though all beside you leave with me,
That which was your's thro' life's long pain,
    Is your's through all eternity.

In the next two years, others in the Park House family, those who had known Emmy even more intimately than Lucy had, virtually canonized her memory. On 24 July 1869 Ellen reminded Edmund of how on "the corresponding Sunday to this last year" he and she and Emmy had been together "sitting under that tree in the Buxton garden, while our dear one read to us some Wordsworth— the Ode to Immortality [*sic*] was one & it is seven months this day since that new life opened for her dear child. Every day at Buxton" seemed "so fresh in view, though as if separated by many years now, yet every new place & thing, or even any plant in the hedges I want to turn around & point out to her." Near the first anniversary of the death Ellen wrote again: " . . . If there is anything dear Edmund for which I could feel more than unspeakably thankful, it was that you were able to come in time to carry away some of our precious one's loving & tender words, and her pure faith, gathered out of those few days of darkness, & which I feel ought to be a light for all the end of my life." Zilly wrote too, characteristically comparing herself disadvantageously with the beatified sister: "I am never without thinking of her, and yet I feel unable to think of her as I would. I long to be like her by being like the Saviour whom she followed, but I feel immeasurably distant through my own nature of selfishness." She thought

Edmund could not "know the feeling I have of being lost in myself, because you have always lived so much more for others." But, wisely, Zilly admonished Edmund, "Keep this letter to yourself, please." (In short, it should not be shown to her mother.) Cecilia's own more forthright grief and depression were perhaps no more unhealthy. She too thought that Emmy, "that lovely one," was in heaven, "very very near to Christ & I believe granted to pray for us." But even that consolation was scant: "I am better than I expected . . . in this long (as it seems to me) & bitter trial. When I see the streets here & see the clogs of men & every thing moving, I feel with Lear, Why should a dog a horse a rat have life and thou no breath at all." Ellen a year later was again observing the death's anniversary: "These days are so sad & yet so full of our dear one, that I feel I cannot write of anything else."

Edmund preserved two letters of condolence from cherished friends who blended their own sorrows with unique appreciations of him. Florence Bairdsmith extended "loving tender sympathy and prayers" but could "suggest no comfort in this life for such an unutterable sorrow." With a phrase from *In Memoriam*, she reinvoked her own bereavement: "Through seven long years I have not found the 'far off interest of tears.' How can I hope it in many more years for one whose life is in his love as I know yours is?" The octogenarian Erskine of Linlathen, two years after burying his lifelong companion sister, had "long learned to consider the love of any human being—as one of God's great gifts—being a pledge as it were of his own love—but there is a great difference in the degree of value which we must attach to these gifts." He could "truly say" that Edmund's "friendship & tender attentions" had been "most refreshing and comforting during the last few years—most dear to my heart—healthfully stimulating to my capacity of thought." A "heavy burden" was "laid upon man—& whilst he remains in this fleshly tabernacle, he seems rarely enabled to shake it off," yet there was "surely attainable a peace of God which passeth all understanding—& which can make the most galling yoke easy, & the heaviest burden light. God grant it to you & me—& to all mourners."

Seeking change, during part of the summer of 1869, Edmund took his sister Emily and Zilly for a tour on the Continent, including a visit to his much-loved Bonn. Such journeys had their discomforts, potential or real. Cecilia wrote, "I shall be glad to hear that you get comfortable lodgings without insects like fleas & Bugs no one can gain strength while fleas & Bugs are about." Whatever the prevalence of such entomological pests, Venables learned that at least once in France the travelers were "driven by noise from lodgings to a hotel."

At summer's end a year later, Edmund, Cecilia, and Lucy (then seventeen) visited the Tennysons for two weeks in their new home at Aldworth on Blackdown, where Emily Tennyson was "thankful" they were "the better" for their visit. They had always been "most true & loving friends."[42]

Glasgow University that year, 1870, had finally moved into an ornate building at its new location on Gilmorehill. When the term opened, it was Edmund,
in his sixtieth year and beginning his thirty-third in the Greek chair, who was
selected to deliver the introductory address.[43] The core of his message was the
deeper values of the three divisions of study under the faculty of Arts.

The natural sciences, he reminded his hearers, needed no apologists in Glasgow, "the city of Watt." In the sciences one learns "that science is linked to
science: in the grand concatenation disclosed by gradual discovery, sciences
originally separate become one; laws at first apparently distinct reveal themselves as but special applications of the same law. The recently completed
Atlantic Cable was one "crowning manifestation of the power which, by
stooping to nature's laws, has learnt to regulate nature's processes."

Edmund turned next to "Mental Philosophy," his own second love. What
was "nearer to man than man? and what can he care to know, if his own nature,
with all its yearnings and aspirations, is to remain for ever unknown?" That
most human yearning to know ourselves has "inspired the oldest poems of our
race that survive, where deep thought is strongly and confusedly entwined with
the wildest imagery." We are foolish if we "sneer at these early essays of
reason seeking with two dauntless wings to scale the empyrean." People who
scoff at the Egyptian and the Greek "can but feebly apprehend the deeper truth
and holiness of Christianity." Edmund praised recent historians of pre-Socratic
philosophy (these included his recently dead friend Ferrier). It was equally
important that in modern times "one nation should enter into the mind of
another"—Edmund would have been thinking primarily of the British studying the Germans—"when each has sought to approach truth from different
sides."

Almost inseparably linked to philosophy was Edmund's own calling, the
study of language, that "symbol and foremost instrument of thought, so essentially incorporated with it that we seek in vain to imagine how one could exist
without the other." The "more we feel that our race is one . . . a brotherhood of pilgrims whose paths, though separate, converge and point alike to the
same crowning height—the more shall we prize the power which enables us to
read the thoughts and acts of long-vanished generations that have helped us
onward to all we now possess of worth or excellence." Acquainting ourselves
with ancient works of genius will enable us to contemplate genius if in our own
time such should appear. Compare Homer and Milton. "What can, in many
ways, be more unlike . . . what more perfect than either? Homer swift-flash-
ing in radiance of beautiful strength; Milton stern in august majesty, clothed
with thunder." Yet any who have studied them both "will have found his
admiration of either confirmed and deepened by the contrast." So also in comparing Aeschylus or Sophocles with Shakespeare. The "imaginative wealth of

one generation is not, indeed, reissued, but becomes fruitful, and multiplies the wealth of another." No longer did scholars "fancy Latin derived from Greek or Greek from Latin": now they knew that "both these noble languages belong to a wide family of cognate tongues, whose origin is traced to the far East, and whose domain embraces the largest portion of Europe and most of Asia." Here was a truly exciting, relatively new, scholarly development:

> It would seem as if our time were providentially summoned to explore this region of historical science. In our day, languages whose existence had sunk out of human remembrance have, after the dumbness of centuries, again become vocal to the understanding. The long-buried re-orient dawn has smitten Memnon's statue, charming it once more into speech. The Egyptian, Assyrian, Persian records are read and interpreted; men who breathed and thought 5000 years ago tell us on stone or paper their doings, their household ways, their experiences of earth, their hopes for eternity. To those who seriously reflect on these vast treasures so recently unearthed, it can seem scarcely an hyperbole to speak of modern research having annihilated space and time.

Such "wonders" had been opened to view by "cautious, slowly advancing, imaginative, critical investigation, adding one proof to many others that to divorce the imaginative from the critical spirit is to do violence to nature."

Therefore in "all the lines of thought" much had been done, but "infinitely more" remained. "Newton's simile" held "good for all time: the ocean of truth spreads before us, children picking up pebbles on the shore that hint at the vaster wonders which the boundless deep embraces." There should be no complacent extolling of one's own age, "as though *we* stood at the top of knowledge." The present age should adopt "the high vocation of intellect and mental culture," knowing it "a sacred duty—a duty to ourselves, our race, and our Maker." Such culture was "destined to raise us higher and higher in the scale of being, if by persevering use of our native powers we make these glorious gifts our own, in the true sense in which what is originally not his own, but wholly given, can be called a finite being's own." All should "strive to realise the lofty conception expressed by the great poet of our time, growing [the lines are from *In Memoriam*]

> 'Not alone in power
> And knowledge, but by year and hour
> In reverence and in charity.' "

In 1872 Tennyson published "Gareth and Lynette," intended at the time, although he later changed his plan, to be the last composed of the *Idylls*. Edmund's lofty conceptions both of poetry and of womanhood were offended by Lynette's persistently coarse mocking of her supposed kitchen-knave knight. The poem seemed "in general extremely fine," he wrote, "hardly an expression that is not chiseled out into clearest keenness, & rich in condensed strength." Gareth's "modest heroism" was presented "with surpassing light & grace." But if "the lofty lady" that Lynette styled herself "had shown her haughtiness in another way than talking such a mass of scullery slang it seems to me the poem need not have lost in effect what it wd gain in pleasantness." Good poetry "is too good to be thrown away upon vulgar railing of ill conditioned hussies." One could only hope that, outside the poem, "Arthur in his justice doomed her to serve as kitchenmaid for a year under some Mrs. Kay or Lady Blanche."[44]

Illnesses continued with little abeyance to afflict the Lushingtons. Ellen's health, especially, steadily deteriorated. In September 1871, Venables recorded, she had a "diagnosis of consumption," and all feared she was dying. In May 1872 she was "looking thin and weak," in November 1873 so weak that she was hardly able to move, and in November 1874, "quite helpless." At that point she was only fifty-three. Some time before the autumn of 1875, she became, and remained, completely unable to walk, although she would live on, mentally alert, until 1886.

Edmund himself, before the end of the 1850s, had begun experiencing a rheumatic condition in a knee, sometimes diagnosed as gout. During midsummer 1864, although normally an enthusiastic walker, he resorted to a pony chaise for getting about his estate. Again in 1866 Venables found him "very lame," in 1868 "painfully" so, and in 1872 hardly able to "walk at all."

But the cruelest of blows, the one that for Edmund and Cecilia would crown all previous ones, fell in the autumn of 1874. Details are sparse, but evidently Cecilia had been anxious since at least 1869 concerning Lucy's susceptibility to coughing. Her twenty-first birthday occurred on 20 January. She wrote her father from Edinburgh on 24 February, describing an entertainment or concert that she had enjoyed, but ended, "I do not feel any better yet for the medicine but I daresay I shall soon." In early June, Venables noted, "Lucy apparently in danger." With some fluctuations she progressively worsened until she died on 1 October—according to her death certificate of "tubercular disease." During her life, since early childhood, she had lived comparatively little at Park House. Venables, with all his frequent visiting there, including summer visits, could comment upon her death, "Though I knew her little, the intolerable grief it causes is to me a great trouble." The fairest inference from that and numerous other indications seems to be that Cecilia herself, since 1860, had spent relatively little time in her nominal home. Lucy had been the only one of Cecilia's four children whom she could always unambiguously consider her own. Her namesake, "Zilly," since 1856 the heir-apparent to Park House, was by the time of Lucy's death twenty-eight years old. Ironically, as Cecilia's long life would spin itself ever more vaguely out, she would become in extreme old age more Zilly's child than the reverse.

A week after Lucy died, Edmund wrote to the Tennysons. Cecilia seemed "as well as I cd have hoped—no doubt she is not well but she has often been more ill with no such compelling cause." Her physician's medication had helped her sleep. Zilly "in another way" was "perhaps even more shattered; it is more difficult for her to obtain sleep, but I trust the terrible strain is yielding to time & fit remedies." Ellen's "constant weakness" made "difference in her state less conspicuous," but she was "manifestly" in grief. Cecilia had stayed away from the funeral, which was attended by Franklin, and by Tom's son Godfrey, as well as Maria, Emily, Zilly, Mr. Sankey (the physician), "old Watson, and several maidservants." Cecilia was generally "calm & can talk of other subjects; alone with me she often breaks out into passionate grief, wh perhaps is best." She seemed "quite making up her mind to go with me to Glasgow, whither Tilly [Matilda Tennyson] will accompany us." He hoped that plan was best, but the Tennysons should "not let anything be written about it . . . it might unsettle her; she partly dreads it & might take against it." Numerous letters had comforted her by showing "how many persons prized & loved our Lucy—& I am sure she is earnestly wishing to bear God's will aright & as far as may be do His work."

Edmund had just seen Alfred's new volume; he had known and loved the "exquisite" Swainston Garden lines (with their tribute to Henry, along with Hallam and Simeon). "The Voice and the Peak" was to Edmund "quite new, & it seems to me like a wild & mighty psalm, in truest harmony with all our present thoughts and feelings."[45] On Christmas day he wrote from Glasgow that "Cissy has been very poorly indeed, & I have been forced to call in a medical colleague to give her advice. She likes him & I hope he is doing her some good." She had been "terribly deprest at times," but could "sometimes be rather more cheerful—but she dislikes Glasgow as much as ever & is persuaded it always makes her ill. She has not been able to get out of doors for more than a fortnight."[46] Edmund himself had rheumatism in his right arm.

There would be no more winters in Glasgow for either Cecilia or Edmund. Sensibly, that next summer he would retire, at the age of sixty-four, after thirty-seven years in the chair of Greek.

Several letters among his papers thank him and Cecilia for copies of a song, both words and music, by Lucy. Through her sister, Anne Weld, Emily Tennyson, being ill, conveyed her admiration "for the words" and "their striking fitness to what has come to pass." Alfred wished to say "that he thinks the song very pretty no small praise for him." Florence Bairdsmith had been "greatly struck at the wild tenderness, so like a prophetic cry for those whom she has left sorrowing." When Edmund felt he could, would he "tell dear Mrs. Lushington of my tender and deep sympathy. I will not write to her because one fears to so highly strung a nature as hers a letter coming at a wrong time." The song, but not the music, survives in a manuscript:

The Petition

Bury me not in the cathedral old,
The resting place of warriors bold,
Where the cold stone figures in armour lie
With their rigid faces upturned to the sky,
Nor in the cold vaults underground,
Where all is dark and still around,
But bury me where the wildflower grows,
Bury me where the violet blows.
Nought over my head but the pure blue sky,
No stone to mark the spot where I lie
Where the wild wind goes sweeping by,
And the nightingales sing a lullaby,
Lay me down quietly, & leave me to rest,
That violets and daisies may bloom on my breast.

Perhaps of greater interest in our story are certain of Lucy's poems in her privately printed posthumous collection depicting imagined persons that seem at least partially modeled after members of the family. Seventy-two trimeter lines entitled "A Character" poignantly suggest her Aunt Emily:

Yes, I knew her story,
 Understood by few;
Little of life's glory
 Had she, and she knew
Much of self-repression,
 Little of delight;
Thus was her expression
 Oftener calm than bright.
Others when in sorrow
 Told to her their grief,
Strength from her to borrow,
 And thus found relief.

She gave them comfort, but never spoke of the "want and pain" in her own life. Those who thought her "strong and brave" "passionless and cold" did not know "what had taught her/Passion to withhold." She desired "not to fail in duty," although "life's beauty/Once past closely by her." On occasions "strong feeling/Broke thro' self-control,/Some slight chance," through a "dilation" of eyes, paling of cheek, compression of lips revealing her soul. Through loving her, the narrator had learned "how to comprehend" the "character," as she patiently faded. Another poem, a sonnet describing a depressive individual, must surely contain traces of the writer's mother:

> Her eyes are dim with looking long in vain,
> Her feet are weary, climbing up the hill,
> Her heart is heavy with a weight of ill,
> A nameless burden of unspoken pain.
> She goes her way alone, nor doth complain,
> And from her daily work she doth not cease;
> She hath no wish for pleasure, only peace,
> And knows on earth that her desire is vain.
> She makes no murmur, and she doth not weep,
> Her sorrow is too great for any tears;
> But she is tired of smiling day by day,
> She fain would lose all consciousness in sleep,
> All memory of past and present fears
> In dreamless rest, which shall not pass away.

Undoubtedly for Cecilia, but perhaps also for a few cherished others, Lucy wrote the poem "Unity":

> No joy can make your spirit bright
>   And not make mine the brighter too;
> And nought can give my heart delight
>   But finds a sympathy in you.
>
> No darkness passes o'er your soul
>   That doth not cast a shade on mine;
> No sorrow o'er me hath control
>   But you that sorrow half divine.
>
> No cloud upon your brow has place
>   But on mine own a sadness lies;
> No smile can ever cross my face
>   But is reflected in your eyes.

No chord within your heart is moved
    But vibrates in mine own again;
So are we one, O best beloved,
    In every joy, in every pain.

Probably the most moving is Lucy's self-portrait, entitled "To——":

When haply on this little book,
    Although it is a thing of nought,
Your eyes may give a passing look,
    O think of me one kindly thought.
Think, she has all the faults of youth,
    Is wilful, wayward, passionate,
But those she loves she loves in truth,
    And never will her love forget.

And she will strive, when far away,
    In all to make a rightful choice,
To live in hope from day to day,
    And in God's goodness to rejoice;
To be, tho' in the world, not of—
    That is her aim, tho' oft forgot—
To keep her heart a well of love,
    Amid all changes changing not.

Sir Charles Tennyson, who knew Lucy's book, viewed it judiciously. Her "poems suggest that the death of her sister Emily had been a severe blow from which she never wholly recovered. They shew also that she had a good ear and a highly sensitive temperament. Was there more? Had she a gift which time might have matured into solid achievement?" He felt, and I concur, that "a fair sample of the whole—suggests this possibility."[47]

"What does it mean?" Edmund at the age of four had habitually asked about "any new word or expression." As he neared sixty-four, bereavement was no new word, yet it called anew for interpretation. A manuscript written in his hand, entitled "Dec. 31, 1874," preserved his unpretentious attempt. Death may or may not mean passing over into celestial bliss. If for any, then surely for pure-hearted Lucy. But surely love itself is eternal. All love, if true—each child's for parents, theirs for her or him, theirs for one another, their friends' for them, theirs for the friends—concentrically broadens out, deepens, becomes part of cosmic love's eternal storehouse, constantly drawn upon, never depleted:

O lost to us when claimd above
　　We miss thee ever, as we must,
Whose every word was tender love,
　　Whose latest thought was holy trust.

So sweet a death, so peaceful breath
　　I have not witnessed ebb away;
If bliss is sure to spirits pure,
　　Dear, thou art blest with God to-day.

Old year is changing into new,
　　Time hastens, hurrying off so much,
Our love to all the good & true
　　Time, the great spoiler, cannot touch.

Our love still deepens on & on,
　　And shalt, till time himself's no more,
Our love for all our dearest gone
　　Time for Eternity doth store.

On the reverse side of the paper and in a different stanza form, Edmund wrote
six more lines:

Dear for thy own & for thy Mother's sake,
Dear for thy brother & thy sister gone,
Like theirs thy light is spent wh brightly shone;
Dear for all loving breath that with me ache,
　　Thy image folds all dearness into one,
　　And melts in love that points to God's own throne.

XII

Park House and Boxley Churchyard

1875–1893

$\mathbf{A}$T GLASGOW UNIVERSITY an era in classical education was ending. In April 1875 Edmund memorialized the University Court for permission to retire: he had "taught during thirty-seven sessions," had reached his sixty-fifth year, and as his physician, the beloved Dr. John Brown, duly certified, had become "permanently disabled for the performance of the duties of his office . . . from frequent and severe attacks of gout." The court, with the University Senate "unanimously and cordially concurring," voted him the honorary degree of LL.D.[1] From 14 May he would receive an annual pension slightly above £862 (two-thirds of £1,293, his average annual earnings for his final five years, including the rental of £100 for his university house).[2]

Unfortunately, at Park House there was all too little likelihood of serene retirement for Edmund and Cecilia. Neither advancing age nor calendar-round propinquity was designed to charm away old tensions between the nominal mistress, nearing fifty-eight, and her three sisters-in-law, all in their mid- or later fifties. On 10 May, with the reunion looming, Venables could hardly believe it was his "last time of visiting Park House on the old footing which has lasted so many years."

But in reality, the next decade brought less of a change to either Cecilia or the others than might have been anticipated. She soon substantially removed herself, quietly residing most of the time at Dover with her maid and frequently with her sister Matilda. Evidently, her emotional health remained least impaired when she could live, as she had done most of the time since 1860, with only one or two other persons. Venables's journals and Edmund's letters reveal the general pattern, although Cecilia may have sojourned at Park House during certain gaps in the record.

She arrived with Edmund from Scotland on 20 May. By 19 June, when Venables and James Bryce came by the same train, she had left for Dover, where Edmund joined her during part of July. She probably returned some time around December, when Venables had a "distressing" letter from Ellen and another from Franklin, "about P.H." On the thirty-first Venables complained, "The year closes very gloomily, P.H. shut to me"; and on New Year's day, "Everything wrong at P.H." But by late April he felt free to visit, after being away, including three months in Wales, for nine months, the "longest interval since 1839." On 31 July, Cecilia returned, but had left again before mid-November, when Venables came for a week. On 3 May 1877 he wrote, "Mrs. L. coming back at last"; she was still there on 20 June. Clues are lacking for the remainder of that year. For the three years between March 1878 and June 1881, there are no positive indications that Cecilia saw Park House at all. Venables visited freely during March, April, June, and July 1878, never mentioning her; Edmund was with her at Dover in November; she was absent from Park House at Christmas. By Edmund's own account she had remained at Dover throughout the "long, bitter winter" of 1879,[3] and was still there in May. He stayed with her in parts of July and August, and again in November. Venables visited Park House periodically through the spring and early summer of 1880. And so it seems to have gone until 28 June 1881, when "Mrs. L. came home." She was still home, or there again, at the end of the year, when Venables spent ten days there, but without seeing her once, since she was ill and keeping to her room. During the first five months of 1882, Venables himself was dangerously ill in Wales. When he returned to England, Cecilia was back at Dover. She and Edmund visited the Tennysons at Farringford in August or September,[4] after which she seems to have been at Dover for most or all of 1883. Zilly was with her during April, Edmund with her in July, and writing her at Dover in August. At the end of that year, we lose our chronicler, when Venables's surviving journals cease. Cecilia and Edmund, in his first eight years of retirement, seem to have lived apart no less, if not actually more, than previously.

Edmund's honorary LL.D. from Glasgow was followed in 1876 by an honorary D.C.L. from Oxford. By then he had become deeply immersed in a new scholarly interest, Egyptology, a pursuit seriously begun before he left Glasgow. No later than 1872 he had joined the Society of Biblical Archaeology, founded by the eminent Egyptologist Samuel Birch (1813–85), of the British

Museum, under whose auspices Edmund eventually published six scholarly articles containing his own translations from the hieroglyphics.[5] To his Park House
library he brought an impressive array of German, French, and English books
and journals about Egyptian antiquities, which his family enjoyed calling his
"golden calves."[6] When portions of his library were auctioned in 1929, the
catalog listed no fewer than 185 volumes in Egyptology. And in 1980 Mr. Frank
H. Mitchell of Sandling, near Park House, recalled that after the Lushington
family sold the estate in 1936, a lot of old notebooks filled with hieroglyphics
were left behind, perhaps inadvertently, and unceremoniously dumped by the
new occupants into an old quarry pit.

   While Edmund was passing through late middle age when he began studying
the Egyptian language, the study itself was scarcely emerging from its infancy.
The great pioneering works in the field, Jean François Champollion's *Grammaire
Egyptienne* and *Dictionnaire Egyptienne*, were not published until after his death in
1832; and they remained under the shadow of fierce criticism until vindicated in
the 1860s and later by scholars such as Karl Richard Lepsius (1810–84), and
Gaston Gaspero (1846–1916). Not yet by anyone had the grammar of the language been adequately described. For a conscientious translator like Edmund,
much remained at best conjectural.[7] In the extensive notes appended to his
translations, his forthright tentativeness is almost as interesting as the half-
mythical battle histories emerging from the texts. "Of this usage," he writes,
"no instance is known to me; still it suits the context." Or, "A phrase follows
which perplexes me," and then forty-six lines discussing his perplexity and
referring to the contributions of seven earlier scholars concerning various aspects of the problem. Again, "I cannot feel confident that the right interpretation is yet discovered. The words given above may vaguely convey the general
meaning." Or even more frankly, "The text here is very obscure. . . . I
doubt if my reading of Sallier can be right." Yet here and there he permits
himself to disagree with established authorities, even with an H. K. Brugsch or
Birch. Perhaps more than a century later these articles would retain for specialists little more than retrospective interest; but from a biographical perspective,
their worth is immense. Since Edmund did not publish in his own field of
Greek, these pieces document uniquely his admirable blend of intent concentration, unpretentious integrity, and wholehearted, if understated, affection for
all the phenomena of ancient language.

   In retirement Edmund entered all the more heartily into fraternal association
with Cecilia's brothers and sisters. In October 1875 he wrote the eldest, Frederick, then briefly in England from his home on Jersey. Could he and his daughter
spare a few days for Park House? "I have seen this year four brothers Charles
Alfred Arthur Horatio—a pleasure now too seldom granted me—& should not

willingly miss the sight of the other one."⁸ Frederick did not come, but until near the end of Edmund's life, his letters to Frederick were frequent and full, conveying news not only about the Lushington family and old Cambridge friends but about the Tennyson brothers and sisters as well. In fact, Edmund, a Tennyson by adoption only, seems to have appointed himself a sort of clearing-house for informing Tennysons about other Tennysons.

A mutually amused epistolary camaraderie flourished between Edmund and Charles Tennyson Turner. Charles, at tiny Grasby in his remote wolds parson-age, remained the most conventionally scholarly of the Tennysons. Edmund could indulge a heavyhanded playfulness by sending him versified epistles al-ternating English doggerel with Greek, Latin, and German. He would twit Charles on his stodgy theological conservatism, and Charles would return goodnatured volleys at Edmund's German-conditioned heterodoxy:

> There was a wight what lost his sight at Tubingen & Bonn
> And then avouched he'd not be couched—for oculist was none
> In English parts, if it were so, but seeing as he did
> As clear as Hegel Strauss or Baum he valued not a "quid"
> The "crumbe" of old Mother Church, with which she fondly feeds
> The addle-brains of British clerks, to keep them up to creeds.

"But," Charles wrote, "you seem to have an attachment at times to really orthodox books—which puzzles me. Am I to judge you by 'the Christ of His-tory,' St. Augustine, Thomas A Kempis or by your anti-Christian squibs?" In another interchange Edmund characterized Charles in pseudo-Byronic coup-lets:

> His thousand virtues soil'd by but one crime—
> The crime, indeed, was one that rightly shocks ye,
> The man was deeply tinged with Orthodoxy.
> Well—Orthodoxy the sole fault he had?
> *Bad*—but for British parson not *too* bad.
> Let's hope he sometime of this sin repented,
> And from his narrow bleareyed sect dissented.

More soberly, in the same letter Edmund remonstrated against Charles's unjust censure of Frederick Temple: "I am curious & really anxious to know on what grounds you speak of Temple's name as 'out of tune with Xtian faith'—this is to me incomprehensible & I seek for light & think any one who has read his ser-mons wd be greatly surprised at such an expression."⁹

By early 1878 both Charles and his careworn Louisa, Emily Tennyson's sister, had suffered breakdowns—Louisa's involving mental depression—and

left Grasby for their last time. Martin writes that Charles "went slowly down-
hill from general debility to seizures and paralysis in the last month or two"
before dying on 25 April 1879.[10] Both at Bristol, where at first he stayed, and
finally at Cheltenham, his physician had been Alfred's old friend Dr. Ker,
brother-in-law of Mary Tennyson Ker. At first Harriet Tennyson, Arthur's
wife, nursed him; and when she became disabled with bronchitis, Edmund
came out to relieve her.[11] From his letters to the Tennysons, it appears that he
was again at the bedside when Charles died. "Dear Mary" Ker had been "admirable in her devoted attention." Charles himself throughout had exhibited
"unfailing sweetness amid much suffering." His nurse declared "she never saw
anyone so gentle & considerate of others, never knew anyone like him. His
tender gratitude for any little help was exquisitely beautiful, & his cheerfulness
& humour kept up its native grace to the last." Charles had yearned that his
later sonnets might be published. "Every line," as Edmund read them, "seemed
to bring himself before me with wonderful vividness; each word seems a living
utterance of his inmost being, alike in playful or solemn, always gracious
mood." Louisa, confined at Salisbury, had not been informed: "We thought it
much better that the information should come from you."[12] In less than a
month, poor Louisa was buried beside her husband.

Enclosed in Edmund's letter to Alfred and Emily was an elegy he had written
for Charles, in fifty-eight quiet couplet lines. "Sweet friendship" had given
him no dearer friend than this one, with his "rich rare wit," his "heart's pure
warmth," his "unalloy'd" graciousness—one whose "childlike simpleness of
truth / Reveal'd his mind's unfailing youth." The elegy memorializes the dead
friend's "grand thought weighted brow," his ever guileless, never spiteful
manner of speech, his poetic gift—"lightnings of poetic thought," fanciful,
tender, reverent. His face in death carried a "strange & awful loveliness /
Attuned by death's grave earnestness / To holier beauty"—a "pure chill
beauty" that relieved sorrow and quickened "trust / That while thy dust descends to dust, / Even now thy soul is glorified, / Friend, brother, lover, angel
guide."

Since Dr. Ker had refused payment for his medical services, Edmund initiated and coordinated a Tennysonian group gift for him. "I think," he wrote
Frederick, "if you and Alfred take part all the brothers & sisters will be glad to
contribute something—few things wd gratify me more."[13] Alfred broke ranks
and sent a set of his own works, but the others jointly sent a "handsomely bound
copy" of the nine-volume Dyce's Shakespeare, which the doctor warmly acknowledged. Since Franklin Lushington was one of the trustees of Charles's
will, Edmund wrote Frederick several letters concerning the distribution
among the heirs and the disposal of the Grasby property.[14]

In 1875, soon after Alfred published his first play, *Queen Mary*, Edmund happily transmitted its commendations by two of his scholarly friends. The drama's "simplicity," "realism," and "self-restraint" had surprised the professor of moral philosophy at Glasgow. The laureate had "resources that have never been shown." And "leaving out of question Shakespeare's endless luxuriance & life" (hardly trivial omissions), the professor thought the play came "nearer to Shakespeare in grasp of the situation than any other drama" he had seen in English. Also the formidably learned and hard-to-please Bishop Connop Thirlwall, whom Edmund had seen at Bath (then seventy-eight, almost totally blind, in the last year of his life), had "heard Q Mary read to him & hoped to hear it again & was rather sorry" Tennyson "had not tried the dramatic line sooner."[15]

Edmund himself in early 1877 hailed the second play, *Harold*: its "greatness" struck him "quite as forcibly as ever or more so—& its beauty—I shd only waste time in trying to say how much I feel & admire these." But if Alfred would bear with him, could later editions not contrive to show "more of the struggle" in Harold's mind before he "seems to yield too easily" and "half abandons Edith and takes Aldwyth" for his consort? Could the thing not be done with "some grand soliloquy here and there" to "make the change less abrupt & be in itself a further help to portray his nobleness?" The action was "almost too rapid & anything that wd make Harold's weakness in the points in which he is weak less palpable wd make him more interesting as well as nobler." Characteristically too, Edmund yearned for Tennyson to magnify his glorification of ideal womanhood. "Sweet and beautiful" as Edith was, one saw "too little of her to know her as she deserves to be known."[16]

In late February came the wedding of Lionel Tennyson to Eleanor Locker, daughter of Tennyson's friend Frederick Locker (later Locker-Lampson), in Westminster Abbey, with Edmund and Cecilia present.[17] A son was born before the end of the year, and before the next year ended, a second son, who would become Sir Charles Tennyson, barrister, businessman, biographer of Tennyson and his family, and warmhearted encourager of Tennysonian scholars. The godfather of the infant Charles was Edmund. It is ironical that Sir Charles, whose fine memory remained proverbial until his death in his ninety-eighth year, worried about having no recollection of Cecilia, although he was almost thirty before she died.[18] Most probably he never saw her. She traveled very little during his boyhood, and evidently by the time of his adulthood, she seldom if ever left Park House.

Toward the end of 1879, Zilly at thirty-three became a published author when the firms of Griffith and Farran in London and E. P. Dutton in New York jointly issued her brief work of fiction, *Fifty Years in Sandbourne*, less chokingly sentimental than its plot might have made it. Its theme is endurance of suffering: a young woman learns to bear the death of her new husband and years later the simultaneous drowning of twin sons, one of whom from his sagacious vicar had learned to bear the double loss of ability to walk and, consequently, of the woman he loved. Edmund explained to Frederick Tennyson that Zilly's story was "her own," the seaside town of Sandbourne being based upon Eastbourne, "a place familiar to her from early childhood, & to me from sixty years back."[19] Frederick, preoccupied as always with Swedenborgianism, wrote to Zilly, acknowledging her "picturesque and pathetic sketches," then launching into one of his compulsive theological disquisitions: " 'Trust in the Lord' seems to be the keynote of your little book—the golden threads which run through the dark web of your village histories and thus redeem them from the outer darkness of gorgeous tragedy. . . . But who is this Lord?" To assist his niece with that supreme question, Frederick dispatched a book "which within the framework of a slight tale embodies in the form of a sort of Platonic dialogue the teachings of the Higher Christianity or New Church which is making its way slowly into all churches and must prevail being truth itself."[20]

Zilly's response, affectionate but independent, paid tribute to her own liberal nurturing as daughter of the Lushingtons and of Park House. Frederick's Swedenborgian book "might be useful to some persons who are, or fancy themselves to be, unbelievers," but it was "hardly what I feel in any way fitted to my own needs." The "narrow, bigoted tone against which it declaims never was in my bringing up or my belief." She had "known too much of love and sorrow to be able to find comfort in any but the widest conception of the love of God." To her, George Fox's words, "I saw an ocean of darkness and death; but an infinite ocean of light and love which flowed over the ocean of darkness," were "a grand expression of the one hope which makes life endurable with patience."[21]

One of the bitterest disappointments of Edmund's retirement years was the fiasco of the botched attempt of the Conservative student faction at Glasgow in the spring of 1880 to nominate Tennyson to succeed Gladstone in the lord rectorship, ending in Tennyson's embarrassed withdrawal and the election of John Bright. Hallam Tennyson's terse account is, by the most charitable reckoning, an innocuous obfuscation of a complex sequence of events: "He [Tennyson] had understood that the invitation had come from the whole body of students irrespective of political party. The manifesto of the Glasgow Independent Club recognized his condition. He found however that he had been put forward as a nominee of the Conservative party and at once withdrew."[22] In reality, the Independent Club had become significant participants in the farce only *after* Tennyson's withdrawal—not before. The documents, no fewer than fifteen letters and two telegrams at the Tennyson Research Centre,[23] establish that two members of the Conservative Club first visited Tennyson at Farringford, accurately presented themselves as spokesmen for the Conservatives, correctly informed him that the Liberals were nominating the controversial Bright, but succeeded in persuading the poet that he would be almost universally accepted on purely literary, rather than political, grounds. Several weeks after Tennyson's final refusal, Matthew Fraser, the Conservatives' chief spokesman, wrote to plead with him for a short statement vindicating Fraser and his associate of having dealt underhandedly:

> I would respectfully ask you in a short note which might be published simply to state that the deputation which waited on you *did not* deceive you (1st) as to their being representatives of the Glasgow University Conservative Club (2nd) as to their wishing you to be the nominee of that Club and (3rd) as to Mr. Bright being already in the field. I would not have made this application to you had I not believed that it was my duty to do so in the interests of our Club, and I feel sure that you will not allow us to lie under the imputation of having acted deceitfully.[24]

It seems improbable that Tennyson provided the statement; but it would have been sheer effrontery for Fraser to request it if the claims had been untrue.

The Conservatives had, nevertheless, been rash and obtuse, having returned to Glasgow and euphorically issued a hastily edited circular embellished with rhetoric that the Liberals would certainly construe as generally political and specifically anti-Bright:

> Though mingling little in the turmoil of the world, the Poet-Laureate has never hesitated to give forcible expression to his opinions regarding England's place among the nations of Europe. With lofty scorn he has denounced that insular selfishness which would leave England without a foreign policy. His belief in those great constitutional principles which have made our country what it is is none the less unwavering because it is seldom openly declared.[25]

After such baiting, the Liberals felt gloriously liberated to counterattack, both on the quadrangle and in Glasgow newspapers. They were not impeded by Fraser's belated announcement on 3 May that Tennyson had agreed to stand only if "we would promote his candidacy on purely literary grounds. Every one will at once admit that we could have no other object in view in nominating Mr. Tennyson, and we intend strictly to conform to his expressed intentions." One valiant Liberal, not much bolder than some others, volleyed back, "But since Mr. Tennyson has consented to be the nominee of a purely political party . . . he must be prepared to accept" a "crushing . . . defeat." Unwise

Tennysonian supporters began fiercely berating Bright as a preacher of "peace at any price," a Philistine scorner of higher education, a demagogue outside the Commons and a propagandist within it for his own "opulent trading and manufacturing class."

Tennyson withdrew in a letter to Fraser published in the *Times* (London).[26] He could not "appear what I have steadfastly refused to be—a party candidate." The "mere fact of a contest between . . . a nominee for a Liberal and . . . for a Conservative Club leads, I suppose, inevitably to this conclusion in the minds of the public." Furthermore, several years earlier he had declined to be the candidate of the Glasgow Liberals. (Strictly speaking, that claim was only partly true.)[27] But he would "gladly accept a nomination . . . at any time" from a "body of students, bearing no political name" or from "both Liberals and Conservatives" jointly recognizing only "the literary merits you are good enough to appreciate." Thereupon, the Conservatives proposed to withdraw and turn over the poet's cause to the Independent Club; but at that, the most activated Liberals hooted that transparently the Tories were pandering to the Independents by offering to fight under their colors.

It was Tennyson's unwillingness to accept the sponsorship of the Independents that most painfully disappointed Edmund. "His letter said *at any time*, not *another time.* . . . After the offer thrown out in the letter it will be very hard on his loyal supporters if he withdraws."[28] On 10 May, Edmund had begged Tennyson: "I say, earnestly, pray do not do this—it would have the worst effect possible; it would tend to damp the generous ardour felt for high literary achievement & it would grieve me deeply." The university would "lose what would be an honour to herself, & proferred by the young men to you in a spirit of becoming & true admiration." On the eleventh he argued: "If the honest feelings of the students is in favour of electing the Country's highest name in literature, who has a right to say that the contest is made a political one?" Tennyson's "retiring after giving his assent would absolutely be fatal to literary eminence being ever considered as the chief ground on wh students might venture to bring forward a candidate." To himself it would be "most painful," both on "public and on personal grounds."[29]

On the twelfth an editorial writer in the *Glasgow Herald* wistfully summed up the case. Tennyson would have to "wait long for that halcyon period when strife of parties is silent in the College quadrangle, and the student youth of polemical and political Scotland emulate each other in recording their votes for men distinguished by learning and genius, and the peaceful arts." Tennyson's election would have been a great honor to the university, "but we cannot say that in withdrawing from a political contest he has taken a course in which any of his real friends will disagree with him."

Even Edmund—and Tennyson never had any friend more real—achieved greater detachment by early June, admitting that the greatest offender had been the Conservatives' circular with its "phrases obviously . . . poking at the opposite side," giving "colour to the plea that the contest must take the form of political antagonism." Tennyson might have acted differently if the circular had only generally "described Mr. T's writings as inspired with noble and patriotic feeling." But "declarations . . . from all sides that it could not help being a party candidature . . . carried against what I could say."[30]

Early that October, Edmund's mellowed thoughts turned backward forty-two years when he found himself spending some pleasant hours with the two other men who in 1838 had most desired the Glasgow Greek professorship. One of them, A. C. Tait, archbishop of Canterbury, whom Edmund had several times briefly met, had invited him and Zilly to Addington Park, the archdiaconal palace. Then thoughtfully, Tait had invited his old Oxford friend Robert Lowe (Lord Sherbrooke), Edmund's former bitter rival. As Edmund informed Alfred, the three aging men, "Archy, Bob, & I drove under 3 umbrellas in a pony chaise. . . . The rain was steady & sharp enough to put out any lingering sparks of our ancient antagonisms." "Archy" had been "very kind & social, with a good deal of anecdote & humour, I like him very much, & Lowe was affable and pleasant."[31] To Hallam, Edmund ponderously quipped, " . . . You will at once admit the cogency of the argument that if I had not become Grk. Prof. I should probably have been either Archbishop of Canterbury or Chancellor of the Exchequer—or possibly both."[32]

Enthusiastically Edmund hailed Tennyson's admirably varied 1880 volume, *Ballads and Other Poems*, his first new collection in eight years. Edmund, perhaps predictably, preferred the contrived melodrama of "The Sisters" (classing it with "Enoch Arden wh I always thought one of your noblest poems in pathos & grandeur") to the starker, innovative "Rizpah," because the "real blank verse" in "The Sisters" pleased him more than "the other metre, however admirably managed." Predictably too he admired the metaphysical "De Profundis," comparing it with "sundry short poems of Göthe." He had no toleration for "shallow & narrow criticism" that objected to metaphysical ideas in verse: it might "just as fairly be said" that Hamlet had "no right to think or utter many of his speeches." He praised "all the little dedicatory poems . . . very tender & graceful," and "The Voyage of Maeldune"—"wonderfully fine and imaginative," with "a wizard roll in the verse suiting so wild a story." Such martial poems as "The Ballad of the Revenge" and "The Defence of Lucknow" reinforced his patriotic bellicosity against uncontrolled terrorism in Ireland and Gladstone's apparently spineless foreign policy around the world: "our sham Government, wh lets half Ireland be enslaved by the hatefullest tyranny,

& truckles to murderous ruffianism, blind to the shame & guilt of doing nothing to stop triumphant savagery." Some of "this volume might at least teach those who have forgotten it what brave men can do." In the same letter Edmund was the one to inform the Tennysons about Arthur Tennyson's recent illness and, indeed, the latest mailing address of Arthur and his wife, Harriet.[33]

In the spring of 1883, Venables, almost seventy-three, finally retired from the Parliamentary Bar, after having been honored at a Bar dinner. In September, Edmund and Zilly spent two weeks with him at the family estate at Llysdinam, Newbridge-on-Wye, where a new church built for the parish by Venables himself had recently been dedicated.

Tennyson that August had gone at the queen's invitation for a friendly conversation in her own room at Osborne. Edmund, receiving Alfred's account, wrote, "It makes one's love of the Queen still warmer if that were needed, to know how truly she can know & honour true greatness & nobleness when she has an opportunity of meeting them."[34] When later that year Tennyson, probably at the direct behest of the queen, was raised to the peerage, Edmund rejoiced "that you are to keep your true name, the name loved & admired for 50 years, with no mean additions." Alfred had made unsuccessful overtures toward discomfiting his cousins by appropriating the name Tennyson d'Eyncourt. Edmund felt a "profound . . . sense of relief" that it would not be so.[35]

Soon he had to turn from felicitating one Tennyson brother to consoling another, Frederick, upon the death of his wife, Maria. It was an uneasy task, so divergent were his own tentative views of the afterlife from Frederick's. He could only "offer my earnest wishes that all the earthly comfort possible may come to you from the love of those nearest you who are left, & that comfort from a higher source may not fail, as I trust it never does those who seek for it, as you will, in a true spirit."[36] Cecilia, without inhibitions, poured out her heart: her brother's was "a sorrow which time can never *really heal.*" It was nine years "since I lost my Lucy. No human being ever loved me as she loved me, except my Mother. Your loved one has met our Mother & my Lucy up above. Oh that we were there with them." Maria had been "all in all" to Frederick, as "Lucy was to me, therefore *I know* your sorrow. . . . 'Tis better to have loved and lost / Than never to have loved at all.' "[37]

In April 1884 death came quickly to Mary Ker, the eldest Tennyson sister, three months after Frederick's Maria. "Words can say little," Edmund wrote the doubly bereaved old man. "Even if I had better mastery of thm, I could not express my deep sympathy with you." Within a few weeks all "the shadowy fleetingness of life, and at the same time its awful reality," had been pressed upon him through the deaths of three who had been "intimately known & dear." About a week before Mary, "there was Monteith," his friend through

fifty years "of intimacy," like Mary "seeming quite well a few days before, &
like her succumbing with strange swiftness to congestion of lungs." And poor
Francis Garden (son of Monteith's elder sister and a fellow Apostle) was "lingering on, lying conscious but hardly able to speak, peacefully sinking."[38]

Alfred's mediocre short plays *The Cup* and *The Falcon* left Edmund in a quan-
dary. It was never comfortable either to dispraise, or ignore, his sensitive
brother-in-law; but *The Cup* he could honestly commend only mildly, *The Falcon* hardly at all. It was "always a grief . . . not to be able wholly to sympathize with & admire whatever you write, but I believe you would rather have
my true feelings exprest than mere vague compliments." Alfred had "accustomed" him to "such an ideal of perfection that I feel intitled to look for what I
have almost universally found & love to find."[39]

After the great crowd at the wedding of Hallam Tennyson and Audrey
Boyle in Westminster Abbey in June 1884 had blocked Edmund and Cecilia
from greeting the Tennysons, Edmund wrote to reassure them of his love. "It
was hard to bear not to be able to see & speak to you & Emmy. . . . See *you*
indeed I did & the two little boys in front of you, but I never did catch a glimpse
of her." Perhaps, though, it would be "easier to say this in writing than it would
have been to say anything in the midst of the crowd." He could express "but
feebly" all that he felt and wished for them, "all that the memory of quiet
Shiplake [the Tennysons' wedding] of that morning & of the years that have
past since brought before my mind during the solemn service." The "journey &
everything" had been "much of a trial" for Cecilia; she was not well, but he
trusted she might soon recover strength.[40]

By then half through his seventy-fourth year and well into the tenth of his
uneventful retirement, Edmund would have harbored no aspirations beyond
the ancient rituals of routinely living, extending and receiving affection, gradually aging, eventually dying. With his long-beloved studies to occupy his
thoughts, and nourish his soul, he could not have yearned for more. But fate was
reserving for him one final happy surprise. On 6 November that year, Henry
Fawcett, the elected lord rector of Glasgow University, a man who had risen
above the handicap of total blindness to become a respected economist and
public servant, died of congestion of the lungs within nine days of the statutory
date for a rectorial election. Thoughts at Glasgow may well have reverted four
years to the unfortunate contretemps when Tennyson might have accepted the
honor had it been extended nonpartisanly and unanimously. But could anybody
confidently depend upon the temperamental poet, now a peer, to make up his
mind on such brief notice to accept? Certainly he would not give the customary
rectorial address, for he had so stipulated in 1880. But from a sense of duty
would not his scholarly brother-in-law, beloved at Glasgow, accept and speak?
Unanimously, the students elected Edmund. He confided to a nephew of Ceci-

lia's that he would have "preferred remaining quiet & not coming again into this sort of publicity"; but it would be "a very great pleasure to meet so many of my old friends and colleagues together," perhaps for the last time.[41]

As Edmund approached the podium on 26 March 1885, he seemed momentarily "dazed" (perhaps merely fighting back tears?), until his former student and longtime colleague William Thomson (later Lord Kelvin) stepped up to reassure him. One report years later claimed that inconsiderately noisy students drowned out parts of the speech; another report maintained that the noise was merely their "enthusiastic reception."[42] The address[43] carried echoes of Edmund's 1870 dedicatory speech, but the later, and shorter, discourse began more confidently and remained almost uniformly eloquent, conveying, as Lewis Campbell described it, "the experience and authority of age."[44]

Edmund exhorted his hearers to fortify one another's zeal for learning: "Communion of mind with mind is the most powerful help to mental growth . . . in such intercourse he who gives receives, and is made richer in giving what awakens new life in another." Learning is progressive: "Every decad [sic], almost every year, opens new vistas through which the piercing eye . . . may look forward bright in the hope of adding something more to the store of accomplished good to mankind; for in knowledge as in nature, nothing is unfruitful."

"What," he asked, "is this being of ours which thinks, plans, and wills? What means it? Whither tends it? This, the question of questions, from far distant periods, souls possess with profound genius have dared to ask and yearned for a reply." The early Greek philosophers led to Plato and Aristotle, through whose "unsurpassed lucidity of diction . . . we are led into the very foundry of ideas, and can follow the subtle process of new-born thought growing clearer to itself, and shaping language into its close-fitting outward venture." In literature "the creations of imaginative art, in clear-eyed intelligence and vivid description of man's life and doings, in the mastery of potent words, spurring men on to noble deeds, in all outcomings of mental activity, we have models of high excellence preserved to us, which should deepen our obligation to the great minds of bygone eras."

The old classicist pleaded against innovative proposals to replace teaching of the ancient languages with study of the classics in translation. Surely not even the "best translation into a foreign tongue could do full justice either to Shakespeare or Burns." Only through the originals could one fully realize the "stormy concentrated strength" of the "battle-music" in Homer; the "stern and awful moral grandeur" of Aeschylus; the "calm, solemn, piously tender earnestness" of Sophocles; the "simple, open-eyed, truth-loving curiosity" of Herodotus; the "grave, lofty thoughtfulness" of Thucydides; or the "burning words in which the pure, high-souled Demosthenes strove to wake a noble, but half-enervated and easily deluded community, to a living sense of their inherited glories and duties."

Knowledge was advancing dramatically through archaeological explorations, the "excavation of magnificent buildings, the discovery of sites and localities, long known and unsuspected," the unearthing and reading of "inscriptions in manifold dialects." Recent developments in comparative philology had enabled men to "trace in divers languages, by carefully analyzing their inmost form and structure, the brotherhood which comprehends us as members of one large family."

No less important was the burgeoning study of English literature. The "more we grow familiar with the life-teeming freshness of Chaucer, the better shall we be prepared to appreciate the peerless sovereignty of Shakespeare" and "the severe sublimity of Milton." Burns and Wordsworth were "two morning stars of a new dawn of poetry"; and the prematurely dying Shelley and Byron were succeeded by equally worthy youthful poets "who have created new forms of beauty and loftiness . . . teaching that the guiding light for poet and for man should be 'self-reverence, self-knowledge, self-control' "(that quotation, of course, was from Tennyson's "Oenone"), and that "beauty is the most beautiful when it reflects the inner essence of goodness."

In all knowledge, "though 'the scale is infinite,' we may yet draw nearer to the light, and obtain in drawing nearer the assurance of an inexhaustible light beyond. The most expanded knowledge, gazing from afar towards the immeasurable height above, is also the most humbling." Students should "never forget that it is a sacred and humbling duty to improve and strengthen the faculties given you; that they are bestowed for a high purpose . . . extending beyond any limits of time; that every human soul bears the seed of a boundless destiny . . . for each one to nourish and rear into fulness of growth and make fruitful of abiding good, by faithful, unwavering devotion to truth and duty."

Four nights later at Maclean's Hotel, Edmund's old students gave him a dinner attended by more than 120 men. The printed toast list[45] included a sonnet (no author given):

> Our dear old Master! little changed the face
> Which had such charm for us in vanished days,
> How sweetly fell thy sparing words of praise,
> How lashed thy tongue whate'er was mean or base!
>
> Few were the students on whose hearts no trace
> Was left of contact ever wont to raise;
> The boldest shrank before thy quick eye's blaze,
> And all revered thy dignity and grace!

And now there comes to thee in green old age
The crowning honour of an honoured life,
The choice of thee has blotted from the page
All politics and every dream of strife;
Lord Rectors may have boasted greater fame,
None ever bore a nearer or a dearer name.

The usual monotonous toasts lauded the queen; the army, navy, and volunteers; the Scottish universities; the professions (clergy, law, medicine, education); the commercial interests (so important to Glasgow); and the new lord rector himself. The chairman, James A. Campbell, M.P., declaimed that "under Professor Lushington we all learned from a living example what was meant by the enthusiasm of scholarship and the graces of culture." His unanimous election by students who had never known him was "sufficient testimony" to his merits. From their fathers many had heard of the "professor who . . . had cast such lustre on the University." Edmund, responding, expressed his pleasure in "grasping the hands of those whom I count as my friends." If some of their names and faces had been forgotten, his "interest in their fortunes and their kindness" would "ever be unforgotten." He memorialized his beloved late colleague William Ramsay, whose "kindly, benignant, and ever-ready and ever-wise help and counsel" had smoothed the way for him when he first arrived in Scotland. All the love and praise his listeners had extended would remain "a stimulus" to him. It would be "base to have received such affectionate and warm commendation without doing the utmost that lies within me to prove that it is not entirely without meaning."[46]

All the ceremonies concluded, Edmund worked his leisurely way back to Park House—first to Edinburgh, where he had "almost as many old friends to see as at Glasgow"; then to Northumberland to visit Venables's widowed sister-in-law; thence to London for a few days with Franklin; on down to Bournemouth ("quite new to me, & interesting in many ways"), where Zilly had been staying for her health; finally to Alfred and Emily at Aldworth, their mainland home high on Blackdown in Sussex. Alfred was "very well," Emily "undoubtedly much better than she has been," and "Hallam & his bride seemed very happy in each other."[47]

Back at Park House in May, he felt obliged on principle to disappoint Cecilia's sister, Emily Jesse, by refusing to contribute to her fervently cherished cause of antivivisection. Her letter to him probably resembled one she wrote Frederick at about the same time. She and Richard, her navy captain husband, had "lately been so thoroughly horrified and almost palsy stricken" by the findings of the Royal Commission on Vivisection that they had "begun the fight against such devilish deeds direct from the mouth of Hell. I said the other day to Richard that if I could commit a murder the victim would be a vivisector." Frederick contributed a sovereign (about ten shillings).[48] Edmund sent an apology: "It grieves me to have to decline to accede to a request which I well know you make from pure benevolence." But he was unconvinced that the antivivisectionist movement was "altogether right, or that wanton cruelties are in the habit of being practised by such men as Sir John Paget & others." It seemed "a very difficult point to determine how far pain which we unscrupulously give in obtaining animal food for ourselves is permissible or otherwise for the sake of being able to relieve severe human suffering." Not being "free from doubt," he would have to abstain.[49]

Edmund, then seventy-five, would live for another eight years, three of them as his old university's lord rector, cheerfully free from duties to perform.[50] Less agreeably, he suffered his share of financial losses as a rural landowner during the agricultural depression of the latter 1880s—plots of land unrented, tenants unable to pay, hops rotting on vines for want of a tolerable market price. "It is really a very serious business," Franklin wrote Venables in 1887, "for so incapable an innocent as Edmund to have a 250 acre farm with 30 acres of hops thrown into his hands [unrented] at his time of life, and I don't see how he is to be helped out of it."[51] Fortunately, during these years Cecilia, living less at Dover and more with him at Park House, seems to have been relatively undepressed although never physically healthy. Zilly's health too was often precarious. Edmund himself, until his final two years, seems to have remained comparatively well except for recurrent lameness.

Of his three remaining sisters, Ellen, the youngest, was first to die, on 14 January 1886, after decades of semi-invalidism still only sixty-four. Replying to spiritistic consolations from Frederick, Edmund spoke merely of "a field for reverent loving hope" that "beloved beings who have past away from sight of our corporeal eyes" may be "yet present spiritually, wielding gracious & helpful influence to draw us on to good." That possibility could hardly be denied by any one "who has felt the beneficent spell of the earthly intercourse with pure & noble characters." Actually, "no science can explain how the miracle of soul communing with soul is effected," even through "the medium of sense—*how* it is that certain pulses of the air convey to my mind the thoughts of another mind." No "less" then, "*without* the evidence of sense this marvel of spiritual communion may be accepted & looked to as one of God's methods of reaching our spirits, & drawing them up to Himself."[52] All of which was much too tentative for such a forthright supernaturalist as Frederick. On another occasion Frederick described a friend who had "proclaimed himself an Agnostic—and it would seem that all Agnostics—or sceptics—for they are convertible terms—do not agree as to their scepticism." This one was "not a Materialist but did not believe an iota of Spiritualism—for which he substituted a belief in Metaphysics—precisely resembling Edmund Lushington in that respect."[53]

Weak-eyed Maria, most serene of the sisters, would live on until 19 January 1891, eleven days short of her seventy-fifth birthday. For several months, as Edmund reported, she was bedridden, "but not often suffering pain or illness, cheerful & taking interest in everything around her, eager to help in any way that she possibly could, as in knitting woolen things for poor people, & our labourers." Three days before the end, a stroke paralyzed her left side, impairing her speech. On her last evening she asked Edmund to read James Montgomery's hymn " 'Forever with the Lord'—and indeed if ever those words may apply to a human being they may fitly be spoken of her whose life was so deeply loving & unselfish, actively devoted to the good of others, a beautiful & holy life, such as must purify & help Godward the spirits of those who knew her."[54] Unfortunately, when Emily died on 3 April 1893 at seventy-five, Edmund himself would be too ill to pen her eulogy. The Kent *Messenger* only partially supplied the need: an "estimable lady, who though she led a rather retired life, was a keen sympathizer with the poor and needy in their troubles and trials."

On 6 October 1888, as Edmund informed Frederick, death had taken Venables, "one of the truest friends & most genuine noble-hearted men that ever lived." Although seventy-eight and gradually failing, he had spent a late-August week at Park House, driving daily with Edmund and walking vigorously two or three miles. He proceeded to the Tennysons at Aldworth, but almost immediately fell ill, hurried back to London, seemed to be improving, but had "a bad fall, & was unconscious . . . longer than . . . in 2 or 3 earlier falls," then two days later died. "With no family was he for many years on terms of more intimate friendship than ours, the change & loss to us is exceeding great, & yet it is surpassing strange." That Maria, recently quite ill, survived him "like many other surprises . . . presses upon us the mystery of life & death & of all things—a mystery to whose darkness we must bow till it be finally dissolved, as we hope it may, into reconciling light."[55]

Frederick, almost seventy-eight, had published no poems for three decades when Edmund in the spring of 1885 began urging him to do so: "I earnestly wish & exhort you to think of publishing another volume of poems. You must have plenty at hand well worthy of it." Edmund had "seen some very beautiful ones, & wish I had seen more, but you have lived so remote from many who care for you. . . . You owe it to yourself & to the Power who bestowed the gift of poesy on you not to let it be hidden under a napkin."[56] On 17 November 1887, after Frederick had authorized Hallam Tennyson to ready a blank-verse volume based upon Sapphic materials, Edmund wrote Frederick to raise some questions of Greek mythology and suggest greater compression—good advice for so profuse a poet—and even some omissions.[57] By August 1888 the project, largely transferred from Hallam to Hardwick Rawnsley, was dragging on; the book remained unpublished; and Frederick had turned eighty-one. Edmund had urged Hallam to "quicken the Revd sonneteer [Rawnsley] in the business," but had received no reply. It seemed "important that no time should be lost—it would be a most grievous loss if the whole were to come to nothing."[58] Two months later Edmund had again urged Hallam "to poke up H. Rawnsley about your poems, & he promised to attend to it—people are sometimes unaccountably slow."[59] On 18 July 1889, with Frederick's eyesight failing, Edmund sent him several pages of general criticisms, urging still further cutting and compressing.[60] By late October, with the *Isles of Greece* manuscript in some kind of shape at last and Walter Ker, Mary Tennyson's son, seeing it through the press, Edmund was back urging the old poet to start preparing another volume.[61]

With Frederick's book finally published, Edmund could happily relay appreciations from his friends. He cheered Frederick on to anticipate later editions by rounding up all the typographical and other errors in the first, a list of which he enclosed.[62] By then Edmund himself was eighty and his own health in decline. His letters to Frederick ceased, or have not survived. Frederick, fated to outlive him by almost five years, would publish two more new volumes (the last when eighty-eight), before dying in 1898 in his ninety-first year.

Alfred with his surprising poetic fecundity in old age required no prodding. Edmund could comment, generally with satisfaction, as each new book appeared. He rejoiced in the "undecaying strength" of *Tiresias and Other Poems* (1885)—"all . . . rich in power & grace." "The Ancient Sage" was "the grandest & dearest poem of the volume." He heartily welcomed two older poems, published at last: "Early Spring," a "delicate flower of exquisite beauty wh in its earliest shape I had by heart between 40 & 50 years ago," and "Tiresias," enhanced by the new dedication and requiem, both for FitzGerald. "The Wreck" and "Despair," with "all their deep pathos & beauty," were "almost too painful" (a lenient verdict upon both). In "Balin and Balan" Edmund, characteristically squeamish about less-than-lovely female characters, "wd gladly have seen less of Vivien or dispensed with her presence altogether. She made herself hateful enough years ago in Merlin & needed not to be held up to detestation again."[63] (But as Alfred had projected the total *Idylls*, the newer poem, preceding the older, would be introducing Vivien.) Edmund, writing to Frederick, pronounced "Crossing the Bar" in Alfred's 1889 volume "one of the sublimest utterances I know on the awful subject—his own line is applicable to it 'In its simplicity sublime'—& all the poems are well worthy of him, tho' the subject of some has a kind of ghostly weirdness wh almost checks the pleasure wh the skill & fineness of treatment call forth."[64] To Alfred himself in April

1892 Edmund praised "The Foresters" as "a work of rich & strong imagination": "it would be no use attempting to dwell on passages here & there of remarkable beauty." Edmund himself had been ill and was just reaching the "point at wh I manage a walk out of doors for ¼ of an hour or so, at a very feeble pace. . . . You see I am not nearly up to what I could do when last at Aldworth, tedious enough, but it's no use grumbling."[65]

In April 1886 Alfred, at age seventy-seven, had suffered one of the greatest sorrows of his life in the death at sea of his son Lionel. Edmund, so acquainted with such sorrows and their nuances, did not write until early June. His silence, he explained, had "been from no lack of the deepest sympathy, but from exceeding tenderness of sympathy . . . lest at such a time any words, even the most loving, might painfully jar upon you." But for himself "long silence" was "hard to bear when the heart overflows with affectionate longing for the relief & comfort of one surpassingly dear." Now he would "utter a brother's loving hope, that you have found an image comforting the mind, & that God given strength is yours to bear one of the bitterest griefs destined to life on earth." For himself Alfred's "words . . . spoken or written" had been "over & over again of blessed helpful virtue & strength . . . as to many others." He and Alfred "so rarely" met "now, & life is so uncertain, that I could not bear longer leaving unspoken something of my soul's inmost yearnings to be a very brother & friend to one who commands my entire reverence & love—much as I fall short of being what I would."[66]

As improbable as it may seem, the mild Edmund's fierce loyalty to Alfred extending itself to Alfred's friends, prompted him in 1889 to contemplate publishing an undistinguished set of rhymes rebuking an emotional indiscretion committed by Robert Browning, another of Alfred's friends, against the recently deceased Edward FitzGerald. The story has several times been tediously told of how Browning, aging and tired, unfortunately discovered a thoughtlessly misogynist remark in an 1861 letter of old Fitz that Aldis Wright, editor of his letters, had inadvertently neglected to delete: "Mrs. Browning's Death is rather a relief to me, I must say: no more Aurora Leighs, thank God!" and more to the effect that female poets might better be employed minding "the Kitchen and their children; and perhaps the Poor."[67] In an understandable rage Browning fired off a tasteless rhymed squib to the *Athenaeum*, which he almost immediately, but too late, attempted to retrieve[68]:

To Edward Fitzgerald

I chanced upon a new book yesterday:
I opened it, and, where my finger lay
    'Twixt page and uncut page, these words I read

—Some six or seven at most—and learned thereby
That you, Fitzgerald, whom by ear and eye
   She never knew, "thanked God my wife was dead."

Ay dead! and were yourself alive, good Fitz,
How to return you thanks would tax my wits:
   Kicking you seems the common lot of curs—
While more appropriate greeting lends you grace:
Surely to spit there glorifies your face—
   Spitting from lips once sanctified by Hers.

ROBERT BROWNING

Seeing the verses and "stirred" with "indignation" and "grief that a great man should so degrade himself," Edmund penned some "lines" of his own:

Peace, angry Bard,! can spitting ease thy pain?
Shall nobler minds such temper not disdain?
Homeric gods condemn'd when Hector bled,
Insensate vengeance on the senseless dead:
In outrage which serene Olympians blame
Can Christian born Achilles take no shame?
Back, with the scorpion poison sheath'd again,
Or plant its sting in thy own heart & brain.
On one dead man, who never sought to hurt,
What generous pen could savage rancour blurt?
Great as thou art, why stoop to be so small?
Thy phrenzied spite with chasten'd soul recall.

Edmund sent his piece to Hallam with instructions to send, or not send, it to "the St. James or any other paper," but to keep it strictly anonymous.[69] He later told Frederick that Browning's lines had offended him "as a gross outrage on the feelings of all of" Fitz's friends, "especially on Alfred considering the warm regard shown in the dedication to Tiresias." But Alfred had "thought the subject had better be let to rest."[70] No doubt Edmund was grateful for Alfred's wisdom a few weeks later when Browning died. He had been a "true & great poet," Edmund wrote Frederick; "the wish that his faults were fewer" could not "blind one to the splendour of all that was good & great in him, & he must rank with those rare souls who are the salt of the earth."[71]

For Alfred's eighty-third, and last, birthday, 6 August 1892, Edmund wrote a brief and beautiful greeting:

You will probably today be receiving many letters of friendly congratulation from divers quarters—none I am sure more loving and earnest than this. May the day be blest to you and all who are dear to you and may the year bring more blessings as it goes forward must be the warm wish of all who have felt the knowledge of you and your writings to be among the greatest blessings of their life.

Year after year my deep love and admiration has grown, tho' I have not often of late had the opportunity of expressing it, as we now so seldom meet—but I think you know how largely indebted to you I feel for whatever is best and truest in myself—a debt one cannot hope to repay.

Edmund was "sorry to learn from Arthur's wife" that Alfred was again unwell, so soon after "the newspaper reports had so constantly spoken of your being perfectly well." Cecilia had "pains in her knees which are troublesome, but she can take a fair amount of walking and is cheerful." He himself could "only walk about 10 minutes after my drive and do not improve much. . . . Now I hope that before long I may hear of your being a great deal better. Hallam you will write and tell me, won't you?"[72]

When Alfred died at Aldworth on 6 October, exactly two months after his birthday, Hallam, no doubt overwhelmed with preparations for the mammoth funeral in Westminster Abbey, telegraphed Edmund. Would he communicate the news to the five surviving Tennyson brothers and sisters? The new Lord Tennyson was tacitly confirming the pivotal family position his affectionate uncle-by-marriage had gradually established by thoughtfully keeping the never very clannish Tennysons in touch with one another. Edmund wrote to Frederick and to the wives of Arthur and Horatio, who would know how best to tell their husbands. Zilly and her aunt Emily Lushington wrote to Matilda, whom Edmund had already written that morning after receiving a letter from Hallam's wife, Audrey. "Your Aunt C," he informed Hallam, was "greatly afflicted," but bearing up "quite as well as I cd have expected." Fortunately, she had been "for the last 3 or 4 days in somewhat better health than she often is—had she been as ill as she sometimes is the shock wd have been more intense & overwhelming." She would "sometimes" say, "I foreboded it all," and would "dwell on the comfort & support he was to her from earliest childhood—'he has never been out of my thoughts' is one of her expressions." Edmund wished Hallam to know "one little thing wh possibly may not be quite without interest." Earlier that week he had dreamed of "walking & talking with your Father & I kissed him." After waking he could recall "no other part of the dream, but this was perfectly clear to my memory, & I am glad to have had the dream." In Greek, he added, "The dream is of God."[73]

From Cecilia herself a letter survives, as brief as it is earnest, to Emily Tennyson, dated only "Nov. 1892": "Only a line to say that I know that God is helping you as he is helping me and Tilly [Matilda]. We both send dearest love.

I am so glad you have your Hallam with you. Tell him I hope to remember some past things, for the history." She enclosed some verses she had made on the day after Alfred died:

> Oh my brother gone to where
> The Brother Christ and angels are,
> Our Christ will meet thee, thou wilt find
> One ever loving, tender, kind;
> To *love* him will be ecstasy
> No want in that bright destiny
> No longing for the past, for there
> All is joy, no pain, no care,
> The summit of thy bliss will be
> To love thy Lord with ecstasy.[74]

The purest of high-Victorian bardolatry, already outdated in that decade of Oscar Wilde, informed a letter from Zilly to Hallam, a fortnight after the death. "Hitherto the days" had been "too sacred" to "break in upon. . . . All these days our thoughts have been centred on your home—where that great soul—to whom were entrusted such mighty gifts of power and influence among men—was passing thro' the Shadow into Light." When "the final tidings reached us," she had "felt thrilled thro' and thro' with holy awe and solemn triumph that one so nearly related to me, and so marvellously endowed, should have received the last great call into the last ocean of Everlasting Life." What a "glorious Destiny" it had been for "nearly 60 years to be a light and guide to human beings without number—helping them out of sin, out of misery, out of even suicide—helping them towards Truth, towards Holiness, towards Christ." And then she referred to Edmund. She could "enter deeply" into Hallam's "love and . . . loss—for, like yourself for so long, I am daily and hourly watching over a beloved father, whose hold on life seems to become more frail and precarious every week."[75]

Edmund by then was feebly advancing toward eighty-two. As his sister Emily wrote Emily Tennyson, he had "a good deal of business to attend to, but rest of mind & body" were "both very needful to him." She and "dear Zilly" were watching him constantly "lest he would do anything to hurt his heart or give him cold."[76] (Evidently Emily and Zilly were agreed that Cecilia, who was "quite as well as one could at all hope" and "less excitable than we feared she might be," had enough to do in keeping well herself without trying to look after her husband. But there was nothing new in that: for decades the family, wrongly or rightly, had thus regarded Cecilia.)

On 10 January, Edmund entered his eighty-third year. Of his final months few details survive. The *Glasgow Herald* later reported that a few months before his death he had fallen down a staircase in his house. In May he had written "hopefully of improvement to an old student in Glasgow," but "unfavourable symptoms intervened." His grief at Emily's unanticipated dying in early April must have been compounded by his own inability as head of the family to attend her funeral. Now, of his parents' twelve offspring, only Franklin and he, the firstborn, remained. It may have been after that, although possibly sooner, that his superb mind began breaking, leaving him with the delusion (as Zilly informed a cousin) "that someone was following him about trying to kill him."[77] Or the delusion may have been confined to the week of delirium preceding his death on 13 July.[78]

The Maidstone newspapers reported the brightness of the weather on the afternoon of the funeral, and the freedom from "obtrusiveness or display." Seven mourning carriages and seven private conveyances moved across the mile between Park House and Boxley churchyard. Cecilia was not in the party, nor evidently was Franklin, presumably ill, although his wife, Kate, rode in the first carriage with Zilly, Hallam Lord Tennyson, and Tom Lushington's son, the Reverend Godfrey Lushington. A "number of the villagers and old retainers of the family were present in the church and at the graveside eager to show the esteem and respect for the deceased gentleman and his family." After a simple service the coffin, "covered with beautiful white wreaths and crosses," was placed in the family vault out in the churchyard, "a large brick structure containing already fourteen coffins," including Emily's, deposited there three months before. Inside the church, on the right wall near the altar, Edmund's tablet, with others of his family, reads (in part): "For thirty-seven years Professor of Greek in Glasgow University and afterwards elected Lord Rector. . . . A man of vast learning, rare humility, and wonderful influence for good."

Edmund's obituary article in the *Classical Review* (7:425–28), which I have several times cited, was composed by his former Glasgow pupil and longtime friend, Lewis Campbell, for many years professor of Greek at St. Andrews University. Despite several peripheral inaccuracies, it is the best treatment of Edmund's life that I have seen. On 1 October death claimed another of Campbell's former Greek professors and personal friends, a man more eminent than Edmund, Benjamin Jowett, master of Balliol College, Oxford, and superb translator of Plato, Aristotle, and Thucydides. For him too Campbell wrote the *Classical Review* memorial article (7:474–76). With affectionate admiration for his scholar-friends, Campbell essayed a comparison to set forth the peculiar strengths of both. Jowett, he had decided, "had far more alertness and elasticity of intellect, more fertility of resource, wider aims, more comprehensive

FIG. VII. Boxley Parish Church. 1971. Photograph by author.

sympathies,—though perhaps not more power of suspending judgment,—than Lushington had. But those who from 1845 to 1865 came from 'prelections' in the Glasgow private Greek class to the Balliol lecture room . . . did not feel the same certainty of touch, the same unfailing strength of presentation."

Cecilia when widowed was three months short of seventy-six. Of all surviving documents throughout her life referring to her—letters, journal entries, or reminiscences—few are without some reference to her poor health. During her marriage, a long half-century, her valetudinarianism had been virtually perpetual. Yet, ironically, she would live on for nearly sixteen more years before dying, quite senile, in the spring of 1909 in her ninety-second year. The most interesting detail of Edmund's will is a codicil requiring his widow, so long as she continued to live at Park House with their daughter (heir to the estate), to pay £200 a year "as a contribution . . . to the general expenses of keeping up the house." Should she live elsewhere, the £200 would be paid to her in addition to the £400 she had always received under the marriage settlement. Expenses would "press far more heavily on my daughter than they did on me, as my yearly pension of £862 ceases with my life, & rents of late years have so greatly diminished." Furthermore, his now deceased sisters had "regularly contributed to the general expenses, & it seems to me but fair that my widow should likewise in this way help to lighten the burden falling on my daughter." The "£400 of the settlement" would help her meet various personal expenses" that he "used to defray for her," including medicine, various Maidstone bills, and her maid's wages.[79]

It is unfortunate that the only really vivid descriptions we have of Cecilia emanate from her extreme old age: a formidable figure clumping about Park House with her omnipresent walking stick, unintentionally terrifying the children (grandchildren of Tom), curiously prodding them with the stick, breaking into Zilly's teas to point it at visitors while demanding to know who they were, complaining vaguely to Zilly that nights were dark, or pitifully talking to the Woolner bust of little Eddy while stroking its head.[80] Death came mercifully. Her sister and longtime companion, Matilda, her senior by a year, would outlive her by four, finally dying in 1913 at approximately ninety-seven. Among the floral pieces at Cecilia's funeral in Boxley church was one from Franklin's widow and two daughters (last of his family, he had died in 1901, after having been knighted for his service as London's chief metropolitan magistrate). Almost too painfully appropriate was the line of a quatrain accompanying the flowers: "Rest comes at last, though life be long and dreary."[81]

Shortly after her mother's death, Zilly turned over the Park House estate to her cousins, Tom's sons. She died, aged seventy-four, in 1921 at her beloved Eastbourne. Finally, in 1936, the estate passed out of the Lushington family and has since been taken over by the British Army, with Park House itself becoming a hospital during World War II, and subsequently an officers' mess.

When I was courteously conducted through it on a bright summer afternoon in 1979, I and my designated escort, the cultured and genial mess sergeant, were at that hour the only persons inside the spotlessly clean, eerily silent building. And were there no ghosts? No, none at all, not even in the room that once housed Edmund's assiduously accumulated, now irretrievably dispersed library, not even in that corner, whichever one it was, where he often settled himself to pen his restrained letters of heartfelt admiration to Tennyson. Biographers desiring ghosts must toil to assemble their own, recruited unwillingly from whatever documents chance to survive. Prosperos *manqués* most biographers are, whose reluctant actors melt away, all too nimbly, into the thinnest of air.

To literary historians Park House is most noteworthy, if at all, for Tennyson's frequent, occasionally extended, visits there. Yet during his final forty years, those of his eminence, he seldom came. Our biography of Edmund and Henry has attempted to return the place to the Lushingtons themselves, to bring them back and plant them there, however insubstantially, again. Laboring to receive them into one's mind, contriving to live with them thus, one eventually comes to love them all, compassionately and fiercely love them, including Venables and the Tennysons. Various brands of otherworldly goodness seem to characterize each one.

Yet we forget at our peril that they themselves were not, any of them, expansively gregarious persons. The extraordinariness of Edmund's and Henry's and Venables's intellects, and the daunting genius of Tennyson, push them beyond our comfortable reach. And the year-round residents of Park House formed a tiny, self-contained world to which cards of admission were not freely obtained.

Edmund Henry, sire of the clan, one who had intimately experienced and outlived sore frustration and heartbreaking grief, sought for himself and his family a happy, love-permeated refuge from the rude world outside its flower-bordered gates. Even after his death (though his wife still lived), the atmosphere of the place, its gladdening "mode of life," seemed so ideal to Venables as to make the ordinary world, after a visit to Park House, virtually unendurable. Yet from a different vantage point, in 1861, after the atmosphere had been recurrently weighted with death, Edward Lear, an overly devoted friend of Franklin but otherwise outside the circle, found them "a cold lot, the Park House Lushingtons—& being so are providentially spared much trouble. They have hearts for themselves. Let us hope they will sit in a happy circle in heaven—& admit nobody beyond the outside limit."[82]

The Lushington sisters emerge in the carefree morning of their lives, almost too euphoric with affection and fanciful humor. In their twilight (about 1885), old Arthur Tennyson's young second wife smugly perceived the three surviving sisters as nothing else but "doleful": "I am sure that if I stayed there long I should do something to startle those solemn old Miss Lushingtons [ages 69, 68, and 64], it is more like a house of the dead than anything else. I should think those old dames were never joyous children."[83] One itches, of course, to choke the babbler for her dull insensitivity. Had her "old man," as she fliply called her husband, never informed her about Eddy and Emmy and Lucy—to say nothing of Louy and Henry and Tom? What reserves of love and diminishing energy those spinster aunts and sisters had expended upon those six bereavements! Yet Mrs. Arthur too, like the solemn oldsters she derided, has faded, secure from menacing biographical fingers, into air.

Two scenes among others remain etched in one's imagination, symbols of the brighter and darker surfaces of the Park House story. The first is the joyous "hubbub" on the day before Cecilia's and Edmund's "first great dinner party"—everybody talking at once, while Alfred Tennyson sat on his "corner of the sofa the only one perfectly quiet, deep in a book." In the second, nocturnal, scene, a senile Cecilia gropes in with her walking stick from wandering about the lawn: " 'Very dark tonight, Zilly,' to which Zilly would invariably reply, 'Of course it is dear. The sun has gone down.' "[84]

Abbreviations Used in the Notes

Persons

AHH	Arthur Henry Hallam
AT	Alfred Tennyson
CTT	Charles Tennyson Turner
EFG	Edward FitzGerald
EHL	Edmund Henry Lushington
ELL	Edmund Law Lushington
ET	Emily Tennyson (Alfred's wife)
FL	Franklin Lushington
FT	Frederick Tennyson
GSV	George Stovin Venables
HT	Hallam Tennyson

Printed Materials Most Frequently Cited

Alfred Tennyson	Tennyson, Charles. *Alfred Tennyson*. London: Macmillan, 1949.
Background	Tennyson, Charles, and Hope Dyson. *The Tennysons: Background to Genius*. London: Macmillan, 1974.
Cambridge Apostles	Allen, Peter. *The Cambridge Apostles: The Early Years*. Cambridge: Cambridge University Press, 1978.
DNB	*Dictionary of National Biography*
Friends	Tennyson, Hallam Lord, ed. *Tennyson and His Friends*. London: Macmillan, 1911.
Italian War	Lushington, Henry. *The Italian War, 1848–9, and the Last Italian Poet*. Edited by George Stovin Venables. Cambridge: Macmillan, 1859.

Jrnl ET	Tennyson, Emily Lady. *Lady Tennyson's Journal.* Edited by James O. Hoge. Charlottesville: University Press of Virginia, 1981.
Ltrs AHH	*The Letters of Arthur Henry Hallam.* Edited by Jack Kolb. Columbus: Ohio State University Press, 1981.
Ltrs AT	*The Letters of Alfred Lord Tennyson.* Edited by Cecil Y. Lang and Edward F. Shannon, Jr. Vol. 1, *1821–1850.* Cambridge, Mass.: Harvard University Press, 1981.
Ltrs EFG	*The Letters of Edward FitzGerald.* Edited by Alfred McKinley Terhune and Annabelle Burdick Terhune. 4 vols. Princeton, N.J.: Princeton University Press, 1980.
Ltrs ET	*The Letters of Emily Lady Tennyson.* Edited by James O. Hoge. University Park: Pennsylvania State University Press, 1974.
Ltrs to FT	Schonfeld, Hugh J., ed. *Letters to Frederick Tennyson.* Published by Leonard and Virginia Woolf at the Hogarth Press, London, 1930.
Little Wars	Lushington, Henry. *A Great Country's Little Wars: or England, Affghanistan and Sinde.* London: John W. Parker, 1844.
Mats	[Tennyson, Hallam, ed.] *Materials for a Life of AT Collected for My Children.* 4 vols. Printed 1894–95.
Mem. AT	Tennyson, Hallam Lord, ed. *Alfred Lord Tennyson: A Memoir by His Son.* 2 vols. London: Macmillan, 1897.
"Mem. HL"	Venables, George Stovin. "Memoir of Henry Lushington." In *The Italian War, 1848–9, and the Last Italian Poet,* by Henry Lushington. Pp. ix–ci.
"Narrative ET"	"Emily Tennyson's Narrative for Her Sons." Edited by James O. Hoge. *Texas Studies in Language and Literature* 14 (1972): 93–106.
Poems AT	*The Poems of Tennyson.* Edited by Christopher Ricks. London: Longman Group, Ltd.; New York: W. W. Norton and Co., 1969.
Sketch EHL	[Lushington, Ellen Eliza.] *A Sketch of Edmund Henry Lushington.* Maidstone: Frederick Bunyard, 1881.
Testimonials	*Testimonials in Behalf of Edmund Law Lushington, M.A., Fellow of Trinity College, Cambridge, Candidate for the Office of Greek Professor in the University of Glasgow.* 1838.
Unquiet Heart	Martin, Robert Bernard. *Tennyson: The Unquiet Heart.* Oxford: Oxford University Press, 1980.

Locations of Manuscript Materials

BL	British Library
GUA	Glasgow University Archives
Lilly	Lilly Library, Indiana University
NLW	National Library of Wales, Aberystwyth
PRO	Public Records Office, Kew Gardens
TRC	Tennyson Research Centre, Lincoln
Trinity	Trinity College Library, Cambridge

Notes

For dated references within the text to George Stovin Venables's journals at the National Library of Wales and the privately held Lushington family papers, no notes are provided. For my major published sources of primary materials and biographical information concerning the Tennysons and the Lushingtons, I have given publishers' names with the list of abbreviations preceding these notes. For reasons of economy I am omitting publishers' names for all other books cited below.

I Family Background and Early Childhood to 1823

1 Arthur Bryant, *Years of Victory (1802–1812)* (London, 1944); *The Age of Elegance (1812–1822)* (New York, 1950).
2 *DNB*; Lord [John] Campbell, *Lives of the Chief Justices* (Boston, 1873), 4:102–254; Albert N. Imlah, *Lord Ellenborough: A Biography of Edward Law, Earl of Ellenborough, Governor General of India* (Cambridge, Mass., 1939)—a study of the son that includes a balanced view of the father.
3 George Philips to EHL, 15 May 1811, Lushington family papers; indications in various other letters in that collection and in the Liverpool Papers, BL.
4 *DNB*; William Paley's memoir of Bishop Law in Law's *Considerations on the Theory of Religion*, ed. George Henry Law (London, 1820); Charles T. Abbey, *The English Church and Its Bishops* (London, 1887), 1:224, 241, 2:245–51; my study of several of Law's books.
5 Ronald S. Crane, "Anglican Apologetics and 'Progress,' " in *The Idea of the Humanities and Other Essays* (Chicago, 1967), 1:251–87, esp. 287.
6 Mrs. Hicks Beach, *The Yesterdays behind the Door* (Liverpool, 1956), pp. 64–65.
7 Much of the early Lushington genealogy is from Foster's *Baronetage*.
8 For an interesting link between Sir Edmund and the Lushingtons, see Roger G. L. Lushington, "The Tankards of Sir Edmund Berrie Godfrey," *Connoisseur* 190 (1975): 258–65.

9   *Alumni Cantabrigiensis.*

10 Peter Campbell Scarlett, *A Memoir of the Right Honourable James Scarlett* (London, 1877), p. 45. James Scarlett refers to his close friendship with EHL.

11 Lord Campbell, 4:109–11.

12 For Whishaw see W. P. Courtney, "A Memoir of John Whishaw," in *The "Pope" of Holland House: Selections from the Correspondence of John Whishaw and His Friends 1813–1840*, edited and annotated by Lady Seymour (London, 1906), pp. 19–37.

13 PRO Series CO 54 and 55, 1802–9. During nearly two weeks I intensively studied these records, but space limitations forbid details. At least three books have touched upon EHL's story; but none has had the background, or the apparent motivation, to try to understand the man. See Colvin R. de Silva, *Ceylon under the British Occupation* (Colombo, 1953), 1:317–25, an attempt at an evenhanded account; C. Willis Dixon, *The Colonial Administrations of Sir Thomas Maitland* (London, 1939), pp. 89–93, a capable treatment despite several factual errors, but entirely from Maitland's point of view; and a shoddy piece of melodramatic posturing, Walter Frewer Lord, *Sir Thomas Maitland: The Mastery of the Mediterranean* (London, 1897), pp. 108–14.

14 Alfred P. Wadsworth and Julia de Lacy Mann, *The Cotton Trade and the Industrial Lancashire 1600–1780* (Manchester, 1931), pp. 288–301.

15 *Sketch EHL*, pp. 9–10. Through the gracious generosity of Mr. Frank H. Mitchell, of Sandling near Maidstone, I have a copy of this rare book.

16 Lennox A. Mills, *Ceylon under British Rule, 1795–1932* (Oxford, 1933), pp. 27–51, esp. 47.

17 PRO, CO 54–34, 6 March 1809, EHL's court decision in the dispute.

18 PRO, CO 54–31, Gov. Maitland to Alexander Johnston, ca. Feb. 1809.

19 BL Addl MSS 38255, Liverpool Papers, correspondence between Lds Liverpool and Ellenborough, 25 Dec. 1813, 10 Jan. 1814, 14 Jan. 1814, and Addl MSS 38256, 22 Jan. 1814. Various letters between Ellenborough and EHL, in the Lushington family papers. Liverpool promised to increase the Civil List when possible.

20 BL Addl MSS 38256, Liverpool Papers, 31 July 1814: a note between two Treasury clerks requests "the Christian name of Mr. Lushington the late Chief Justice of Ceylon—I want it for the purpose of its being inserted in a Treasury Warrant." On the back in another hand: "Edmund, Henry." Also another note: "A Pension to Mr. Lushington of 300 £ a year gross." But in an earlier letter, BL Addl MSS 38258, Liverpool Papers, 25 July 1814, Ellenborough proposed EHL's appointment to the Colonial Board of Audit, which he soon received, stipulating that "his appointment would relieve the pension fund, from the charge . . . which your Lordship had the goodness to make upon it, at my instance at the beginning of the present year."

21 *Sketch EHL*, p. 14.

22 "Mem. HL," pp. xii–xiii.

23 Ibid., p. xxi.

24 R. L. Archer, *Secondary Education in the Nineteenth Century* (Cambridge, 1921), p. 96. See also J. R. de S. Honey, *Tom Brown's Universe: The Development of the English Public School in the Nineteenth Century* (New York, 1977), p. 126: "Boys of five, six, seven, and eight . . . were not unknown in Arnold's Rugby or Keate's Eton."

25 Esp. Gordon N. Ray, *Thackeray: The Uses of Adversity* (1811–1846) (New York, 1955), pp. 79–100, and bibliographical notes, pp. 450–53.

26 Mrs. Charles Brookfield's *The Cambridge Apostles* (New York, 1906), pp. 347–48, claims that "the three lads," Thackeray, Venables, and Henry, "formed a happy and affectionate triumvirate united by similar tastes and a common implacability towards Dr. Russell," all of which may or may not be true. In adult life Venables tended to defend Russell.

II Charterhouse School 1823-1828

1   William Haig-Brown, *Charterhouse Past and Present* (Godalming, 1879), pp. 150–51.
2   Gerald S. Davies, *Charterhouse in London* (London, 1921), p. 273.
3   Ibid., pp. 265–66.
4   Jonathan Gathorne-Hardy, *The Public School Phenomenon, 597–1977* (London, 1921), p. 70.
5   T. Mozley, *Reminiscences, Chiefly of Oriel College and the Oxford Movement* (Boston, 1882), 1:158.
6   Davies, pp. 266–67.
7   See J. R. de S. Honey, *Tom Brown's Universe: The Development of the English Public School in the Nineteenth Century* (New York, 1977), p. 164, on epidemics in the schools. Davies (p. 267) possessed a letter from our period about an outbreak of scarlet fever in one of the houses: "The patients were crammed into an upper room which had direct communication with the box room. So they lay, and so they recovered."
8   Martin Farquhar Tupper, *My Life as an Author* (London, 1886), pp. 14, 21.
9   *The Works of William Makepeace Thackeray*, Cornhill Edition (New York, 1923), 20:405–6.
10 Tupper, p. 17.
11 Davies, p. 265.
12 Gordon N. Ray, *Thackeray: The Uses of Adversity* (New York: 1955), p. 80.
13 Haig-Brown, p. 150; Davies, p. 265.
14 Mozley, 1:171–73.
15 Ray, pp. 81, 451n. Quotations from Ray, who cites Davies, "Thackeray as a Carthusian," *Greyfriar* 2 (1890–95): 62; Henry L. Thompson, *Henry George Liddell* (London, 1899), p. 6; and Henry L. Phillott, "Some Carthusian Reminiscences," *Greyfriar* 2 (1890–95): 75.
16 Mozley, 1:171.
17 Mozley, *Reminiscences, Chiefly of Towns, Villages, and Schools*, 2d ed. (London, 1885), 1:v–vi, in a letter to Mozley from W. W. Wingfield, who was at Charterhouse from 1822 to 1832.
18 Ray, 80: Thackeray was in the seventh form in 1823, and in the fifth in 1824, having come up from the twelfth in 1821, and the tenth in 1822.
19 Thackeray, *Pendennis*, 1st ed. (London, 1849), 1:15, deleted from later editions.
20 Davies, pp. 271–72. In 1826, three years after our boys' first year, the room held fifty-five first-form boys and fifty-four auditors from the top of the second. And in 1823 the total enrollment of the school was fifteen more than in 1826.
21 Ray, p. 96, following Phillott, pp. 75–76.
22 Haig-Brown, p. 149.
23 Davies, p. 264.
24 Edward C. Mack, *Public Schools and British Opinion, 1780–1860* (New York, 1939), p. 165; Lionel Stevenson, *The Showman of Vanity Fair: The Life of William Makepeace Thackeray* (New York, 1947), p. 15; Ray, p. 95; Tupper, p. 14.
25 *Pendennis*, 1:16–17.
26 Tupper, pp. 15–16.
27 Ray, p. 95.
28 Mozley, *Reminiscences . . . Towns*, 1:388, 391–92.
29 Davies, p. 271.
30 Lewis Campbell, "Obituary, the Late Professor Lushington," *Classical Review* 7 (1893): 427.
31 Samuel Berdmore (1740–1802), headmaster from 1769 to 1791, and "loved by the pupils" (Haig-Brown, p. 148).
32 Mozley, *Reminiscences . . . Towns*, 1:394.
33 Ibid., 1:396.

34 GUA, George Henry Law to Duncan Macfarlan, Macfarlan Private Collection.
35 *Testimonials*, p. 14.
36 "Mem. HL," pp. xiv–xv.

III Park House and Trinity College 1828–1838

1 Auction announcements from 1827 and 1936, preserved at Park House, copies provided by S.Sgt. R. D. Lucas, 36 Engineer Regt., Invicta Park, Maidstone.
2 Marriage settlement, ELL and Cecilia Tennyson, 12 Oct. 1842, Kent County Archives.
3 *Testimonials*, p. 3.
4 D. A. Winstanley, *Early Victorian Cambridge* (repr. 1940 ed., New York, 1977), pp. 65–71.
5 R. Robson, "Trinity College in the Age of Peel," in *Ideas and Institutions of Victorian Britain*, ed. Robert Robson (New York, 1967), p. 325.
6 David Newsome, *Godliness and Good Learning: Four Studies on a Victorian Ideal* (London, 1961), p. 11.
7 *Ltrs AHH*, p. 244.
8 Augustus J. C. Hare, *Memorials of a Quiet Life* (repr. 9th Engl. ed. New York, n.d.), p. 191 and passim.
9 Robert O. Preyer, "Breaking Out: The English Assimilation of Continental Thought in Nineteenth-Century Rome," *Browning Institute Studies* 12 (1984): 59–63.
10 See Charles Richard Sanders, *Coleridge and the Broad Church Movement* (Durham, N.C., 1942), pp. 123–46.
11 *Ltrs AHH*, pp. 344, 347n.
12 Emerson Marks, *Coleridge on the Language of Verse* (Princeton, N.J., 1981), pp. 6–7.
13 Most significantly the new annotated edition of *Biographia Literaria*, ed. James Engell and W. Jackson Bate, *Collected Works of Samuel Taylor Coleridge*, vol. 7, pts. 1, 2 (Princeton, N.J., 1983). Also Paul Hamilton, *Coleridge's Poetics* (Stanford, Calif., 1983); Michael Kent Havens, "Coleridge on Language and Imagination," Ph.D. diss., Cornell University, 1980 (Ann Arbor, University Microfilms); and three older studies: James Holly Hanford, "Coleridge as a Philologian," *Modern Philology* 16 (1919): 119–40; Joshua H. Neumann, "Coleridge on the English Language, *PMLA* 63 (1948): 642–61; and L. A. Willoughby, "Coleridge as a Philologist," *Modern Language Review* 31 (1936): 176–201.
14 *Ltrs AHH*, pp. 263.
15 Ibid., pp. 263, 270.
16 Evidently in his third year, when his chances would have been best, he was disqualified on a technicality, possibly insufficient residence time owing to illness in the spring of 1829. A letter from Tom to Henry in 1834 recalled "the experience of the severe restrictions which would not allow" Edmund to sit for the Battie Scholarship. It illustrated "that many acts which appear harsh are performed in accordance with the letter though not the spirit of the law."
17 Newsome, pp. 92–147; Arnold's testimonial, p. 98.
18 "Mem. HL," p. xvii.
19 Ibid., p. xviii.
20 Ibid., p. xix.
21 *Sketch EHL*, p. 25.
22 "Mem. HL," p. xx.
23 Ibid., p. xxvi.
24 *Mem. AT*, 1:201.
25 *Mats*, 1:244–45.

26 *Ltrs AHH*, p. 30; *Unquiet Heart*, p. 69.
27 The *Wellesley Index* attributes the review to W. J. Fox.
28 *Mem. AT*, 1:20.
29 *Mats*, 1:245.
30 George O. Marshall, Jr., "Textual Changes in a Presentation Copy of Tennyson's *Poems* (1830)," *University of Texas Library Chronicle* 6:3 (1959): 16–19.
31 J. Willis Clark, *Old Friends at Cambridge and Elsewhere* (London, 1900), p. 99.
32 M. L. Clarke, *Greek Studies in England 1700–1830* (Cambridge, 1945), pp. 38–39; R. M. Ogilvie, *Latin and Greek: A History of the Influence of the Classics in English Life from 1600–1918* (London, 1964), pp. 102–3.
33 W. D. Paden, *Tennyson in Egypt: A Study of the Imagery in His Earlier Work* (repr. 1942 ed., New York, 1971), p. 158n.
34 *Journal of Philology* 7 (1877): 164.
35 *Testimonials*, p. 4.
36 *Cambridge Apostles*, p. 7. My general statements in this chapter concerning the Apostles are heavily indebted to this book.
37 Trinity, Houghton Papers, HO 8/85, 24 Sept. 1933, Francis Garden to Milnes.
38 *Testimonials*, pp. 4, 5, 11.
39 Ibid., p. 15.
40 Ibid., pp. 18–21.
41 Ibid., p. 4.
42 Alfred Friendly, *Beaufort of the Admiralty: The Life of Sir Francis Beaufort 1774–1857* (New York, 1977), pp. 298–99.
43 "Mem. HL," pp. xxii–xxiii.
44 Published Cambridge and London, 1838.
45 *British and Foreign Review* 7 (1838): 678–93, authorship verified in Trinity, Houghton Papers, Kemble to Milnes, HO 13/119, n.d., 13/120, June 1838.
46 *Friends*, p. 92n.
47 "Mem. HL," pp. xxvi–xxviii.

IV The Glasgow Professorship 1838–1875

1 J. D. Mackie, *The University of Glasgow 1451–1951: A Short History* (Glasgow 1954), pp. 247–48, 269–72. Between 1761 and 1858 nine new "regius professorships" were created, but not made part of the "faculty." Reforms imposed by the crown in 1858 reduced the power of the faculty and put all professors on equal footing.
2 Ibid., p. 247.
3 David Murray, *Memories of the Old College of Glasgow: Some Chapters in the History of the University* (Glasgow, 1927), pp. 197–98. [K. H. Boyd,] "College Life at Glasgow," *Fraser's Magazine* 53 (1856): 508. Author identified by *Wellesley Index* (brackets not used in later citations).
4 Boyd, pp. 508, 519.
5 Mackie, p. 247.
6 Boyd, p. 506.
7 [John Stuart Blackie,] "Scottish University Reform," *North British Review* 23 (1855): 98–99. Author identified by *Wellesley Index* (brackets not used in later citations); P. A. Wright-Henderson, *Glasgow and Balliol and Other Essays* (Oxford, 1926), p. 17.
8 Boyd, pp. 506–7.
9 [John Gibson Lockhart,] *Peter's Letters to His Kinfolk*, 1st American ed. from 2d Edinburgh ed. (New York, 1820), p. 85.

10 James Coutts, *A History of the University of Glasgow from Its Foundation in 1451 to 1909* (Glasgow, 1909), p. 346.
11 Blackie, pp. 77–78.
12 Boyd, p. 518.
13 Murray, p. 201.
14 C. J. Fordyce, "Classics," in *Fortuna Domus: A Series of Lectures in Commemoration of the Fifth Centenary of Its Foundation* (Glasgow, 1952), p. 38.
15 Quoted by Mackie, p. 280.
16 Boyd, pp. 505–6.
17 *DNB*.
18 Lockhart, pp. 488–89.
19 Daniel Keyte Sandford, *Inaugural Lecture Delivered in the Common Hall of the University of Glasgow, November the 6th, 1821* (Glasgow, 1822).
20 Sandford, *Preliminary Lecture, Delivered in Common Hall of the University of Glasgow, November the 7th 1826; comprising a View of the Course of Study Performed in the Greek Class* (Edinburgh, 1826).
21 Edited by himself: *Extracts from Various Greek Authors, with Notes and a Lexicon. For the Use of the Junior Greek Class in the University of Glasgow* (Glasgow, 1823). Sandford also authored two other books for his Glasgow students—a manual for Greek composition, and an introduction to Greek prosody.
22 Boyd, pp. 508, 518–19.
23 My statements concerning Peel and his circle are heavily indebted to two books by Norman Gash, *Mr. Secretary Peel* (Cambridge, Mass., 1961), and *Sir Robert Peel* (London, 1972).
24 GUA, Fac. Mtg Notes, 1 Apr., 8 Apr. 1834.
25 GUA, Fac. Mtg Notes, 2 Sept. 1834.
26 GUA, Tait to Principal Macfarlan, 9, 12 Feb. 1838.
27 GUA, Campbell to Macfarlan, 19 Feb. 1838.
28 Murray, p. 202.
29 James Winter, *Robert Lowe* (Toronto, 1976), p. 14.
30 GUA, Clerk to Macfarlan, 15 May 1838. For details of the liberal activities of Edmund's distant relatives, Dr. Stephen and Charles Lushington, see *DNB* for the former. Two prominent half-uncles of Edmund's were also named Stephen and Charles, but certainly were not radicals.
31 Gash, *Sir Robert Peel*, pp. 151–56.
32 Bernard Aspinwall, "The Scottish Dimension: Robert Monteith and the Origins of Modern Roman Catholic Social Thought," *Downside Review* 97 (1978): 52.
33 William John Lushington to EHL, 8 Aug. 1838: " . . . By that Night's Post I likewise wrote to Lord Lyndhurst & Goulburn to thank them for their kind exertions in his favour & attributed the completion of all our wishes in some degree to their efficient cooperation."
34 Gash, *Sir Robert Peel*, p. 716.
35 GUA, Fac. Mtg Notes, 1 Aug. 1838.
36 Ibid.
37 "On Scottish University Tests," *North British Review* 12 (1849–50): 273.
38 Coutts, pp. 419–21.
39 Murray, pp. 203–4.
40 *Considerations on the Propriety of Requiring a Subscription* (Cambridge, 1774), pp. 2–5, 14, 23.
41 *Inaugural Lecture on the Study of Greek, Delivered in the Common Hall of Glasgow College on Thursday, Nov. 8, 1838* (Glasgow, 1839).
42 William Young Sellar, "John Campbell Shairp," in *Portraits of Friends*, by Shairp (Boston, 1899), p. 17.

43 *In Memoriam*, "Epilogue," lines 37–40.

44 ELL's statement in *Mats*, 1:250.

45 Boyd, p. 508.

46 Murray, pp. 198–99.

47 Boyd, p. 507.

48 Murray, pp. 198–99.

49 Silvanus P. Thompson, *The Life of William Thomson, Baron Kelvin of Larg* (London, 1910), 1:10, 85, 163.

50 Professor Knight, *Memoir of John Nichol, Professor of English in the University of Glasgow* (Glasgow, 1896), pp. 88–92.

51 Ibid., pp. 90-91.

52 Fordyce, pp. 37–38.

53 *Classical Review* 7 (1893): 88–92.

54 Sellar, p. 18.

55 H. A. L. Fisher, *James Bryce (Viscount Bryce of Dechmont, O.M.)* (New York, 1927), pp. 17–18.

56 Knight, p. 185, quoting "Mr. Dunn, the Scottish school inspector."

57 *Friends*, p. 94.

58 Gilbert Murray, "Autobiographical Fragment," in *Gilbert Murray: An Unfinished Autobiography, with Contributions by Friends*, ed. Jean Smith and Arnold Toynbee (London, 1960), p. 94.

V The Old Order Changeth 1839–1841

1 *Sketch EHL*, pp. 29–36.

2 MS marriage settlement, ELL and Cecilia Tennyson, Kent County Archives, Maidstone. Two of the properties (here indicated by "perhaps") appear in one section but not another.

3 "Mem. HL," p. xxv.

4 For more concerning the Eglinton Tournament, see Mark Girouard, *The Return of Camelot* (New Haven, Conn., 1981), pp. 92–110.

5 Trinity, Houghton Papers, HO 15/81, 11 Aug. 1839.

6 Ibid., HO 15/82, 24 Sept. 1839.

7 "Mem. HL," p. xxvi.

8 *Mem. AT*, 1:201.

9 "Mem. HL," p. xxiv.

10 Ibid., pp. xcv–xcvii.

11 Trinity, Houghton Papers, HO 15/83, HO 15/85, n.d., but evidently ca. 1841.

12 "Mem. HL," pp. xv, xvi.

13 Ibid., p. xxvi.

14 *Mem. AT*, 1:182.

15 *Friends*, p. 92n. HT's note states erroneously that AT dedicated *In Memoriam* to HL. It was, of course, *The Princess*, 2d ed.

16 *Cambridge Apostles*, pp. 214–15, 259n.

17 "Mem. HL," p. xvi.

18 *Unquiet Heart*, p. 251.

19 *Mem. AT*, 1:201-2. ELL's account is so vague about the date that it is not certain that any househunting visits occurred before the summer of 1841.

20 *Testimonials*, pp. 19–20.

21 Trinity, Houghton Papers, HO 15/77.

22 Ibid., HO 45/14.

23 *Classical Review* 7 (1893): 426–28.

24 Published by Cambridge University Press. For ELL's review see *British and Foreign Review* 12 (1843): 515–42.
25 *DNB*; also D. A. Winstanley, *Early Victorian Cambridge* (Cambridge, 1940), pp. 298–301, 304.
26 Concerning De Quincey, I depend heavily upon Horace Ainsworth Eaton, *Thomas De Quincey: A Biography* (New York, 1936). See also John Mack, "Thomas De Quincey and Two Glasgow Professors, II, De Quincey and Lushington," *Glasgow College Courant* 2:1 (1941): 26–31.
27 Eaton, p. 397.
28 See *Ltrs AT*, 1:187, 22 Feb. [1841].
29 *Ltrs AT*, 1:191.
30 Ibid., 1:192.
31 *Mem. AT*, 1:204.
32 *Ltrs AT*, 1:192.
33 Ibid., 1:193–94.
34 *Mem. AT* 1:204.
35 *Mats*, 2:254.
36 Trinity, Houghton Papers, HO 15/86, 7 Sept. [1841]; HO 15/84 [late Aug. 1841].
37 *Mats*, 2:248.
38 Letters from there in *Ltrs AT*, 1:198–200.
39 *Mem. AT*, 1:202.
40 *Ltrs AT*, 1:200–201.

VI A Wife Ere Noon 1842

1 Trinity, Houghton Papers, HO 15/87, 9 Jan. 1842.
2 *Ltrs AT*, 1:200–201.
3 For Spedding's date of departure, see *Friends*, p. 415. See also *Ltrs EFG*, 1:315, including n.2, for EFG's assistance. Martin, *Unquiet Heart*, p. 261, erroneously asserts that Spedding was present in March and "patiently advised" AT about "revisions and helped him smooth out the rough spots."
4 *Unquiet Heart*, p. 263.
5 *Mem. AT*, 1:201–2.
6 An undated letter from HL to ELL, enclosed in an envelope postmarked 8 July 1841 and addressed in HL's hand (Lushington family papers), speaks of "Alfred's coming with or without Mr. [Charles Tennyson] Turner to look at houses."
7 *Unquiet Heart*, p. 35.
8 *Alfred Tennyson*, p. 46.
9 *Ltrs AT*, 1:14, 30 Oct. 1827.
10 Ibid., 1:20, 5 Dec. 1827.
11 Ibid., 1:28, 25 Feb. 1829.
12 Ibid., 1:29–30, 27 Feb. 1829.
13 Ibid., 1:45, 5 July 1830.
14 *Unquiet Heart*, p. 131.
15 "Narrative ET," p. 95.
16 *Ltrs AHH*, p. 361n.
17 *Friends*, p. 91.
18 *Ltrs AT*, 1:113.
19 *Background*, pp. 145–46.
20 Ibid., pp. 147–48.

21 TRC, Cecilia to Susan Haddlesey, 11 April [1838], transcribed here from MS, but edited with corrected punctuation in *Ltrs AT*, 1:159–60.
22 *Ltrs AT*, 1:151.
23 TRC, Cecilia to Susan Haddlesey, postmarked 1 Dec. 1837, appears also with corrected punctuation, *Ltrs AT*, 1:155.
24 *DNB.*
25 *Little Wars*, pp. 23, 144.
26 "Mem. HL," p. xxix.
27 *Little Wars*, p. 2.
28 John Killham, *Tennyson and "The Princess": Reflections of an Age* (London, 1958), pp. 44–63.
29 Correctly given by Edmund in *Mats*, 1:249, and in *Alfred Tennyson*, p. 185, as confirmed by Boxley parish register, courtesy of the Reverend Malcolm Bradshaw in a letter to me in 1983. Erroneously given by *Ltrs AT*, 1:212, and *Poems AT*, p. 981.
30 For an exposition of the influence of Chambers's *Vestiges of Creation* upon these lines, see *Poems AT*, pp. 986–87n.
31 See especially *Background*, pp. 149–59, and relevant correspondence in *Ltrs AT*, 1:183ff.
32 *Ltrs AT*, 1:205–7.
33 Ibid., 1:207–8.
34 Ibid., 1:213.
35 *Unquiet Heart*, pp. 270–72.
36 *Ltrs EFG*, 1:459n; *Ltrs AT*, 1:133n.
37 *Ltrs AT*, 1:222–23.
38 Ibid., 1:222–23.
39 Ibid., 1:221–22, 194.
40 Ibid., 1:186.
41 *Mem. AT*, 1:221.
42 Christopher Ricks, *Tennyson* (New York, 1972), p. 181.
43 *Ltrs to FT*, p. 58.

VII An Ill-Fated Heir and a Stillborn Book 1843–1844

1 *Christian Remembrancer*, 5 (1843): 197–222.
2 Ibid., pp. 606–39; 6 (1843): 1–41. All my quoting and summarizing will be from the book version, *Little Wars*.
3 *Little Wars*, pp. 2, 8.
4 *Mats*, 1:250.
5 *Ltrs to FT*, pp. 57–58.
6 *Unquiet Heart*, p. 274, places the move in November or December, but ELL (See *Mats*, 1:251) said it was "in the later part of the season" (i.e., at the end of summer), and that he and Cecilia, returning to Glasgow, stayed with the family at Cheltenham "from Oct. 9 to Oct. 12."
7 I cannot identify her.
8 See *Ltrs AT*, 1:219–20, AT to Aubrey De Vere, 17 Sept.: "I am down here at St. Leonards with the Lushingtons."
9 *Mats*, 1:251.
10 Possibly AT was simply thinking about Carlyle's *Past and Present*, then recently published, ominously picturing England (book 1, chapter 2) in its "soft-hung Longacre vehicle of polished leather . . . beautifully" rolling "towards the *road's end*," where "the abyss yawns sheer."
11 *Ltrs AT*, 1:255–26.

12 "Mem. HL," p.xxx.
13 Trinity, Houghton Papers, HO 15/94.
14 *Ltrs AT*, 1:229n.
15 *Unquiet Heart*, p. 281.

VIII *The Princess* and a Maltese Appointment 1845–1847

1 *Ltrs AT*, 1:231–32.
2 Ibid., 1:234.
3 *Unquiet Heart*, pp. 283–84.
4 John Killham, *Tennyson and the Princess* (London, 1958), p. 174.
5 TRC, ELL to HT, 10 Jan. 1885.
6 *Mem. AT*, 1:247.
7 Ibid., 1:263.
8 Killham, pp. 7, 16–17.
9 Ibid., p. 247n.
10 *Jrnl ET*, pp. 60–62. While writing "Merlin and Vivien," AT was reading *Hamlet, As You Like It, Much Ado about Nothing*, and *Measure for Measure*; while writing "Lancelot and Elaine," he was reading *The Merchant of Venice, A Midsummer Night's Dream, Richard II, Samson Agonistes*, and *Comus*.
11 *Ltrs AT*, 1:237n.
12 Ibid., 1:238.
13 Ibid., 1:28, 238n.
14 "Narrative ET," 101.
15 *Ltrs AT*, 1:242n.
16 *Mem AT*, 1:203.
17 *Ltrs AT*, 1:238.
18 *Mem. AT*, 1:203.
19 *Ltrs AT*, 1:243n.
20 Ibid., 1:242, 244, 245.
21 Ibid., 1:249.
22 Extracted in *ibid.*, 1:250–51.
23 *Ltrs to FT*, p. 74.
24 *Ltrs AT*, 1:258–61.
25 Ibid., 1:262–65.
26 Historical summary based upon Norman Gash, *Mr. Secretary Peel* (Cambridge, Mass., 1961); quotation on p. 477.
27 Number explicitly stated in GSV's journal, 1 June; oddly, in his "Mem. HL," p. xxxii, he recalled the count as "five or six hundred signatures," but possibly this total included the petitions circulated at Cambridge.
28 "Mem. HL," pp. xxxii–xxxiii.
29 *The Broad and Narrow Gauge: or Remarks on the Report of the Gauge Commissioners* (London, 1846), and *Postscript on the Gauge: Evidence, Witnesses and Judges* (London, 1846).
30 "Mem. HL," pp. xxxiii–xxxvi, and GSV's journal, 3–18 March 1846, NLW.
31 Jack Simmons, *The Railway in England and Wales 1830–1914* (Leicester, 1978), pp. 39–43.
32 See E. T. MacDermott, *History of the Great Western Railway*, Vol, 1, *1833–1863* (London, 1927), pp. 31–37, 200–247.
33 *Observations on the Report of the Gauge Commissioners* (London, 1846), cited in MacDermott, 1:235.

34 See Simmons, pp. 170–72.

35 Ibid., p. 47.

36 GUA, Fac. Mtg Notes, 19 Feb. 1847.

37 *Ltrs AT*, 1:273–74.

38 Ibid., 1:274–76.

39 In T. Wemyss Reid, ed., *Life, Letters, and Friendships of Richard Monckton Milnes*, 3d ed. (London, 1891), 1:381; Milnes gives the correct figure.

40 PRO, Kew Gardens, HL to Colonial Office, received 12 May 1847, with notation by Lord Grey, the only letter I located pertaining to HL's appointment.

41 Not said by FL to Brookfield, as *Unquiet Heart*, p. 309, has it, nor said by "the spritely and rather malicious" Mrs. Brookfield herself, as unfortunately reported in *Background*, p. 168.

42 Charles and Mary Brookfield, *Mrs. Brookfield and Her Circle* (London, 1905), 1:212–13.

43 *Background*, p. 168.

44 *Jrnl ET*, p. 16.

45 *Unquiet Heart*, pp. 322–33.

46 *Alfred Tennyson*, pp. 239–40; *Unquiet Heart*, p. 321.

47 *Papers Relating to Malta, ordered by the House of Commons to be Printed*, 27 May 1869, pp. 3–4. For historical background see also Edith Dobie, *Malta's Road to Independence* (Norman, Okla., 1962), p. 17ff; Hilda I. Lee, "The Development of the Malta Constitution, 1813–1849," *Melita Historica* 1 (1952): 7–18; "British Policy towards the Religion, Ancient Laws, and Customs in Malta 1824–1851," *Melita Historica* 4:1 (1964): 11–18; Henry Seddall, *Malta: Past and Present* (London, 1870), pp. 240–59.

48 Trinity, Houghton Papers, HO 15/104, 21 Oct. [1847].

49 "Mem. HL," pp. xxxix–xl.

50 *Papers Relating to Malta*, pp. 31–32.

IX A Precarious Stability 1848–1853

1 Trinity, Houghton Papers, HO 15/78.

2 "Mem. HL," pp. liii–lvi, lxv–lxvi.

3 Ibid., p. xlviii.

4 Printed without author or date by McGowan and Co., Great Windmill St., London.

5 Tipped-in versified inscription by FL, "Eastertide 1895," in ET's specially bound copy of *Joint Compositions*, TRC.

6 *Cambridge Apostles*, pp. 119–23.

7 *Unquiet Heart*, p. 125, citing letter, James Spedding to Edward Spedding, 5 Dec. 1830, Spedding family papers.

8 *Sketch EHL*, p. 18.

9 Concerning the council see "Mem. HL," pp. xli–xliv; H. Bowen-Jones, J. C. Dewdney, and W. B. Fisher, *Malta: Background for Development* (Durham, Engl., n.d. [ca. 1960]), p. 127; Edith Dobie, *Malta's Road to Independence* (Norman, Okla., 1962), pp. 17–18.

10 Trinity, Houghton Papers, HO 15/106.

11 Dobie, p. 19; "Mem. HL," p. xliv; Henry Seddall, *Malta: Past and Present* (London, 1870), p. 249.

12 "Mem. HL," pp. xliv–li; Seddall, pp. 246–56. For a more recent, more impartial account, see Hilda I. Lee, "British Policy towards the Religion, Ancient Laws, and Customs in Malta, 1824–1851," *Melita Historica* 4:1 (1968): 10–18.

13 Trinity, Houghton Papers, HO 15/105.

14 "Mem. HL," p. lxi.

15   Trinity, Houghton Papers, HO 15/105.
16   "Mem. HL," p. lxi.
17   *Poems AT*, p. 932n.
18   Ibid., p. 932n.
19   *Jrnl ET*, pp. 16–17; "Narrative ET," p. 101.
20   The list of five adults in *Mem. AT*, 1:329 should have also included the presiding vicar, Drummond Rawnsley, and his wife Catherine (ET's cousin). See also *Ltrs AT*, 1:331.
21   *Unquiet Heart*, p. 334, gives no source for this plausible piece of trivia.
22   *Ltrs AT*, 1:328.
23   TRC, 10 July 1850.
24   *Jrnl ET*, p. 20.
25   *Ltrs ET*, p. 48.
26   *Ltrs AT*, 1:342 (Phipps to AT), date of receipt from *Jrnl ET*, p. 21.
27   *Mem. AT*, 1:336.
28   *Jrnl ET*, p. 21.
29   FL, with Henry Maine, would compose Harry Hallam's memoir.
30   "Narrative ET," pp. 104–5; *Jrnl ET*, pp. 23–26.
31   "The Struggle of Italy," *Edinburgh Review* 93 (Jan. 1851): 33–71; "The Defeat of Italy," *Edinburgh Review* 93 (April 1851): 498–534, reprinted in *Italian War*.
32   William Ewart Gladstone, *A Letter to the Earl of Aberdeen on the State Prosecutions of the Neapolitan Government* (London, 1851).
33   *A Detailed Exposure of the Apology Put Forth by the Neapolitan Government in Reply to the Charges of Mr. Gladstone* (London, 1852).
34   TRC, 20 Sept. 1852.
35   Trinity, Houghton Papers, HO 15/110.
36   *Unquiet Heart*, pp. 315–16.
37   Both letters at TRC.
38   Republished by GSV in *Italian War*, pp. 217–78.
39   TRC.
40   A portion had appeared earlier in the form of letters to the *Morning Chronicle*.
41   "Mem. HL," p. lxxiii.
42   TRC, ELL to AT, 19 Nov. 1853.
43   James Coutts, *History of the University of Glasgow 1451–1909* (Glasgow, 1909), pp. 411, 548; James Murray, *Memories of the Old College of Glasgow* (Glasgow, 1927), p. 332.
44   Professor Knight, *Memoir of John Nichol* (Glasgow, 1896), pp. 118–21.
45   Trinity, Houghton Papers, HO 15/112.

X The Shadow Feared of Man 1854–1860

1   *Jrnl ET*, p. 32.
2   "Mem. HL," p. lxxxi.
3   Ibid., pp. lxxxi–lxxxii.
4   Letters in the Lushington family papers. Permission to quote from letters by the Tennysons is by kind permission of Lord Tennyson and the Lincolnshire Library Service.
5   TRC.
6   Charles Francis Atkinson, "Crimean War," *Encyclopedia Brittanica*, 11th ed.
7   Also published again and cited here in *La Nation Boutiquière, and Other Poems Chiefly Political*, by

Henry Lushington, with a preface; [and] *Points of War* by Franklin Lushington (Cambridge, 1855).

8 The certificate of death gives the cause of death as "albuminaria"—a symptom rather than a disease—indicating urinary disorder, compatible with the severe edema mentioned in accounts of the boy's illness. Infection from initial cysts on the back, requiring lancing, could have invaded the kidneys. I have discussed the case with Herald Habenicht, M.D., a pediatrician.

9. NLW, Llysdinam B2334, dated only "Wednesday, May."

10 "The Muster of the Guards," in *La Nation Boutiquière.*

11 A. Dwight Culler, *The Poetry of Tennyson* (New Haven, Conn., 1977), p. 205.

12 NLW, Llysdinam, B2333, 2334.

13 "Mem. HL," p. lxxxix.

14 TRC, Edward Lear to ET, 23 July 1855.

15 "Mem. HL," p. xc.

16 Located for me by Daniel Ranisavljevic, nephew of my colleague Professor Daniel Augsburger.

17 Seen at Llysdinam Hall, Newbridge-on-Wye, in 1982; may by now have been added to Llysdinam papers at NLW, Aberystwyth.

18 *Jrnl ET*, p. 50.

19 TRC, GSV to ET, 2 Oct. 1855.

20 NLW, Llysdinam B2621, 5 Oct. 1855.

21 TRC, ELL to ET, 1 Nov. 1855.

22 NLW, Llysdinam B2608, 18 Dec. 1856.

23 Trinity, Houghton Papers, HO 45/64.

24 TRC, 15 July 1856.

25 *Poems AT*, p. 1465.

26 TRC.

27 *Jrnl ET*, p. 94.

28 NLW, Llysdinam B2616.

29 TRC, ELL to ET, 11 June 1859.

30 GUA, Fac. Mtg Notes, 17 Oct. 1856.

31 TRC.

32 TRC, ELL to ET.

33 TRC, 28 Nov. 1856

34 TRC, ELL to ET, 10 Aug. 1858.

35 Dr. Robert Lee (1793–1877), who was later brought from London to Park House to examine her, was a gynecological specialist.

36 *Jrnl ET*, pp. 70–71.

37 NLW, Llysdinam B2622, 21 May [1856].

38 TRC, ELL to AT, 3 March 1856.

39 TRC, ELL to AT, 15 July 1856.

40 TRC, ELL to ET, 31 Aug. 1858.

41 TRC, ELL to ET, 11 June 1859.

42 TRC, FL to ET, 18 Jan. 1857.

43 TRC.

44 GUA, Fac. Mtg Notes, 21 Oct. 1859.

45 TRC, ELL to ET.

46 TRC, ELL to ET.

XI Middle Years, More Sorrow 1860–1874

1   TRC, ELL to ET.
2   Ibid., 28 May 1860.
3   TRC, ELL to AT, 13 Feb. 1861.
4   Ibid., 18 April 1861.
5   TRC, ELL to ET, 5 Dec. 1861.
6   Ibid., 5 Feb. 1862.
7   Ibid., 23 Dec. 1862.
8   Ibid., 4 Feb. 1863.
9   Ibid., 25 Dec. 1863.
10 Ibid., 4 Jan. 1865.
11 Ibid., 9 May 1965.
12 Ibid., 7 Jan. 1866.
13 Ibid., 6 April 1866.
14 E. M. Sellar, *Recollections and Impressions* (Edinburgh, 1907), pp. 106–8.
15 *Jrnl ET*, p. 150.
16 Ibid., p. 157.
17 Ibid., p. 177.
18 Ibid., pp. 187–88.
19 Ibid., p. 200.
20 Ibid., pp. 250–51.
21 TRC, ELL to AT, 1865 (?).
22 TRC, ELL to ET, 7 Jan. 1866.
23 Ibid., 24 Sept. 1864.
24 Ibid., 5 Feb. 1862.
25 Ibid., 4 Feb. 1863.
26 Ibid., 6 April 1866.
27 Ibid., 4 Feb. 1863.
28 Ibid., 5 Dec. 1861.
29 Ibid., 24 Sept. 1864.
30 Ibid., 20 Jan. 1862.
31 *DNB.*
32 Horace Ainsworth Eaton, *Thomas De Quincey: A Biography* (New York, 1936), p. 440n.
33 Sellar, pp. 72–73, 107–8.
34 "Introductory Notice," in *Lectures on Greek Philosophy*, by James Frederick Ferrier, ed. Sir Alexander Grant and E. L. Lushington, 2d ed. (Edinburgh, 1875), pp. vii–xliv.
35 *Testimonials of J. F. Ferrier, B.A., Oxon, Professor of Moral Philosophy and Political Economy in the University of St. Andrews, Now a Candidate for the Chair of Moral Philosophy in the University of Edinburgh,* 1852, pp. 18, 21.
36 David Shaw, *Tennyson's Style* (Ithaca, N.Y., 1976), pp. 165–67, 241, 275, 296–97.
37 TRC, ELL to ET, 20 Feb. 1855; 19 April 1855.
38 *Jrnl ET*, p. 41.
39 Ibid., p. 137.
40 "Introductory Notice," pp. xxi–xxii.
41 L.M.L., *Verses*, printed for private circulation only (Maidstone, 1880).
42 *Jrnl ET* p. 310.
43 *Introductory Address Delivered at the Opening of the University of Glasgow Session 1870–71* (Edinburgh, 1870).

44 TRC, ELL to ET, 27 Oct. 1874.
45 TRC, ELL to AT and ET, 8 Oct. 1874.
46 TRC, ELL to AT.
47 *Background*, pp. 170–71.

XII Park House and Boxley Churchyard 1875–1893

1   GUA, Senate 1873–76, 1 or 15 April 1875.
2   GUA.
3   Lilly, ELL to FT, 17 May 1879.
4   Lilly, E. Louisa (Mrs. Arthur) Tennyson to FT, Sept. 1882.
5   "The Third Sallier Papyrus, Containing the Wars of Ramses II against the Cheta," *Transactions of the Society of Biblical Archaeology* 3:83–103 (read 6 Jan. 1874); "Fragment of the First Sallier Papyrus," ibid., 4:263–66 (read 7 Dec. 1875); "The Victories of Seti I, Recorded in the Great Temple of Karnak," ibid., 6:509–34 (read 1 April 1879, based upon hieroglyphic transcriptions from six published sources, but the first consecutive translation published in any language); "The Stele of Mentuhotep," ibid., 7:352–69 (read 7 June 1881); "Hymn to Ra-Hamarchis," *Records of the Past: Being English Translations of the Assyrian and Egyptian Monuments, Published under the Sanction of the Society of Biblical Archaeology* 8 (1876): 129–34; "Sepulchral Inscription of Panehsi," ibid., 12 (1881): 137–43. See TRC, ELL to AT, 13 Jan 1877: "I have ordered to be sent to you the 8th vol. of Records of the Past wh I hope may be found to contain some things not entirely uninteresting to read."
6   *Classical Review* 7 (1893): 427.
7   In 1910 the *Encyclopedia Britannica*, 11th ed., 9:58, declared that only then was it beginning to be possible to determine "the exact interpretation of historical documents on Egyptian monuments and papyri." Earlier, "the supposed meaning of these was extracted chiefly by brilliant guessing, and the published translations of even the best scholars could carry no guarantee of more than approximate exactitude, where the sense depended at all on correct recognition of the syntax."
8   Lilly, ELL to FT, 11 Oct. 1875.
9   TRC, ELL to CTT, 17 April 1873.
10 *Unquiet Heart*, p. 526.
11 Harriet (the first Mrs. Arthur) Tennyson to FT, 23 April 1878.
12 TRC, ELL to AT, 27 April 1879. *Unquiet Heart*, p. 526, says that Louisa was confined on the Isle of Wight, but ELL's letter twice places her at Salisbury.
13 Lilly, ELL to FT, 17 May 1879.
14 Ibid., 1 June, 20 Aug., 17 Oct. 1879.
15 TRC, ELL to Lionel T, 13 July 1875.
16 TRC, ELL to AT, 13 Jan. 1877.
17 Recorded in GSV's journal, 28 Feb. 1878.
18 Sir Charles Tennyson, "The Somersby Tennysons," Christmas Supplement, *Victorian Studies*, 1963. In a memorable but too brief conversation with me at the White Hart Inn at Tetford, near Somersby, in August 1975, Sir Charles said, "I *ought* to remember her, but I don't."
19 Lilly, ELL to FT, 13 Nov. 1879. Unfortunately, *Background*, pp. 171–74, mistakenly attributes to Zilly's mother (the two names, of course, being identical) the authorship of this book and two others by Zilly, *Margaret the Moonbeam* (1881) and *Over the Seas and Far Away* (1882).
20 Lilly, FT to Zilly L, 3 Dec. 1879.
21 Lilly, Zilly L to FT, 12 March 1880.

22 *Mem. AT*, 2:242–43. Neither *Alfred Tennyson* nor *Unquiet Heart* mentions the episode.

23 TRC, ELL to HT, 26 April; Matthew Fraser to AT, 3 May; Fraser to AT, 4 May; Fraser to HT, 5 May; J. P. Nichol to AT, 8 May; Fraser to AT, 8 May; ELL to AT, 10 May; ELL to HT, 11 May; Fraser to HT, 11 May; ELL to HT, 15 May; ELL to HT, 17 May; ELL to HT, 18 May; ELL to HT, 24 May; Nichol to HT, 29 May; Fraser to AT, 14 June; telegram, date illegible, Fraser to AT; telegram, Fraser to AT, 10 May.

24 TRC, Fraser to AT, 14 June 1880. See also the account by Fraser's associate, George F. A. Macnaughton, *Tennyson: An Interview—Episode in a Glasgow University Rectorial Election* [Glasgow, 1928].

25 Quoted in a letter to the *Times* (London), 15 May 1880.

26 The *Times*, 11 May 1880; also *Mem. AT*, 2:243.

27 See above.

28 TRC, ELL to HT, 17 May 1880.

29 The three letters all at TRC.

30 Professor Knight, *Memoir of John Nichol* (Glasgow, 1896), 202–3

31 TRC, 18 Oct. 1880.

32 TRC, 13 Oct. 1880.

33 TRC, ELL to AT, 8 Dec. 1880.

34 TRC, ELL to ET, 13 Aug. 1883.

35 TRC, ELL to AT, 30 Dec. 1883.

36 Lilly, ELL to FT, 28 Jan. 1884.

37 Lilly, Cecilia L to FT, [1884].

38 Lilly, ELL to FT, 9 May 1884.

39 TRC, 1 March 1884.

40 TRC, ELL to AT, 27 June 1884.

41 TRC, ELL to Eustace Jesse, 25 Nov. 1884.

42 David Murray, *Memories of the Old College of Glasgow* (Glasgow, 1927), p. 202; Lewis Campbell, "Obituary: The Late Professor Lushington," *Classical Review* 7 (1893): 426.

43 *Address Delivered on Thursday, 26th March 1885, on His Installation as Lord Rector of the University of Glasgow* (Glasgow, 1885).

44 Campbell, p. 426.

45 Glasgow University Library has a copy.

46 *Glasgow News*, 31 March 1885.

47 Lilly, ELL to FT, 15 May 1885.

48 Lilly, Emily Jesse to FT, 20 April, 30 April 1885.

49 Lilly, ELL to Emily Jesse, 8 May 1885.

50 TRC, ELL to Eustace Jesse, 25 Nov. 1884.

51 NLW, Llysdinam 2328, 2330, FL to GSV, 18 Sept. 1886, 22 Dec. 1887.

52 Lilly, ELL to FT, 21 Feb. 1886.

53 Lilly, FT to Mary Brotherton, 6 Aug. 1889.

54 Lilly, ELL to FT, 26 Jan. 1891.

55 Ibid., 12 Oct. 1888.

56 Ibid., 15 May 1885.

57 Lilly.

58 Lilly, ELL to FT, 18 Aug. 1888.

59 Ibid., 12 Oct. 1888.

60 Lilly.

61 Lilly, ELL to FT, 22 Oct. 1889.

62   Ibid., 26 March, 29 April 1891.
63   TRC, 18 Dec. 1885.
64   Lilly, ELL to FT, 19 Dec. 1889.
65   TRC, 8 April 1892.
66   TRC, 8 June 1886.
67   *Ltrs EFG*, 2:407–8.
68   Published on 18 July 1889. For Browning's attempted retrieval, see William Irvine and Park Honan, *The Book, the Ring, and the Poet: A Biography of Robert Browning* (New York, 1974), pp. 513–14.
69   TRC, 16 July 1889. ELL's verses are in the Lushington family papers.
70   Lilly, ELL to FT, 22 Oct. 1889.
71   Ibid., 19 Dec. 1889.
72   TRC, 5 Aug. 1892.
73   TRC, ELL to HT.
74   TRC, [Nov. 1892].
75   TRC, 20 Oct. 1892.
76   TRC, 25 Oct. 1892.
77   TRC, Eustace Jesse's "Annales Tennysoniana."
78   *Ltrs ET*, p. 364.
79   Kent County Archives.
80   *Background*, pp. 174–75.
81   *Maidstone and Kentish Journal*, 25 March 1909.
82   TRC, Lear to ET, 6 March 1861.
83   Lilly, E. Louisa Tennyson to FT [May 1885?].
84   *Background*, p. 175.

Index